PRAISE FO

Protecting Human Rights in Occupied Palestine

"No one is better qualified than these three eminent authors, models of integrity and professionalism, to evaluate the facts and give the world an objective assessment of the legal and political conundrum surrounding the tragedy of the Palestinians, enumerate the gross violations of international law and human rights law committed against them, and address issues of Apartheid, war crimes and crimes against humanity."

ALFRED DE ZAYAS, Former UN Independent Expert on the
Promotion of a democratic and equitable international order

"This is a unique and essential book. It is a devastating record of two decades of dramatically deteriorating Palestinian reality while these three lawyers in succession were the United Nations' eyes and ears on the state of affairs of fundamental rights. Highly readable, meticulously researched, the details of illegality and unspeakable cruelty on every page are an unanswerable indictment not only of Israel's politicians, judiciary and military leaders, but of every member of the United Nations who had these reports year after year. With a few honourable exceptions they utterly failed to stand up to the implacable determination of the United States and its Western allies to blank this disgrace out of current consciousness. This remarkable history book cannot so easily be ignored."

VICTORIA BRITTAIN, Former Associate Editor, *The Guardian*

"It is one of the supreme ironies of contemporary international relations that the very state created by the United Nations has become the principal suppressor of the legitimate rights of the Palestinian people that the UN today seeks to protect. It shows that in the ultimate analysis it is power politics that determines how the UN acts. In spite of this reality, the UN through various instruments, channels, and committees has tried to do what little it can to defend the position of the Palestinians. This book is a tribute to those efforts which is why it deserves to be read by the world at large."

DR. CHANDRA MUZAFFAR, President,
International Movement for a Just World

"This powerful book brings together the experiences and conclusions of three outstanding scholars of international law and activists in the field of human rights as they sought to document and combat Israeli violations of human rights. The book not only highlights the failure of the UN to act on the recommendations of their reports, it also offers hope by concluding that ultimately international opinion will prevail, and states will have no alternative but to conclude that Israel, like South Africa, is guilty of instituting an apartheid system. The book makes a strong and unique contribution to furthering that hope."

RAJA SHEHADEH, Palestinian Lawyer, Writer,
Co-Founder Al-Haq, and winner of Britain's 2008 Orwell Prize.

"This book harnesses the remarkable collective experiences and wisdom of three authors, whose contributions served as the backbone of discussions on Palestine in leading international legal and political institutions. The edifice of their collective work is proof that, despite the skewed power dynamics at the United Nations, a morally driven international law is still possible. This book is a historical document that reflects on the troubled and challenging past, but also offers a roadmap towards a future in which just peace is an achievable goal."

RAMZY BAROUD, Author and Editor, *Palestine Chronicle*

"A ground-breaking and timely contribution from three eminent UN Special Rapporteurs on the Occupied Palestinian Territories (OPT), forging deep critical insights into the regulatory complexities of Israel's administration of the OPT. As such, the book offers important new insights into the UN geopolitical landscape from the perspective of the rapporteurs, where both the struggles and opportunities of the UN institutional system are explored in detail. The book highlights the importance of the Special Rapporteurs as front-line defenders pushing for the justice they believe in, against systems that do not always work as promised. The support of the Special Rapporteurs to the Palestinian people and Palestinian civil society throughout the years has been pivotal, and continues in the product of this excellent text."

SHAWAN JABARIN, General Director of Al-Haq

Protecting Human Rights in Occupied Palestine

WORKING THROUGH THE UNITED NATIONS

Richard Falk | John Dugard | Michael Lynk

Clarity Press, Inc.

© 2022 Richard Falk, John Dugard, Michael Lynk

ISBN: 978-1-949762-54-9
EBOOK ISBN: 978-1-949762-55-6

In-house editor: Diana G. Collier
Book design: Becky Luening

Library of Congress Control Number: 2022948171

Clarity Press, Inc.
2625 Piedmont Rd. NE, Ste. 56
Atlanta, GA 30324, USA
https://www.claritypress.com

To the People of Palestine in their struggle
for fundamental rights

TABLE OF CONTENTS

PART IV
Joint Concluding Statement

ACKNOWLEDGMENTS

The three of us, during our periods as Special Rapporteur on the situation of human rights in the Palestinian territory occupied since 1967, are grateful to many people for assistance rendered to us in the course of carrying out duties. We received much help in carrying out our missions and the preparation and presentation of our reports, and wish to acknowledge this with gratitude as it made the difficulties associated with the special rapporteur position logistically and substantively manageable, and more effective, as well as more enjoyable.

John Dugard wishes to thank Darka Topali for her consistently first-class assistance in all things pertaining to the special rapporteur mandate. In addition, he wishes to thank Darka, Ali Hotari and Andy Clinton for their comradeship, guidance and protection on never to be forgotten journeys though occupied Palestine. Thanks, too, to Linnea Arvidsson for her assistance in the last year of my mandate. And, finally, my thanks go to my wife, Ietje, for accompanying me enthusiastically and bravely on my visits to Palestine.

Richard Falk wishes to single out staff members of the Office of the UN High Commissioner for Human Rights (OHCHR), Linnea Arvidsson, Kevin Turner, and Kiyohiko Hasegawa, not only for their assistance and dedication to human rights, which often went beyond the line of duty, but also for their friendship that definitely eased the pressures that came with the position.

Along the same lines, Michael Lynk would like to thank Katharine Marshall, Anis Anani, Abigail Eshel, Sarah Jacquier Nobel, Audrey Rinaldi and Junko Tadaki for their invaluable assistance to his work and to their steadfast commitment to human rights. Their professionalism made a huge contribution to the work of the mandate, and their friendship certainly made the burdens of the work bearable and even enjoyable.

The three of us wish to acknowledge the UN High Commissioners of Human Rights who presided over the OHCHR, with its headquarters in Geneva, during our terms of service:

Louise Arbour, Zeid Raad Al Hussein, Navi Pillay, and Michelle Bachelet. Each provided in their own distinctive ways inspiring leadership and consistent support to each of us in carrying out HRC's most controversial and contested mandate, and they did so in an atmosphere fraught with geopolitical pressures. If they had been any less steadfast and dedicated to human rights, our roles would have become less manageable and certainly less professionally useful and personally fulfilling.

We are also most grateful to Francesca Albanese, the new special rapporteur for occupied Palestine, for contributing an illuminating, generous, and gracious Foreword, and wish her well in continuing this challenging work of informing the UN and civil society about developments in occupied Palestine, especially the depiction of Israeli patterns of Israeli violation of fundamental Palestinian rights, including the right of self-determination.

Finally, we owe an enormous debt to Diana Collier and her team at Clarity Press. We are so grateful to Diana for dealing with our often confusing and complex manuscript in a most constructive and always friendly manner that definitely improved the overall text. As important, was her enthusiastic support for our project.

Any collaborative venture of this type poses challenges of fortitude, commitment, and friendship, and we think that, despite some bumps in the road, we emerged very pleased with the process and results.

Richard Falk
John Dugard
Michael Lynk

FOREWORD

Francesca Albanese[1]

Protecting Human Rights in Occupied Palestine is destined to become a staple in any scholar's library on Palestine. I had eagerly anticipated the release of this book, but it surpassed my already-high expectations. The last three Special Rapporteurs on the situation of human rights in the Palestinian Territories Occupied since 1967—whom I believe are also the most influential—are renowned international law scholars who have contributed to uplifting and shifting the debate concerning Israel/Palestine, one too often encroached upon by prejudice and polarized narratives. I salute their decision to come together to share their experiences in both separate and joint assessments. Their uniquely informed perspectives allow the reader to appreciate not only their individual contributions as Mandate Holders, but also the aggravating situation in both the Occupied Palestinian Territory and in the Israel "control room" of its illegal occupation, creeping annexation, and decades-long brutalization of the Palestinian people. With its authors committed to the primacy of international law as the force that should delimit and orient politics in the pursuit of justice, this book bears witness to how each of them advanced a unified vision for the mandate.

The structure of the book helps the reader—even the least familiar with the Human Rights Council and the work of special rapporteurs—to appreciate the significance and functions of such a complex mandate, the common challenges that have persisted throughout the past three terms, and the distinctive obstacles confronting each rapporteur. In a unique interweaving of sophisticated woof and warp, the reader is introduced to the UN "special rapporteurship," revealing how its characteristics—including its independence, given that the position is voluntary

---

1 In 2022, Francesca Albanese was elected by the Human Rights Council to be the Special Rapporteur on the situation of Human Rights in the Palestinian Territories Occupied since 1967 for a three-year term, renewable for another three years.

and unpaid—can make distinctive contributions within the UN system. The authors' own experiences, emerging from the personal accounts in the essays, demonstrate the added value of the special rapporteur's mission as part of the UN and operating under its aegis and authority, but also garnering additional respect and esteem by virtue of the holder's expert status, authority, individual commitment, and exemption from the disciplines of the international civil service to which UN employees are subject.

Part I of the book depicts the gravity of the human rights violations in the Occupied Palestinian Territory through the three special rapporteurs' individual experiences. The fragmentation of Palestinian land and people imposed by a variety of Israeli policies and measures include: the separation wall and its associated closure regime; the encroachment of the settlement enterprise in the West Bank including East Jerusalem; the rather unique explicit claim of ethnic supremacy in Israel's 2018 Basic Law implemented at the expense of the Palestinian indigenous population; the ongoing and cynical destruction of Palestinian social fabric and attempted erasure of Palestinian culture and identity; the imprisonment of entire generations of the occupied Palestinian population including children as a cruel means of intimidation, punishment, and control; the degrading living conditions in Gaza, which stand as a stain on our consciousness for every day that its two million inhabitants remain imprisoned by a brutal and unlawful blockade; the pervasive impunity that feeds the hubris that—as the Israel/Palestine situation sadly reminds us—regrettably inhabits the belly of all humanity.

In Part II, the book sheds light on the worsening situation in the Occupied Palestinian Territory, transitioning from John Dugard's to Michael Lynk's mandate, by means of a sensitive selection from the Special Rapporteurs' Annual Reports to the Human Rights Council and General Assembly, spanning more than two decades (2001–2022). Through this period the crime of apartheid moved from being a mere suspicion as inferred by Special Rapporteur Dugard in 2007 to become a more violent, vicious and fully documented reality, as was often denounced by Special Rapporteur Falk throughout his mandate (2008–2014).

A recurrent claim in the special rapporteurs' reports—which this book vividly illustrates—is the unwillingness of the international community to enforce international law and consensus even in the face of this deteriorating human rights' reality. The persistent lack of accountability and impunity of Israel points to the irresponsible role of the international community, exhibited by its complicit inaction, a role occasionally interrupted, at best, by mere rhetorical condemnations.

Part III of the book highlights, in my mind, how each rapporteur made a unique contribution to the mandate by being true to his own distinctive personality. Soft-spoken and reflective, Professor John Dugard, a major contributor to the development of international law as a member of the UN International Law Commission, brought gravitas and wisdom to the mandate. As a special rapporteur, his early critique of the closure of Gaza and of the so-called "unilateral disengagement" by Israel in 2005—which he showed did not lead to an end of the Israeli control over or responsibility as occupant of Gaza—acted as an early warning to the UN, which has eventually proven to be politically perceptive and legally persuasive. As early as 2007, John Dugard, who had seen the dismantlement of apartheid in his homeland South Africa, had warned that some of Israel's practices in occupied Palestine resembled that of Apartheid South Africa. By 2021, the argument that the widespread and systematic discrimination imposed, by a multitude of Israeli laws, policies and military orders, over the Palestinians, amounted to the crime of apartheid, could no longer be concealed from objective observers.

Where Dugard impressively uplifted the mission of justice and accountability that a special rapporteur on the Occupied Palestinian Territory must pursue, Professor Richard Falk, as his successor, strengthened that aim with his innate "militant commitment" to the legal profession. Radical, fearless, and revolutionary, Richard Falk has inspired generations of human rights lawyers, activists and researchers, injecting humanism, elegant legal prose and activism to the functioning of special rapporteur. Never sparing to tell the truth in its naked form as he saw it, Richard Falk exposed to the fullest the unlawfulness and immorality of many

Israeli practices, which he did not hesitate to denounce as "ethnic cleansing," "apartheid," "colonization," and more. He interpreted its mandate to its fullest extent, transcending its limitations, always keeping the Palestinian people, including the refugees, at the core of his call for justice. Falk's reports and work admirably called out Western actors who, perhaps due to a mixture of guilt over the Holocaust and white supremacist opportunism—had turned a blind eye to decades of violations of international law by Israel at the expense of the Palestinians' rights, aspirations and claims for justice. Undaunted in the pursuit of the truth, Falk faced the fury of wealthy and rapacious self-defined "human rights groups," whose purpose is in fact to shelter Israel from any critique in the UN and elsewhere. For six years, Richard Falk became the target of their hatred and false allegations, while the reputational damage they inflicted on him may have enabled some UN member states already so inclined to disregard the Mandate Holder's communications. Since the Falk years as special rapporteur, Israel has intensified its adversarial position at the UN towards the Mandate and refuses to cooperate or engage in constructive dialogue.

Professor Michael Lynk—an engaged labour lawyer and academic whose passion for justice has shone throughout his career—was confronted with that same reality. Continuing its approach during the Falk period, Israel countered Lynk by an adamant refusal to authorize his entry to the Occupied Palestinian Territory because of an alleged (undocumented and false) "anti-Israel" bias. Stepping into a UN mandate that had become a minefield, facing relentless vitriolic attacks by vociferous pro-Israeli groups, Michael Lynk succeeded in the mammoth task of "resetting the tone" of the debate involving the special rapporteur. He proved to be an authentic trailblazer, with his innovative, strategic approach to analysis of complex developments, structuring his reporting around key core issues and messages, and mapping pragmatic ways to overcome present wrongs. Michael Lynk navigated political obstacles tactfully, and skilfully built a base of consensus that nonetheless allowed him to launch a series of powerful *j'accuse* in each and every report he produced. He articulated the illegality of the Israeli occupation with unprecedented clarity, challenging the very assumption that the occupation continues to be tolerated by the Palestinians, given its length and nature, and addressing Israel's failure to abide by international law. He also exposed the many forms of collective punishments imposed on the occupied Palestinians, including through the illegal settlements, which he carefully presented as amounting to war crimes. He also courageously denounced the European Union, the U.S., the World Bank, and the Quartet as the "enablers" who allow Israel to maintain a brutal regime of control and domination—only later defined as Apartheid in his last report—over the Palestinians under occupation. While accomplishing all of this, he still managed to leave the mandate with the full respect of those who had received his strong criticism. Not less remarkably, Michael Lynk also managed to "mainstream" the call for justice and accountability in occupied Palestine (for brevity) across the UN special rapporteur system, with unprecedented numbers of independent experts often joining his calls for justice to the Palestinian people.

Through the three Rapporteurs' testimonies and selections from their most influential reports, the book reveals how they fulfilled their responsibilities as special rapporteurs with impressive continuity and faithfulness. Together, this book is a unique account of twenty years of history of the Palestinian people under occupation through the lens of international law, which has been manifested more in terms of its absence and violations than by its regulatory, principled and redressing power to the Palestinians, over the course of more than a century. Civil society, academics and policymakers active in and on human rights and justice for Palestine/Israel and the Palestinian people will find much inspiration in this book and treasure it as an enduring legacy of the three Rapporteurs. Hopefully this book will also further encourage academia and scholars to use international law as an organic matrix for the holistic protection of rights and freedoms, overcoming the limitations to which sectoral legal interpretation of individual bodies of law (e.g. IHL, international human rights law and international criminal law), tend to lead, thereby submitting to the rigors of legal discipline in an often ahistorical and decontextualized setting.

The final pages of this book, where the authors' accomplishments, disappointments and perspectives are summarized, left me with a sense of urgency concerning "what must be done." As the new Special Rapporteur on the Occupied Palestinian Territory as of May 2022, and the first woman to have taken such a daunting responsibility, I am wholeheartedly committed to discharge this mandate with the same integrity, rigor and wisdom of my predecessors: using the law to call out the missteps and pitfalls of politics and humanity to expand and strengthen the basis of support in order to realize the call of my mandate, using all institutional avenues, mechanisms and human networks to advance this case.

Together with John, Richard and Michael, I am deeply concerned with the worsening reality for the Palestinians living under occupation and for any human rights defenders standing up for them. The current regional and international geopolitical constellations certainly leave no space for optimism. And yet, like them, I strongly believe that justice cannot be delivered anywhere if Palestine continues to be left to bear the wounds inflicted on her and her ongoing generations by over one hundred years of colonialization. I am profoundly convinced that while we cannot turn the clock back and make fully right the many wrongs punctuating the past of that tormented part of the world that we learned to call Israel/Palestine, *there is* a just way out.

For, I believe, humanity and respect for everyone's life and dignity can and must be restored, and that in the future, Israel and Palestine shall offer a demilitarized horizon for all their children and youths, hopefully with the mental boundaries and the construct of opposing "identities" fading from sight, until that becomes a distant nightmare of the past. If justice is given a chance to flourish, the stimulating central message of this book will be finally vindicated.

Francesca P. Albanese,
Ariano Irpin

INTRODUCTION

PROTECTING HUMAN RIGHTS IN OCCUPIED PALESTINE: PERSPECTIVES OF UN SPECIAL RAPPORTEURS

Richard Falk, John Dugard, Michael Lynk

The UN Human Rights Council has adopted an innovative approach to factfinding and legal analysis in relation to violations of basic human rights. The work of such inquiries is carried out by independent experts, officially called special rapporteurs (SRs), who are known within the UN as "mandate-holders." These individuals are presupposed to have a professional background relevant to their mandate. SRs are now selected through an elaborate vetting process, which includes a selection committee of ambassadors who are themselves appointed by the president of the Human Rights Council (HRC), which itself consists of 47 member states elected by the General Assembly, taking due account of geographic representation. This Selection Committee forwards its recommendations regarding appointments in a rank-ordered form to the president of the HRC, who in turn serves in that role for one year and is a diplomat who represents one of the member States. The president has the discretion to ignore or re-rank the SR recommendations put forward by the committee, and in controversial instances, is often encouraged to do so by interested governments. The SR's recommendation is then presented to the HRC for a vote. At the time of the initial appointment the SR must be backed by a consensus of the membership, which has been interpreted to mean that a single dissenting view will block the candidate, although abstaining votes will not. Once selected the SR is eligible for reappointment for a second three-year term, which requires

1

only majority approval. This has been routinely given even for a controversial mandate such as this one devoted to a consideration of Israeli violations of international human rights standards.

The appointment process varied for the three of us. Especially in the years during John Dugard's SR mandate, the process was more influenced by those NGOs active in monitoring the work of the Human Rights Council. Governments at that stage played varied roles, but the Palestine Authority, which until 2012 was treated as a non-state actor, was nevertheless influential in giving or withholding its support from a nominated candidate. Because of widespread civil society interest in upholding human rights in the Occupied Palestinian Territories, NGOs were particularly active on both sides of these issues in relation to this mandate—either protective of Israel's behavior or extremely critical of it—compared to the other country mandates.

The role of SR has attained increasing prominence in recent years reflecting their reputation as both independent and expert, enabling them to provide valuable and trustworthy information to governments, civil society, and the media with respect to compliance with international human rights standards. As non-salaried UN appointees, these individuals are prohibited from having any connection with governments, including their own, and are not subject to civil service discipline by the UN. Even the UN Secretary General lacks the authority to dismiss an SR, and on occasion openly resists pressures by invoking this lack of authority. An SR can be challenged, censured, or even dismissed if found by the HRC to be exceeding the terms of the mandate, which specifies the scope of permissible inquiry. Because the work of SRs is often taken seriously in public discourse, a government subject to criticism is more likely to strike back, giving this analytic and professional activity an inevitable political edge. More attention and greater credibility have brought more controversy surrounding the work and person of the SR.

The media, many NGOs, and a variety of governments have come to rely on the work of the SRs to shape responses to a variety of human rights issues. Many countries lack the capabilities to carry out international investigations of human rights issues on their own, given the wide range of issues and countries covered, and this limitation can be addressed by the efforts of SRs. At present, there are 44 thematic SRs and an additional 12 whose mandate is geographically confined to the human rights circumstances of a particular country. The country mandates tend to be established only if a large number of governments view the human rights of that society as problematic.

Special rapporteurs, despite holding unpaid positions, nevertheless accept burdensome duties as mandate-holders, including the annual preparation, submission, and presentation of two comprehensive reports describing and analyzing their concerns and making recommendations within the scope of their mandates. One report is delivered to a plenary session of the Human Rights Council in Geneva and the other is made to the Third Committee of the General Assembly at UN Headquarters in New York City. The reports normally reflect mission trips undertaken by SRs to gather information about new developments and listen to recent complaints by thematic rapporteurs pertaining to a particular human right and to human rights trends, developments and recommendations pertaining to a particular State, in the case of country rapporteurs. A limitation on the work of the SRs arises because their visits to a country depend on it expressing its formal consent, either in the form of an invitation from the government or consent to admission to carry out a UN mission. In other words, the SR for a particular right or country cannot carry out an on-site visit without the prior approval from the government whose records are being appraised. Invitations to thematic rapporteurs are often not forthcoming, especially from governments that would expect a negative assessment. And for country rapporteurs, permission can be withheld and cooperation refused, thereby greatly hampering the quality of the work, but yet not necessarily weakening the purpose of the mandate, which seeks to highlight serious patterns of human rights valuations, coupled with recommending steps to achieve compliance.

As this is an official undertaking of the UN, there is some confusion between the right of a Member State to not extend an invitation even when requested and its legal obligation as a UN member to cooperate with the official work of the Organization. This confusion reflects a fundamental UN tendency to, wherever possible, reconcile sovereign rights with UN activities that are perceived as intruding upon territorial forms of governance. The work undertaken by each SR is carried out in coordination with the valuable research and logistical assistance of well-trained human rights officers attached to the Office of the High Commissioner for Human Rights (OHCHR) located in Geneva. Release of SR findings, concerns, and recommendations to the media, although discouraged earlier, have become accepted as an important dimension of the SR work, and helps explain the rise in awareness and influence of this UN mechanism, which nevertheless remains virtually unknown to the general public.

The mandate for occupied Palestine

The mandate for Palestine, formally known as "Special Rapporteur on the situation of human rights in Palestinian Territory occupied since 1967," raised special problems from the moment of its establishment in 1993. The initiative arose from widespread concerns about the prolonged Israeli occupation of the territories occupied as a result of the 1967 War, which did not lead to the expected early Israeli withdrawal to pre-war "green line" borders, and to widespread international objections to the practices and policies imposed on the Palestinian civilian population in the occupied territories of the West Bank, Gaza, and East Jerusalem. The UN has always been closely connected with this unresolved situation confronting the Palestinian people with continuous hardships that can be traced back at least as far as the failure of the UN partition plan endorsed in GA Res. 181 to be implemented with respect to Palestinian rights, especially the right of self-determination. It is also relevant that the Security Council, in the aftermath of the 1967 War, reached a rare unanimous decision in SC Res. 242 with respect to achieving a peaceful future for both Jews and Arabs that has yet to be realized despite the passage of more than a half century. Under these circumstances, Palestinian grievances intensified, and the UN was under particular pressure to respond.

The mere existence of the Mandate was predictably controversial from the moment it was proposed and established in 1993. As might be expected, it was the vehement opposition by Israel, with support from the United States and some European countries, that made this mandate a site of struggle, especially in recent years when its reports became influential. Singling out Israel for such special scrutiny was allegedly expressive of an anti-Israel UN bias, sometimes claimed to reflect anti-Semitism. Defenders of establishing a special rapporteur mandate to evaluate complaints about Israel's compliance with international law generally and the Fourth Geneva Convention in particular pointed both to the lengthy occupation and to the special unfulfilled UN responsibility for protection of Palestinian rights. This monitoring impulse was reinforced by persuasive evidence that Israeli policies were giving rise to serious patterns of Israeli non-compliance with its obligations as the Occupying Power of the West Bank, Gaza, and East Jerusalem since the conclusion of the 1967 War. Such concerns often emphasized opposition to Israel's gradually revealed ambitions for encroachment and even annexation of the Occupied Palestinian Territory, especially in the West Bank, which were seen as irreversible violations and obstacles to finding a peaceful solution to the conflict based on an independent sovereign state with borders set by the contours of these occupied Palestinian territories.

There were also objections to the framing of the mandate as applicable *only* to Israeli violations, thereby exempting Palestinian behavior from formal scrutiny, with respect to allegations directed at either the Palestinian Authority, Hamas, and/or Islamic Jihad. Despite this framing, our evaluation as SRs of charges against Israel was contextualized, if appropriate, by reference to unlawful Palestinian behavior.

Examining the experience of three special rapporteurs for occupied Palestine

The three authors of this book served successive terms as SRs for occupied Palestine in the period from 2001 to the present, with a brief interlude in 2014–2015 during which period Makarim Wibisono, a diplomat who had previously been Indonesia's ambassador to the UN, held the post. Wibisono resigned in frustration after believing that Israel had not followed through on pre-appointment pledges to cooperate with the mandate if he became SR. The three of us faced similar constraints in efforts to fulfill the obligations of the mandate, which was to gather evidence relating to Israeli violations of human rights in occupied Palestine by reference to international humanitarian law as primarily set forth in the Fourth Geneva Convention addressing situations of belligerent occupation, the laws of war, and international human rights law.

Among the three of us, John Dugard was least obstructed in the discharge of his duties as SR, being tacitly allowed access to the occupied Palestinian territories, although without tendering formal approval. Neither Richard Falk nor Michael Lynk were given access, and Falk was detained and expelled in December 2008 when seeking entry. Lacking access, which depended on Israeli consent and cooperation, it was necessary to do factfinding to the extent possible by meeting Palestinian human rights experts and witnesses in neighboring countries, which proved to be feasible for purposes of preparing reports. The failure to benefit from visiting Palestinians living under occupation clearly diminished the quality of our reports with respect to testimony and direct observation. At the same time, with respect to assessing Israeli compliance with international law, the combination of documentary materials and numerous meetings with persons familiar with the human rights situation daily challenging Palestinians living under occupation enabled us to form a clear picture of the factual character of various human rights grievances of Palestinians living under conditions of belligerent occupation. We, as SRs, found that our contacts with representatives of Palestinian and Israeli NGOs were valuable, providing sufficient evidence to allow appraisals of Israeli behavior to be made with high levels of confidence as to their accuracy and coverage.

The oral presentation of written SR reports to the HRC and GA were accompanied by what was called, in UN parlance, "interactive dialogues," in which representatives of countries posed questions or made short comments and SRs were given an opportunity to respond. The format was useful in surfacing concerns and raising issues calling for further discussion but were limited by time constraints that often made it difficult for SRs to cope adequately with the many issues raised. There was also a limited opportunity given at the HRC to accredited NGOs to pose their questions or offer comments. Again, to some extent this was a useful effort intended to give a degree of participatory role to representatives of civil society, yet it also created occasions for certain abuses of the intended dialogic process by way of facilitating defamatory attacks on SRs by NGOs with strong alignments with the country being criticized. In these regards this mandate was different from that of any other due to the intensity of both polarized views of the underlying conflict and the greater media interest in the main conclusions of the reports.

We accepted the appointment to be an SR with an awareness that the mandate would arouse strong sentiments of emotional support for and against the critical conclusions reached by our reports, feeling that it was worthwhile to compile as best we could an honest and objective assessment of alleged Israeli violations of the human rights of Palestinians living under conditions of prolonged occupation. Although attacks by those siding with Israel dominated news coverage, we were gratified that our reports were cited in the work of prominent NGOs and relied upon by some governments. We believe this commitment was worthwhile not only for its own sake, but to give us and others a much better understanding of how the UN operates with respect to issues of this kind and to provide all concerned with a better appreciation of the relevance of international law to the highly politicized set of relationships between Israel and the Palestinian people. Our overall experience as SRs closed some doors, but opened more than it closed, and contributed an invaluable real-world dimension to our more conventional academic pursuits carried on in classrooms, libraries, and scholarly conferences.

We decided to collaborate in sharing this experience by producing this book. We are motivated by a series of overlapping goals. Our primary goal is to show through our reports that Israel is legally responsible for the violation of basic Palestinian rights during the course of over 50 years of occupation. A secondary goal is to show how the UN has created the position of SR to gather useful knowledge about patterns of compliance and non-compliance with respect to human rights and in countries where such issues are particularly salient. Further goals involve evaluating whether such work has beneficial effects with respect to encouraging higher levels of compliance, with special reference to the problematic relationship between Israel and the United Nations, and particularly the HRC. Finally, we believe that the position of SR has provided an authoritative resource for civil society, media, and governments in strengthening global solidarity initiatives of a nonviolent kind that call for the application of pressure to induce compliance with international humanitarian law and human rights standards.

Explaining the undertaking

Our book is divided into three distinct parts.

Part I consists of essays by each of the three authors that summarizes their distinct experiences during their tenure as SR for occupied Palestine.

Part II consists of extracts from the reports that illustrate the patterns of violation that were found to be most significant, recognizing that the assertion of control by the Occupying Power and the resistance by the occupied society vary through time. This middle section of the book is the core of the presentation. It illustrates that certain legally questionable policies and practices, including establishment of Jewish settlements, imposition of collective punishment, use of excessive force, and house demolitions are persistent patterns of behavior. The extracts also illustrate issues that arise in specific contexts such the periodic military incursions on Gaza or more recently, the withholding of vaccines during the COVID pandemic. This section includes criticisms of the political organs of the United Nations for their failure to respond meaningfully to Israel's violations of human rights in occupied Palestine.

Part III is made up of individual essays by the authors assessing the effects and value of their work as SR, with emphasis on what was accomplished and what was disappointing. Attention is also devoted to what improvements can be made in the operation of the mandate, including with the dissemination of the results and their integration with parts of the UN other than the HRC. In a sense, these essays seek to evaluate the experience of being an SR in the context of Israel/Palestine, focusing on human rights, international law, and the pursuit of justice. Although Palestine is admittedly a special case for several reasons, its role and limitations illuminate the wider significance of one type of information-gathering and expert analysis that assume many forms within the UN System.

Experiences of Three Special Rapporteurs

CHAPTER ONE

PROTECTING HUMAN RIGHTS IN OCCUPIED PALESTINE
John Dugard (2001–2008)

Today there is intense competition for special rapporteurships of the Human Rights Council, including the Special Rapporteur on the situation of human rights in the Palestinian territories occupied since 1967. Candidates apply for the post and lobby in a public process with the support of NGOs and, hopefully, their own governments.[1] It was not so in 2001 when the Commission on Human Rights (replaced by the Human Rights Council in 2005) was required to appoint a new special rapporteur for the situation of human rights in occupied Palestine.

I was at the UN headquarters in Geneva in June 2001 to attend the annual session of the International Law Commission, of which I was a member. Earlier that year I had served as member and chair of a Commission of Inquiry (together with Richard Falk and Kamal Hossain) into violations of human rights committed by Israel in the course of the Second Intifada.[2] I knew that the Commission was considering appointing a new special rapporteur and I had heard a rumor that I was being considered. But I did not take this seriously, as I assumed that I would not be appointed without first being asked if I was available. So it came as a surprise when, on 22 June 2001, I was approached by the chair of the Commission, Leandro Despouy of Argentina, with the news that I had been appointed as special rapporteur with the unanimous

---

1 Neither Richard Falk nor Michael Lynk enjoyed the support of their own governments, but candidates for many other special rapporteurships have been actively supported by their governments.

2 See *Report of the Human Rights Inquiry Commission Established Pursuant to Commission Resolution 5/1 of 19 October 2000, E/CN.42001/121,* 16 March 2001.

support of all regional groups. When I complained that I had not been consulted and did not have time for the post, he informed me that the South African government would be embarrassed if I declined because it was to host the World Conference against Racism in Durban later that year. This led me to assume that South Africa had lobbied on my behalf, but I was informed by the South African ambassador in Geneva that this was not the case. NGOs, I was later informed, had pressed for my appointment on the basis of my work on the Commission of Inquiry into the Second Intifada. I accepted the appointment for a year, hoping that I might be able to contribute in some small way to the plight of the Palestinians.

Shortly after I had been appointed, I paid a courtesy call to the ambassador of Israel to the UN in Geneva. To my surprise he informed me that as a South African, who did not require a visa, I was always welcome to visit Israel and the Occupied Palestinian Territory (OPT). Nevertheless, he made it clear that Israel did not recognize my mandate and that I would not be able to meet with any member of the Israeli government.

I visited the OPT twice a year for about seven to ten days. I found visits, researching and writing reports and presenting them to the Commission on Human Rights in March each year and to the Third Committee of the General Assembly in October–November each year, difficult to reconcile with my teaching and work at the International Law Commission, so after a year I seriously considered resigning. Before doing so, however, I wanted the opinion of my wife, Ietje, and I suggested that she accompany me on a visit to the OPT to help me assess the situation. She came, saw, and said that in all conscience I could not resign. So it was that, with the permission of the UN, Ietje accompanied me on one visit each year and became my most critical adviser.

Unlike my successors I was able to visit the West Bank, East Jerusalem, Gaza—and Israel itself—without difficulty. Despite its vigorous criticism of my reports, the Israeli government placed no obstacles in the way of my visits. I sent the Israeli ambassador in Geneva a copy of my proposed itinerary and on a number of occasions Foreign Ministry officials helped us when our passage through checkpoints was blocked. I even received an apology from the Foreign Ministry when I was nearly hit by a tear-gas canister fired by the IDF when I was observing a protest meeting on the West Bank.

I was accompanied on my missions by my UN assistant, Darka Topali; a security adviser, Andy Clinton; our Palestinian driver and trusted adviser, Ali Hotari; Ietje and a member of OCHA (the Office for the Co-ordination of Humanitarian Affairs) or UNRWA.

Being allowed to visit the OPT meant that I was able to see the situation for myself and to collect information firsthand from Palestinian officials, informed interlocutors, and ordinary people—farmers, teachers, doctors, patients, businessmen, school children—all of whom had a story to tell.

We travelled extensively in Palestine: from Jenin in the north to the Hebron Hills in the south, from Qalqilya in the west to Jericho in the east. Over the years I visited every part of Palestine, its cities, towns and villages, its fields and mountains. We stayed at the wonderful American Colony Hotel in East Jerusalem, close to the Old City. When not in Jerusalem we stayed in Gaza City and visited the towns and villages of the coastal belt.

We visited the refugee camps of Jabalia, Balata and Aida and listened to the refugee narrative. We spoke to the wounded in hospitals and heard graphic accounts of torture from former detainees. We walked through destroyed homes and saw olive trees uprooted by settlers.

We met with members of the Palestinian Authority and the governors of many cities. President Yasser Arafat, confined by the IDF to the Muqata, his headquarters in Ramallah, always had time to meet us. This was probably because, as it was the policy of the United States and Israel to isolate him, it meant that most visiting foreign leaders and diplomats refused to meet with him. I also met with Ismail Haniya of Hamas in Gaza City, despite protests from UN officials that it was UN policy not to engage with Hamas.

Other interlocutors included members of UN agencies, lawyers, NGO staff, university academics and independent commentators such as Hanan Ashrawi and Mustafa Barghouti.

This meant that my reports to the UN were less concerned with broad political or legal analysis of the occupation and more with providing an account of what I had seen and heard. I saw it as my duty to inform the world of what was happening in Palestine. At the same time, I saw it as my role to bring the UN to the people of Palestine and to show them that the UN cared about their plight—even if I had serious doubts on this score, myself.

My mandate was one-sided in the sense that it required me to investigate and report on violations of human rights by Israel only, and not on violations committed by the Palestinians.

On occasion I ignored this direction and criticized Palestinian militants for firing rockets from Gaza and the Palestinian Authority for its execution of convicted criminals. These criticisms were not well received by the Palestinian Authority or Arab states.

My reports covered a broad spectrum of human rights law and international humanitarian law arising out of the occupation. The standards by which I measured Israel's conduct were those contained in the principal international human rights treaties, to which Israel was a party, customary international humanitarian law and the Fourth Geneva Convention with its provisions on the law of occupation and the treatment of civilians in occupied territories. Israel argued that although it was a party to the Fourth Geneva Convention the Convention did not apply to Palestine because the Convention applied only to the occupation of States and Palestine was not a State at the time of its occupation in 1967—an argument rejected by the International Court of Justice in 2004.[3] Inevitably the occupation and Israel's obligations as the Occupying Power featured prominently in my reports.

Obtaining facts to support my findings and criticisms presented little problem. Visits to the OPT allowed me to collect information from a wealth of sources: victims, eyewitnesses, journalists, lawyers, doctors, teachers, farmers, informed persons from UN agencies and NGOs (both Palestinian and Israeli), Palestinian government officials, independent interlocutors, press reports, and UN and NGO reports.

---

3 *Legal Consequences of the Construction of a Wall in the Occupied Palestinian Territory,* 2004 ICJ Reports 136, para. 101.

My reports focused on a wide range of violations of international law by Israel as Occupying Power. Violations of human rights law covering civil and political, economic, social, and cultural rights were examined throughout occupied Palestine. There were many violations of international humanitarian law (IHL) in the West Bank and East Jerusalem but most violations occurred in Gaza. The issues that received the most attention were "the Wall," settlements, house demolitions, freedom of movement, terrorism, Gaza and apartheid, and these will be the main focus of what follows. Other issues that I regularly followed and monitored were prisoner's rights, torture, criminal justice, and the treatment of children. Selections from my reports that follow provide evidence of my concern for these subjects.

The Wall

In 2002 Israel began the construction of a wall or barrier to separate the West Bank from Israel. Israel initially described it as security barrier designed to protect Israel from Palestinian "terrorists." Had this been a genuine security wall it would have been built along the Green Line, the recognized boundary line between Israel and the West Bank, and no one could have objected. But instead, 80 percent of the approximately 700 kilometers Wall was to be built within Palestinian territory, encircling more than sixty major Israeli settlements with 85 percent of the settler population and seizing ten percent of Palestinian land.

In 2002 I was taken to see marks on hills near Qalqiliya and Tulkarm which indicated clearly that Israel intended to build the Wall well within Palestinian territory. This led me to embark upon a campaign to draw attention to the Wall. I wrote an op-ed for the *International Herald Tribune* in which I condemned the Wall as an act of annexation.[4] The Israeli ambassador to the United Nations complained about the op-ed to the Secretary-General but I responded that comments of this kind fell within my mandate. In my September report of 2003 I wrote that the Wall was "a visible and clear act of territorial annexation under the guise of security."[5]

4 2/3 August 2003.
5 E/CN.4/2004/6of 8 September 2003, para. 6.

In previous years I had reported to the Third Committee of the General Assembly in New York but in September 2003 the bureaucracy of the High Commissioner of Human Rights sought to prevent me from travelling to New York. In exasperation I sought the support of the Egyptian ambassador who mobilized the Arab group to override this decision. This was the first time that I was given reason to suspect that there was an obstructive presence in the Office of the High Commissioner. At the Third Committee I repeated my charge that the Wall was an act of annexation. It agreed and referred the matter to the General Assembly, which duly condemned the Wall, called on Israel to stop its construction and requested the Secretary-General to report back to the General Assembly on Israel's response.[6]

While I was in New York in 2003, I lobbied delegates to support a request for an advisory opinion from the International Court of Justice to pronounce on the legality of the Wall, should Israel fail to heed the call of the General Assembly to dismantle the Wall. As expected, Israel ignored the General Assembly's admonition and on 8 December the General Assembly adopted a resolution which welcomed my report to the Third Committee and asked the International Court of Justice to give an advisory opinion on the question: "What are the legal consequences arising from the construction of the Wall being built by Israel, the Occupying Power, in the Occupied Palestinian Territory?"[7]

In July 2004 the International Court of Justice rendered its Opinion.[8] By fourteen votes to one it held that the Wall was illegal, that Israel should stop building the Wall and dismantle what it had built and should pay compensation to those who had suffered as a result of its construction. The Court relied on my September 2003 report in its assessment of the impact of the Wall on Palestinian communities living near to the Wall. The Opinion was approved by the General Assembly in a resolution that included members of the European Union. Predictably Israel and the United States

---

6 A/Res/ES-10/13 of 21 October 2003.

7 Resolution ES-10/14 of 8 December 2003.

8 *Legal Consequences of the Construction of a Wall in the Occupied Palestinian Territory,* 2004 ICJ Reports 136.

rejected the Opinion and the United States made sure that it did not feature in the decisions of the Security Council or the Quartet—a body comprising the United States, Russian Federation, United Nations, and European Union set up in 2002 to advance the peace process in the Middle East.

An advisory opinion is advisory and not binding. But the treaties on which the Opinion was based—the Fourth Geneva Convention and the International Covenant on Civil and Political Rights—*are* binding. Accordingly, I argued that the UN as an institution, including the Secretary-General, were bound by the Opinion. Despite this Secretary-General Kofi Annan, advised by his senior advisers and legal counsel, disregarded the Opinion in his decision-making on the Middle East. And, of course, the Quartet did likewise. With this example, States too soon came to disregard the Opinion.

The Wall remained a principal focus of my concerns through-out my rapporteurship. I reported regularly on the construction of the Wall and on its impact on Palestinian communities living in the shadow of the Wall. The Wall not only seized some of Palestine's most fertile agricultural land, but it also incorporated over forty Palestinian villages, with a population of some 50,000, in the so-called "seam zone" or "closed zone," that is, the area between the Wall built in Palestinian territory and the Green Line, the official border.

Severe restrictions were placed on Palestinians living in the "seam zone" and those with farmlands in the zone. Palestinians (but not Israelis or tourists) were obliged to obtain a permit to live, visit or farm in the area and major obstacles were placed in the way of obtaining such a permit. Moreover, it became difficult for those living in the "seam zone" to access hospitals, clinics, schools, employment, and markets in the West Bank. On my visits to the OPT I spent a considerable portion of my time in the "seam zone" speaking to communities about the hardships they suffered and observing the enforcement of the restrictions on movement within the zone. I was horrified to observe school children crossing the border from the seam zone to schools in the West Bank closely watched by armed Israeli soldiers. One village that I visited regularly, Jayyus, was situated on the Palestinian side of the Wall, with a population of 32,000, mainly farmers separated from their farmlands, greenhouses, and wells by the Wall. We were always hospitably received by the elders of the village who gave graphic accounts of the hardships inflicted on them by the Wall. They looked to me as an agent of the UN to do something about their plight, but all I could do was to report on what I had seen and heard, knowing full well that the UN would do nothing.

The Wall has become a *fait accompli*. The United States has ensured that the Security Council, the UN Secretariat, the Quartet and European States have made no attempt to enforce compliance with the Opinion. While in New York I pursued the question of compensation for the victims of the Wall, but it was not until 2007 that the new Secretary-General, Ban Ki-Moon, appointed a board to oversee this process. Little has been done on this front as the UN remains unwilling to confront Israel on this issue. After 2005 the Israeli government acknowledged that it regards the Wall as the future border of the state of Israel and little attempt is made today to justify this act of *de facto* annexation as a security measure.

Settlements

Settlements have grown exponentially since the occupation of the OPT in 1967. Today there are some 300 settlements—150 officially recognized and 150 so-called settler outposts that are not officially recognized by the Israeli government but are condoned and even supported. There are some 665,00 settlers in the West Bank and East Jerusalem. When I became special rapporteur there were fewer than 400,000 settlers in the West Bank, East Jerusalem and Gaza. Israel withdrew its settler population of some 7,000 from Gaza in 2005.

My reports regularly condemned the illegality of the Israeli settlements. This was understandable because settlements are so clearly illegal. Settlements violate Article 49(6) of the Fourth Geneva Convention, which prohibits the transfer of citizens of an Occupying Power into an occupied territory and are today a criminal offense in the Rome Statute of the International Criminal

Court.[9] The International Court of Justice unanimously found settlements to be unlawful in its 2004 Opinion[10] and resolutions of both the General Assembly and the Security Council have declared them unlawful.

The settlements, perched on the top of Palestine's beautiful mountain tops were an ever-present eyesore. On occasion we drove through the major settlements of Ariel, Ma'ale Adumim, and Kiryat Arba in our UN vehicle but it was clear that we were not welcome to spend time viewing the neat houses, spacious gardens and suburban facilities. These settlements provided evidence of suburbia at its best.

Settler violence was a frequent occurrence. Settlers regularly attacked Palestinians, destroyed their olive trees (in 2005, 900 trees were destroyed in the village of Salem, near Nablus), and damaged their property. Hebron, with its settlements and Yeshiva (mainly it seemed for Americans from Brooklyn) in the center of the city, was notorious for settler violence. We had some evidence of this while visiting Hebron with the Temporary International Presence in Hebron (TIPH), a body of law enforcement officers drawn from several countries with the mandate of keeping the peace in the city. We were spat on and abused and our vehicle was spray painted. There we saw the refuse from settlers deposited on the streets of the city and anti-Palestinian graffiti on the walls—including a slogan with historical connotations—"Gas to the Arabs." Also renowned for settler violence were the South Hebron Hills. There we visited At-Tuwani where we heard reports that settlers had beaten and terrorized schoolchildren on their way to school; wells and fields had been poisoned; and sheep and goats stolen and poisoned. Villagers confirmed reports from other parts of the OPT that the IDF had done nothing to prevent settler violence.

I continued to condemn the settlements as illegal, and towards the end of my mission I described them as the new colonialism. In one of my last reports, I declared that Israel practiced apartheid in the course of its occupation, but I failed to show clearly that the settlement enterprise was responsible for a system of apartheid. I

---

9 Article 8(2)(viii).

10 2004 ICJ Reports 136, para. 120.

was not unaware of the fact that settlements produced a colonial regime akin to apartheid as I had known it in South Africa. Indeed, the similarities between the occupation of Palestine and apartheid South Africa had become clear to me in my earliest visits to the region, well before I was appointed as special rapporteur. My failure to make the comparison more forcefully was motivated by the knowledge that the influence of my reports would suffer if I likened Israel's occupation to the hated policy of apartheid.

Demolitions

Israel justifies its demolitions of Palestinian homes on three grounds: military necessity, the ground raised by Israel to justify its destruction of homes and property in military operations; administrative sanction, Israel's explanation for its destruction of homes built in East Jerusalem and Area C of the West Bank (rural Palestine over which Israel has full control according to the terms of the Oslo Accords); and collective punishment, the destruction of the home of a family of whom a member has committed an offense against the Occupying Power (a policy abandoned in 2005 but revived in 2014). I saw ample evidence of this policy which has been inflicted on thousands of Palestinians.

In April 2002, the IDF launched a brutal offensive against militants living in the refugee camp in Jenin. Using armed Caterpillars, the IDF destroyed some eight hundred dwellings and rendered 4,000 homeless. When we visited Jenin in August 2002 the refugee camp was a wasteland with refugees living in tents. Still worse was the destruction inflicted on Rafah in the Gaza Strip in 2005. Tanks, F16 Fighter Aircraft, Apache helicopter gunships and the ubiquitous bulldozer destroyed 298 homes housing over 2,000 persons. We visited Rafah shortly afterwards and saw the homes, government buildings and schools that had been reduced to rubble.

Israel is determined expand its presence by means of settlements in East Jerusalem and Area C of the West Bank. As a corollary it seeks to prevent Palestinians from building houses and structures in these areas. This it does by refusing permits to build and by destroying anything built without a permit.

Over 1,000 homes were destroyed in the West Bank while I was special rapporteur. I saw the consequences of such destructions in the Jordan Valley and other parts of Area C and spoke to community leaders unable to build schools because of this policy. We visited the ruins of the Hadidiya Bedouin community's structures near Tubas, which had been destroyed at the request of a nearby settlement. Humanitarian considerations were abandoned by Israel in its quest for expansion in Area C of the West Bank and East Jerusalem. The policing of this policy was characterized by a vindictive pettiness. We visited a house owner in Area B, in which Palestinians were permitted to build, who had planted geraniums outside his house, which fell within Area C. The Israeli Defense Forces (IDF) destroyed the geraniums on the ground that they had been grown without a permit!

The condemnation of house demolitions in my reports resulted in my being invited by the Israeli Law, Constitution and Justice Committee to address the Knesset in 2005 on this subject. An objection from the Israeli government to having anything to do with me was rejected on the ground that a legislative committee was not bound by a decision of the executive. I opened the debate with a highly critical account of Israel's demolition practices. I expected to be savagely criticized but found that my criticisms were soon outdone by speakers from the Israeli communist party and Arab members of the Knesset. This experience illustrated the contradictions in Israeli society and the extent to which freedom of expression prevailed in Israel itself.

Freedom of movement

I paid particular attention to the restrictions on freedom of movement in the West Bank and Gaza because these practices resembled South Africa's notorious pass laws restricting the movement of black South Africans, and provided evidence, to which my reports drew attention, of the similarities between apartheid in the two countries.

Like black South Africans under apartheid Palestinians are obliged to carry permits and to present them at checkpoints and to members of the occupying force when requested. Whereas the discriminatory South African system was transparent and regulated by accessible legislation, the Israeli system is characterized by bureaucratic complication and obfuscation. To make matters worse the Israeli system is mainly enforced by a system of checkpoints where permits are required, and vehicles and luggage are searched. Everyday thousands of Palestinians must pass through checkpoints to travel from home to work, to reach schools and hospitals and to visit friends and family. Every day Palestinians waste hours in this way.

In 2007 there were 80 permanent manned checkpoints, in addition to over 500 obstacles to travel—unmanned locked gates, concrete blocks and ditches. Delays at checkpoints are endemic. Even ambulances are held up for hours. Between 2000 and 2006, 68 women gave birth at checkpoints; there were 35 miscarriages; and five died in childbirth. Checkpoints were mainly manned by young IDF conscripts who saw it as their task to humiliate Palestinians as much as possible. Strangely, no attempt was made to conceal this brutish behavior when we were observing and monitoring the major checkpoints. Finally, there were separate—good—roads for settlers and bad roads for Palestinians, a form of discrimination unknown in apartheid South Africa.

Terrorism

Israel and its allies are quick to condemn Palestinians' resort to violence as terrorism. But they refuse to acknowledge that many of Israel's actions, particularly its assaults on Gaza, may likewise be characterized as terrorism. I drew attention to this in my reports and recalled the use of violence that probably qualified as terror by resistance movements in occupied Europe during World War II. I also reminded Israel of the way in which Jewish resistance movements, led by two future Prime Ministers of Israel, had resorted to terrorism against the British administration. These comparisons and reminders were not well received, and I was accused by Israel and the United States of being soft on terrorism.

Gaza

When I first visited Gaza at the start of the Second Intifada in 2001 it was a boom town with a cosmopolitan atmosphere that accommodated Palestinian government ministries and UN agencies. It was a Mediterranean coastal city with hotels and restaurants buzzing with visitors. Its streets were crowded, and I had the terrifying experience of being driven though its traffic in a special Arafat-ordained motorcade at high speed with the horn replacing the brake. It had an air of excitement, anticipation, and prosperity.

There were still Israeli settlements in Gaza, such as Netzarim, with white-washed bungalows and spacious gardens. The security presence around them was intense. The IDF escorted settlers whenever and wherever they went, resulting in major traffic jams. The IDF swept the agricultural land and demolished homes in an ever-expanding area surrounding the settlements.

Gaza was the home of Hamas and in the early days of the Second Intifada it was the scene of many skirmishes with the Israeli security forces. IDF activity came to focus heavily on Gaza, because it was used for firing rockets into Israel.

In August 2005 Israel withdrew its settlements from Gaza. This was the end of the colonization of Gaza but not of the occupation. Gaza remained an occupied territory over which Israel retained effective control, the test for occupation. Initially there was joy that Israel had left. Led by James Wolfensohn, former head of the World Bank, a concerted effort was made to improve the quality of life in Gaza. A commitment was secured from Israel that it would allow travel to the West Bank and funds were raised to allow Palestinians to farm the properties vacated by settlers. At this time, I visited greenhouses producing vegetables and flowers for export to Israel.

It soon became clear that this euphoria was misplaced. Israel reneged on its promise to allow travel to the West Bank; the export of produce was severely restricted; and the import of goods was also restricted. Then in January 2006 elections were held in Palestine, which independent observers hailed as free and fair. But Hamas won and this was unacceptable to Israel and the Western

States. Israel, the United States, the EU, and Canada withdrew funding and labelled Hamas a terrorist organization. A government of national unity was established for Palestine comprising Hamas, Fatah, and independents but this was short-lived. Israel, the United States, and the EU made sure of this.

In June 2006 Israel launched two military offensives on Gaza—Operation Summer Rains and Operation Autumn Clouds— to recover an Israeli held hostage by Hamas. Aerial bombing was accompanied by low-flying F16s breaking the sound barrier and causing frightening sonic booms; heavy bombing destroyed Gaza's power plant leaving half the population with no electricity; pipelines and sewerage were damaged; agricultural land was bull-dozed; homes, schools, hospitals, and mosques were destroyed; and hundreds of civilians were killed and wounded.

I visited Gaza every year from 2001 to 2007 and saw its transformation from a bustling coastal territory to a besieged land whose people lived in fear of another Israeli offensive. I saw the devastation caused by Israel's invasions, visited hospitals where the wounded lay dying, talked to bereaved families and teachers whose schools had been damaged, and factory owners whose factories had been destroyed. I visited an UNRWA girls' school short-ly after Operation Summer Rains and heard young girls speak to counsellors about their experiences, fears and hopes. They wanted to be treated like children in other parts of the world. But this was not to be as they grew up in fear and hatred for an occupation that had stolen their childhood.

Gaza was not safe. On my last day as special rapporteur in September 2007, Ietje and I were suddenly rerouted by our security officer as we left Gaza City for the Erez crossing to avoid an IDF missile attack. Later we heard that twelve people had been killed on the road we were to have taken.

In June 2007 Hamas seized power in Gaza and the situation deteriorated further under an Israeli blockade. The people of Gaza resigned themselves to a future without hope. But worse was yet to come.

Apartheid

The evidence of apartheid in occupied Palestine is clear for those who wish to see. There are two separate racial groups. The Jewish group, comprising settlers and their IDF protectors, enjoys privileges and rights denied to the Palestinian group. They are allowed to build homes in the West Bank and East Jerusalem without fear of demolition; to travel freely to their work, schools, shops and hospitals on good roads free from checkpoints; they are free to express their political views and to assemble to voice their protests; they are subject to Israeli criminal and civil law and exempt from the harsh injustices of military courts; and, above all, they are free from harassment by the IDF. Palestinians, on the other hand, are not free to build homes and risk inevitable demolition if they build without permission; they are forcibly relocated to meet the needs of settlers; they are subjected to multiple obstacles when they seek to travel anywhere; they are subjected to a harsh military law and to military courts that make no pretense of applying fair trial procedures; they are denied the right to express their views and to assemble peacefully; they are subject to arbitrary search, arrest, imprisonment and torture; and they are fearful of military interventions and offensives that make no distinction between combatants and law-abiding civilians.

In short, Palestinians are discriminated against and persecuted because they are Palestinians. They are subjected to inhumane acts, and this occurs, according to the definition of apartheid in the Rome Statute of the International Criminal Court, "in the context of an institutionalized regime of systematic oppression and domination by one racial group over another racial group."[11]

I had witnessed and opposed apartheid in South Africa for forty years. I had experienced the arbitrariness and discrimination of an apartheid regime.[12]

I know apartheid when I see it. I likened the restrictions on movement of the Palestinian people to the pass laws of apartheid

---

11 Article 7(1)(j) and (2)(h).

12 For an account of my life in South Africa, see John Dugard, *Confronting Apartheid: a Personal History of South Africa, Namibia and Palestine* (Johannesburg: Jacana, 2018).

South Africa in my report of 2004, which resulted in a report in *Haaretz* titled "UN agent: Apartheid regime in Territories worse than in South Africa." [13] However, I refrained from making a general comparison of apartheid in South Africa and Palestine or from examining Israeli practices in occupied Palestine in the context of the crime of apartheid. This silence, which was wrong, was prompted by a fear that my reports would be taken less seriously by governments if I labelled Israel's occupation as a form of apartheid. In January 2007, however, I did address this issue head-on when I concluded that Israel's laws and practices in occupied Palestine resembled apartheid in South Africa and probably fell within the definition of the crime of apartheid.

---

13 Column by Aluf Benn, August 2004

CHAPTER TWO

ON BECOMING AND BEING SPECIAL RAPPORTEUR FOR OCCUPIED PALESTINE

Richard Falk (2008–2014)

Prelude

It was early in 2008 that I started receiving phone calls at my home in California asking me if I would accept an appointment as special rapporteur for occupied Palestine if the position was offered to me. I knew that I had the backing of the Palestinian Authority delegation, which apparently mattered, although Palestine was at the time neither a member of the Human Rights Council in Geneva or of the United Nations. I also knew that Israel had been opposed to the existence of such a mandate and had become vocally unhappy about the critical reports submitted by John Dugard, whose tenure as SR was about to expire in the Spring of 2008. I anticipated that this campaign to identify a candidate for the position who was considered sympathetic with Israel's approach to occupation would have the full support of the United States and quite likely the EU. As I was accustomed to Israel getting its way at the UN on appointments to sensitive positions, especially when that enjoyed the support of Washington, I never took my prospects seriously. Besides, I was aware that there were many other qualified candidates under consideration. My expectation was that someone with a less controversial profile on the Israel/Palestine relationship would be offered the position, probably a compromise between the choice of the Palestinian Authority and Israel.

For these reasons, it came as a surprise when I received a congratulatory phone call informing me that I had been selected by the Human Rights Council by the required consensus, that is, with no negative votes. Canada had spoken against my appointment in the discussion preceding the vote but abstained when the votes were recorded. Had Israel been a member of the HRC it would not have hesitated to vote "no." So would the United States, had it not withdrawn as a member of the HRC during the presidency of George W. Bush, ironically in protest against the alleged bias against Israel. But for this fortuitous circumstance, I would never have had the opportunity or challenge of serving as SR for six strenuous years.

The senior American ambassador to the UN at the time was John Bolton. He was hardly flattering in his over-the-top remarks about my appointment, saying that "it illustrated what was wrong with the UN," adding for good measure that I was "a fruitcake." I suppose he meant to call attention to what he considered my zany views on a range of world issues. Because Dugard had left such a favorable impression during his six years in the position, especially in pro-Palestinian NGO circles and activists around the world, my appointment was greeted with suspicion, given the energy Israel was known to have devoted to finding a new SR to their liking. Added to this, I received a flurry of hate mail, including death threats, from those who viewed criticism of Israel, especially by a Jew such as myself, as tantamount to ethnic treason. I was categorized by such inflammatory labels as "self-hating Jew" and "anti-Semite."

Not to be outdone, Israel issued a formal statement by way of its Defense Ministry denouncing my appointment and declaring the government's refusal to cooperate with the UN in relation to the Mandate on Palestine as long as I was SR. Without additional explanation, the formal statement merely alleged "bias" on my part as the justification for non-cooperation. Of course, I was not surprised by this show of embitterment, although given Israel's continued willingness to allow Dugard to visit the occupied Palestinian territories even after he began submitting his critical reports, I hoped for the best. Indeed, officials at the HRC headquarters in Geneva mistakenly expected this informal low-profile *de facto* cooperation with Israel would continue, but it was not to be for me or my successors.

I think Israel changed its tactics partly because it came to understand the acute difficulty of reconciling its policies with widely accepted international interpretations of international human rights standards. Perhaps I personified these frustrations; the objections to my appointment coincided with Israel and its important NGO vehicle in Geneva, UN Watch, seeking to wound the messenger rather than refute the message as well as to champion the view that harsh criticism of Israel is "anti-Semitism." What continues to be noteworthy is that neither Israel nor its supporters make any effort to demonstrate that the criticisms are maliciously false and without evidence. Criticism, as such, is rather addressed by dismissing the critic as an anti-Semite, whether deserved or not.

Against this background, I wondered whether I had been imprudent to let my candidacy go forward because I had viewed my prospects as dim and felt pleased even to be nominated. Beyond this, I was teaching at the Santa Barbara campus of the University of California and involved in several demanding research projects on a variety of other subjects of interest to me and taking time for the two missions per year plus the preparation and presentation of two reports on the overall human rights situation in occupied Palestine seemed to exert undue work pressure at a time in life when sensible persons are finding satisfying ways to enjoy retirement.

At the same time, as a longtime student of international institutions and international law, I welcomed the chance to become better informed about the UN *from within* and to report on the specifics of Israel's violations of human rights in the West Bank, East Jerusalem, and Gaza, the three territories occupied by Israel in the 1967 War. I also had not altogether given up hope that a sustainable and just peace could be agreed upon. It was widely accepted internationally at the time that these territories constituted the geographic basis for a political compromise with Israel that would result in the Palestinian people finally gaining a sovereign state of their own and Israel would presumably achieve greater security if an agreement was reached. As long ago as 1988 the Palestinians had signaled a willingness to accept such an arrangement although it meant settling for 22 percent of historic Palestine, less than half of what the UN in 1947 had put forward as a fair division of the territory in its then controversial partition resolution. It seemed like an interesting time to be involved with this long Palestinian struggle for attaining basic rights. In addition, I felt bound by my word that, if selected, I would accept the position.

Of course, I was already on record on the issue, through academic publications, and by way of a 2000 UN three-person factfinding mission to Gaza chaired by Dugard on behalf of the HRC. The report was critical of Israel's behavior as Occupying Power from the perspective of international humanitarian law, as substantially codified in the Geneva Convention of 1949 and the two additional Protocols of 1977. When the membership of the mission was announced at a public meeting of member governments of the HRC, the Israeli ambassador asked for the floor although Israel was not a member. He objected to the mission, singling me out as unfit due to bias to serve in such an investigative role. Mary Robinson, the former president of Ireland, then UN High Commissioner for Human Rights, came to my defense by rejecting the objection, and the mission went ahead. Our report, as expected given what was known, was highly critical of the manner by which Israel was discharging its role as Occupying Power in Gaza, especially its consistent reliance on excessive force and collective punishment.

Those appointed to be SR are assessed as qualified based on their credentials as experts, and if an academician, this meant by reference to relevant publications and professional affiliations. It was my judgment, then and later, that bias is measured by inflammatory or manifestly misleading distortions of facts or through the presentation of strained and irresponsible interpretations of the applicable law. In the context of the Palestinian Territories Occupied since 1967, Israel itself makes little substantive effort to reconcile its occupation policies with international law. My claim was and is to be *objective*, and unbiased, following the evidence rather than being bound by preconceptions.

In fact, as I often contended, in the case of occupied Palestine the fact/law nexus was so persuasive that it was not even necessary to be balanced for a professional investigator to find against Israel on the main Palestinian human rights grievances. Even an expert who was a 90-percent Israeli partisan, yet 10-percent openminded and objective would reach the same critical conclusions as had I and other SRs. In this sense an objective critic of Israel should not be viewed as anti-Israeli but as performing as a professionally qualified expert. Thus, its ad hominem attacks against me for such reporting exhibited Israel's adoption of a politics of deflection that dodges material allegations of international law violations by seeking to discredit their source, not their substance. In my judgment, the quality of SR reporting should be assessed by standards of accuracy, fairmindedness, reasonableness, coverage, interpretative coherence, and conceptual clarity. The credibility of an SR is also relevant, and the balancing of my reputation as a scholar against my tendency to support controversial interpretations of international events is a fair matter of concern, but one for others to determine in their search for the best candidate. I would only point out in my defense that I am only controversial in Western mainstream venues, and quite the contrary in most non-Western settings. This was frequently confirmed by the support and encouragement I received during my six years as SR from a variety of representatives of HRC members.

I had experienced a similar personal attack when I was invited in 1968 by the International Commission of Jurists, a respected NGO based in Geneva, to be an official observer of a major political trial in South Africa of leading political figures in South West Africa (now Namibia) during the height of apartheid. I submitted my report based mainly on several weeks of observations of the treatment of black African defendants at the trial, and interviews with the lawyers and presiding judge. The South African government officially responded to my report by attacking me as wielding "a poison pen," suggesting that I would be prosecuted criminally if I dared to set foot in South Africa ever again. In other words, where the prevailing pattern of control is oppressive there is no objective or responsible alternative for an observer than to report the existing conditions, which from the perspective of those administering the situation is tantamount to a subversion of legitimate governance arrangements. That my resume would reinforce an impression of opposition to racism reveals a commitment to widely endorsed ethical values and legal norms, not bias. Such a view does not imply that defenders of apartheid or of Israeli policies and practices should be deprived of their day in court, or that there may not be legalistic, moralistic, and even political arguments supportive of a defense of apartheid as an acceptable mode of control in a multi-ethnic society or a society subject to belligerent occupation, depending on specific circumstances. Unlike South Africa, Israel refuses to acknowledge that it relies on racist categories in organizing societal life for Jews and Palestinians and treats allegations of "apartheid" as anti-Semitic smears undeserving of a substantive response. South Africa, in contrast, made no democratic pretensions, arguing that what it called "separate development" for whites and blacks was a preferable way of organizing its multi-ethnic society, although it obscured the discriminatory and exploitative nature of the way separate development was implemented.

Of course, the UN takes sides in matters involving human rights that reflect a normative consensus among its members, which is resisted by outlier states that insist on respect for sovereign rights and compliance with Article 2(7) of the UN Charter that prohibits the UN from interfering in matters within the domestic jurisdiction of its members. The UN is itself manipulated by geopolitical forces that lead it to focus on some issues and ignore others. Given the history of Palestine since the collapse of the Ottoman Empire at the end of World War I, it seems persuasive to contend that the UN had a special responsibility, as bestowed by the League of Nations, for finding a peaceful and just solution to the still unresolved struggle between Jews and Arabs for the control of historic Palestine. The need to exercise this responsibility has been reinforced by Israel's military occupation of territories set aside by the UN as the basis of a Palestinian sovereign entity for more than 50 years. One aspect of discharging this responsibility is by way of the Human Rights Council, and its innovative reliance on SRs to provide periodic factual and legal reporting on Israel's compliance with international human rights standards, including international humanitarian law, in its prolonged administration of these Palestinian Territories Occupied since 1967.

Early trials and tribulations: Expected and unexpected

Once appointed, I anticipated hostility from expected quarters in Geneva and New York and was not disappointed. UN Watch wasted no time in mounting a defamatory attack not only in the time allotted to NGOs in the interactive dialogue involving questions from members and answers from SRs in response to the presentation of annual reports to the HRC but also by derogatory letters sent to top people in the UN Secretariat and to the diplomatic representatives of Israel's strongest supporters. What surprised me was that such personal attacks were taken seriously without any effort to check on their accuracy or reasonableness. I was particularly disturbed by the fact that the HRC president presiding over the Geneva meetings—who holds a one-year position that rotates—allowed these vindictive personal attacks to continue uninterrupted in time set aside for dialogue about substantive issues. Otherwise, by and large, the UN staff in Geneva, which gave efficient logistical support to SRs, arranged agendas of meetings and travel schedules, exhibited a commitment to the work of promoting human rights and in my experience were helpful in the drafting and revising of reports.

Offsetting the unpleasantness, I encountered private expressions of encouragement from important officials at OHCHR and at UN Headquarters in New York City. I received many private expressions of admiration for enduring the public abuse and reassurances about the importance of the work. At one point, perhaps taking pity or maybe seeking to remove an irritant from the scene, the High Commissioner, Navi Pillay, asked to meet with me and expressed her sympathy for being a target of attacks that had nothing to do with my performance as a SR, and suggested if I found the situation too difficult, I should consider resigning and another less contentious position could be found for me. I appreciated the empathy of the offer, but was determined not to let the dirty tactics of my critics lead me to give up my role as SR. In fact, I never seriously considered resignation as a result of the pro-Israeli campaign being orchestrated by UN Watch, although I was distressed that it had as much resonance as it did with the U.S. delegation and the diplomatic representatives of such conservative governments as those of the UK, Canada, and Australia, as well as with right-wing European political leaders. Although the depth of the vitriol and persistence of the attacks, emulated by a variety of other Zionist venues, surprised me somewhat, being attacked came as no surprise. In fact, as time passed, and the ferocity of the attacks increased, I reasoned to myself that I must be doing an effective job in my SR work to be the target of such venom.

What did come as an unwelcome surprise were unexpected tensions with the Palestinian Authority, whose representatives had strongly supported my selection, but soon came to regret it. I reasoned that the PA, having made a political investment in my appointment by overcoming opposition, felt entitled to provide guidance as to my approach to the work of the mandate. This attempted guidance collided with my understanding that the position of SR was one of complete *political independence*, including from UN officialdom and from sponsoring governments, which was part of the rationale for making the position unpaid and not subject to civil service discipline. There were, to be sure, subtle pressures exerted from within the UN, especially by more senior staff eager to avoid stepping on the toes of those with political leverage within the Organization, but they were indirect and discreet.

In my early years as SR the tensions with the PA were much more intense. My first misstep from the PA perspective was to propose in my first report to the HRC that my mandate be expanded to include Palestinian violations of human rights in the Occupied Territories. I thought that this was appropriate, besides having the side benefit of depriving critics of their main argument that Israel was being singled out in an unfair manner. The PA delegation was furious and succeeded in mobilizing widespread opposition to my proposal from Arab and some Asian countries. I was somewhat surprised that the EU was silent during the discussion. Friendly delegates told me in private that it had been such a challenge to establish this mandate on occupied Palestine that they were fearful that any modification of its coverage might lead to its termination. I was also told that it would be appropriate for me to mention PA encroachments on human rights in conjunction with the discussion of Israeli violations, and this did prove to be a practicable compromise course of action.

I later managed to anger the PA more by mentioning in my report the role of Hamas in the governance of the Gaza Strip. My term as SR started in 2008, shortly after Hamas' victories in the Gaza elections of 2006, leading to Israel imposing a blockade in 2007 while Hamas succeeded in prevailing over Fatah in a struggle for political control of Gaza. The PA was so enraged by this turn of events that they took the unusual step of exercising their right to delay the publication of my report, and informally suggested that I resign my position. Although somewhat shaken, I was determined to hang on and not succumb to the pressure. Later on, a new ambassador took charge of the PA delegation, and we developed cordial and cooperative relations, especially with the junior diplomats. We discussed policy differences, which arose from time to time. The PA was not happy about my public criticisms of their willingness to shelve the 2009 Goldstone Report, thereby foregoing any effort to implement its recommendations stemming from the Israeli Cast Lead military operation in Gaza that began at the end of 2008. By and large we went on to develop such a good working relationship that at the end of my six year term, I received a message of thanks for my role as SR from Mahmoud Abbas and a PA farewell dinner in Geneva.

Quite a different tribulation arose from some miscalculations in Geneva about how to handle Israel's objection to my appointment. The expectation was that Israel would not agree to cooperate in an affirmative manner but would rather continue their pattern of response to Dugard by placing no obstacles in my path with respect to conducting annual visits to the three occupied Palestinian territories covered by the mandate. The first mission, scheduled for early December 2008 was designed to establish contact with a wide range of NGOs and political representatives in occupied

Palestine, including the Ramallah leadership of the PA. As with Dugard, my proposed agenda for the mission was submitted to the Israeli Embassy in Geneva for their consideration, and as had been their past practice with Dugard, no approval or disapproval was forthcoming. The OHCHR interpreted this lack of response as tacit approval of my agenda. I was somewhat hesitant about this reaction, given the way Israel had reacted to my appointment, and was reluctant to make the long trip from Santa Barbara, California if I was to be denied entry. However, I was then persuaded that Geneva was probably right, and the responsible thing for me to do was to test the waters.

And what a test it was! I was accompanied by a staff assistant and an inexperienced security officer from the OHCHR. When we landed at the airport, they had no trouble with immigration and went ahead to pick up the luggage. I was told to sit in a nearby chair by the Israeli official at the entry window. I then sat there for several hours. Finally, I was summoned to the immigration window, informed that I had been expelled, and furthermore, would be detained at a facility close to the airport. An official from the Ben Gurion Airport security accompanied me to recover my luggage. He was polite and even somewhat apologetic, explaining that the order expelling me came from the Foreign Ministry and had somewhat surprised the Security people, given my status as leading an official UN mission. Be that as it may, my computer and cell phone were confiscated (later returned after being scrutinized) and I was whisked off to the detention facility a few miles away. I was led into a second-floor locked cell, which had five other detainees, smelled of urine, and was illuminated by bright lights which were not dimmed during the night. It was frustrating overall, but making the best of it, I engaged my cellmates in lively conversation for the next 15 or so hours before being sent back to the U.S. I returned via New York City to California. The then current president of the General Assembly, Miguel d'Escoto Brockman, the former Foreign Minister of Nicaragua and a friend, proposed arranging a press conference devoted to my expulsion from Israel. I was so exhausted from the ordeal that I begged off, probably irresponsibly as it was an opportunity to illustrate Israel's unwillingness to live up to its legal obligation as a member of the UN to facilitate, or at least not obstruct, its official undertakings.

In my early years as SR I was disappointed by the OHCHR in several respects. First of all, on my failed mission to Israel, the accompanying assistants quite unprofessionally went ahead to their hotel in Jerusalem, and washed their hands of my fate, claiming there was nothing they could do as it was a weekend and the UN offices in Geneva were closed. It was left to my wife back in California and a friend in the U.S. to activate the American Embassy in Tel Aviv. This initiative seemed to account for an abrupt change in tone by the detention guards, who then accorded me a kind of respect. It also hastened my departure from the airport, which was quicker and easier than ever before as there was no passport check or exit questioning, which was customary when leaving Israel.

A second disappointment occurred when my experience—which was indirectly a humiliation of the UN—was brought to the attention of the OHCHR and failed to produce a response. This UN non-response expressed weakness, essentially an unwillingness to step on geopolitical toes.

There was also a media angle that confirmed my worst suspicions, particularly the treatment accorded my expulsion by *The New York Times*. Maybe I should not have been surprised. After all, I had collaborated on two books scrutinizing their approach to foreign policy issues in the Middle East. The *NYT* reported my expulsion without bothering to get my side of the story, while taking at face value what the Foreign Ministry told their correspondent: a total lie to the effect that I had been formally warned before the mission not to attempt to enter Israel. As mentioned, there had been no hint of a negative reaction when the mission agenda was submitted to the Israeli Embassy. The issuance of visas to my assistants was taken as a further positive signal in Geneva that we would not encounter difficulties upon arrival. When I contacted the *Times*, requesting an opportunity to set the record straight, the request was rejected without explanation.

Despite these trials and tribulations, I never gave serious thought to resigning. On the positive side, it was an important learning experience both with respect to the nature of the Israel occupation and more generally with regard to how the UN operates in a sensitive policy area where strong geopolitical pressures exist. It provided me with some insight into what the UN can and can't do, and to why the Organization is at once indispensable and disappointing. I came to understand that where geopolitical pressures collide with human rights, or more generally with the UN Charter and international law, the UN remains important, but only in the symbolic domains of political life where issues of legitimacy and legality are sorted out. Here, Palestinian legal, moral, and political entitlements are clarified, the discourse within the UN is influenced, and pro-Palestinian civil society activism is reinforced and encouraged. I felt that, as someone prepared to take the heat that honest and accurate reporting produced, it would be irresponsible for me to resign, risk having the mandate politicized in Israel's favor, while vindicating the tactics of my detractors.

The challenges of performance

Against this background of exclusion from entry to the Palestinian Territories, and the disappointing failure of the UN to challenge Israel's uncooperative behavior, I was forced to adapt to the situation. There was no point in trying to visit the West Bank, East Jerusalem, and Gaza directly by way of Israel as it was virtually certain that I would again be denied entry. This deprived me of direct testimony from the victims of Israel human rights violations, and exposure to the existential experiences of living under the constraints of prolonged occupation. I know from John Dugard and other SRs that such direct contact is an invaluable element in effectively discharging the role of SRs, especially in situations as tense as that existing in the Israel/Palestine setting. At the same time, I was not completely disadvantaged, having visited all three territories on recent previous occasions subsequent to 1967, and being in contact with many resident Palestinians who were allowed by Israel to travel internationally, although living under occupation.

I went about configuring the factfinding missions in the neighboring countries of Egypt, Jordan, and Lebanon where I could most conveniently meet with Palestinians, occasional Israelis, and individuals working on behalf of NGOs active in the Occupied Territories. After the Arab uprisings in 2010–2011 the Egyptian government became cooperative, facilitating visits to Gaza by way of the Rafah crossing. The logistics turned out to be difficult as the road trip from Gaza to Rafah was considered dangerous, and mission visits were twice cancelled for security reasons. When approval was finally given for me to visit Gaza in 2012, our UN cars were escorted by two Egyptian armored vehicles driving ahead and behind. We made the trip to and from Gaza safely. It turned out to be worthwhile as it gave me the bitter taste of what an ordeal the occupation had become on a daily basis for the long captive civilian population of Gaza. Additionally, it turned out to be an opportune time for an in-depth visit, coming shortly after a massive Israeli military attack under the code name of Operation Pillar of Defense. We were able to see with our own eyes several sites of devastation as well as talk with families who had lost close relatives on attacks targeting residential neighborhoods. Israeli "disengagement" from Gaza in 2005 had turned out to be mainly a matter of redeployment of troops on the Israel side of the border, which, together with a blockade imposed two years later, created what became known as the world's largest open-air prison in the world. During my week in Gaza, in addition to the pervasive fear of Israeli attacks and surveillance from the air and the aura of captivity, I feared the daredevil road navigation of my UN drivers.

In matters of substance, thanks to the excellent staff work of my dedicated assistants in Geneva, the missions to the area surrounding occupied Palestine were very useful, as well as informative and interesting beyond the terms of the mandate. The fact that my terms as SR overlapped the Arab uprisings that erupted in late 2010, added a dimension to my mission visits, especially to Egypt, which I visited several times during the course of the six years. These uprisings were generally supported by Palestinians I encountered. This made sense. The early outcome of these Arab uprisings suggested greater responsiveness to pro-Palestinian public opinion on the Palestinian struggle by the new leadership in the Middle East, which was particularly evident in Egypt. This hopeful development would not last long, given the policy reversals accompanying a series counter-revolutionary developments in the ensuing years. Already in 2013, the coup in Egypt led the authoritarian Sisi leadership to restore collaborative ties with Israel, once more impinging on both the usefulness of missions carried out in Cairo and the provision of a potential gateway to Gaza.

The missions taken during my two terms as SR were all outside the territorial venue of the mandate. While they served to collect useful information, they probably contributed less to the reports presented each year to the Human Rights Council and Third Committee of the General Assembly than would have been the case, had I had the benefit of testimony of victims of human rights abuses from those on the scene who could describe Israeli behavior. In practice this meant that it seemed appropriate to use my discretion in calling attention to aspects of the situation facing the Palestinian people, including the prolonged character of the occupation, which were not themselves considered a violation of human rights. The military administration of the West Bank, in particular, had denied Palestinians, who were living within the framework of belligerent occupation, their fundamental human rights since 1967. The Fourth Geneva Convention governing Belligerent Occupation had been conceived as a temporary legal framework for the aftermath of war in which occupation was to cover a rapid transition from war to peace. It became increasingly evident during my time as SR that Oslo diplomacy had failed, and no end was in sight for the occupation.

This understanding of the occupation was reinforced in this instance by the international legal consensus embodied in SC Res. 242 that territory could not be acquired by force, and hence there existed no justification for a prolonged occupation, and worse, for annexation claims. Yet the language of Geneva Convention did not directly address prolonged occupation and left open the permissible length of occupation. I made many efforts to call this situation to the attention of the UN, and although the feedback I received from government representatives was favorable, nothing concrete happened. Now after 55 years of Israeli occupation, which has included many serious violations of the central guidelines of international humanitarian law, the situation remains dormant, and the political will to end international acceptance of continued occupation and demand Israeli withdrawal seems absent.

In my role as SR I attempted to engage relevant NGOs in challenging this underlying condition, including the International Committee of the Red Cross, but met with either indifference or, in the case of ICRC, an evident anxiety that any move of the sort I was recommending would have the appearance of being "political"—as antagonistic to Israeli policies, and hence disturbing to the ICRC comfort zone as a neutral arbiter.

I also pressed the political organs of the UN as hard as I could on the troubling nexus between the establishment of Jewish settlements in the West Bank and East Jerusalem and increasing evidence that rather than withdrawal, Israel was creating a set of circumstances that exhibited an increasingly acknowledged annexationist agenda, which surfaced as explicit Israeli policy after 2014 when my mandate ended. Yet this incipient circumstance of an expanding settlement phenomenon, combined with an unwillingness by the UN or important governments to challenge Israel, disturbed me for two major reasons: first, the settlements were a flagrant, continuing violation of Article 49(6) of Geneva IV, and second, allowing the settlements to expand further both revealed an Israeli intent to prevent the emergence of a viable independent Palestinian state, hence striking a fatal blow against the "two-state solution," which continued to be the explicit goal in UN circles. Feeble UN reactions to these fundamental threats to Palestinian self-determination were very discouraging and led me to reach the conclusion that the fate of the Palestinian struggle increasingly depended on civil society activism, including the exertion of pressure on the UN.

During my period, the plight of the two million Palestinians living in Gaza often preoccupied me and deeply influenced the composition of my reports. The most basic issue was to reassert the applicability of international humanitarian law to Gaza despite Israel's claim that it had relinquished its role as Occupying Power by withdrawing its troops and dismantling its 18 settlements in 2005. The Israeli view was internationally rejected given Israel's control over Gaza's borders, airspace, and access from sea, as well as its total control over entry and exit of persons and goods. In UN settings Gaza continued to be viewed as occupied. In my efforts to delineate a human rights perspective that explained the reality facing the people of Gaza I emphasized the reliance by Israel on many types of collective punishment, a direct violation of Article 33 of Geneva IV. Israeli reliance on excessive force in reaction to resistance by Gazans, even including nonviolent forms of resistance, was reinforced by periodic major IDF operations launched against Gaza.

Gaza issues were further aggravated by the Israeli unwillingness to negotiate long-term ceasefire agreements with Hamas.

In my visits to Egypt and on one occasion to Qatar, I had the opportunity to have serious conversations with Hamas leaders living in exile and was convinced of their resolve to hitherto pursue their liberationist goals by political means and avoid the massive suffering that violence has brought to Gaza. I found Israel's undisguised refusal to explore this possibility of creating a more peaceful relationship with Gaza deeply disturbing, as was the American diplomacy that followed Israel's lead. For a combination of reasons, having little connection with Israeli security, Tel Aviv seemed determined to disallow Hamas's efforts to alter its "terrorist" identity and rejected its numerous pleas to replace armed struggle by diplomacy.

There was less occasion in these years to focus on the situation of Palestinians in East Jerusalem, but I took note of similar trends toward unlawful annexation of the territory accompanied by Israel's formal claims to govern the whole of Jerusalem as an integral portion of Israel, its "eternal capital." A number of regulations that discriminated against Palestinians living in East

Jerusalem were also evident. These added up to a subtle form of ethnic cleansing, undermining the stability of Palestinian residence and associated property rights.

Concluding remarks

Taking due account of the restraints on my performance resulting from the denial of access to the Occupied Palestinian Territories, it still seemed possible to prepare reliable comprehensive reports of Israeli violations of international human rights standards in their role as Occupying Power. There were ample demonstrations, as well, that the relevant parts of the UN system were aware of this state of affairs but lacked the will and capabilities to do much about the situation on the ground except to allow a documentary record to be made in the form of my SR reports.

On UN sidelines in Geneva and New York there existed a growing appreciation of the role, responsibility, and opportunities for civil society activism in relation to the Palestinian struggle for national rights. Yet I continue to believe that SRs have played important roles in these unresolved circumstances of fundamental denials of human rights by providing governments, NGOs, and the more independent media platforms with objective and apolitical confirmations of alleged abusive circumstances. It is the effectiveness of this under-appreciated informational role played by the UN System that helps explains Israel's recourse to its provocative campaign to discredit the mandate and personally attack SRs doing their job.

CHAPTER THREE

WORKING WITHIN THE UNITED NATIONS HUMAN RIGHTS SYSTEM

Michael Lynk (2016–2022)

Introduction

On 25 March 2022, I delivered my twelfth and final report to the UN Human Rights Council in Geneva as United Nations Special Rapporteur on the situation of human rights in the Palestinian territory occupied since 1967. The focus of this last report was on apartheid in the Occupied Palestinian Territory (OPT), a topic that I never thought I would be addressing when I was first appointed to the mandate in 2016 (more on this later). In my concluding comments to the council, I stated that:

> I would not be here in front of you today delivering a report on how an unrelenting occupation has metasta-sized into apartheid had the international community taken its own laws seriously 45 and 35 years ago when the Security Council and the General Assembly began to adopt the first of their many resolutions critical of the Israeli occupation. International law is not meant to be an umbrella which folds up at the first hint of rain.

In many ways, that day encapsulated the numerous experiences I had encountered as special rapporteur during the previous six years of my mandate: strong endorsements for my findings by regional and international human rights organizations; *pro forma* statements of support by member states at the Council from the developing world; hostility from a handful of private groups whose *raison d'être* is to vigorously defend the Israeli occupation

46

from any criticism, however accurate, however measured; and diplomatic laryngitis by member states from Europe and North America. Throughout my years as special rapporteur, I sought to maintain a sharp focus on what I have called the accountability crisis: the titanic gap between the applicable rules of international law and UN resolutions addressing Israel's illegal occupation of Palestine, and the remarkable unwillingness of the international community to enforce any of its own laws and resolutions. And yet, as with my previous calls for meaningful accountability, my meetings during that week in Geneva with diplomatic representatives of Western countries were met with silence and a shrug, their tribute to the framework of international law that, in the Middle East, is closer to power than it is to justice.[1]

At its very best, the United Nations has provided an indispensable forum for the Question of Palestine to be addressed and for the right of Palestinian self-determination to be endorsed and pursued. The highest aspirations of the modern human rights movement and international law have been expressed in the hundreds of resolutions adopted by the General Assembly and the Human Rights Council (and its predecessor) in support of Palestinian rights over the past half century. The General Assembly has repeatedly accepted that the United Nations bears a permanent responsibility for the Question of Palestine until it is resolved in all its aspects.[2] And the United Nations has devoted meaningful resources, through its offices and agencies located in Jerusalem, Ramallah, Gaza and elsewhere in Palestine and the region, to monitoring the Israeli occupation, funding and managing social development projects, issuing comprehensive human rights reports, acting as a good office and attempting to ensure, with indifferent support from the international community, the well-being of the Palestinian refugees.

---

1 Jean Allain, *International Law in the Middle East* (Routledge, 2004).

2 A/RES/76/10 (3 December 2021): "Reaffirming the permanent responsibility of the United Nations with regard to the question of Palestine until it is resolved in all its aspects in accordance with international law and relevant resolutions."

But, as I discovered during my experiences as special rapporteur, the United Nations is rarely at its very best when it comes to the Question of Palestine. Far more often, the UN has been desperately hobbled by its political inability to act upon its many resolutions to demand that Israel halt its *de jure* and *de facto* annexation of Palestine, end its occupation, and clear the path for Palestinian freedom. The United States has been at the heart of this institutional inertia; its zeal to shield Israeli intransigence through its Security Council veto has prevented any meaningful action by the one legislative organ of the United Nations that possesses the power to act decisively against an international outlier. For the UN, this inability to effectively press Israel to end the orphaned political status of the Palestinians has acutely stained its reputation and prestige. As Kofi Annan, the former Secretary General of the United Nations, acknowledged in his memoirs, this failure has been, for the UN: "... a deep internal wound as old as the organization itself, given that the Arab-Israeli conflict began at the very inception of the UN—a painful and festering sore consequently felt in almost every intergovernmental organ and Secretariat body."[3]

My appointment as special rapporteur

In March 2016, I was unanimously selected as the seventh special rapporteur for human rights in the OPT by the United Nations Human Rights Council. My immediate predecessor, Makarim Wibisono, had resigned after less than two years in the mandate, citing Israel's refusal to allow him entry into the occupied territory as his breaking point.[4]

At the time of my selection, I had been a Canadian law professor for 17 years, teaching and writing in the areas of Canadian labor law, constitutional law, and human rights law. I had also

---

3 Kofi Annan, *Interventions* (Penguin, 2012), at 254.

4 Makarim Wibisono, "My resignation as UN human rights rep in occupied Palestinian areas," *AA New Analysis Desk*, 15 January 2016 ("I am left with a sense of...deep regret that the non-cooperation by Israel with my mandate, as well as other United Nations mandates which it dislikes, signals a continuation of a situation under which Palestinians suffer daily human rights violations under the Israeli occupation.").

been an active labor arbitrator, adjudicating differences between employers and unions. In addition to my professional and academic work in Canadian law, I had a long-standing interest in Israel and Palestine: in the late 1980s, I worked for the United Nations in Jerusalem during the first Palestinian intifada;[5] I invigilated the 1996 Palestinian elections on behalf of the Canadian government; and I had written a number of articles for academic publications on international law and the Israeli occupation.

Controversy, in the form of allegations generated by several pro-Israel non-governmental organizations which persistently attacked the United Nations and the international human rights movement, arrived within hours of my appointment. Among other sins, these organizations alleged that I had once compared the Israeli settlements to Nazi Germany. I had done nothing of the sort, and the slur could only have been made by taking my writings on the legality of the Israeli settlements entirely out of context.[6] A quip attributed to Mark Twain is *à propos* to those circumstances: "A lie travels half-way around the world before truth gets a chance to put its pants on."

Nonetheless, conservative members of the Canadian Parliament and the Canadian foreign minister, Stéphane Dion, relying on the unfounded allegations, began tweeting against my selection (although Canada had played no role in either my application or the Council's decision), and questions were asked in the Canadian House of Commons. In response, I gave interviews to the national Canadian media,[7] unsolicited letters of support on my behalf were sent to the foreign minister by Canadian parliamentarians and law professors and by John Dugard and Richard Falk, and I spoke with the foreign minister's senior staff. In my

5 Michael Lynk, "Vignettes of Nablus" (1990), 20:1 *Journal of Palestine Studies* 101.

6 Michael Lynk, "The Wall and the Settlements," in *Implementing the ICJ Advisory Opinion* (United Nations, 2005) was a principal focus of these attacks.

7 Michael Harris, "Dion might owe the UN's new Palestinian expert an apology," *iPolitics*, 29 March 2016; Patrick Martin & Michelle Carbert, "UN appointment of Canadian professor creates controversy," *Toronto Globe & Mail*, 30 March 2016; Michael Harris, "Vindication for Michael Lynk—and Dion, an elbow in the eye," *iPolitics*, 31 March 2016.

comments, I pointed out that I would be approaching my work as special rapporteur with an open mind, but not with an empty mind. The tempest in the teapot soon evaporated.

But this initial brush with the professional defenders of the Israeli occupation cast a sharp spotlight for me on how well organized this lobby is in North America and Europe. No other serious international human rights crisis generates such a mobilized and impactful pushback. Each time that another report, full of verified facts and unimpeachable legal analysis, is issued by the United Nations or by regional and global human rights organizations addressing Israel's abusive conduct of its occupation, a predictable *sturm und drang* ensues. (Barack Obama, in his presidential memoirs, acknowledged this very point regarding Israel and domestic American politics.)[8] This has meant that Western diplomats in New York and Geneva, and some senior UN officials, all too often approach the issue with hesitancy, angst and considerable reluctance. As just one illustration: Western states in recent years have supported every accountability mechanism established by the Human Rights Council regarding the conflicts in Belarus, Burundi, Myanmar, Syria, Venezuela and Yemen; yet, when the creation of a Commission of Inquiry to examine the root causes of the Israeli-Palestinian conflict was adopted in May 2021, five of the Western members on the Council opposed it, and the other seven abstained on the vote.[9]

Working within the United Nations human rights system

During my six years working within the United Nations human rights system as special rapporteur, I addressed a number of human rights trends in the OPT through my twice-annual reports, as well as through UN press statements, letters and media interviews. My reports—delivered in March of each year to the

---

8 Barack Obama, *A Promised Land* (Crown, 2020), at 633: "...normal policy differences with an Israeli prime minister ...exacted a domestic political cost that simply didn't exist when I dealt with the United Kingdom, Germany, France, Japan, Canada, or any of our other closest allies").

9 A/HRC/RES/S-30/1 (28 May 2021) (Adopted 24-9-14).

Human Rights Council in Geneva and in October to the Third Committee of the General Assembly in New York—spoke both to conceptual legal issues involving the occupation (the illegality of the occupation, accountability, apartheid, the Israeli settlements, and collective punishment) and to the distressing social and economic features of Palestinian life under Israeli rule (the precarious position of human rights defenders, and the occupier's violations of the Palestinians' rights to development, to water and natural resources, and to health).

This occupation has become the best-documented (but, alas, far from the best-reported) conflict in the modern world. Since Israel did not permit me to enter the Palestinian territory, I have been grateful, when writing my own reports and statements, for the high-quality reports issued by Palestinian, Israeli and international human rights organizations, by the United Nations, and by some independent institutes. As well, the intrepid journalism and analysis practiced by Al-Shabaka, 972+ magazine, *Haaretz,* the Foundation for Middle East Peace, the European Council on Foreign Relations and Mondoweiss, among many others, kept me immensely well-informed about events and trends on the ground. Among the mainstream media, I read *The New York Times, The Guardian, Foreign Affairs* and *Foreign Policy* daily to gauge the establishment perspective, although the depth of their coverage of Israel and the OPT has been declining in recent years.

While I had many encounters within the United Nations system regarding Israel and Palestine, four issues stand out that are worth discussing in some detail.

The database on business enterprises in the Israeli settlements

During the same week that I was selected as special rapporteur, the Human Rights Council directed the UN High Commissioner for Human Rights to produce a database of "all business enterprises" engaged in the Israeli settlements in the OPT.[10] The purpose of the database was to shine a light on those companies—Israeli and

---

10 A/HRC/RES/31/36 (24 March 2016).

international—whose economic activities and investments were facilitating the growth of the settlements, thereby contributing to their well-documented violations of Palestinian human rights in East Jerusalem and the West Bank.[11] This spotlight was influenced by the 2011 UN Guiding Principles on Business and Human Rights,[12] which directed all business enterprises to refrain from contributing to human rights abuses arising from conflict. Yet, the Council's vote on the database displayed the ongoing timidity of the West towards creating even a modest form of accountability regarding the Israeli occupation. The resolution was adopted 32–0, with 15 abstentions: all 11 members of the Council from Europe or elsewhere in the developed world abstained.

The creation of a business activity database focused on a crisis conflict zone with myriad human rights abuses was not new for the United Nations. The Security Council had commissioned a substantive report in 2003 by a panel of experts highlighting 75 international businesses engaged in the illegal exploitation of natural resources in the Democratic Republic of the Congo.[13] The Human Rights Council issued major reports in 2018 and 2019 respecting 59 foreign businesses involved with companies controlled by the security forces in Myanmar, which were implicated in mass human rights violations in the country's western and northern states.[14] But neither of these reports triggered the sustained backlash that the Israeli settlements database provoked: among the over-the-top invectives hurled at it were "blacklist," "economic terrorism" and "modern anti-Semitism." It was none of these things: it had no judicial or remedial powers, it did not call for a boycott of the settlements (although the Security Council has directed UN member states to distinguish between Israel and

---

11 See the 2013 report of the independent fact-finding mission created by the HRC to investigate the Israeli settlements, which called for the monitoring of business activities in the settlements: A/HRC/22/63. It stated that the impact of the settlements on the rights of the Palestinians was "pervasive and devastating."

12 United Nations Office of the High Commissioner for Human Rights, *Guiding Principles on Business and Human Rights* (New York and Geneva, 2011).

13 S/2003/1027.

14 A/HRC/39/CRP.3; A/HRC/42/CRP.3

the settlements on several occasions)[15] and describing actions to address Israel's illegal settlements as antisemitic is not only intended to divert attention from the well-established human rights harm being caused to the Palestinians, but it also dishonors the important work being done to challenge the very real anti-Jewish bigotry that exists in the world.

Three issues regarding the database greatly concerned me as special rapporteur. First, the High Commissioner's Office took almost four years to release the database. Part of the delay can be explained by the obvious concern to develop a rigorous methodology and to triple-check its gathered information respecting what business enterprises were actually operating in the Israeli settlements. But this alone does not explain the inordinate length of time it took for the database to appear. The High Commissioner's Office—both under Zeid Ra'ad Al Hussein and his successor, Michelle Bachelet—encountered enormous lobbying pressure, led by the United States and Israel, to derail the database from ever seeing the light of day. And, perhaps in reaction to the lobbying pressure, the resources devoted by the High Commissioner's Office and the Human Rights Council to creating the database were scant and insubstantial in comparison to the importance of the work.[16]

My second concern related to the High Commissioners' conservative approach to the database's mandate. When it was released in February 2020,[17] it identified 112 businesses involved in the settlements. Of these, 94 were Israeli, and the rest were from the U.S., the United Kingdom, France, the Netherlands, Thailand, and Luxembourg. Among the listed companies were Airbnb, Booking.com and Expedia. But there were also glaring, and inexplicable, omissions. The German-owned Heidelberg

---

15 UNSC Res. 2334 (23 December 2016 ("Calls upon all States . . . to distinguish, in their relevant dealings, between the territory of the State of Israel and the territories occupied since 1967"); UNSC Res. 465 (1 March 1980) ("Calls upon all States not to provide Israel with any assistance to be used specifically in connexion with settlements in the occupied territories").

16 The High Commissioner acknowledged the slim resources devoted to the database's creation in his 2018 interim report: A/HRC/37/39, para. 62.

17 A/HRC/43/71 (12 February 2020).

Cement company, which operates stone quarries in several Israeli settlements in the West Bank, was missing from the database.[18] So, too, was FIFA, the international governing body of football/ soccer, which permits its Israeli subsidiary, the Israeli Football Association, to include six teams based in the Israeli settlements, in violation of FIFA's own statute.[19] And, probably due to a highly cautious interpretation of its mandate resolution, there was no mention of the scores of foreign registered pro-Israel charities and not-for-profits who funnel enormous sums of donations annually to the Israeli settlements.[20]

And third, and most concerning: the database has become, since its release in 2020, a virtual dead letter. Although the 2016 Human Rights Council resolution called for the database to be updated annually, no resources were subsequently allocated to it either by the Council or the High Commissioner's Office. In my final meeting with the High Commissioner in March 2022, I urged her to devote the necessary funding and personnel to revitalize the database and honor the 2016 resolution. She explained that, for a variety of technical reasons, it was not possible to do so—a procedural justification that obscures a human rights failure. Although the database was never going to be more than a small step towards holding Israel accountable by directing international attention towards the scale of corporate involvement in the settlements, it was nevertheless a highly visible signal that demonstrated that defiance of international law by an acquisitive Occupying Power would not go unanswered.

Not being admitted into Israel and the OPT

When I first met the staff at the Office of the High Commissioner for Human Rights in 2016 shortly after my appointment, I was briefed on the many procedures accompanying

---

18 "The Israeli Exploitation of Palestinian Natural Resources, Part II: Heidelberg Cement," *Who Profits,* (online, last review: 22 August 2022).

19 "FIFA will not take action on Israeli settlement teams," Business & Human Rights Resource Centre (business-humanrights.org)

20 Elena Hodges, "Hidden in Plain Sight: US Nonprofits as Drivers of Illegal Israeli Settlements" *Just Security,* 10 June 2022.

the mandate. Among the challenges now facing me, one of the greatest was Israel's steadfast refusal to cooperate with the special rapporteur mandate and to deny my access to the OPT. This non-cooperation had begun with Richard Falk's mandate, and continued with that of his successor, Makarim Wibisono. On several occasions, I met with either the High Commissioner or the Deputy High Commissioner in Geneva to urge them to press Israel to allow me access to the OPT. After all, the UN General Assembly has directed Israel to fully cooperate with my mandate, including by allowing me entry into the OPT.[21] The unwillingness of the senior OHCHR leadership to expend any political capital on this request not only hindered my work, but it also reflected the unwillingness of many senior leaders within the UN to challenge Israel's strong sense of exceptionalism.

This institutional timidity has not served the UN's mission to protect and promote human rights well. After Richard Falk was refused entry to the OPT in 2008 without great protest from the UN, Israel went on to deny any cooperation with, and entry into the country for, a variety of special human rights supervisory mechanisms established by the Human Rights Council over the next 13 years. These include the separate panels of experts appointed to investigate the Israeli wars on Gaza in 2008–2009 and 2014, the human rights impact of the Israeli settlements in 2013, and the mass shootings at the Gaza frontier against largely unarmed Palestinian civilians in 2018. As well, Israel refused any cooperation with the Commission of Inquiry formed in 2021 to investigate the root causes of the Israeli-Palestinian conflict. The one UN human rights mechanism whose presence Israel has tolerated in the OPT—the OHCHR country office in Palestine, with offices in Ramallah, Gaza, East Jerusalem and Hebron—has also been impacted by this timidity: in 2021, Israel refused to renew the visas for the 12 international UN staff assigned to the country office, and they were forced to leave Palestine and work remotely from their homes abroad. Quiet diplomacy has its place and value but, in these circumstances, it has too often become

---

21 UNGA Resolution 71/98 (6 December 2016), para. 5.

a justification for the UN's reticence to meaningfully confront Israel's obstructiveness.

My human rights mandate would have been enriched, had I been permitted to make annual visits to the OPT. Had I been allowed, I would have spoken with victims of human rights abuses. I would have met with the valiant advocates working for Palestinian, Israeli, and international civil society organizations in their home settings. I would have witnessed the demographic transformation of Palestine through the constantly expanding settlements. And I would have hopefully had the opportunity to exchange views with the Israeli government and military to learn more about their *weltanschauung* and their understanding of the future of the occupation. As it was, I travelled every year (before the pandemic) to Amman, where civil society organizations and UN officials in turn travelled from the OPT to provide me with detailed briefings on the current human rights trends. These visits, together with the excellent reporting on the occupation by civil society, enabled me to write comprehensive reports for the UN, full of detail and analysis, but without the human faces and stories which would have personalized the modern ordeal of Palestine.

Security Council Resolution 2334 and the American shield

In late March 2022, as I was delivering my final report to the Human Rights Council in Geneva, the United Nations Security Council in New York was convening its quarterly meeting to re-view Israel's compliance with Resolution 2334.[22] This resolution had been adopted by the Council in December 2016 in the waning weeks of the Obama Administration. As an illustration of the ex-traordinary diplomatic armor the United States extended to shield Israel by its veto power (by both Democratic and Republican administrations), this has been the only resolution critical of Israel adopted by the Security Council since January 2009.

Resolution 2334 was the Council's brusque rebuke of Israel's ongoing misconduct as the Occupying Power. It called the Israeli

---

22 UN Security Council Resolution 2334 (23 December 2016).

settlements "a flagrant violation under international law," and stressed that, by "dangerously imperiling" what is left of a two-state solution, they are "entrenching a one-State reality" in Israel and Palestine. It demanded that Israel "immediately and completely cease all settlement activities" in the OPT. It directed all States to "distinguish, in their relevant dealings, between the territory of the State of Israel and the territories occupied since 1967." And, in the penultimate paragraph of the Resolution, the Council requested the UN Secretary-General to report to the Council every three months on the implementation of its directions.

What was initially a triumph of responsible diplomacy by the world's single most powerful political body would soon become another exercise in the inexhaustible capacity of leading political decision-makers on the Israeli occupation to avert their gaze away from the facts proliferating in front of their noses. In each of the subsequent 20 quarterly meetings on Resolution 2334, beginning in March 2017, the UN Secretary General or his Special Coordinator for the Middle East Peace Process (MEPP) had reported that Israel had taken no steps to comply with the direction of the Security Council, that Israel instead was escalating its approval and construction of new settlement units, and that no member state had acted upon the direction to distinguish between Israel and the Occupied Palestinian Territory. Following each of these reports, the Council took no further action to demand Israeli compliance with its directions beyond some criticisms in the minor key.

The 21st quarterly meeting of the Security Council on Resolution 2334 was held on 22 March 2022. By now, the quarterly reports had become the Council's version of Groundhog Day: the same grim facts on the ground, the same warnings about the relentless settlement expansion, the same condemnation of Israeli and Palestinian violence, the same concern about the viability and necessity of a two-state solution, and the same acknowledgement that no action had been taken by anyone. In his briefing at this meeting, Tor Wennesland, the UN Special Coordinator for the MEPP, stated, in the same antiseptic language, that Israel continued to be in breach of the Council's direction respecting the settlements:

> Security Council resolution 2334 (2016) calls on Israel to "immediately and completely cease all settlement activity in the Occupied Palestinian Territory, including East Jerusalem" and to "fully respect all of its legal obligations in this regard." No such steps were taken.[23]

This language was virtually interchangeable with each of the previous 20 reports delivered to the Security Council on 2334. The passive voice invariably used was either: "No such steps were taken," or "No such steps were taken during the reporting period." In the statements that followed the report, many of the 15 Council members spoke about the need for a conducive atmosphere for stability and calm, to curb settler violence, to refrain from any unilateral actions and to acknowledge the deteriorating humanitarian situation in Gaza. Beyond a few voices, no one called for accountability for Israel's plain defiance of the Council's clear demands in the Resolution.[24]

On the fifth anniversary of the adoption of Resolution 2334 in December 2021, I had issued an official statement as special rapporteur, noting that every quarterly report had concluded that Israel was non-compliant with every one of the directions of the Security Council. I pointed out that the international community has no strategy, no Plan A, to end the world's longest military occupation. I then asked, in light of the relentless settlement expansion: "Is it not clear by now that the Israeli political leadership has no interest, and no incentive, to end the occupation?"[25]

---

23 "Briefing by UN Special Coordinator for the Middle East Peace Process Tor Wennesland to the UN Security Council Briefing, 22 March 2022."

24 Settlement Expansion Fuelling Violence in Occupied Palestinian Territory, Middle East Peace Process Special Coordinator Warns Security Council | UN Press.

25 United Nations Special Rapporteur OPT, "Five Years after UNSC Resolution 2334, International Accountability to End the Israeli Occupation is More Important Than Ever" (online, last review, 7 September 2022).

The primary responsibility for this paralysis at the Security Council rests with the United States. After he left office as UN Secretary General, Ban Ki-moon lamented the "political cover provided by successive U.S. governments to Israel," which is "partly to blame for this lack of accountability."[26] In his presidential memoirs, Barack Obama observed that America's shielding of Israeli violations of international law meant that "our diplomats found themselves in the awkward position of having to defend Israel for actions that we ourselves opposed."[27] In response, one might ask, as American political scientist Shibley Telhami has done: "If an American president cannot leverage this extraordinary and unprecedented support to advance core American values, what hope is there for succeeding anywhere else?"[28]

In May 2021, tensions in occupied East Jerusalem escalated over attempts by Israeli settlers to displace Palestinians from their homes in Silwan and Sheikh Jarrah. This led to rockets being fired by Hamas at Israeli civilian targets and an overwhelmingly disproportionate military response by Israel, culminating in an 11-day military assault on Gaza, killing approximately 260 Palestinians, injuring more than 1,900, displacing more than 75,000 from their homes and causing immense property damage. The diplomatic role of the United States was distressingly familiar: at the Security Council, it blocked both a draft resolution seeking a ceasefire and even the issuance of a Council statement, arguing that these would only alienate Israel.[29] This time the buffer allowed Israel to sustain its assault on Gaza until it had achieved most of its military goals, in the face of broad diplomatic and public opinion seeking to end the violence and the mounting civilian death toll.

Since the Israel occupation began in June 1967, the United States has regularly allowed the Security Council to adopt resolutions critical of Israel—77 in total—but it has also used its veto, or the threat of its use, to thwart the ability of the Security Council

---

26 Ban Ki-Moon, *Financial Times* (29 June 2021).

27 Barack Obama, *A Promised Land* (Crown, 2020), p. 627.

28 *Boston Globe*, 19 May 2021.

29 International Crisis Group, *Beyond Business as Usual in Israel-Palestine* (August 2021).

to enforce any of these resolutions. Since 1972, it has formally vetoed 44 resolutions critical of Israel, which is more than half of the 82 total vetoes it has cast during that period of time. Thirty-one of these vetoes dealt with the Israeli occupation of Palestine.[30] No other permanent member of the Security Council has ever cast even a single veto respecting a resolution critical of Israel.[31] As Kofi Annan observed in his memoirs: "The United States wielded its veto to protect the Israelis even from reasonable scrutiny and pressure, paralyzing the Council on one of the world's central conflicts."[32]

Apartheid

When I was appointed as special rapporteur in 2016, the thought that I would devote one of my reports on apartheid in the OPT was the furthest thing from my mind. Using the language of apartheid, I thought, would surely only harden diplomatic hearts and close doors. My initial strategy was to focus on international humanitarian law (the laws of war and occupation) and international human rights law in my reports to the United Nations and my relationships with UN member states. For me, this was so self-evidently the obvious approach. After all, virtually every country in the world accepted that Palestine was occupied, the Fourth Geneva Convention applied in full, the settlements were profoundly illegal, the Palestinians were entitled to self-determination and Israel's occupation was rife with human rights abuses. We shared a common language. All I had to do, I thought, was to employ this rights-based framework to write clear reports, devise workable policy recommendations and call upon member states to commit themselves, in the words of Martin Luther King's 1968 Mountaintop speech, to be true to what they had said on paper.

By the time my mandate was ending, I had changed my mind. Two developments explain this *volte-face*. First, I was

---

30 Most of the other vetoed resolutions critical of Israel dealt with Israel's invasion of Lebanon in 1982 and its subsequent occupation.

31 "The Israeli Exploitation of Palestinian Natural Resources: Part II," *Who Profits* (online, last review: 22 August 2022)

32 *Interventions* (Penguin, 2012) at 256.

deeply, if guilelessly, surprised by the utter unwillingness of most member states in the developed world—Europe, North America and Oceania—to accept that the solemn obligations of international law entailed the responsibility to impose accountability on UN member states who persistently disobey international law and UN resolutions. Indeed, Article 25 of the UN Charter states that: "The Members of the United Nations agree to accept and carry out the decisions of the Security Council in accordance with the present Charter." Israel has defied scores of Security Council resolutions since the early 1970s demanding that it undo its illegal annexation of East Jerusalem, end its illegal settlements, and wind up its occupation. Yet, Western countries have treated Israel as an important strategic, technological, military, and political partner with a democratic framework and "shared values," marred only, perhaps, by a regrettable approach towards the Palestinians. As the intrepid Israeli journalist, Gideon Levy, has written: "No country is as dependent on the support of the international community as Israel, yet Israel allows itself to defy the world as few dare."[33] With five years under my belt as special rapporteur, I began to accept the futility of persuading Western member states to energetically confront Israel through the plentiful tools of international humanitarian and human rights law, even as I continue to believe that these tools remain an important legal foundation for holding Israel to account.

The second reason for my new openness to considering the apartheid framework were the proliferating and indisputable facts on the ground. Albert Camus once wrote that calling things by their wrong name only adds to the afflictions of the world. I came to accept that international humanitarian law could no longer adequately capture the new legal and political reality in the OPT. The Israeli occupation—which is required to be temporary and short-term under international law—has become indistinguishable from annexation and apartheid. When I became special rapporteur in 2016, there were 400,000 Israeli settlers in the West Bank, and 220,00 in East Jerusalem. By 2022, at the end of my mandate, the

---

33 Gideon Levy, "Netanyahu's Right: The Occupation Can Actually Go on Forever," *Haaretz*, September 25, 2016.

settler population had reached 485,000 and 230,000, respectively. These settlers live outside of Israel's recognized international borders yet enjoy full Israeli citizenship rights in Jewish-only communities, while the five million Palestinians among them live under either Israeli military law or under a truncated form of precarious residency rights. Israeli political leaders openly proclaimed that the country's rule over the Palestinians and their land is permanent, and no genuine Palestinian state would emerge,[34] with little pushback from the West. When the facts change, so must our minds.

By 2022, the vocabulary for understanding the situation in Israel and the OPT was changing rapidly. Two of my distinguished predecessors—John Dugard and Richard Falk—had written persuasively about the prevalence of apartheid in the OPT.[35] Beginning in 2020, a number of regional and international human rights organizations issued reports concluding that apartheid existed, either in the West Bank (Yesh Din) or in the entire area between the Mediterranean and the Jordan (Al-Haq, Addameer, Al-Mezan, B'Tselem, Human Rights Watch and Amnesty International). As well, some prominent Israeli figures were coming to the same conclusion: as one example, Michael Ben-Yair, a former Attorney-General of Israel, wrote in 2022 that Israel had become: "an apartheid regime...a one state reality, with two different peoples living with unequal rights."[36]

In my report, I followed the path of the international human rights community in adopting the legal definition of apartheid laid out in the International Convention on the Suppression and

---

34 Prime Minister Benjamin Netanyahu stated in 2018 that the Palestinians could have a "state-minus," where Israel would maintain security control over all of the Palestinian territory: *Jewish Telegraphic Agency*, 24 October 2018. In 2022, Prime Minister Naftali Bennett said that: "I oppose a Palestinian state, and I am making it impossible to conduct diplomatic negotiations that might lead to a Palestinian state": *Al-Monitor*, 31 January 2022.

35 John Dugard and John Reynolds, "Apartheid, International Law and the Occupied Palestinian Territory" (2013), *European Journal of International Law* 24:3, 867; Richard Falk and Virginia Tilley, *Israeli Practises towards the Palestinian People and the Question of Apartheid* (UN ESCWA, 2017).

36 Michael Ben-Yair, *TheJournal.ie*, 10 February 2022.

Punishment of the Crime of Apartheid[37] and the Rome Statute of the International Criminal Court.[38] This meant that my starting analytical point was not whether Israel's practices in the OPT resembled apartheid South Africa, but whether the evidence of the practices of the Israeli occupation satisfied the three-part legal definition in these two binding international documents. I concluded that the facts on the ground met this legal definition. (See my application of the three-part test in Part II of this book.)

My apartheid report received more international media and civil society coverage than any of my previous reports. Much of it was positive. *The New York Times* covered its release,[39] after previously ignoring—to its shame—the comprehensive reports on apartheid issued by Human Rights Watch in 2021 and Amnesty International in early 2022. Following the 2017 Falk/Tilley report on Israeli apartheid prepared for the UN Economic and Social Commission for West Asia, which the UN leadership quickly smothered at the instigation of the Trump Administration,[40] my report was the second within the UN system devoted to the topic. Although criticized by the usual suspects, my report was left to stand unscathed, partly because of the autonomy enjoyed by UN Special Procedures within the UN human rights system and partly because of the rapid sea-change in international opinion towards Israel and its systemic discriminatory practices. In one of my many interviews following the release of the report, I said that, if there is a better term in the international vocabulary to describe the situation of two different peoples living in the same political space yet living in sharply segregated communities and having access to vastly different legal and social rights based solely on their ethnicity and nationality, then I would be happy to use that term. Until then, apartheid is the appropriate word.

---

37 (1973), 1015 UNTS 243, entered into force 18 July 1976. As of 1 February 2022, 110 states ratified the *Convention*.

38 (1998), 2187 UNTS 3, entered into force 1 July 2002. As of 1 February 2022, 123 states had ratified the *State*.

39 Patrick Kingsley, "UN investigator accuses Israel of apartheid, citing permanence of occupation" *The New York Times* (23 March 2022).

40 Richard Roth, "UN report on Israeli 'apartheid' sets off diplomatic fireworks," *CNN Politics*, 17 March 2017.

Conclusion

Wherever I went through the hallways of the United Nations Secretariat Building in New York or the council rooms at the Palais des Nations in Geneva to meet senior leadership, I would encounter a strong sense of fatalism whenever the issue of Israel and Palestine arose. One of the Secretary-Generals that I met said to me in a moment of candor: "How does one ever solve an issue like this? Is there really an answer?" On another occasion, a senior official at the OHCHR offered an impromptu lecture on the philosophy of despair, explaining to me how a cynical worldview actually heightens the search for pathways to address the Israeli occupation. An ambassador in New York from a country which was sitting as a non-permanent member of the Security Council from the developing world told me that no amount of valiant diplomacy was going to give birth to a real Palestinian state, given the American possessiveness of the file. Accordingly, he added, we should all get used to the fact that conflict-management and criticism without consequences, sprinkled with the ritual references to a future two-state solution, would be the operative framework well into the future.

And yet, within the middle and lower ranks of the OHCHR staff and among UN officers in other agencies which work on the Question of Palestine, I encountered a much more positive and determined outlook towards the future of the struggle. My reports on the frail state of health services in the OPT, the collective punishment of Gaza and the shrinking space for human rights advocates in Israel and Palestine owed much to the diligent professionalism of the UN officers in Ramallah, Jerusalem, and Geneva. "You are saying what we wish we could say," I heard from them on regular occasions. Witnessing the lived reality on the ground, as those living in the OPT did from their various vantage points, these UN officers—Palestinian, Israeli, and international—often represent the very best of the UN's guiding mission: promoting peace, securing human rights, advancing the rule of law and furthering human security for all.

PART II

Selections from Annual Reports to the Human Rights Council and General Assembly

CHAPTER FOUR

SELECTIONS FROM THE REPORTS OF SPECIAL RAPPORTEUR JOHN DUGARD

(2001–2008)

The Wall, 2003

E/CN.4/2004/6 of 8 September 2003, paras. 6–16

The Wall as an act of annexation

This report was relied upon by the International Court of Justice for its finding that the Wall was illegally constructed in Palestinian territory: *Legal Consequences of the Construction of a Wall in the Occupied Palestinian Territory,* 2004 ICJ Reports, 136, para. 133.

6. Language is a powerful instrument. This explains why words that accurately describe a particular situation are often avoided out of fear that they will too vividly portray the situation which they seek to depict. In politics euphemism is often preferred to accuracy in language. So it is with the Wall that Israel is presently constructing within the territory of the West Bank. It goes by the name of "Seam Zone," "Security Fence," or "Separation Wall." The word "annexation" is avoided as it is too accurate a description and too unconcerned about the need to obfuscate the truth in the interests of anti-terrorism measures. However, the fact must be faced that what we are presently witnessing in the West Bank is a visible and clear act of territorial annexation under the guise of security. There may have been no official act of annexation of the Palestinian territory in effect transferred to Israel by the construction of the Wall, but it is impossible to avoid the conclusion that we are here faced with annexation of Palestinian territory.

7. Israel is presently building a wall between Israel and the West Bank that, when completed, will be some 450 (possibly 650) kilometres in length. At the time of writing some 150 kilometres have already been completed and building constructors are working frenetically to finish it as soon as possible. At times this barrier takes the form of an eight-metre-high wall (near Qalqiliya). Mostly it takes the form of a barrier some 60 to 100 metres wide, which includes buffer zones with trenches and barbed wire, trace paths to register footprints, an electric fence with sensors to warn of any incursion, a two-lane patrol road and fortified guard towers at regular intervals. No-go areas of over 100 metres wide on each side of the barrier will be policed by IDF. Israel has undertaken to install some 27 agricultural crossings and 5 general crossings for traffic and persons through the barrier but as yet little progress has been made on these crossings.

8. Possibly, the Wall will assist in the achievement of the government's publicly declared goal—to prevent suicide bombers from reaching Israeli territory. Even this, however, is doubted by some who point to the fact that most suicide bombers have passed through checkpoints and that the Wall will not deter persons determined to cross into Israel to commit acts of terrorism. That this is a valid complaint is borne out by the comment of the Israeli State Comptroller in his report of July 2002 that "IDF documents indicate that most of the suicide terrorists and car bombs crossed the seam area into Israel through the checkpoints, where they underwent faulty and even shoddy checks."

9. The Wall does not follow the Green Line, that is, the 1967 boundary between Israel and Palestine which is generally accepted as the border between the two entities. Instead, it follows a route that incorporates substantial parts of Palestine within Israel. At present the Wall intrudes six to seven kilometres within Palestine, but there are proposals to penetrate still deeper into Palestinian territory in order to include the settlements of Ariel, Immanuel and Kedumim. In some places the winding route creates a barrier that completely encircles Palestinian villages while at many points it separates Palestinian villages from the rest of the West Bank and converts them into isolated enclaves. Qalqiliya, a city

with a population of 40,000, is completely surrounded by the Wall and residents can only enter or leave through a single military checkpoint open from 7 a.m. to 7 p.m. Palestinians between the Wall and the Green Line will effectively be cut off from their land and workplaces, schools, health clinics and other social services. Much of the Palestinian land on the Israeli side of the Wall consists of fertile agricultural land and some of the most important water wells in the region. The Wall is constructed on Palestinian lands expropriated by Israeli military order, justified on grounds of military necessity. Many fruit and olive trees had been destroyed in the course of building the barrier. B'Tselem, a leading Israeli human rights NGO, estimates that the barrier will cause direct harm to at least 210,000 Palestinians living in 67 villages, towns and cities.

10. Palestinians, unconvinced by Israel's assurances that they will be allowed to pass through the crossings to be erected in the Wall, are moving from their homes in the affected areas to the security of what remains of Palestine. It is reported that already some 600 shops and enterprises have closed in Qalqiliya as a result of the construction of the Wall. The Wall will therefore create a new generation of refugees or internally displaced persons.

11. It is impossible to give complete facts about the Wall as its final trajectory is still surrounded in secrecy and uncertainty. The path of the Wall changes regularly in response to demands from settlers and other political interest groups within Israel. There is no transparency surrounding the construction of the Wall and its final course seems to be known only to an inner circle of the military and political establishment within Israel. It is, however, widely expected that, following the completion of the Wall separating Israel from the western side, an eastern wall will be constructed along the mountain range west of the Jordan Valley which will separate Palestine from the Jordan Valley.

12. The Wall must be seen in the context of settlement activity and the unlawful annexation of East Jerusalem. Settlements in East Jerusalem and the West Bank are the principal beneficiaries of the Wall, and it is estimated that approximately half of the 400,000-settler population will be incorporated on the Israeli side

of the Wall. Needless to say, it is extraordinary that such action should be taken to incorporate illegal settlements that form the subject of negotiations between Israel and Palestine. The Wall will be built at great cost to Israel: it is projected that US$1.4 billion will be spent on its construction. This simply confirms the permanent nature of the Wall.

13. The Wall has serious implications for human rights. It further restricts the freedom of movement of Palestinians, restricts access to health and education facilities and results in the unlawful taking of Palestinian property. However, the Wall has more serious implications as it violates two of the most fundamental principles of contemporary international law: the prohibition on the forcible acquisition of territory and the right of self-determination.

14. Like the settlements it seeks to protect, the Wall is manifestly intended to create facts on the ground. It may lack an act of annexation, as occurred in the case of East Jerusalem and the Golan Heights. But its effect is the same: annexation. Annexation of this kind goes by another name in international law—conquest. Conquest, or the acquisition of territory by the use of force, has been outlawed by the prohibition on the use of force contained in the Kellogg-Briand Pact of 1928 and Article 2, paragraph 4, of the Charter of the United Nations. The prohibition on the acquisition of territory by force applies irrespective of whether the territory is acquired as a result of an act of aggression or in self-defence. The Declaration on Principles of International Law concerning Friendly Relations and Cooperation among States in accordance with the Charter of the United Nations (General Assembly resolution 2625 (XXV) of 24 October 1970, annex) declares that "the territory of a State shall not be the object of acquisition by another State resulting from the threat or use of force. No territorial acquisition resulting from the threat or use of force shall be recognized as legal." This prohibition is confirmed by Security Council resolution 242 (1967) and the Oslo Accords, which provide that the status of the West Bank and Gaza shall not be changed pending the outcome of the permanent status negotiations. The Geneva Convention relative to the Protection of Civilian Persons in Time of War (the Fourth Geneva Convention)

provides that protected persons in an occupied territory shall not be deprived of the benefits of the Convention "by any annexation ...of the occupied territory" (art. 47).

15. The right of self-determination is closely linked to the notion of territorial sovereignty. A people can only exercise the right of self-determination within a territory. The amputation of Palestinian territory by the Wall seriously interferes with the right of self-determination of the Palestinian people as it substantially reduces the size of the self-determination unit (already small) within which that right is to be exercised.

16. The Special Rapporteur submits that the time has come to condemn the Wall as an act of unlawful annexation in the language of Security Council resolutions 478 (1980) and 497 (1981) which declare that Israel's actions aimed at the annexation of East Jerusalem and the Golan Heights are "null and void" and should not be recognized by States. Israel's claim that the Wall is designed entirely as a security measure with no intention to alter political boundaries is simply not supported by the facts.

The Wall, 2004

E/CN.4/2004/6/Add 1 of 27 February 2004, paras. 8–31

Facts, harmful effects and violations of international law

8. In his report of 8 September 2003 the Special Rapporteur described the nature of the Wall. At times it takes the form of an eight-metre-high concrete wall, at other times it takes the form of a barrier some 60–100 metres wide with buffer zones protected by barbed wire and trenches and patrol roads on either side of an electric fence. The first phase of the Wall, running for 180 kilometres, has been completed. It is estimated that, when completed, it will be 687 kilometres in length, penetrating some 22 kilometres into Palestinian territory at one point to include the settlements of Ariel, Immanuel and Kedumim. The United Nations Office for the Coordination of Humanitarian Affairs (OCHA) estimated in

its report of 9 November 2003, that approximately 680,000 persons—that is 30 percent of the population of the West Bank—will be directly harmed by the Wall; 280,000 Palestinians living in 122 towns and villages will be enclosed in the area between the Wall and the 1949 Armistice Line or Green Line (the *de facto* border between Israel and Palestine) or in enclaves completely surrounded by the Wall while another 400,000 living to the east of the Wall will need to cross it to get to their farms, jobs and services. Other studies put the estimated number of Palestinians likely to be affected by the Wall at over 860,000, that is, about 36 percent of the population. OCHA estimates that 14.5 percent of West Bank land (excluding East Jerusalem) will lie between the Wall and the Green Line. Estimates of this kind may not be completely accurate. However, they are supported by studies from reliable sources and it is significant that they have not been seriously challenged by Israel.

9. Israel has designated the area between the Wall and the Green Line as a "Closed Zone" in which Israelis may travel freely, but not Palestinians. Thus, over 13,500 Palestinians who live in the "Closed Zone" are obliged to have permits to live in their own homes. (See Order Regarding Security Regulations (Judea and Samaria) (No. 378) 5730-1970 [Declaration concerning Closing an Area No. S/2/03 (Seam Zone)]). This means that it has become a privilege for Palestinians to live in their own homes while Israelis have the right to travel freely in this area. Surely this provides yet further evidence of Israel's intention to annex this territory?

10. Palestinians living within the West Bank with farms inside the "Closed Zone" require permits to cross the Wall into this zone, as do others from the West Bank who wish to visit the Zone for personal, humanitarian or business reasons. To make matters worse, passage through the wall or barrier at checkpoints is administered in an arbitrary manner, apparently designed to pressure Palestinians into leaving their homes to relocate on the other side of the wall, thereby creating a new generation of internally displaced persons.

11. The barrier has been, and is being, built with no regard for the environment. Beautiful hills and valleys have been scarred by the wide barrier. Thousands of olive and citrus trees have been uprooted and fertile agricultural land reduced to a wasteland. There is no evidence that Israel carried out an environmental impact assessment before it embarked on the construction of the Wall.

12. In his earlier report the Special Rapporteur described the construction of the wall in Palestinian territory as an act of *de facto* annexation in violation of basic norms of international law. The International Court of Justice has been asked by the General Assembly to give an advisory opinion on this subject and, at the time of writing this report, this has still to be done. The view of the Special Rapporteur on this subject remains unchanged. Indeed, his view has been strengthened by his visit to several sections of the Wall inside Palestinian territory in the Qalqiliya/Tulkarm region, which cannot be explained in terms of security.

13. Most of the Wall is built in Palestinian territory. Where the Wall penetrates Palestinian territory it snakes around villages, separating villages and people from agricultural land. Security could just as easily, and probably more effectively, have been achieved by building the Wall to the west along the Green Line. It is difficult to resist the Palestinian claim that the Wall has been built in this way in order to put agricultural land out of the reach of farmers—and within the reach of settlements adjacent to these lands. Israel clearly wants land, not people. Hence the construction of the Wall around villages, leaving land on its westward side to Israel. Enclaves within the Closed Zone between the Green Line and the wall cannot be explained in terms of security. What conceivable security goal does the enclave enclosing the village of Ras-A-Tira achieve? Is it not easier to explain enclaves of this kind as a measure to isolate villages so that their inhabitants will ultimately withdraw to the eastern side of the Wall, leaving more vacant land to Israel? And is not this the fate intended for villages like Jubara in the Closed Zone? How is the Wall separating Palestinians at Abu Dis in Jerusalem to be justified on security grounds? If the purpose of the Wall is to prevent Palestinian suicide bombers from

crossing into Israel, why is Israel unconcerned about the security risk posed by the thousands of Palestinians who are situated in villages on the Israeli side of the Wall (between Green Line and Wall)? Or is the final aim to compel them to relocate to the West Bank side of the Wall? These are questions that must be satisfactorily answered by Israel if it is to persuade the international community that the latter is confronted with a good faith attempt to provide security for its people rather than forcible territorial expansion.

14. Israel claims that the taking of land for the purposes of the Wall has been done in accordance with due process of law; and that the people affected have been treated humanely, particularly in respect of the granting of permits and access to schools and medical facilities. The Special Rapporteur found no evidence to substantiate these claims.

15. The justification advanced by Israel for the seizure of land between the Green Line and the Wall is security. Notices of land seizure in many instances have simply been served by placing an order of seizure under a stone or on a tree. Sometimes the order is written in Hebrew only, with no Arabic translation. In theory, the seizure of the land is temporary, until 31 December 2005, but there is every likelihood that such seizures will be renewed. Thus it seems that this is a case of confiscation by construction. Owners are given one week in which to lodge an appeal, but this has not occurred in most instances for reasons ranging from shortness of notice, lack of funds to prosecute an appeal properly, to the widespread distrust of the Israeli judicial system resulting from the lack of success of Palestinian landowners in other cases involving the taking of land. The process of land taking has also been destructive. Olive and citrus trees have been uprooted—and sometimes sold in Israel! The Special Rapporteur visited an area near the Wall at Al-Jarushiya where 30 dunums of olive trees had been destroyed by error in the course of construction of the Wall.

16. The Wall may be crossed at checkpoints only. These checkpoints are infrequent—only 31 in the first 180 kilometres—and most open for limited periods of the day only. Consequently, farmers generally have to travel great distances to reach their

lands adjacent to their homes, but on the other side of the Wall. Schoolchildren likewise have to travel considerable distances to reach school. Checkpoints are staffed in an intimidating manner: those crossing the barrier are carefully searched, at gunpoint. The situation is aggravated by the arbitrary manner in which gate crossings are opened. During October 2003 gates were closed for several weeks because of Jewish holidays. Moreover, gates are not regularly opened at the scheduled time or kept open for the scheduled period of time.

17. Farmers separated by the Wall from their land require permits to farm their land. In many instances, permits are refused. Reasons advanced for refusal are:

(a) Failure to prove ownership—a difficult requirement in a country with archaic land ownership laws and one in which landowners often leave their land to several sons without formal registration of ownership;

(b) Security—interpreted generously by the IDF to exclude anyone with a security record;

(c) Age—in practice elderly farmers receive permits but not their younger, able-bodied sons who might constitute a security risk.

18. Permits are not granted to those who rent land only. Nor are they granted to labourers to cultivate land or to harvest crops. To aggravate matters, permits are sometimes granted for very short periods, normally from two to six months. The Special Rapporteur met a farmer granted a permit to farm his land for only 12 days. The system is administered in a highly bureaucratic manner in which applicants are required to provide clear evidence of their residence and land ownership and to satisfy the IDF that they pose no security risk. As a result, farms are sometimes worked by men seen as too old to be a security risk or boys who have received permits to attend school in the Closed Zone. Moreover, permits are often denied to heavy vehicles to cross the Wall.

19. The permit system has already had a devastating effect upon agriculture in Palestine. Citrus trees are dying due to lack of

irrigation. In the village of Jayyus, 90 percent of the guava crop was lost, and poultry farming is coming to an end in the Closed Zone and enclaves because of the impossibility of providing food for poultry. There is a marked decline in agricultural productivity and production as many crops and orchards to the west of the Wall remain uncultivated by their owners who live on the eastern side of the Wall. Inevitably, this decline in food production from the agricultural heartland of Palestine will have serious consequences for the Palestinian people.

20. In some instances children are required to cross the barrier to attend school. The school at Azzun Atma, for instance, has 219 pupils of whom 80 live in Beit Amin on the other side of the Wall. The Special Rapporteur saw school crossings at Beit Amin/Azzun Atma, at Atiya/Ras-A-Tira and Jubara. Permit policy varies from place to place. In some places the crossing point simply keeps a list of children's names, while in other places permits are required for children over the age of 12. Children not infrequently have to wait for long periods of time at crossing points, without shelter from the rain. There are serious complaints of harassment of children at such crossing points. The Special Rapporteur's observation of the school crossing at Atiya/Ras-A-Tira was painful: he saw young girls carefully searched by one soldier while another pointed a gun at her. Parents are not given permits to visit their children's school. (Would such a practice be tolerated by Israeli parents?) The Al-Quds University of Abu Dis is also directly affected by the Wall. Students will be obliged to travel considerable distances to reach a campus which, geographically, is not far from their homes.

21. There are no hospitals in the Closed Zones. Those living in such zones must therefore cross the barrier at a checkpoint to reach hospitals. Inevitably, this causes delays in emergency situations and there are already reports of deaths en route to hospital. A stark example of the change in access to hospitalization is presented by Abu Dis. Before the construction of the Wall residents might be treated at a hospital in Jerusalem. Now they must travel to Bethlehem—a journey of some two hours along a poor road and through checkpoints. Although there are primary health-care clinics isolated between the Wall and the Green Line they do not

extend to ophthalmology, gynaecology, dermatology, paediatrics or diabetes services. Many clinics do not offer medication and there are difficulties in gaining access to pharmacies. Moreover, many doctors do not live in the same village as their clinic and have the usual problems in gaining access to their clinic.

22. Family life is a victim of the Wall. Within the Closed Zone not all members of a family are granted permits to reside within the Zone. In some localities, such as Jerusalem, married couples are divided by their identity documents. The husband may have a West Bank identity document, the wife a Jerusalem identity document. Such couples will either have to move to the West Bank or face separation. Moreover, the quality of family life suffers from unnecessarily long journeys to reach checkpoints to work or to school. Visits to family members resident on the other side of the Wall are subject to the usual uncertainties of the permit system.

23. The permit system regulating movement between the Wall and the Green Line and into the Closed Zone is intrinsically unfair and arbitrarily administered. There are different kinds of permits. (Lily Galili, writing in *Haaretz* on 13 February 2004, estimates that there are 11 different kinds of permit for persons wishing to visit the Closed Zone!) If they are granted, they are granted for short periods of time and require repeated renewal with all the attendant bureaucratic difficulties. Often, they are refused without reason or no apparently good reason. They subject the freedom of movement of Palestinians to the whim of the Occupying Power. The uncertainty and unpredictability of the permit system creates anger, anxiety, and humiliation.

24. The Wall aggravates a humanitarian crisis that is already acute in the West Bank as a result of curfews, closures, and checkpoints. The cities of Qalqiliya and Tulkarm have become ghost towns: their commercial life has been destroyed by their isolation from the West Bank, while farmers in the vicinity of these cities are no longer able to market their produce. Some 600 shops have reportedly closed in Qalqiliya and an estimated 6,000 persons have left the area.

25. At present those affected by the Wall are determined to stay. But there is a real possibility that the residents of villages

within the Closed Zone, and those near to the Wall who have been separated from their lands, will admit defeat, and move east, the victims of strangulation by permit, intimidation, and isolation. Palestinians in Jerusalem face a similar fate. The Wall at Abu Dis has already led to a 60 percent depreciation in property values and both residents and shopkeepers now contemplate migration. "Voluntary" population transfer of this kind is seen by Palestinians as the principal aim of the Wall.

26. The immediate beneficiaries of the Wall are the settlers: 54 settlements containing 142,000 settlers (that is 63 percent of the West Bank settlement population) will find themselves on the Israeli side of the Wall, with the prospect of access to and, in due course appropriation of new land separated from its Palestinian owners. The rhetoric of a "freeze on settlements" has lost its meaning and settlements feel free to expand, both in terms of new buildings and asserted security zones. Settlements may be illegal in terms of the sixth paragraph of article 49 of the Geneva Convention relative to the Protection of Civilian Persons in Time of War of 12 August 1949 (the Fourth Geneva Convention), but they have achieved a new recognition and status under Israeli law as a result of the Wall. However, it is important to stress that the illegal nature of settlements makes it impossible to justify the penetration of the Wall into Palestinian territory as a lawful or legitimate security measure to protect settlements. This also applies to the building of the Wall within the illegally annexed part of East Jerusalem.

27. The Special Rapporteur is compelled to conclude, on the basis of evidence made available to him and the benefit of on-site inspection, that the Wall does not serve a legitimate security purpose when it enters into Palestinian land. Rather, this penetration seems designed to expand Israeli territory and to bring illegal settlements into Israel. It must therefore be seen as an instrument of annexation, in violation of international law. As shown above, the Wall has serious implications for human rights and international humanitarian law. Space does not permit a detailed account of the norms violated. The following violations are, however, the most obvious.

28. *General international law.* As pointed out in the report of 8 September 2003, the construction of the Wall constitutes *de facto* annexation of Palestinian territory by forcible means and therefore violates the prohibition on the acquisition of territory by forcible means contained in Article 2 (4) of the United Nations Charter and General Assembly resolution 2625 (XXV) of 24 October 1970 on the Declaration on Principles of International Law concerning Friendly Relations and Cooperation among States in Accordance with the Charter of the United Nations. (See further E/CN.4/2004/6, para. 14.)

29. *International humanitarian law.* The Wall violates, directly or indirectly, a number of important principles of international humanitarian law. These include the prohibition on annexation of occupied territory (Fourth Geneva Convention, art. 47), on settlements (ibid., art. 49, sixth paragraph), on confiscation of private property (The Hague Regulations, respecting the Laws and Customs of War on Land, art. 23 [g] and 46), on mass forcible transfers of the population of occupied territory (Fourth Geneva Convention, art. 49, first paragraph) and on the destruction of private property where such destruction is not "rendered absolutely necessary by military operations" (ibid., art. 53). The Wall has also resulted in the failure on the part of Israel to facilitate the education of children and to ensure that the occupied population has adequate food and medication, in violation of articles 50 and 55 of the Fourth Geneva Convention.

30. *International human rights law.* A number of basic human rights are violated as a result of the Wall. These include freedom of movement, and the rights to family life, to work, to health, to an adequate standard of living, including adequate food, clothing and housing, and to education. The prohibition on discrimination contained in many international conventions is clearly violated in the Closed Zone in which Palestinians, but not Israelis, are required to have permits.

31. *The right of self-determination.* As pointed out in the report of 8 September 2003, the Wall interferes with the Palestinian right of self-determination as it substantially reduces the size of

the self-determination unit within which the right is to be exercised (E/CN.4/2004/6, para. 15).

The Wall, 2006
E/CN.4/2006/29 of 17 January 2006, para. 16

Not a security measure

16. In past years the Special Rapporteur has visited sections of the Wall, complete or under construction, in the north (Al-Mutilla, Tulkarm, Jubara, Ar-Ras, Qalqiliya, Jayyus, Habla, Ras-A-Tira, Azzun Atma, Beit Amin, Iskaka), the centre (Beit Surik, Biddu, Qalandia, Ar-Ram, Anata, Abu Dis, Bethlehem, Al-Walaja) and the south (Hebron hills). On this occasion he visited Biddya, Bil'in, Ar-Ram, Qalandiya, Shuafat, Anata, Abu Dis, Al-Eizariya and Bethlehem. The Special Rapporteur has repeatedly expressed the opinion that many sections of the Wall appear to have been built for reasons other than security. Observations on the present visit confirmed this view. The Wall near Bil'in has clearly been constructed to allow for the expansion of the Modi'in settlement. The construction of the settlement of Matityahu East in the Modi'in bloc is there for all to see and provides the obvious explanation for the Wall. (The Special Rapporteur was tear-gassed by the Israel Defense Forces/Border Police while viewing the wall near Bil'in and a demonstration in the vicinity of the Wall.) Even more grotesque is the suggestion that the Wall around Abu Dis, Anata, Shuafat and Al-Eizariya is being constructed for security purposes when it separates Palestinian from Palestinian. Here the clear purpose of the Wall is to reduce the number of Palestinians in East Jerusalem. A recent publication of B'Tselem and Bimkom ("Under the guise of security; routing the separation barrier to enable the expansion of settlements in the West Bank," December 2005) confirms that the principal purpose of the Wall is to protect settlements and to provide for settlement expansion. The Israeli High Court in part acknowledged this in *Mara'abe v. The Prime Minister of Israel* H.C.J. 7957/04 when it held that the Wall might

legitimately be built to protect settlers (paras. 20–21). Further evidence that the Wall is not intended as a security measure has come from a statement by the Israeli Minister of Justice, Tzipi Livni, who stated on 30 November 2005 that "one does not have to be a genius to see that the fence will have implications for the future border. This is not the reason for its establishment, but it could have political implications" (*Haaretz*, 1 December 2005). The time has, therefore, come to accept that while the wall may serve a legitimate security purpose when it follows the Green Line, when it enters Palestinian territory it serves different goals, namely, territorial expansion and the protection of settlements.

The Wall, 2008

A/HRC/7/17 of 21 January 2008, paras. 36–39

Humanitarian consequences

36. The Wall that Israel is at present building, largely in Palestinian territory, is clearly illegal. The International Court of Justice in its Advisory Opinion on the construction of the wall found that it is contrary to international law and that Israel is under an obligation to discontinue construction of the Wall and to dismantle forthwith those sections that have already been built. Israel has abandoned its claim that the Wall is a security measure only and now concedes that one of the purposes of the Wall is to include settlements within Israel. The fact that 83 percent of the West Bank settler population and 69 settlements are enclosed within the Wall bears this out.

37. The Wall is planned to extend for 721 kilometers. At present 59 percent of the wall has been completed and 200 kilometers have been constructed since the International Court of Justice handed down its Advisory Opinion declaring the Wall to be illegal. When the Wall is finished, an estimated 60,000 West Bank Palestinians living in 42 villages and towns will reside in the closed zone between the Wall and the Green Line. This area will constitute 10.2 percent of Palestinian land in the West Bank. There

are, however, suggestions that the route of the Wall will be revised to include additional Palestinian lands in the south-eastern West Bank near to the Dead Sea. If this plan is implemented some 13 percent of Palestinian land will be seized by the Wall. The closed zone includes many of the West Bank's valuable water resources and its richest agricultural lands.

38. The Wall has serious humanitarian consequences for Palestinians living within the closed zone. They are cut off from places of employment, schools, universities and specialized medical care, and community life is seriously fragmented. Moreover, they do not have 24-hour access to emergency health services. Over 100 persons residing in the closed zone have not received permits to leave the area. Palestinians who live on the eastern side of the Wall but whose land lies in the closed zone face serious economic hardship, as they are not able to reach their land to harvest crops or to graze their animals without permits. Permits are not easily granted and the bureaucratic procedures for obtaining them are humiliating and obstructive. The Office for the Coordination of Humanitarian Affairs (OCHA) has estimated that only about 18 percent of those who used to work land in the closed zone before the construction of the Wall receive permits to visit the closed zone today. The opening and closing of the gates leading to the closed zone are regulated in a highly restrictive manner: in 2007 OCHA carried out a survey in 67 communities located close to the wall which showed that only 19 of the 67 gates in the wall were open to Palestinians for use all the year round on a daily basis. To aggravate matters Palestinians coming into and out of the closed zone are frequently subjected to abuse and humiliation at the gates by the IDF. Hardships experienced by Palestinians living within the closed zone and in the precincts of the Wall have already resulted in the displacement of some 15,000 persons.

39. The plight of the village of Jayyus, visited by the Special Rapporteur on 30 September 2007, illustrates the hardships faced by communities living near to the Wall, but in the West Bank. The 3,200 residents of Jayyus are separated by the Wall from their farmland; 68 percent of the village's agricultural land and its six agricultural wells lie in the closed zone between the Wall and the

Green Line and are off limits to those without a visitor's permit. Scores of greenhouses are situated in the closed zone, producing tomatoes, cucumbers and sweet peppers, which require daily irrigation. Only about 40 percent of the residents of Jayyus are granted permits to access farms, and gate opening times are both limited and arbitrary. By August 2004, one year after the construction of the Wall, local production had fallen from 7 to 4 million kilograms of fruit and vegetables. The situation has further deteriorated over the past three years.

The Wall, 2007

A/62/275 of 17 August 2007, paras. 31–32

Compensation for damage caused by the Wall

31. In its 2004 advisory opinion the International Court of Justice held that Israel has the obligation to make reparations for the damage caused to Palestinians by the construction of the Wall. Where restitution of property is not possible, stated the Court, Israel "has an obligation to compensate, in accordance with the applicable rules of international law, all natural and legal persons having suffered any form of material damage as a result of the Wall's construction" (2004 ICJ Reports 136, para. 153). In 2004 the General Assembly directed the establishment of a United Nations Register of Damage Caused by the Construction of the Wall in the Occupied Palestinian Territory and the establishment of a board to administer this register. As this decision was not implemented for more than two years, on 15 December 2006 the General Assembly at its tenth emergency special session, in resolution ES-10/17, requested the Secretary-General to report within six months on the progress made in this respect. In compliance with this request the Secretary-General appointed, on 10 May 2007, Harumi Hori of Japan, Matti Paavo Pellonpää of Finland and Michael F. Raboin of the United States to membership of the Board. The Board met from 14 to 16 May 2007 and plans to meet again in August/September.

32. Compensation for violation of the human rights of Palestinians and the violation of rules of international humanitarian law arising from the construction of the Wall is a human rights issue which clearly falls within the present Special Rapporteur's mandate. The Special Rapporteur shares the concerns expressed by stakeholders and civil society about the Board and its functions. First, there is the opaque manner in which the Board was appointed. Many United Nations officers who hold similar positions are elected to office; others are appointed after wide consultation. The failure of the Secretary-General to employ a more transparent method of appointment, coupled with the fact that all the members of the Board, however well qualified they undoubtedly are, are nationals of States from the North with close relations with Israel, inevitably means that members of the Board will have to overcome the misgivings of stakeholders and civil society. Secondly, there are serious doubts about how the Board will perceive its role. What criteria will it adopt for eligibility and verification of claims? Will it consider non-material damages such as the effects on mental health and family life? Or will it confine itself to material damage? Will it insist on gaining access to the Occupied Palestinian Territory to fully assess the damages involved? Or will it defer to Israel when it is refused access? Will it ensure that Palestinians are informed about their right to claim? Will there be consultation with civil society?

The Wall, 2008
A/HRC/7/17 of 21 January 2008

The failure of the United Nations to implement the advisory opinion of the International Court of Justice on the Wall

50. On 8 December 2003 the General Assembly requested an advisory opinion from the International Court of Justice on the legal consequences arising from the construction of the Wall being built by Israel in the OPT (Resolution ES-10/14). Fifty

States and international organizations gave written statements to the Court and 15 States and international organizations made oral statements before the Court. The Court provided an advisory opinion (*Legal Consequences of the Construction of a Wall in the Occupied Palestinian Territory*, 2004 ICJ Reports 136) by 14 votes to 1, which answered many of the legal questions that have been raised over the past 40 years. The principal findings of the Court were as follows:

(a) The Palestinian people have the right of self-determination (para. 118) and the exercise of this right is violated by the construction of the Wall (para. 122);

(b) Israel is under a legal obligation to comply with the Fourth Geneva Convention in the OPT (paras. 90–101)—a unanimous finding;

(c) Settlements are illegal as they violate article 49 (6) of the Fourth Geneva Convention (paras. 120–21)—a unanimous finding;

(d) Israel is bound by international human rights conventions in the OPT (paras. 102–121)—a unanimous finding—and consequently its conduct is to be measured against both international human rights conventions and the Fourth Geneva Convention;

(e) The regime in force in the closed zone between the Wall and Green Line violates the right to freedom of movement contained in article 12 of the International Covenant on Civil and Political Rights (paras. 133–36) and the right to work, health, education and an adequate standard of living contained in the International Covenant on Economic, Social and Cultural Rights (paras. 132, 135–37);

(f) The destruction of property for the construction of the Wall violates article 53 of the Fourth Geneva Convention and cannot be justified on grounds of military necessity or national security (paras. 132–37);

(g) The Wall cannot be justified as an exercise in self-defense (paras. 138–39);

(h) The annexation of East Jerusalem is illegal (paras. 75, 122);

(i) The construction of the Wall by Israel in the OPT, including in and around East Jerusalem, and its associated regime are contrary to international law; and Israel is obliged in law to cease the construction of the Wall, to dismantle it and to make reparation for the construction of the Wall (para. 163);

(j) All States are under a legal obligation not to recognize the illegal situation resulting from the Wall and to ensure compliance by Israel with the Fourth Geneva Convention (para. 163);

(k) The United Nations, especially the General Assembly and Security Council, should consider what further action is required to bring an end to the illegal situation resulting from the construction of the Wall and associated regime, "taking due account of the present Advisory Opinion" (para. 163).

51. On 20 July 2004 the General Assembly adopted Resolution ES-10/15 which called for Israel to comply with the Advisory Opinion of the International Court of Justice. This resolution was adopted by 150 votes to 6 (Australia, Micronesia, Israel, Marshall Islands, Palau, United States) with 10 abstentions. The Russian Federation and member States of the European Union voted in favor of the resolution.

52. Since 2004, the Advisory Opinion has been ignored by the Security Council. While the General Assembly (Resolution of 10 December 2007) and Human Rights Council (HRC Resolution 2/4 of 27 November 2006) have passed several resolutions reaffirming the Opinion, no attempt has been made by the Security Council to compel Israel to comply with the Opinion or to remind States of their obligation to ensure compliance by Israel with the Fourth Geneva Convention. The reason for this is not hard to find. The Security Council is prevented from giving its backing to the Opinion by the United States, which has refused to accept it. Similarly, the United States prevents the Quartet from taking steps

to implement the Opinion. No statement issued by the Quartet has ever acknowledged the Opinion (see, for example, the statement of the Quartet of 23 September 2007).

53. Although the Advisory Opinion of the International Court of Justice is an authoritative statement of the applicable law and is designed to contribute to the framework for peace in the Middle East, it is not legally binding on States. In law, the United States is well within its right to refuse to accept the Opinion in the Quartet. The same applies to the Russian Federation and the European Union—although both have compromised themselves by giving approval to the Opinion by supporting General Assembly resolution ES-10/15 and subsequent resolutions. The position of the United Nations is, however, very different. The International Court of Justice is the judicial organ of the United Nations. Moreover, the General Assembly has by an overwhelming majority repeatedly given its approval to the Opinion. This means that it is now part of the law of the United Nations. As such the representative of the United Nations in the Quartet—the Secretary-General or his representative—is in law obliged to be guided by the Opinion and to endeavor in good faith to do his or her best to ensure compliance with the Opinion. If the Secretary-General (or his representative) is politically unable to do so, he has two choices: either to withdraw from the Quartet or to explain to his constituency—"we the peoples of the United Nations" in the language of the Charter—why he is unable to do so and how he justifies remaining in the Quartet in the light of its refusal to be guided by the law of the United Nations. The first course is possibly unwise at this time as this would deprive the United Nations of a role in the peace process. This makes the second course essential.

54. For 40 years the political organs of the United Nations, States and individuals have accused Israel of consistent, systematic and gross violations of human rights and humanitarian law in the OPT. In 2004 the judicial organ of the United Nations, in its Advisory Opinion, affirmed that Israel's actions in the OPT do indeed violate fundamental norms of human rights and humanitarian law and cannot be justified on grounds of self-defense or

necessity. If the United Nations is serious about human rights it cannot afford to ignore this Opinion in the deliberations of the Quartet, as it is an authoritative affirmation that Israel is in serious breach of its international commitments. Failure to attempt to implement, or even to acknowledge, an advisory opinion dealing with international humanitarian law and human rights law, brings the very commitment of the United Nations to human rights into question.

Settlements, 2004
E/CN.4/2005/29 of 7 December 2004, paras. 27–30

The incorporation of settlements by the Wall

27. The course of the Wall indicates clearly that its purpose is to incorporate as many settlers as possible into Israel. This is borne out by the statistics showing that some 80 percent of settlers in the West Bank will be included on the Israeli side of the Wall. If further proof of this obvious fact is required, it is to be found in an article by Benjamin Netanyahu, Minister of Finance of Israel and former Prime Minister, in the *International Herald Tribune* of 14 July 2004, in which he wrote: "A line that is genuinely based on security would include as many Jews as possible and as few Palestinians as possible within the fence. That is precisely what Israel's security fence does. By running into less than 12 percent of the West Bank, the fence will include about 80 percent of Jews and only 1 percent of Palestinians who live within the disputed territories."

28. Settlements are, of course, unlawful under international law. This was the unanimous view of the International Court of Justice in its advisory opinion. The Court found that "the Israeli settlements in the Occupied Palestinian Territory (including East Jerusalem) have been established in breach of international law," and that "the route chosen for the wall gives expression in loco to the illegal measures taken by Israel with regard to Jerusalem and the settlements" (2004 ICJ Reports 136, paras. 120 and 122).

Moreover, Judge Buergenthal, the sole dissenting judge, stated that he agreed that article 49, paragraph 6, of the Fourth Geneva Convention applied to the Israeli settlements in the West Bank from which it followed "that the segments of the Wall being built by Israel to protect the settlements are ipso facto in violation of international humanitarian law" (Dissenting Opinion, para. 9).

29. Despite this, there is overwhelming evidence of settlement expansion in the West Bank. No longer does the government of Israel even pay lip service to its claim of several years ago that it would "freeze" settlement expansion. In August, the government of Israel granted 2,167 permits to settlers to build apartments in Palestine (*International Herald Tribune*, 24 August 2004, p. 5). The Prime Minister, Ariel Sharon, has furthermore announced that in return for dismantling settlements in the Gaza Strip and four small settlements in the northern West Bank (Ghanim, Khadim, Sa-Nur and Homesh), the remaining settlements in the West Bank would be consolidated and expanded. According to the report of the Director-General of ILO to the 92nd session of the International Labour Conference, "the settler population has continued to increase rapidly, at an annual rate of 5.3 percent in the West Bank and 4.4 percent in Gaza since 2000, reaching close to 400,000 persons in the occupied Palestinian territories. This is equivalent to 6 percent of the Israeli population and 11.5 percent of the Palestinian population in 2002. The increase in the settler population has been much faster than population growth in Israel (at 1.4 percent per year over 2000–2002), thereby indicating more than natural demographic growth, even allowing for higher fertility among settler families" ("The situation of workers in the occupied Arab Territories," ILO, June, para. 39).

30. Settler expansion has unfortunately been accompanied by settler violence. Numerous incidents have been reported of settler attacks on Palestinians and their land and it is reported that there has been a 20 percent increase in settler violence. Recently, settlers have prevented Palestinians from harvesting the olive crop. Settler behaviour is particularly disgusting in Hebron where settlers continuously harass Palestinians and damage their property. The Special Rapporteur had first-hand experience of this

when the vehicle in which he was travelling with the Temporary International Presence in the City of Hebron (TIPH) was spat upon by settlers and splattered with paint. Obstacles placed in the road by settlers were not removed, despite a request by a TIPH official. On the contrary, members of the IDF laughingly indicated their approval of the action of the settlers and refused to intervene, despite Israel's legal obligation to cooperate with TIPH. As settlers are present in the OPT with the government's approval and as inadequate steps are taken to curb their actions, the government of Israel must accept responsibility for their actions.

Settlements, 2006
E/CN.4/2006/29 of 17 January 2006, para. 29

Settler violence with special reference to Hebron

29. Settler violence remains a serious problem. Prosecutions of settlers are rare and it seems that settlers are able to terrorize Palestinians and destroy their trees and crops with impunity. Nine hundred olive trees in the West Bank village of Salem, near Nablus, were destroyed in the course of 2005. In the southern Hebron hills, visited by the Special Rapporteur in June 2005, schoolchildren are terrorized on their way to school; wells, fields and sheep have been poisoned; many sheep and goats have been stolen (B'Tselem, "Means of Expulsion: Violence, harassment and lawlessness against Palestinians in the Southern Hebron Hills," July 2005). The worst settler violence is to be found in the city of Hebron, where settlers occupy key buildings within the centre of the old city. From these settlements they terrorize the few Palestinians that have not left the old city and assault and traumatize children on the way to school. Obscene, racist graffiti (for example, "Gas the Arabs") adorns the walls of the old city of Hebron. The Israel Defense Forces patrol the city but make little attempt to protect Palestinians from the settlers and fail to remove racist graffiti. In short, the Israel Defense Forces have made themselves a party to the crimes of the settlers.

Haaretz columnist Gideon Levy sums up the situation as follows:

> Every day the settlers torment their neighbours here. Every walk to school for a Palestinian child has become a journey of harassment and fear. Every shopping outing by a housewife is a journey of humiliation. Settler children kicking old women carrying baskets, settlers setting their dogs on the elderly, garbage and faeces thrown from the settlers' balconies into the courtyards of Palestinian homes, junk metal blocking the entrances of their houses, rocks thrown at any Palestinian passer-by—this is the routine of life in the city. Hundreds of soldiers, border policemen and cops witness these actions and stand by idly. ... Israel cannot be considered a State ruled by law, or a democracy, as long as the pogroms continue in Hebron (*Haaretz,* 11 Sept. 2005).

Settlements, 2007
A/HRC/4/17 of 29 January 2007

The new colonialism

32. Jewish settlements in the West Bank are illegal. They violate article 49, paragraph 6, of the Fourth Geneva Convention and their illegality has been confirmed by the International Court of Justice in its advisory opinion on the Wall. Despite the illegality of settlements and the unanimous condemnation of settlements by the international community, the government of Israel persists in allowing settlements to grow. Sometimes settlement expansion occurs openly and with the full approval of the government. As recently as December 2006, the Israeli government officially approved the building of a new settlement—Maskiot—in the northern Jordan Valley. More frequently, expansion takes place stealthily under the guise of "natural growth," which has resulted in Israeli settlements growing at an average rate of 5.5 percent

compared with the 1.7 percent average growth rate in Israeli cities. Sometimes settlements expand unlawfully in terms of Israeli law, but no attempt is made to enforce the law. Outposts are frequently established and threats to remove them are not carried out. As a result of expansion, the settler population in the West Bank numbers some 260,000 persons and that of East Jerusalem nearly 200,000. As indicated above, the Wall is presently being built in both the West Bank and East Jerusalem to ensure that most settlements will be enclosed within the Wall. Moreover, the three major settlement blocks of Gush Etzion, Ma'aleh Adumim and Ariel will effectively divide Palestinian territory into cantons, thereby destroying the territorial integrity of Palestine.

33. In October 2006, the Israeli NGO, Peace Now, published a study which showed, on the basis of government maps and figures, that nearly 40 percent of the land held by Israeli settlements in the West Bank is privately owned by Palestinians (*Breaking the Law in the West Bank—One Violation Leads to Another: Israeli Settlement Building on Private Palestinian Property*). The data shows, for example, that 86 percent of the largest settlement of Ma'aleh Adumim is on Palestinian private property; that 35 percent of Ariel is on private property; and that more than 3,400 buildings in settlements are constructed on land privately owned by Palestinians. The Israeli government maintains that it respects Palestinian property in the West Bank and that it only, on a temporary basis, takes land there legally for security reasons. Moreover, article 46 of the Hague Regulations of 1907, which Israel acknowledges as binding upon it, provides that "private property . . . must be respected" and "cannot be confiscated." Peace Now's disclosure is an embarrassment to the government of Israel, but it is unlikely to respond positively as it has already repeatedly rejected the international community's complaint that settlements are contrary to article 49, paragraph 6, of the Fourth Geneva Convention. This new revelation does, however, serve to further emphasize the illegality of Israel's colonial empire—the settlements—in the West Bank.

34. The history of colonialism shows that there are "good" settlers and "bad" settlers. So it is with Israel's colonists. Many

are ordinary Israelis who have been lured to the settlements by tax incentives and a better quality of life. On the other hand, there is a fanatic minority determined to assert its superiority over the Palestinian population by violent means. Throughout the West Bank there is evidence of settler violence, which often takes the form of destroying Palestinian olive groves or obstructing the olive harvest. Undoubtedly the most aggravated settler behavior occurs in Hebron, where Palestinian schoolchildren are assaulted and humiliated on their way to schools, shopkeepers are beaten, and residents live in fear of settler terror. Despite rulings of the High Court of Justice that it is the duty of the IDF to protect Palestinian farmers from settlers (*Rashad Morar v The IDF Commander of Judea and Samaria* (HCJ 95932/04), there is still evidence that the IDF turns a blind eye to settler violence and, on occasion, collaborates with the settlers in harassing and humiliating Palestinians (Yesh Din, *A Semblance of Law. Law Enforcement Upon Israeli Civilians in the West Bank,* June 2006). Indeed I have witnessed such conduct on the part of the IDF myself in Hebron.

Restrictions on Movement, 2003
E/CN.4/2004/6 of 8 September 2003, paras. 17–21

Checkpoints, curfews and closures

17. Previous reports have described the serious restrictions on freedom of movement imposed on the Palestinian people by the Occupying Power. "Checkpoints," "closures" and "curfews" are words that fail to capture the full enormity of what is happening today in the West Bank and Gaza. A checkpoint is not simply a military outpost on a highway that checks the documents of pedestrians and traffic that seek to proceed along the road. Every day thousands of Palestinians must pass through these checkpoints in order to travel from home to work, to reach schools and hospitals and to visit friends and family. Every day Palestinians are compelled to waste hours passing through these checkpoints. Frequently, Palestinians are obliged to leave their vehicles at one

checkpoint and to walk along dusty roads to another checkpoint to take a taxi to their destination. Accounts of rudeness, humiliation and brutality at the checkpoints are legion. Ambulances are often delayed, and women give birth to children at checkpoints. Checkpoints are not so much a security measure for ensuring that would-be suicide bombers do not enter Israel, but rather the institutionalization of the humiliation of the Palestinian people. Similarly, a curfew is not simply a restriction on leaving one's home. It is the imprisonment of the people within their own homes. Unable to go to work, to buy food, to go to school, to visit hospitals or to bury their dead, they are confined within the walls of their own homes while the IDF patrols their streets. Statistics of checkpoints and curfews cannot accurately portray the obscenity of the situation. Unfortunately, Israelis are protected from seeing what their army is doing to their subjugated neighbor by laws that restrict Israelis from seeing what is happening. The acclaimed Palestinian author, Raja Shehadeh, described the situation in his recent book *When the Bulbul Stops Singing: A Diary of Ramallah Under Siege*: "During the first intifada, the movement of both people into the land of the other continued to be possible. . . . All sorts of relations developed between the people on the two sides of the divide. None of this has been possible this time. With the exception of a few determined Israeli journalists, it was left to the army to present to the Israeli people the reality of the Occupied Territories. The prohibition against travel by both sides to each other's territories meant that the demonization could continue unchallenged."

18. The task of the Special Rapporteur is to report on facts. Curfews continue, but without the severity of 2002. From November 2002 to April 2003, an average of 390,000 civilians were under curfew compared with 520,000 in the second half of 2002. However, people under curfew in Hebron, Jenin and parts of Gaza were frequently under tighter and more continuous curfew in 2003.

19. There are some 300 checkpoints or roadblocks, including about 140 checkpoints manned by the military. However, in late July 2003, a number of roadblocks were removed within the

context of the implementation of the road map. Checkpoints vary in nature and include permanent checkpoints, mobile checkpoints, unmanned roadblocks, dirt walls, earth mounds, concrete blocks, iron gates and trenches dug around villages and towns. Sometimes tanks or military vehicles are used as roadblocks. These checkpoints or roadblocks, around every town and major road junction, divide the OPT internally. Eight commercial checkpoints divide the West Bank into the separate cantons of Hebron, Bethlehem, Jericho, Ramallah, Nablus, Tulkarem, Qalqiliya and Jenin. Each district has one official commercial entrance. Commercial goods must be unloaded and transferred to another vehicle on the other side of the checkpoint ("back-to-back transport"). Checkpoints for ordinary people likewise sometimes require back-to-back transfer. These checkpoints divide the West Bank into a patchwork of cantons. Since March 2002, permits have been required to travel from one district to another. Gaza is totally isolated from the rest of Palestine. It too, however, is partitioned into three separate cantons by checkpoints. These measures have not prevented the movement of militants between different towns or regions or between Palestine and Israel. They do not protect settlements which are already well protected by the IDF. Instead, internal checkpoints restrict internal trade within the OPT and restrict the entire population from travelling from village to village or town to town. They must therefore be seen as a form of collective punishment. Writing in *Haaretz* on 27 July 2003, the columnist Gideon Levy wrote that the purpose of checkpoints is "to make the lives of the local residents as miserable as possible." Unfortunately, the Israeli representatives appearing before the Human Rights Committee on 24 and 25 July 2003 made no serious attempt to address the issue of checkpoints. Indeed, there seemed to be no appreciation on their part of the hardships and humiliation caused by checkpoints.

20. Checkpoints, closures and curfews have had a major impact on the Palestinian economy. According to a World Bank report of May 2003, "The bulk of Palestinian economic losses stem from closure and curfew" (*Twenty-Seven Months: Intifada, Closures and Palestinian Economic Crisis,* Jerusalem, chap 2, para. 2.5). This has resulted in unemployment (which now stands

at 40 percent in the West Bank and Gaza) and poverty (60 percent of the people live on less than US$2 per day; 2 million live in poverty, dependent on food from international donor agencies). Checkpoints and curfews have also led to a drop in health standards resulting from inability to access hospitals and clinics, the impossibility of carrying out health-care programmes (for example, vaccinations) and the psychological trauma arising from the physical, economic and social consequences of occupation. Checkpoints have also resulted in the failure to acquire nutritious food and sufficient clean water. The obstruction of ambulances at checkpoints remains a serious problem. In the past year, about 60 ambulances per month were held up at checkpoints of which a quarter were denied passage. In March 2003, 15 ambulances were fired upon. Children have suffered dramatically. Schools are closed by curfew and checkpoints make it difficult for both teachers and children to reach schools. Twenty-two percent of children under the age of 5 suffer from acute or chronic malnutrition while the breakdown of family life has had a severe impact on children.

21. There is a humanitarian crisis in the West Bank and Gaza. It is not the result of a natural disaster. Instead, it is a crisis imposed by a powerful State on its neighbor.

The Humanitarian Crisis and the Withholding of Funds from the Palestinian Authority, 2007
A/HRC/4/17 of 29 January 2007, paras. 51–54

In January 2006 an election was held in occupied Palestine, which independent observers hailed as free and fair. Hamas won the election but entered into a government of national unity with Fatah. Because Hamas was labelled as a terrorist organization Israel, the U.S., the EU, and Canada withdrew funding for the Palestinian Authority. The January 2007 Report criticized this decision.

51. There is a humanitarian crisis in both the West Bank and Gaza. In Gaza, over 80 percent of the population live below the

official poverty line of US$2.10 per day while in the West Bank 56 percent of households fall below the poverty line. This means that two thirds of all Palestinian households fall below the income poverty line, are dependent on food aid and unable to provide for their basic needs. Health care and education in the West Bank are badly affected by a strike that continued for several months—a strike against the non-payment of salaries by the Palestinian Authority (PA) since March, but also a protest against the international community for withholding funding from the PA. In such a situation it is not surprising that domestic violence and crime is on the increase.

52. In large measure the humanitarian crisis is the result of the termination of funding of the Palestinian Authority since Hamas was elected to office. The government of Israel is withholding from the Palestinian Authority VAT monies amounting to US$50 to 60 million per month which it collects on behalf of the Authority on goods imported into the OPT. In law Israel has no right to refuse to transfer this money, which belongs to the Palestinian Authority under the 1994 Protocol on Economic Relations between the government of Israel and the Palestine Liberation Organization (Paris Protocol). Predictably, Israel justifies its action on security grounds, but the real reason seems to be a determination to effect a regime change. In the process, Israel is violating its obligation as Occupying Power to provide for the welfare of the occupied people. By deliberately making life as difficult as possible for the Palestinian people, by withholding funds and imposing harsh measures on them, Israel has embarked upon a policy of collective punishment in violation of article 33 of the Fourth Geneva Convention. Worse still it is creating a failed state on its own border which augurs ill for both the Occupied Palestinian Territory and Israel itself.

53. Israel is not alone to blame for the crisis in the OPT. Since the election of Hamas in January 2006, the United States, the European Union, and other States have likewise withheld funds from the Palestinian Authority by reason of its failure to recognize Israel, renounce violence, and accept obligations previously assumed towards Israel. The decision of the United States

Treasury to prohibit transactions with the Palestinian Authority has, moreover, resulted in banks refusing to transfer money to the PA. To aggravate matters the Quartet has gone along with this policy of political and financial isolation. In order to mitigate the crisis, the EU has set up a Temporary International Mechanism, endorsed by the Quartet, for the relief of Palestinians employed in the health sector, the uninterrupted supply of utilities, including fuel, and the provision of basic allowances to meet the needs of the poorest segment of the population. Although the EU disbursed US$865 million to the Palestinians in this way in 2006—an increase of 27 percent compared to EU funding in 2005—it has not resulted in the payment of salaries to most Palestinians employed in the public sector. Health-care workers and teachers have received some payments, but well short of their full salaries, and pensioners and social hardship cases have also received an allowance. However, owing to the withholding of tax revenues due to the PA by Israel, most government employees remain unpaid and are experiencing difficulty in paying their basic expenses, such as rent and electricity.

54. In effect, the Palestinian people have been subjected to economic sanctions—the first time an occupied people have been so treated. This is difficult to understand. Israel is in violation of major Security Council and General Assembly resolutions dealing with unlawful territorial change and the violation of human rights and has failed to implement the 2004 Advisory Opinion of the International Court of Justice, yet it escapes the imposition of sanctions. Instead, the Palestinian people, rather than the Palestinian Authority, have been subjected to possibly the most rigorous form of international sanctions imposed in modern times.

Gaza, 2006

E/CN.4.2006/29 of 17 January 2006, paras. 6–11

Gaza following the withdrawal of Israel, January 2006

6. The situation in Gaza has changed dramatically since the Special Rapporteur's previous visit in June 2005. In August/ September, in a highly successful operation, Israel evacuated all of its settlers from Gaza and destroyed all settlements. Shortly thereafter, Israel withdrew its military forces from Gaza. This resulted in the disappearance of a brutal military presence, the removal of checkpoints that had for years thwarted freedom of movement and the conferral of a wide measure of freedom for Gazans.

7. Although Israel exercised strict control over the borders of Gaza following disengagement, on 15 November 2005 an important agreement on borders was entered into between Israel and the Palestinian Authority, facilitated by United States Secretary of State, Condoleezza Rice, and the Quartet's special envoy, James Wolfensohn. This agreement allows Palestinian identity (ID) cardholders to cross to and from Egypt at Rafah at a crossing operated by the Palestinian Authority and Egypt, and provides for the increased export of goods through the Karni crossing and the transit of persons and goods between Gaza and the West Bank by convoys of buses.

8. The withdrawal of the Israel Defense Forces from Gaza has led some to claim that the occupation of Gaza has come to an end. In deciding on this matter regard must be had to whether Israel retains effective control over the territory as this is the test for occupation recognized by international humanitarian law (Article 42 of the Hague Regulations of 1907; *In re List and others (Hostages Trial)* 15 Annual Digest of Public International Law Cases 632, 638).While the Special Rapporteur concedes that the absence of a military Occupying Power in Gaza has removed many of the features of occupation, it is wrong to suggest that the occupation has ended. In the first place, it must be stressed that technological advances since 1949 have changed the whole nature

of control. It is no longer necessary for a foreign military power to maintain a permanent physical presence in a territory to exercise control, as Israel has demonstrated since its withdrawal from Gaza. Sonic booms, which terrorize and traumatize the population (and constitute a form of collective punishment) and the targeted assassination of militants (and innocent bystanders) by rockets fired from the skies, serve as a constant reminder to the people of Gaza that they remain occupied. In the three months following Israel's withdrawal from Gaza, 15 Palestinians have been targeted and assassinated, 18 civilians killed and 81 injured in response to Qassam rockets fired by militants from Gaza. Such actions of the Israel Defense Forces must be viewed in conjunction with the fact that Israel retains control over airspace, territorial waters (fishing is allowed only within 10 nautical miles of the coastline) and external borders. While it is true that the Rafah crossing is now open to Palestinian ID cardholders, Israel reserves the right to complain about who crosses at Gaza and has already done so (the crossing is administered by the Palestinian Authority and Egypt but supervised by European Union inspectors and followed by Israeli officials on TV monitor screens). Karni crossing was largely dysfunctional at the time of writing and allowed passage of only 35 to 40 trucks compared with the 150 trucks promised by the 15 November agreement. This is a serious problem for greenhouse agricultural products harvested in December/January and exported to Israel and the West Bank. The passage of persons between Gaza and the West Bank by bus convoys, scheduled to start on 15 December, has been stopped by Israel, as a result of a suicide bombing in Netanya and Israel's dissatisfaction with the Rafah crossing. (One fears that even if such convoys do commence, they will be frequently suspended for security reasons.) Control is also maintained by means of the Gaza population register, which Israel still administers, thereby allowing it to control the issue of identity documents to Gazans—a precondition for control in and out of the territory. Other facts confirm Israel's control of Gaza: first, Israel still holds some 650 Gazan prisoners, despite article 77 of the Fourth Geneva Convention, which provides for the release of prisoners "at the close of occupation"; secondly, Israel maintains military control over a buffer zone ranging between 150 and 300 metres within Gaza along its eastern and northern borders from which all Palestinians are excluded (farmers are thus denied access to their lands in this zone); thirdly, Israel may, and has already threatened, to cut off electricity supplies to Gaza. Finally, Palestine constitutes a single self-determination unit, comprising the West Bank and Gaza. To suggest that Gaza should enjoy a status different from that of the West Bank would violate the territorial integrity of Palestine and the substantive law of self-determination.

9. Undoubtedly, the nature of Israel's occupation has changed. Many of the provisions relating to the treatment of protected persons in the Geneva Convention relative to the Protection of Civilian Persons in Time of War (the Fourth Geneva Convention) are premised upon the physical presence of the Occupying Power—but not all. For instance, article 27, requiring protected persons to "be humanely treated" and to "be protected especially against all acts of violence" and article 33, prohibiting collective penalties and "all measures of intimidation or of terror-ism," continue to apply and appear to have been violated by sonic booms and targeted assassinations that routinely cause collateral loss of life and injury. The silence of the principal protector of the Fourth Geneva Convention, the International Committee of the Red Cross, on the continuation of the occupation tends to confirm that it does indeed continue.

10. Israel's occupation of both Gaza and the West Bank is un-usual. The occupation of a territory for 38 years and the physical withdrawal of the Occupying Power from a separate part of the occupied territory were clearly outside the contemplation of the drafters of the Fourth Geneva Convention. But despite the unusual features of the Gaza occupation, it remains an occupation as Israel continues to maintain effective control over the territory. It is not a fully liberated part of an occupied territory. Certainly, the mood of the people of Gaza confirms this. They perceive themselves to be still subject to occupation as was repeatedly stressed to the Special Rapporteur on his visit to Gaza.

11. It does not fall within the mandate of the Special Rapporteur to comment on the state of human rights in Gaza under the administration of the Palestinian Authority. However, it is necessary to observe that the present insecurity in Gaza is hardly conducive to human rights. The Palestinian Authority now has the opportunity to recognize civil and political rights, ensure due process of law, advance the rights of women and children and, subject to the restrictions that flow from Israeli control, promote social and economic rights. This opportunity must not be lost.

Gaza, 2006
A/HRC/2/5 of 5 September 2006

Israel's control of Gaza, September 2006

7. The question whether Gaza remains an occupied territory is now of academic interest only. In the course of the cynically named "Operation Summer Rains" IDF has not only asserted its control in Gaza by means of heavy shelling but has also done so by means of a military presence.

8. In August 2005 Israel withdrew its settlers and armed forces from Gaza. Statements by the government of Israel that the withdrawal ended the occupation of Gaza are grossly inaccurate. Even before the commencement of "Operation Summer Rains," Gaza remained under the effective control of Israel. This control was manifested in a number of ways. First, Israel retained control of Gaza's air space, sea space and external borders. Although a special arrangement was made for the opening of the Rafah crossing to Egypt, to be monitored by European Union personnel, all other crossings remained largely closed. The closure of the Karni crossing for goods for substantial periods had particularly serious consequences for Gaza as it resulted in a denial of access to foodstuffs, medicines and fuel. A proposed scheme which would have allowed Gazans to visit family in the West Bank by means of bus convoys was never implemented. In effect, following Israel's withdrawal, Gaza became a sealed-off, imprisoned society. The

effectiveness of Israel's control was further demonstrated by sonic booms caused by its overflying aircraft, designed to terrorize the population of Gaza, regular shelling of homes and fields along the border and targeted assassinations of militants, which, as in the past, were carried out with little regard for innocent civilian bystanders. In one incident in June 2006, a family of seven was killed by IDF shelling while picnicking on a Gaza beach. The actions of IDF in respect of Gaza have clearly demonstrated that modern technology allows an Occupying Power to effectively control a territory even without a military presence.

9. Writing in *Haaretz* on 7 July 2006, the Israeli columnist Gideon Levy summed up the situation in the following language:

"The Israel Defense Forces departure from Gaza . . . did almost nothing to change the living conditions for the residents of the Strip. Gaza is still a prison and its inhabitants are still doomed to live in poverty and oppression . . . Israel left the cage, threw away the keys and left the residents to their bitter fate. Now, less than a year after the disengagement, it is going back, with violence and force."

10. Even before the start of "Operation Summer Rains" Israel had already tightened its control of Gaza in response to the election of Hamas to the Palestinian Authority in January 2006. I visited Gaza on 11 June 2006. For security reasons, I was not permitted to stay overnight, as had previously been my practice during visits to OPT. I visited the Al-Aqsa Martyrs Hospital in Gaza and spoke with the director of hospital services and senior medical practitioners. It was clear that the hospital services faced a crisis resulting from the non-payment of staff salaries and the restrictions placed on the supply of medicines and vaccines through the Karni crossing. It seemed clear to me that the government of Israeli had embarked upon a siege in order to bring about regime change. In the process little attention was being paid to human rights, as shelling and sonic booms violated the fundamental rights to life and human dignity, and even less attention was paid to the constraints of international humanitarian law; it was already clear that collective punishment was to be the instrument used to bring about regime change.

11. On 25 June 2006 a group of Palestinian militants attacked a military base near the Israeli-Egyptian border, which left two Palestinians and two IDF soldiers dead. In retreating, they took Corporal Gilad Shalit with them as captive. They demanded the release of the women and children in Israeli jails in return for his release. This act, together with the continued Qassam rocket fire into Israel, unleashed a savage response from the government of Israeli. In the first place, it arrested 8 Hamas Cabinet ministers and 26 members of the Palestinian Legislative Council in Ramallah. At the time of writing this report, most of them remained in detention. While Israel claims that they are being held because of their support for terrorist activities, it is difficult to resist the conclusion that they are being held as hostages, in violation of article 34 of the Geneva Convention relative to the Protection of Civilians in Time of War (Fourth Geneva Convention). This impression is confirmed by the debate within the government over what to do with them. The Shin Bet security service suggested holding them as bargaining chips under the Unlawful Combatants Law. It seems, however, that the Attorney-General, Menachem Mazuz, has insisted that legal proceedings be initiated against them for membership in a terrorist organization (see *Haaretz*, 30 June 2006). The issue of the arrest of members of Hamas has been aggravated by the arrest of Aziz Dweik, Speaker of the Palestinian Legislative Council, on 5 August 2006 and reports that he has been injured in the course of interrogation.

Gaza, 2008

A/HRC7/17 of 21 January 2008, paras. 9–27

Israel's actions against Gaza and their consequences, 2008

9. In its Advisory Opinion on the construction of a wall in the West Bank and East Jerusalem, the International Court of Justice was not asked to pronounce on the legal status of Gaza. It, possibly therefore, confined its reaffirmation of the occupied

status of the Occupied Palestinian Territory to the West Bank and East Jerusalem (2004 ICJ Reports 136, para. 101). The evacuation of Israeli settlements and the withdrawal of the permanent IDF presence from Gaza in 2005 has now given rise to the argument that Gaza is no longer occupied territory. On 15 September 2005 Prime Minister Sharon told the General Assembly that Israel's withdrawal from Gaza meant the end of its responsibility for Gaza.

10. On 19 September 2007 Israel seemed to give a new status to Gaza when its Security Cabinet declared Gaza to be "hostile territory"—a characterization that was shortly afterwards approved by the United States Secretary of State. Although the legal implications that Israel intends to attach to this "status" remain unclear, the political purpose of this declaration was immediately made known—namely the reduction of the supply of fuel and electricity to Gaza.

11. The test for determining whether a territory is occupied under international law is effective control and not the permanent physical presence of the Occupying Power's military forces in the territory in question (*Armed Activities on the Territory of the Congo (Democratic Republic of Congo v Uganda)*, 2005 International Court of Justice Reports 464, paras. 173–74). Judged by this test it is clear that Israel remains the Occupying Power as technological developments have made it possible for Israel to assert control over the people of Gaza without a permanent military presence. Israel's effective control is demonstrated by the following factors:

(a) Substantial control of Gaza's six land crossings: the Erez crossing is effectively closed to Palestinians wishing to cross to Israel or the West Bank. The Rafah crossing between Egypt and Gaza, which is regulated by the Agreement on Movement and Access entered into between Israel and the Palestinian Authority on 15 November 2005 (brokered by the United States, the European Union and the international community's envoy for the Israeli disengagement from Gaza), has been closed by Israel for lengthy periods since June 2006. The main crossing for goods at Karni is strictly controlled by Israel and since June 2006 this crossing too has been largely closed, with disastrous consequences for the Palestinian economy.

(b) Control through military incursions, rocket attacks and sonic booms: sections of Gaza have been declared "no-go" zones in which residents will be shot if they enter.

(c) Complete control of Gaza's airspace and territorial waters.

(d) Control of the Palestinian Population Registry: the definition of who is "Palestinian" and who is a resident of Gaza and the West Bank is controlled by the Israeli military. Even when the Rafah crossing is open, only holders of Palestinian identity cards can enter Gaza through the crossing; therefore control over the Palestinian Population Registry is also control over who may enter and leave Gaza. Since 2000, with few exceptions, Israel has not permitted additions to the Palestinian Population Registry.

The fact that Gaza remains occupied territory means that Israel's actions towards Gaza must be measured against the standards of international humanitarian law.

12. Israel has taken a number of actions against Gaza since the withdrawal of Israeli settlers and the IDF in 2005.

Military action

13. IDF military incursions into Gaza have continued regularly over the past year; 290 Palestinians were killed in Gaza in 2007. Of this number at least a third were civilians. On 26 September, the day the Special Rapporteur visited Gaza, 12 Palestinian militants were killed by IDF missiles. Since the Annapolis meeting on 27 November 2007, over 70 Palestinians have been killed, of whom 8 were killed in a major military operation in southern Gaza on the day before the first round of talks between Israelis and Palestinians following the Annapolis meeting. A further 13 Palestinians were killed in three separate airstrikes on 18 December. The frequency of targeted killings raises a question as to whether the IDF acts within the permissible parameters for such action laid down by the Israeli Supreme Court in its 2006 judgement on targeted killings.

Or does the IDF act without regard to its own law as well as international law in carrying out targeted killings?

14. In the past two years 668 Palestinians have been killed by Israeli security forces in Gaza. Over half—359 people—were not involved in hostilities at the time they were killed. Of those killed 126 were minors; 361 were killed by missiles fired from helicopters; and 29 of those killed were targeted for assassination. During the same period, Palestinians fired some 2,800 Qassam rockets and mortar shells into Israel from the Gaza Strip. Four Israeli civilians were killed by Qassam rockets and hundreds were injured. Four members of the Israeli security forces were killed in attacks originating from Gaza.

Closure of crossings

15. All the crossings into and out of Gaza are controlled by Israel. Rafah, the crossing point for Gazans to Egypt, and Karni, the commercial crossing for the import and export of goods, are the principal crossing points. They are the subject of the Agreement on Movement and Access, which provides for Gazans to travel freely to Egypt through Rafah and for a substantial increase in the number of export trucks through Karni. Since 25 June 2006, following the capture of Corporal Shalit, and more particularly since mid-June 2007, following the Hamas seizure of power in Gaza, the Rafah crossing has been closed. From mid-June to early August 2007 some 6,000 Palestinians were stranded on the Egyptian side of the border, without adequate accommodation or facilities and denied the right to return home. Over 30 people died while waiting. The Karni crossing has likewise been closed for long periods of time during the past 18 months, and more particularly since mid-June 2007. Karem Shalom and Sufa are now used for the import of goods but the number of trucks bringing goods into Gaza has dropped alarmingly—from 253 a day in April 2007 to 74 a day in November. To make matters worse Sufa is possibly scheduled to close—though on 20 November the Israeli government decided to permit the export of flowers and strawberries from Gaza to Europe via the Sufa crossing. Erez, previously used

as a crossing for persons in need of medical attention in Israel, has also been largely closed for this purpose. On the other hand, in December 2007, Israel allowed several hundred Palestinians who reside abroad to leave Gaza via Israel.

The reduction of fuel and electricity supplies

16. On 19 September Israel declared Gaza to be a hostile territory and announced that, as a consequence, it would reduce the supply of fuel and electricity to Gaza. Ten Israeli and Palestinian NGOs brought an application before the Israeli High Court of Justice to halt the reduction of fuel and electricity on the ground that this constitutes collective punishment and would cause widespread humanitarian damage, but the Israeli High Court has upheld the State's plan to reduce fuel transfers to Gaza. According to the Palestinian Centre for Human Rights fuel supplies have been reduced by more than 50 percent since the decision to cease fuel supplies on 25 October 2007.

Termination of banking facilities

17. Following the designation of Gaza as a hostile territory the only two Israeli commercial banks dealing with financial institutions in Gaza, Bank Hapoalim and Discount Bank, announced that they would cut ties with Gaza. This involves, inter alia, the refusal to clear cheques from Gaza banks and the halting of cash transfers between Israeli banks and Gaza banks. At this stage, the full implications of this decision are not yet clear, but as the Israeli shekel is the official currency in the OPT, in accordance with the Oslo Accords, and must be supplied from Israel, it is likely that this could produce chaos in the Gazan monetary system.

The humanitarian crisis in Gaza

18. Regular military incursions, the closure of crossings, the reduction of fuel and the threat to the banking system have produced a humanitarian crisis, which has the following impact on life in Gaza.

Food

19. Over 80 percent of the population of Gaza is dependent on food aid from the United Nations Relief and Works Agency for Palestine Refugees in the Near East (UNRWA) and the World Food Programme (WFP). This takes the form of flour, rice, sugar, sunflower oil, powdered milk and lentils. Fruit and vegetables are no longer available to supplement these basic rations as farmers do not have the money to get their crops picked and marketed. Few can afford meat, and fish is virtually unobtainable as a result of the Israeli prohibition of fishing. Although critical humanitarian food supplies are being allowed in, only 41 percent of Gaza's food import needs are currently being met.

Unemployment and poverty

20. The closure of crossings prevents Gazan farmers and manufacturers from exporting their goods to markets outside Gaza. It also prevents materials from entering Gaza and this has resulted in the end of most construction works and the closure of factories. On 26 September the Special Rapporteur visited the Karni industrial zone and saw factories that had been closed as a result of the failure to import materials and the prohibition on the export of goods. Factory owners are being held responsible by Israeli buyers for non-delivery of goods caused by the closure. Farmers are without income and some 65,000 factory employees are unemployed. According to the Palestinian Federation of Industries, 95 percent of Gaza's industrial operations have been suspended as a result of restrictions (Report of World Bank, December 2007, para. 13). Fishermen are likewise unemployed as a result of the Israeli ban on fishing along the Gaza coast. On 9 July 2007, UNRWA announced that it had halted all its building projects in Gaza because it had run out of building materials, such as cement. This has affected 121,000 jobs of people building new schools, houses, waterworks, and health centers. In many instances those working in the public sector remain unpaid. Municipal employees in Gaza City have not been paid since March 2007. As

a result, garbage collection services went on strike in November causing a serious threat to health.

21. Poverty in Gaza is rife. Over 80 percent of the population live below the official poverty line.

Health care

22. Health-care clinics are in short supply of paediatric antibiotics, and 91 key drugs are no longer available. Previously, seriously ill patients were allowed to leave Gaza to receive treatment in Israel, the West Bank, Egypt, Jordan and other countries through the Rafah and Erez crossings. Rafah is now completely closed, and the Israeli authorities deny passage through Erez to all but the most "severe and urgent cases." The situation has worsened since the declaration of Gaza as a hostile territory. The World Health Organization reports that while 89.4 percent of patients who applied for permits during the period January-May 2007 were granted permits, only 77.1 percent of those who applied were granted permits during October 2007. This has resulted in a drastic increase in the number of patients who have died as a result of restrictions: according to the Israeli NGO Physicians for Human Rights, since June 2007, 44 people have died as a result of denial or delay of access to medical care by the Israeli authorities and 13 died in November alone. Mahmoud Abu Taha, a 21-year-old patient with stomach cancer, arrived at Erez at 16.00 hours on 18 October with a Palestinian intensive care unit ambulance, escorted by his father. The patient's entry was delayed for two and a half hours, after which the IDF asked the father to cross to the Israeli side of Erez. His son, the patient, was to enter on a walker and not with the ambulance. The patient was denied access after reaching the end of the 500-meter-long tunnel, while the father was arrested by the IDF and held for nine days. On 28 October, a second arrangement for the patient was approved and he was admitted to an Israeli hospital, where he died the same night. In November, hospitals were prevented from carrying out operations as a result of the restrictions placed by Israel on nitrous oxide gas that is used for anaesthetics.

Education

23. Gaza's children in UNRWA schools lag behind refugee children elsewhere, according to UNRWA, as a result of the Israeli blockade and military violence. Students are prevented from studying abroad. In November 670 students were denied permission to study abroad, including six Fulbright scholars.

Fuel, energy and water

24. Gaza is largely dependent on Israel for its supply of fuel and electricity. Already there are frequent power outages as a result of Israel's destruction of the main Gaza power plant in 2006 and subsequent damage to electricity transformers. (For instance, on 14 November the IDF struck an electricity transformer in Beit Hanoun which knocked out power for 5,000 people in the area.) The supply of water is also affected and there is insufficient power for water pumps. As a result, 210,000 people are able to access drinking water supplies for only 1–2 hours a day. Sewage is also a problem: sewage plants require repairs but materials, such as metal pipes and welding machines, have been prohibited by Israel on the grounds that they may be used for making rockets. At present there is a real danger that sewage plants could overflow. Cutting off fuel and electricity will exacerbate an already dangerous situation. It will endanger the functioning of hospitals, water services and sewage, as well as depriving residents of electricity for refrigerators and household appliances. A humanitarian catastrophe is contemplated if Israel continues to reduce fuel and carries out its threat to reduce electricity supplies.

Legal consequences of Israel's actions

25. Israel has largely justified its attacks and incursions as defensive operations aimed at preventing the launching of Qassam rockets into Israel, the arrest or killing of suspected militants or the destruction of tunnels. Clearly the firing of rockets into Israel by Palestinian militants without any military target, which has resulted in the killing and injury of Israelis, cannot be condoned and constitutes a war crime. Nevertheless,

serious questions arise over the proportionality of Israel's military response and its failure to distinguish between military and civilian targets. It is highly arguable that Israel has violated the most fundamental rules of international humanitarian law, which constitute war crimes in terms of article 147 of the Fourth Geneva Convention and article 85 of the Protocol Additional to the Geneva Conventions of 12 August 1949 and relating to the Protection of Victims of International Armed Conflicts (Additional Protocol I). These crimes include direct attacks against civilians and civilian objects, and attacks which fail to distinguish between military targets and civilians and civilian objects (articles 48, 51 (4) and 52 (1) of Protocol I); the excessive use of force arising from disproportionate attacks on civilians and civilian objects (articles 51 (4) and 51 (5) of Protocol I); and the spreading of terror among the civilian population (article 33 of the Fourth Geneva Convention and article 51 (2) of Protocol I).

26. Israel's siege of Gaza violates a whole range of obligations under both human rights law and humanitarian law. The provisions of the International Covenant on Economic, Social and Cultural Rights that state that everyone has the right to "an adequate standard of living for himself and his family, including adequate food, clothing and housing," freedom from hunger and the right to food (art. 11) and that everyone has the right to health, have been seriously infringed. Above all, the government of Israel has violated the prohibition on collective punishment of an occupied people contained in article 33 of the Fourth Geneva Convention. The indiscriminate and excessive use of force against civilians and civilian objects, the destruction of electricity and water supplies, the bombardment of public buildings, the restrictions on freedom of movement, the closure of crossings and the consequences that these actions have upon public health, food, family life and the psychological well-being of the Palestinian people constitute a gross form of collective punishment.

27. Gaza is no ordinary State upon which other States may freely impose economic sanctions in order to create a humanitarian crisis or take disproportionate military action that endangers the civilian population in the name of self-defense. It is an occupied

territory in whose well-being all States have an interest and whose welfare all States are required to promote. According to the Advisory Opinion of the International Court of Justice, all States parties to the Fourth Geneva Convention have the obligation "to ensure compliance by Israel with international humanitarian law as embodied in that Convention." Israel has violated obligations of an *erga omnes* character that are the concern of all States and that all States are required to bring to an end. In the first instance, Israel, the Occupying Power, is obliged to cease its violations of international humanitarian law. But other States that are a party to the siege of Gaza are likewise in violation of international humanitarian law and obliged to cease their unlawful actions.

Jerusalem
E/CN.42006/29 of 17 January 2006, paras. 30–34

The Judaization of the city

30. East Jerusalem is not part of Israel. On the contrary, it is occupied territory, subject to the Fourth Geneva Convention. Unfortunately, Israel's illegal attempt at annexation of East Jerusalem has obscured this truth. As a consequence, world public opinion tends, incorrectly, to treat Israel's occupation of East Jerusalem as different from that of the West Bank and Gaza.

31. Israel has embarked upon major changes to the character of Jerusalem. In essence, these changes are designed to reduce the number of Palestinians in the city and to increase the Jewish population of the city, thereby undermining Palestinian claims to East Jerusalem as the capital of an independent Palestinian State. That this is the purpose of the Wall in Jerusalem was acknowledged by the Israeli Minister for Jerusalem Affairs, Mr. Haim Ramon, on 10 July 2005 when he stated that the route of the Wall would make Jerusalem "more Jewish." He added "The Government is bringing security to the city and will also make Jerusalem the capital of a Jewish and democratic State of Israel."

32. There are already some 190,000 Jewish settlers in Israeli-occupied East Jerusalem. Plans, however, are under way to increase the number of settlers and to extend settlements both to encircle Jerusalem and to cut the West Bank in half. Within the Old City of Jerusalem there are some 80 Jewish settler buildings and institutions. Moreover, there is a plan to build a large new Jewish settlement in the Muslim Quarter near Herod's Gate. Settlement expansion is also evident in neighborhoods surrounding the Old City such as Silwan. Beyond this lie the more established settlements such as Ramot, French Hill, Har Homa and Gilo. The inner circle of settlements will be encircled by the settlement blocs of Givat Ze'ev to the north, Ma'aleh Adumim to the east, and Gush Etzion to the south. Particularly threatening to a future Palestinian State is Ma'aleh Adumim, which is to be expanded by "E1" ("East 1"), a 53-square-mile area larger than Tel Aviv designated to have 3,500 housing units to accommodate 15,000 to 20,000 new settlers. The expanded Ma'aleh Adumim will effectively cut the West Bank in half, separating Ramallah from Bethlehem, with serious economic and political consequences.

33. Conversely, the Palestinian population of East Jerusalem, presently numbering some 230,000, is to be reduced by a number of stratagems. First, by house demolitions. There was a sharp increase in house demolitions in 2004, when 152 homes were destroyed in East Jerusalem. Plans to destroy 88 homes in the Silwan district are presently on hold. Secondly, this population is to be reduced by routing the Wall to the west of neighborhoods previously part of East Jerusalem. Thus, areas such as the Shu'afat camp, with a population of some 55,000, and West Anata are excluded from the East Jerusalem municipality and transferred to the West Bank. Thirdly, this will be done by transferring neighborhoods previously integrated into East Jerusalem into the West Bank by means of the Wall. Neighborhoods such as Abu Dis, Anata and Al-Eizariya fall into this category.

34. The exclusion of large neighborhoods from East Jerusalem and their transfer to the West Bank will cause great suffering to thousands of Palestinians and personal tragedies to many. A sharp distinction is made between Palestinians with blue

Jerusalem ID cards and those with green West Bank ID cards living in East Jerusalem neighborhoods. West Bank ID cardholders, and in due course Jerusalem ID cardholders living to the east of the Wall, will no longer be able to access hospitals and schools in Jerusalem or to work in Jerusalem without special permits to enter Jerusalem. The differences in ID cards will also have a profound effect on family life, as many spouses hold different ID cards. They will be forced to live separately on different sides of the Wall under Israeli law, which prohibits family unification. If one spouse elects to move east of the Wall, he or she will lose his or her rights (such as medical insurance and social security) attached to the Jerusalem ID. In this way Israel hopes to further reduce the Palestinian population of East Jerusalem by compelling spouses to move to the West Bank side of the Wall. The Special Rapporteur visited two of the neighborhoods most affected by the Wall—Abu Dis and Al-Eizariya. There he met husbands separated from their wives and persons separated from their livelihoods, schools, and hospitals in Jerusalem. Words cannot convey the hardships to which Palestinians are subjected in the interests of the Judaization of Jerusalem.

Treatment of Children, 2002

E/CN.4/2002/32 of 6 March 2002, paras. 40–53

Impact of the Second Intifada on children; the administration of justice and children

40. Children have suffered severely from the present crisis in terms of personal safety, family life, physical and mental health, education, and justice. Although Israeli Military Order No. 132 defines a child as someone under the age of 16, the present report accepts the international standard of 18 (article 1 of the Convention on the Rights of the Child, 1989), which is also the position under Israeli law. By this standard, over half the population of Palestine are children.

41. Over 200 of the Palestinians killed since the start of the second intifada in September 2000 have been children, while over 7,000 children have been injured. Of those injured, 500 will experience long-term disabilities. In the early months of the present intifada many children were killed or wounded by the IDF for participating in demonstrations involving the throwing of stones and Molotov cocktails. Live ammunition, rubber-coated steel bullets and tear gas were used to disperse demonstrators in a display of excessive and disproportionate use of force (see report of the Human Rights Inquiry Commission of 16 March 2001, E/CN.4/2001/121, paras. 44–52, 116). In the past year, most of the children killed or injured by the IDF were not engaged in confrontational demonstrations but were victims of shelling by tanks and helicopter gunships, while they were engaged in normal peaceful pursuits. Particularly disturbing are the deaths of five young boys in Khan Yunis on 22 November 2001, caused by a suspicious explosive device, and of three youths crossing a field near Beit Lahia on 30 December 2001, caused by heavy artillery fire. Calls for a full investigation into these deaths have, as yet, not met with a positive response.

42. Inevitably the economic hardships inflicted on the Palestinian community by the "closure" of the Palestinian Territory has had a serious impact on the lives of children. The majority of children in the West Bank and Gaza now live below the poverty line and families are compelled to reduce food consumption. Domestic violence is on the increase and children are becoming increasingly aggressive themselves. Access to hospitals and clinics is obstructed by military checkpoints. And the constant shelling, gunfire and presence of a hostile occupying army has had serious psychological consequences on all, but particularly on children.

43. Education is a top priority in Palestine. There are about 865,500 children enrolled in primary and secondary schools, administered mainly by the Palestinian Authority and UNRWA. Since 1994, many new schools have opened, and student numbers have increased substantially. The Palestinian Authority devotes 13 percent of its budget to education, while more than half of

the UNRWA budget goes to education. Education, at all levels, however, has suffered seriously since 29 September 2000, particularly in the 275 schools, with some 118,600 students, within a 500-meter radius of an Israeli military presence.

44. Some schools have been commandeered by the IDF for use as military outposts; others have been bombed; over a hundred have come under fire, both in the daytime when the schools are in session and at night. On 20 February 2001 the National School for the Blind in the West Bank town of Al-Bireh came under fire for three hours, causing extensive damage and traumatizing the disabled children. On some occasions, the IDF has fired tear gas into schools and ordered children to evacuate. Sometimes schools have been closed by the IDF for alleged security reasons or by the school authorities for the safety of the children. The Al-Khader secondary school in the Bethlehem district, which the Special Rapporteur visited, was closed for 45 days by military order, affecting some 2,500 students. This school has been seriously damaged by the IDF, which has on occasion entered the school premises during teaching hours, assaulted students and used tear gas to disperse students. Schools are also hampered by checkpoints, which prevent both students and teachers from reaching school on time, and by military curfews (particularly in Hebron).

45. The effect of the above actions on education has been severe. Schools have lost considerable teaching time as a result of interruption and closures; absenteeism is rife as schools no longer provide a secure environment; and academic performance has deteriorated. Children are afraid and unable to concentrate. It is impossible to assess the long-term psychological harm caused to children by these assaults on their schools, the killing and wounding of their friends and the growing poverty they experience at home. Many have simply lost their childhood.

Children and the administration of justice

48. Israel is proud of its judicial system and administration of justice. As a nation, Israel is committed to the rule of law and to due process of law in criminal proceedings. There are,

however, serious doubts as to whether this commitment extends to the Palestinian Territory, and particularly to the treatment of Palestinian children in the justice system. Consultations with the principal Palestinian, Israeli and international non-governmental organizations working in this field, the study of their carefully prepared reports, backed in some instances by affidavits from their victims, and interviews with several children who were detained, interrogated and imprisoned, reveals an alarming pattern of inhuman treatment of children under the military justice system in the Palestinian Territory. The Special Rapporteur would have preferred to discuss this matter with the Israeli authorities before reporting on it. Unfortunately, the government of Israel has elected not to cooperate with the Special Rapporteur. In these circumstances, the Special Rapporteur has no alternative but to raise the issue as a prima facie case of inhuman treatment to which the government of Israel should respond.

49. According to the evidence, about 1,000 children under the age of 18 have been arrested and detained since September 2000 in connection with crimes relating to the Palestinian uprising. Most—over 90 percent—have been arrested on suspicion of throwing stones at Israeli soldiers, which carries a maximum penalty of 6 months' imprisonment for a child between 12 and 14, and 12 months imprisonment for a child between 14 and 16. Children are tried in Israeli military courts. There are no military courts or judges designated especially for children, no officers trained specifically for the interrogation of children, no probation officers and no social workers to accompany them. At present about 150 children are in detention or prison.

50. The evidence indicates the following pattern of arrest, interrogation, detention, sentencing and imprisonment. Arrests occur late at night with the maximum disturbance to the family, and children are often assaulted in the process of arrest and on the way to detention centres. Interrogation in order to secure a confession continues for several days and is accompanied by beating, shaking, threats, sleep deprivation, isolation, blindfolding and handcuffing. Detainees are forced to sit or crouch in painful positions ("*shabeh*"), doused with cold water in winter, and shot at

with toy pistols with plastic pellets from close range. Their heads are placed in the toilet and the toilet flushed. Detainees are not permitted to see their lawyers at this stage. Interrogation accompanied by treatment of this kind may continue for several days until a confession is obtained. The Israeli Supreme Court, in its 1999 decision outlawing physical methods of interrogation, accepted that inhuman methods of interrogation qualifying as torture might be employed in a case of "necessity"—where it is imperative to obtain information urgently about the "ticking bomb." This alleged exception to the prohibition on torture is clearly inapplicable where the aim of the interrogation is not to extract information about a ticking bomb but about stone-throwing by children.

51. Following interrogation, children are often detained for several months awaiting trial. When tried they are sentenced to several months in prison: usually between 7 and 12 months in the case of children over 14. In addition, they are usually fined about US$250. They are imprisoned in Israel itself, which makes visits by family and Palestinian lawyers extremely difficult as special permission must be obtained to enter Israel. (Visits arranged by the International Committee of the Red Cross were suspended for several months but have recently been resumed.) These child "political prisoners" are imprisoned with common criminals and complain of assaults perpetrated by both prison guards and common-law prisoners.

52. Complaints about inhuman treatment to medical doctors (both in detention centres and in prison) and to the trial judges in the military courts are generally not investigated or taken seriously.

53. The inhuman treatment of juvenile offenders described above falls short of international standards contained in the Convention on the Rights of the Child (art. 37), the Convention against Torture and Other Cruel, Inhuman and Degrading Treatment or Punishment (arts. 1, 16), the Standard Minimum Rules on the Treatment of Prisoners of 1957 and the Fourth Geneva Convention (arts. 27, 31, 32, 76). These are serious allegations which require a serious response from the Israeli authorities. The Special Rapporteur recommends that the Israeli authorities

conduct a thorough investigation into these allegations (detailed more fully in reports of non-governmental organizations) carried out by an independent body outside the military, police, and prison services. At the same time, immediate steps should be taken to transfer those imprisoned in Israel to prison facilities in the occupied territory (as required by article 76 of the Fourth Geneva Convention) that comply with international standards relating to the imprisonment of children. It is also recommended that the military authorities appoint an Israeli judge or other independent Israeli criminal justice expert outside the military to visit detention centres to monitor interrogations and the treatment of juveniles in detention centres before they are brought to trial.

Treatment of Children, 2004
E/CN.4/2004/6/Add.1, of 27 February 2004 para. 7

IDF attacks on school and children

7. While in Rafah the Special Rapporteur visited UNRWA schools close to the razed zone near the boundary wall. Teachers at one school told of random shooting in the direction of the school that terrorized children and disrupted school activities. Shell holes in the school walls confirmed the veracity of these statements. At another school, teenage girls at a trauma counselling session attended by the Special Rapporteur spoke with tears and pain about their experiences of military occupation: of neighbors shot by the IDF and savaged by IDF sniffer dogs, of homes destroyed without proper notice, and of their desire to live normal lives like children in other countries. To deny childhood to children is unforgivable. Moreover, to create feelings of hatred in the youth of Palestine in this way is impossible to reconcile with the security concerns that Israel claims guide its actions. From the perspective of international law, it must be noted that the actions of the IDF violate many provisions of the Convention on the Rights of the Child.

Treatment of Prisoners, including Torture
EC/N.4/2004/6 of 8 September 2003, paras. 30–32

Torture

30. There are serious complaints about the treatment of prisoners that are supported in varying degrees by respectable non-governmental organizations such as the Public Committee Against Torture in Israel (PCATI), the World Organization against Torture (OMCT), the Defence for Children International—Palestine Section, LAW—The Palestinian Society for the Protection of Human Rights and the Environment, Al-Haq and the Mandela Institute for Human Rights. These complaints cover all prisons and detention centres and include men, women and children held in imprisonment as well as administrative detainees. On the one hand, these complaints cover allegations of overcrowding, disgusting prison conditions and lack of proper medical care. On the other hand, they include serious allegations of inhuman and degrading treatment, sometimes amounting to torture.

31. In 1999 the Israeli High Court of Justice ruled that various methods of torture employed by the General Security Service (GSS), such as violent shaking, covering the head with a sack, tying to a small, tilted chair or position abuse (*shabeh*), sleep deprivation and painful shackling were, when applied cumulatively, illegal. Despite this, there is considerable evidence that these methods are still employed during the interrogation of adults and juveniles. In a publication entitled *Back to a Routine of Torture* covering the period September 2001 to April 2003, PCATI estimated that for the first half of 2003, "each month, hundreds of Palestinians have been subjected to one degree or another of torture or other cruel, inhuman or degrading treatment, at the hands of the GSS and bodies working on its behalf. ... The bodies which are supposed to keep the GSS under scrutiny and ensure that interrogations are conducted lawfully act, instead, as rubber stamps for decisions by the GSS." These allegations are difficult to reconcile with the assurance given by the representatives of the Israeli government before the Human Rights Committee on 24

and 25 July 2003 that allegations of this kind had been properly investigated and proved to be unfounded or justified on grounds of necessity.

32. The Special Rapporteur finds himself in an awkward situation when it comes to assessing evidence of this kind. Allegations of torture and inhuman treatment are supported in varying degrees by highly respected NGOs that have taken statements from former prisoners and consulted with lawyers working within the system. Moreover, there are serious doubts about the impartiality of the investigations of these complaints carried out by the Israeli authorities. The Special Rapporteur is denied access to Israeli prisons and detention centres and to government officials who might assist in the task of assessing the validity of allegations on this subject. The Special Rapporteur therefore urgently calls upon the Israeli authorities either to permit an independent international committee to investigate such complaints or to conduct a full-scale independent judicial inquiry into such allegations itself. It has often been said that the degree of civilization of a state can be measured by the way in which it treats prisoners. At present Israel, which prides itself on a high standard of criminal justice within its own borders, runs the risk of forfeiting this reputation by its consistent refusal to respond to criticisms of treatment of prisoners from the OPT.

Treatment of Prisoners and the Role of Medical Doctors
A/HRC/7/17 of 21 January 2008, paras. 45–48

45. It is estimated that since 1967 over 700,000 Palestinians have been imprisoned. At present, there are some 11,000 prisoners in Israeli jails, a number which includes 376 children, 118 women, 44 members of the Palestinian Legislative Council and some 800 "administrative detainees" (that is, persons not convicted for any offense, held for renewable periods of up to six months). Israel sees such prisoners as terrorists or ordinary criminals who have

violated the criminal law. Palestinians see them as political prisoners who have committed crimes against the occupier. History is replete with examples of such competing perspectives—to cite but South Africa and Namibia as examples. Prisoners are a key issue in any peace settlement. That Israel is aware of this is demonstrated by its release of 779 prisoners (although in November 411 persons were arrested). The release of such a small number of prisoners, however, provides little evidence of a bona fide attempt to reach a peaceful settlement on the part of Israel. To make matters worse prisoners are subjected to humiliating and degrading treatment.

Arrested and detained persons

46. Following arrest, persons are frequently beaten and stripped in a humiliating manner. The interrogation of subjects is then carried out in a degrading and inhuman manner, sometimes amounting to torture. During 2007, two reports published by Israeli NGOs—Hamoked (Center for the Defence of the Individual) and B'Tselem (*Absolute Prohibition: The Torture and Ill-Treatment of Palestinian Detainees,* May 2007) and the Public Committee Against Torture in Israel (PCATI) (*"Ticking Bombs." Testimonies of Torture Victims in Israel,* May 2007)—have shown that arrested persons are subjected to beatings, humiliated, and deprived of basic needs and that persons suspected of having information that could prevent attacks (so-called "ticking bomb suspects") are deprived of sleep for more than 24 hours, beaten and subjected to physical ill-treatment. The treatment of children is equally disturbing. According to Defence for Children International (Palestine Section), children are on average detained for between 8 to 21 days before being brought to court; denied the presence of a parent or lawyer during interrogation; cursed, threatened, beaten, and kept in solitary confinement during interrogation (Semi-Annual Report 2007).

Convicted prisoners and administrative detainees

47. Prison conditions are harsh. Many prisoners are accommodated in tents, which are extremely hot in summer and cold in

winter. Food is poor, resulting in anemia among prisoners, and there is serious overcrowding. Most Palestinian prisoners are held in jails in Israel. This violates article 76 of the Fourth Geneva Convention which requires persons from an occupied territory to be detained in the occupied country, and if convicted, to serve their sentences therein. Family visits are difficult and frequently impossible: all visits for families from Gaza to their relatives detained in Israeli prisons have been suspended since 6 June 2007, affecting some 900 prisoners. On 22 October there was a riot in Ketziot prison in the Negev (in Israel), accommodating some 2,300 prisoners, which resulted in 1 death and some 250 injuries among prisoners.

48. The role of medical doctors in detention centers and prisons requires attention. These doctors witness the result of inhuman treatment—wounds, swollen hands, signs of violence—but remain silent, acting as if they do not know that torture is taking place. This raises ethical questions that in similar circumstances in South Africa were, after years of silence, addressed by the South African Medical Association and international medical bodies. Why, one must ask, has the responsibility of Israeli medical doctors who examine detainees and prisoners not been questioned by the relevant Israeli and international medical professional bodies?

The Killing of Civilians and Assassinations in the Second Intifada
E/CN.4/2004/6 of 8 September 2003, paras. 22–24, 26–28

22. For both human rights law and international humanitarian law the protection of human life is a primary goal. Article 6 (1) of the International Covenant on Civil and Political Rights states that "Every human being has the inherent right to life. This right shall be protected by law. No one shall be arbitrarily deprived of his life." While accepting that combatants engaged in armed conflict would be exposed to life-threatening situations, international humanitarian law seeks to limit harm to civilians by requiring that

all parties to a conflict respect the principles of distinction and proportionality. The principle of distinction, codified in article 48 of Protocol I Additional to the Geneva Conventions of 12 August 1949, requires that "the Parties to the conflict shall at all times distinguish between the civilian population and combatants and between civilian objects and military objectives and accordingly shall direct their operations only against military objectives." Acts or threats of violence the primary purpose of which is to spread terror among the civilian population, are prohibited (art. 51 (2)). The principle of proportionality, codified in article 51 (5) (b), prohibits an attack on a military target "which may be expected to cause incidental loss of civilian life, injury to civilians, [or] damage to civilian objects . . . which would be excessive in relation to the concrete and direct military advantage anticipated." That these principles apply to both Israelis and Palestinians was confirmed by the High Contracting Parties to the Fourth Geneva Convention when, in a declaration issued on 5 December 2001, they called upon both parties to the conflict to: " . . . ensure respect for and protection of the civilian population and civilian objects and to distinguish at all times between the civilian population and combatants and between civilian objects and military objectives."

23. Sadly, neither party to the conflict in the region has paid proper respect to these principles as the death toll has continued to rise. Since the start of the second intifada in September 2000, over 2,755 Palestinians and over 830 Israelis have been killed and 28,000 Palestinians and 5,600 Israelis have been injured. Most have been civilians. Five hundred and fifty children have been killed, of whom 460 were Palestinians and 90 Israelis. The number of Palestinian children killed, mainly in air and ground attacks, has increased in 2003. Within Israel, most deaths have been caused by suicide bombers.

24. The assassination of Palestinian militants has intensified. From October 2000 to April 2003, the IDF has killed more than 230 Palestinians, including 80 children, women and innocent bystanders, in assassination actions. Over 300 persons have been injured in these actions. In the period 10–14 June 2003, the IDF killed 27 Palestinians and wounded dozens of others in a series

of extrajudicial killings carried out by helicopter gunships in the Gaza Strip. These attacks included an unsuccessful assassination attempt on Dr. Abdel Aziz Al-Rantisi, a senior political leader of Hamas. Four people were killed and 35 injured while 29 nearby apartments were damaged. On 12 June 2003, IDF helicopters bombarded the car of Yasser Taha. He was immediately killed, together with his wife and young daughter. In addition, five other civilians were killed in the attack and 36 were wounded, including 10 children. [On 17 April 2004 Dr. Rantisi was assassinated by Israeli Hellfire missiles fired from an AH-64 Apache helicopter at his car. Ed.]

26. Israel justifies its policy and practice of assassinations on grounds of self-defence and claims that it is not possible to arrest and try suspects, particularly where they are in areas controlled by the Palestinian Authority. The evidence on this point is inconclusive as there are certainly some instances in which arrests could have been made in the light of Israel's capacity to exercise its jurisdictional power within the areas controlled in theory by the Palestinian Authority. The failure to attempt such arrests inevitably gives rise to suspicions that Israel lacks evidence to place such persons on trial and therefore prefers to dispose of them arbitrarily.

27. The indiscriminate use of violence is further illustrated by the use of flechette shells in Gaza. The use of such anti-personnel weapons in such a densely populated area as Gaza exposes civilians to great risk and fails to take account of the need to distinguish between civilians and military objectives. On 27 April 2003, the Israeli High Court of Justice refused to intervene in the army's choice of weapons because flechettes are not banned outright under international law.

28. The failure of the IDF to investigate crimes committed by its members in the OPT has long been criticized. In June 2003, this criticism was confirmed when the Judge Advocate General stated that a mere 55 investigations into shooting incidents had been opened since the beginning of the second intifada, resulting in only six indictments (B'Tselem Newspaper, 29 June 2003).

Terrorism

A/HRC7/17 of 21 January 2008, paras. 4–5

A response to the accusation that the Special Rapporteur was soft on terrorism

4. Terrorism is a scourge, a serious violation of human rights and international humanitarian law. No attempt is made in the reports to minimize the pain and suffering it causes to victims, their families and the broader community. Palestinians are guilty of terrorizing innocent Israeli civilians by means of suicide bombs and Qassam rockets. Likewise, the Israeli Defense Forces (IDF) are guilty of terrorizing innocent Palestinian civilians by military incursions, targeted killings and sonic booms that fail to distinguish between military targets and civilians. All these acts must be condemned and have been condemned. Common sense, however, dictates that a distinction must be drawn between acts of mindless terror, such as acts committed by Al Qaeda, and acts committed in the course of a war of national liberation against colonialism, apartheid or military occupation. While such acts cannot be justified, they must be understood as being a painful but inevitable consequence of colonialism, apartheid or occupation. History is replete with examples of military occupation that have been resisted by violence—acts of terror. The German occupation was resisted by many European countries in the Second World War; the South West Africa People's Organization (SWAPO) resisted South Africa's occupation of Namibia; and Jewish groups resisted British occupation of Palestine—inter alia, by the blowing up of the King David Hotel in 1946 with heavy loss of life, by a group masterminded by Menachem Begin, who later became Prime Minister of Israel. Acts of terror against military occupation must be seen in historical context. This is why every effort should be made to bring the occupation to a speedy end. Until this is done peace cannot be expected, and violence will continue. In other situations, for example Namibia, peace has been achieved by the ending of occupation, without setting the end of resistance as a

precondition. Israel cannot expect perfect peace and the end of violence as a precondition for the ending of the occupation.

5. A further comment on terrorism is called for. In the present international climate, it is easy for a State to justify its repressive measures as a response to terrorism—and to expect a sympathetic hearing. Israel exploits the present international fear of terrorism to the full. But this will not solve the Palestinian problem. Israel must address the occupation and the violation of human rights and international humanitarian law it engenders, and not invoke the justification of terrorism as a distraction, as a pretext for failure to confront the root cause of Palestinian violence—the occupation.

The Demolition of Houses
A/HRC/7/17 of 21 January 2008, paras. 41–42

41. The demolition of houses has been a regular feature of Israel's occupation of the OPT. Different reasons or justifications are advanced for such demolitions: military necessity, punishment and failure to obtain a building permit. Although the IDF claims to have discontinued punitive home demolitions, instances of such demolitions still occur.

On 29 August 2007, the IDF demolished seven housing units in the Naqar neighborhood of Qalqiliya, which were home to 48 persons (including 17 children) on the ground that they housed members of the military wing of Hamas. Houses are frequently demolished for "administrative" reasons, on the grounds that no permit has been obtained to build—which Israel defends as a normal feature of town planning. Both law and fact show, however, that houses are not demolished in the course of "normal" town planning operations but are instead demolished in a discriminatory manner to demonstrate the power of the occupier over the occupied.

42. In both East Jerusalem and that part of the West Bank categorized as Area C (60 percent of the West Bank, comprising villages and rural districts), houses and structures may not be built

without permits. The bureaucratic procedures for obtaining permits are cumbersome and in practice permits are rarely granted.
As a result, Palestinians are frequently compelled to build homes
without permits. In East Jerusalem house demolitions are implemented in a discriminatory manner: Arab homes are destroyed but
not Jewish houses (Meir Margalit, *Discrimination in the Heart of
the Holy City,* Al Manar Press, Jerusalem, 2006). In Area C the
IDF has demolished or designated for demolition homes, schools,
clinics, and mosques on the ground that permits have not been
obtained. Between May 2005 and May 2007, 354 Palestinian
structures were destroyed by the IDF in Area C. Many Bedouin
communities have had their structures demolished. In September
2007 the Special Rapporteur visited Al Hadidiya in the Jordan
Valley where the structures of a Bedouin community of some
200 families, comprising 6,000 people, living near to the Jewish
settlement of Roi, were demolished by the IDF. This brought back
memories of the practice in apartheid South Africa of destroying
black villages (termed "black spots") that were too close to white
residents. Article 53 of the Fourth Geneva Convention prohibits the
destruction of personal property "except where such destruction is
rendered absolutely necessary by military operations." According
to B'Tselem, the Israeli Information Centre for Human Rights in
the Occupied Territories, the destruction of homes in the Naqar
neighborhood of Qalqiliya failed to meet this test. The demolition
of homes for administrative reasons can likewise not be justified.
Both East Jerusalem and Area C are occupied territory, in respect
of which the prohibition contained in article 53 applies.

Apartheid, Colonialism, Occupation and Human Rights: Is There Need for a Further Advisory Opinion?
A/HRC/4/17 of 29 January 2007, paras. 49–50, 58–63

49. Article 1 of the International Convention on the
Elimination of All Forms of Racial Discrimination of 1966 defines

"racial discrimination" as meaning "any distinction, exclusion, restriction preference based on race, color, descent, or national or ethnic origin which has the purpose or effect of nullifying or impairing the recognition, enjoyment or exercise, on an equal footing, of human rights and fundamental freedoms in the political, economic, social, cultural or any other field of public life." This Convention only requires States to prohibit and eliminate racial discrimination. Another convention, the International Convention on the Suppression and Punishment of the Crime of Apartheid of 1973, goes further and criminalizes practices of racial segregation and discrimination that, inter alia, involve the infliction on members of a racial group of serious bodily or mental harm, inhuman or degrading treatment, arbitrary arrest or the deliberate creation of conditions preventing the full development of a racial group by denying to such a group basic human rights and freedoms, including the right to freedom of movement, when such acts are committed "for the purpose of establishing and maintaining domination by one racial group of persons over any other racial group of persons and systematically oppressing them." (See, too, the 1998 Rome Statute of the International Criminal Court which recognizes the crime of apartheid as a crime against humanity, Article 7(1)(j).)

50. Israel vehemently denies the application of these Conventions to its laws and practices in the Occupied Palestinian Territory. Despite this denial, it is difficult to resist the conclusion that many of Israel's laws and practices violate the 1966 Convention on the Elimination of All Forms of Racial Discrimination. Israelis are entitled to enter the closed zone between the Wall and the Green Line without permits while Palestinians require permits to enter the closed zone; house demolitions in the West Bank and East Jerusalem are carried out in a manner that discriminates against Palestinians; throughout the West Bank, and particularly in Hebron, settlers are given preferential treatment over Palestinians in respect of movement (major roads are reserved exclusively for settlers), building rights and army protection; and the laws governing family reunification unashamedly discriminate against Palestinians. It is less certain that the International

Convention on the Suppression and Punishment of the Crime of Apartheid is violated. The IDF inflicts serious bodily and mental harm on Palestinians, both in Gaza and the West Bank; over 700 Palestinians are held without trial; prisoners are subjected to inhuman and degrading treatment; and Palestinians throughout the OPT are denied freedom of movement. Can it seriously be denied that the purpose of such action is to establish and maintain domination by one racial group (Jews) over another racial group (Palestinians) and systematically oppressing them? Israel denies that this is its intention or purpose. But such an intention or purpose may be inferred from the actions described in this report.

58. The international community, speaking through the United Nations, has identified three regimes as inimical to human rights—colonialism, apartheid, and foreign occupation. Numerous resolutions of the General Assembly of the United Nations testify to this. Israel's occupation of the West Bank, Gaza and East Jerusalem contains elements of all three of these regimes, which is what makes the Occupied Palestinian Territory of special concern to the international community.

59. That the OPT is occupied by Israel and governed by the rules belonging to the special legal regime of occupation cannot be disputed. The International Court of Justice confirmed this in respect of the West Bank and East Jerusalem in its 2004 Advisory Opinion on the *Legal Consequences of the Construction of a Wall in the Occupied Palestinian Territory* (ICJ Reports, p. 136, paragraph 78), and held that the Fourth Geneva Convention relative to the Protection of Civilian Persons in Time of War, of 1949, was applicable to this Territory (ibid, para. 101). The Security Council, General Assembly and States Parties to the Fourth Geneva Convention have declared that this Convention is applicable to the entire OPT (ibid, paras. 96–99). Moreover, it is not possible to seriously argue, as Israel has attempted to do, that Israel has ceased to occupy Gaza since August 2005, when it withdrew its settlers and the Israel Defense Forces from Gaza. Even before the commencement of "Operation Summer Rains," following the capture of Corporal Gilad Shalit on 25 June 2006, Israel was able to exercise effective control over the Territory by

reason of its control of Gaza's external borders, air space and sea space. Since that date it has exercised its military authority within Gaza by military incursions and shelling, in circumstances which clearly establish occupation.

60. Today there are over 460,000 Israeli settlers in the West Bank and East Jerusalem. Moreover, Israel has appropriated agricultural land and water resources in the West Bank for its own use. This aspect of Israel's exploitation of the West Bank appears to be a form of colonialism of the kind declared to be a denial of fundamental human rights and contrary to the Charter of the United Nations as recalled in the General Assembly's Declaration on the Granting of Independence to Colonial Countries and Peoples of 1960 (Resolution 1514 XV).

61. Israel's practices and policies in the OPT are frequently likened to those of apartheid South Africa (see, for example, Jimmy Carter, *Palestine: Peace, Not Apartheid* (2006)). On the face of it, occupation and apartheid are two very different regimes. Occupation is not intended to be a long-term oppressive regime but an interim measure that maintains law and order in a territory following an armed conflict and pending a peace settlement. Apartheid is a system of institutionalized racial discrimination that the white minority in South Africa employed to maintain power over the black majority. It was characterized by the denial of political rights to blacks, the fragmentation of the country into white areas and black areas (called Bantustans) and by the imposition on blacks of restrictive measures designed to achieve white superiority, racial separation, and white security. Freedom of movement was restricted by the "pass system" which sought to restrict the entry of blacks into the cities. Apartheid was enforced by a brutal security apparatus in which torture played a significant role. Although the two regimes are different, Israel's laws and practices in the OPT certainly resemble aspects of apartheid, as shown in paragraphs 49–50 above, and probably fall within the scope of the 1973 International Convention on the Suppression and Punishment of the Crime of Apartheid.

62. Colonialism and apartheid are contrary to international law. Occupation is a lawful regime, tolerated by the international

community but not approved. Indeed, over the past three decades it has, in the words of the Israeli scholar Eyal Benvenisti, "acquired a pejorative connotation" (*The International Law of Occupation* (1993), p. 212). What are the legal consequences of a regime of occupation that has continued for nearly 40 years? Clearly none of the obligations imposed on the Occupying Power are reduced as a result of such a prolonged occupation (Adam Roberts, "Prolonged Occupation: The Israeli Occupied Territories," (1990) 84 *American Journal of International Law* 44, 55–57). But what are the legal consequences when such a regime has acquired some of the characteristics of colonialism and apartheid? Does it continue to be a lawful regime? Or does it cease to be a lawful regime, particularly in respect of "measures aimed at the occupants' own interests" (Benvenisti, op cit, p 216)? And if this is the position, what are the legal consequences for the occupied people, the Occupying Power and third States? Should questions of this kind not be addressed to the International Court of Justice for a further advisory opinion? It is true that the 2004 Advisory Opinion on the *Legal Consequences of the Construction of a Wall in the Occupied Palestinian Territory* has not had the desired effect of compelling the United Nations to take firmer action against the construction of the Wall. On the other hand, it must be remembered that the United Nations requested four advisory opinions from the International Court of Justice to guide it in its approach to South Africa's occupation of South-West Africa/Namibia. In these circumstances a request for another advisory opinion warrants serious consideration.

63. The Occupied Palestinian Territory is of special importance to the future of human rights in the world. Human rights in Palestine have been on the agenda of the United Nations for 60 years; and more particularly for the past 40 years since the occupation of East Jerusalem, the West Bank and the Gaza Strip in 1967. For years the occupation of Palestine and apartheid in South Africa vied for attention from the international community. In 1994, apartheid came to an end and Palestine became the only developing country in the world under the subjugation of a Western-affiliated regime. Herein lies its significance to the future of human rights. There are other regimes, particularly in

the developing world, that suppress human rights, but there is no other case of a Western-affiliated regime that denies self-determination and human rights to a developing people and that has done so for so long. This explains why the OPT has become a test for the West, a test by which its commitment to human rights is to be judged. If the West fails this test, it can hardly expect the developing world to address human rights violations seriously in its own countries, and the West appears to be failing this test. The EU pays conscience money to the Palestinian people through the Temporary International Mechanism but nevertheless joins the United States and other Western countries, such as Australia and Canada, in failing to put pressure on Israel to accept Palestinian self-determination and to discontinue its violations of human rights. The Quartet, comprising the United States, the European Union, the United Nations, and the Russian Federation, is a party to this failure. If the West, which has hitherto led the promotion of human rights throughout the world, cannot demonstrate a real commitment to the human rights of the Palestinian people, the international human rights movement, which can claim to be the greatest achievement of the international community of the past 60 years, will be endangered and placed in jeopardy.

The Role of the UN in the Protection of Human Rights in the Occupied Palestinian Territory
A/62/275 of 17 August 2007, paras. 46 -50

An appeal to the United Nations to disassociate itself from the Quartet

46. The United Nations is the ultimate protector of human rights in the international community, with its agencies, personnel and political institutions committed to this end. In Occupied Palestinian Territory agencies such as UNRWA, OCHA, the United Nations Development Programme, the Office of the High Commissioner for Human Rights, the World Food Programme, the World Bank, the United Nations Children's Fund, the World

Health Organization, the International Labour Organization and the Food and Agriculture Organization of the United Nations are committed to promoting development and protecting human rights. Dedicated personnel pursue the ideals of the Charter of the United Nations in providing help for a people under occupation. Indeed, it is difficult to imagine how Palestinians could survive without the assistance of bodies such as UNRWA. Unfortunately, the story at the high political level in New York is very different.

47. The Security Council has largely relinquished its powers in respect of the Occupied Palestinian Territory in favor of an amorphous body known as the Quartet, comprising the United Nations, the European Union, the Russian Federation and the United States. The Quartet was informally set up in 2003 without a founding resolution or mandate from either the Security Council or the General Assembly, with the task of promoting peace in accordance with a road map for peace, to which Israel has attached 14 reservations and which is now hopelessly out of date. In his May 2007 End of Mission Report, Alvaro de Soto, former United Nations Special Coordinator for the Middle East Peace Process and United Nations Envoy to the Quartet, stated that "as a practical matter, the Quartet is pretty much a group of friends of the U.S.—and the U.S. doesn't feel the need to consult closely with the Quartet except when it suits it" (para. 63). Despite its dubious constitutionality and the questionable legality of its actions, the Quartet remains unchallenged by the Security Council or the General Assembly.

48. The Quartet does not see it as its function to promote respect for human rights, international humanitarian law, the Advisory Opinion of the International Court of Justice, international law or countless United Nations resolutions on the subject of the Occupied Palestinian Territory. Regular statements by the Quartet make mildly critical reference to the expansion of settlements and the humanitarian situation in the Occupied Palestinian Territory but condemnation of Israel's continuing occupation, and its violations of international humanitarian law (primarily the Fourth Geneva Convention) and human rights is not forthcoming. Moreover, the Quartet has yet to even mention

the Advisory Opinion of the International Court of Justice. Since January 2006 the Occupied Palestinian Territory has been subjected to economic sanctions in the form of the termination of donor aid, the imposition of banking restrictions and the seizure of tax moneys. The United States, the European Union and Israel must take direct responsibility for these actions, but the Quartet must accept indirect responsibility. Most recently, the Quartet has embarked on a course hostile to Palestinian self-determination by giving support to one Palestinian faction, Fatah, at the expense of the other, Hamas, and by making no attempt to restore the unity of the Palestinian people. In the process Gaza seems to have been simply abandoned by the Quartet.

49. The actions of the United States and the European Union within the Quartet can be explained in terms of their own domestic political constituencies and constraints. The Russian Federation seems to be uneasy about its membership of the Quartet and attempts to pursue, without success, an even-handed approach to the situation in the Occupied Palestinian Territory. What then is the position of the United Nations, the guardian of legitimacy enshrined in the Charter, and representative not only of the opinions of the five permanent members of the Security Council but of all 192 members of the Organization? Sadly, the United Nations, acting through the Secretary-General, has ignored the views of the majority of its members and abandoned its role as guardian of international legitimacy. Instead of promoting Palestinian self-determination, striving to end the occupation and opposing the ongoing violation of human rights, the United Nations has chosen to give legitimacy to the statements and actions of the Quartet. The situation is well described by Alvaro de Soto in his End of Mission Report:

> [The Secretary-General] is being used to provide the appearance of an imprimatur on behalf of the international community for the Quartet's positions. This in itself is awkward since the Secretary-General participates in the Quartet not by delegation or mandate from any UN body, leave alone the Security Council, but in

his semi-stand-alone capacity. There are large segments of the international community not represented in the self-appointed Quartet, including the Arab shareholders. Nevertheless, I could live with the arrangements until the point came when the Quartet started taking positions which are not likely to gather a majority in UN bodies, and which in any case are at odds with the UN Security Council resolutions and/or international law or, when they aren't expressly so, fall short of the minimum of even-handedness that must be the lifeblood of the diplomatic action of the Secretary-General" (para. 69).

50. For the past few years the Special Rapporteur has appealed in his reports to the Quartet to show more even-handedness and respect for human rights and the rule of law in both their actions and their utterances. These appeals have been ignored. Now, the former Under-Secretary-General, Special Coordinator for the Middle East Peace Process and Envoy to the Quartet has spoken in stronger language, accusing the Quartet of being led (and coerced) by the United States into adopting positions at odds with the ideals of the Charter, and calling upon the Secretary-General to seriously reconsider continued United Nations membership in the Quartet. In effect, this message has been ignored and the messenger shot (see the statement by Secretary-General Ban Ki-moon at a press conference on 13 June 2007).

Recommendations, 2007
A/62/275 of 17 August 2007, paras. 51–57

At the conclusion of his mandate the Special Rapporteur made a number of recommendations to interested parties:

51. The recommendations or appeals set out below are made to Israel, Palestinian armed groups, States members of the United Nations and the United Nations itself.

To Israel

52. Israel's occupation of the West Bank, East Jerusalem and Gaza is now in its fortieth year. This occupation, which has resulted in numerous violations of international humanitarian law and human rights law, has seriously undermined the integrity and reputation of the State of Israel. Israel is urged to enter into serious negotiations with the Palestinian Authority to bring about the creation of a Palestinian State within the 1967 borders of the Palestinian entity, to end the occupation of the Palestinian Territory and to respect international humanitarian law and human rights law in its dealings with the Palestinian people.

To Palestinian militant groups

53. Palestinian militant groups are urged to end their attacks on civilian targets and comply with international humanitarian law, both within the Occupied Palestinian Territory and Israel.

To States Members of the United Nations

54. States Members of the United Nations are urged to bring pressure on the Quartet to act in an even-handed manner with due respect for human rights and international humanitarian law. They are also urged, as parties to the Fourth Geneva Convention, to ensure that Israel complies with international humanitarian law as embodied in that Convention. (This obligation is affirmed by the International Court of Justice in its Advisory Opinion on the Wall.)

To the United Nations (particularly the Secretary-General)

55. The Secretary-General is urged, as representative of the United Nations in the Quartet, to ensure that the Quartet:

(a) Condemns Israel's violations of international humanitarian law and human rights law (described in the present report) and take measures to ensure that Israel complies with its obligations in this respect;

(b) Accepts the 2004 Advisory Opinion of the International Court of Justice on the Legal Consequences of the Construction of a Wall in the Occupied Palestinian Territory as a juridical basis for its dealings with Israel;

(c) Presses Israel to immediately transfer to the Palestinian Authority all the value added tax and customs duties that it has collected on behalf of the Palestinians in order to ameliorate the humanitarian crisis that prevails in the Occupied Palestinian Territory;

(d) Adopts a fair and even-handed approach to the respective positions of Israel and the Palestinians;

(e) Adopts a fair and even-handed approach to different factions within the Palestinian community, as the United Nations has done in other comparable conflict situations, so that Palestinian self-determination is achieved.

56. If the Secretary-General is unsuccessful in persuading the Quartet to act as proposed above, the United Nations should cease to give its imprimatur to the actions of the Quartet and should withdraw from the Quartet.

To the United Nations (particularly the General Assembly)

57. The General Assembly is urged to request the International Court of Justice to give a further advisory opinion on the legal consequences for the occupied people, the Occupying Power and third States of prolonged occupation.

CHAPTER FIVE

SELECTIONS FROM THE REPORTS OF SPECIAL RAPPORTEUR RICHARD FALK

(2008–2014)

Political Developments: Major Changes in the Setting of Occupation

Report #1: A/63/326, 25 Aug 2008

8. The setting of the occupation is important for a meaningful evaluation of particular events and occupation policies, resistance activities and an assessment of the overall human rights situation, to the extent that the security of the occupier permits. The overall attention to these particular dimensions of the occupation helps keep attention on the centrality of the Palestinian right to and struggle for self-determination under conditions of prolonged occupation. All changes in the wider context of Israeli-Palestinian relations provide insight into the nature of the occupation, both in terms of its oppressive character and the difficulty of improving the conditions of the Palestinian people so long as they live under occupation.

9. Following the breaching of the wall separating Egypt from the Gaza Strip as a result of explosives set by Hamas near the Rafah crossing on 23 January 2008, tens of thousands of Gazans, with some estimates running as high as 500,000, crossed the border into the Egyptian city of Rafah, seeking particularly to buy food, medicines and a variety of consumer goods unavailable in Gaza. When asked by border guards for guidance, the Egyptian President, Hosni Mubarak, was quoted as saying, "I told them, 'Let them come to eat and buy food, then they go back, as long

as they are not carrying weapons.'"[1]* A spokesperson for Hamas is reported to have said, "We are creating facts. We have to try to change the situation, and now we await results. We warned the Egyptian people we are hungry and dying." Many Gazans without political affiliation said in various ways, "This is the best thing Hamas has done." The situation was well summarized by an independent journalist, Allan Nairn, who wrote, "the Gaza wall-breaking was an easy call: no people were killed, some may have been saved, and the spectacle of exodus into Egypt effectively dramatized a gross injustice" Nairn's language captures the main realities illuminated in relation to the occupation, that is to say, exodus and spectacle.[2] It was not possible to witness the events without appreciating the desperation of people long confined by a stultifying occupation that threatens human well-being, even survival, and should not be allowed to endure. In a few days, the Gazans were required to return to Gaza, the wall was repaired and the conditions of siege and confinement were re-established. It is possible that subtle changes for the better resulted from the exodus and spectacle of the departing masses from Gaza, with the events leading to a wider international understanding of the desperate state of affairs produced by the enforced isolation and confinement of the 1.5 million Gazans.

10. No causal connection has been established or acknowledged between the events associated with breaching the Rafah wall and the initiation of secret negotiations under Egyptian auspices in Cairo between representatives of the government of Israel and Hamas, with the objective of establishing a ceasefire agreement that would end the firing of rockets into Israel from Gaza and military incursions and targeted assassinations by Israel in the Gaza Strip. At the same time, it seems difficult to resist the view that the coverage, especially the pictures broadcast worldwide, of the wall being breached, encouraged Israel to be more receptive

1 *The New York Times*, 24 January 2008. *The numbering of footnotes in this chapter follows the sequence of citations in this chapter of selections from the UN Reports, and differs from the numbering in the reports themselves.

2 See Allan Nairn, "Justified Violence: Breaking the Gaza Wall," *The Nation*, 29 January 2008

to long-standing Hamas offers to establish a mutual ceasefire. The negotiations were rather prolonged, but in the end they were successful. On 20 June 2008, a ceasefire was declared, and despite some infractions on both sides, it has generally held.[3] The terms of the ceasefire have not been made public, but it has been assumed by informed observers that a demonstration by Hamas of its will and capacity to enforce the ceasefire on its own militant groups would be matched by an easing of the siege by Israel.

11. Hamas' efforts to enforce the ceasefire have been recognized and reciprocated by Israel in the form of easing the hardships experienced by Gazans. Israel contends that it has increased the supply of food and medicine by as much as 50 percent and is considering further steps designed to ease tensions and hardships. Nevertheless, because the duration and intensity of the siege imposed on pre-existing conditions of widespread poverty and hardship have been so severe, humanitarian conditions inside the Gaza Strip remain dire, and pose great risks of future calamities.

12. An additional aspect of those developments is the implicit recognition by Israel of the *de facto* governance of Gaza by Hamas. According to Meir Javedanfar, a respected Tel Aviv Middle East specialist, "[Hamas] is the power that Israel has to deal with. It's not full diplomatic recognition, but Israel has recognized Hamas as an important party. On some issues it can't be avoided. Israel is showing that its past policy of refusing to talk to militant organizations . . . is not always functional . . . [and has] realized that talking to its enemies is the shortest and most cost-effective path militarily, economically and strategically"[4]

Officially, Israel has not altered its formal position to the effect that Hamas is a terrorist organization, and that the ceasefire agreement should be viewed as a compromise proposal put forward by Egypt and accepted by both sides. Israel continues to insist that Hamas must unilaterally meet three conditions before it will change its formal diplomatic stance. Those conditions are recognition of Israel's right to exist as a Jewish State, affirmation

---

3 For an assessment of the ceasefire, see Uri Avnery, "The Ceasefire," *London Review of Books* 30:15, 31 July 2008.

4 See also articles 51, 52 and 57 of Protocol I to the Geneva Conventions.

of past agreements between the Palestinian Authority and Israel and renunciation of violence.

13. To a certain extent, those recent facts speak for themselves: Hamas has emerged from that process as producing a ceasefire and as a partner with Israel in the administration of joint arrangements.[5]

From the Israeli side, it is also plausible to view the arrangement as an implicit recognition by Hamas of the State of Israel. It is to be hoped that that development creates some prospect that the siege of Gaza will be lifted, international economic assistance restored, and a regime of occupation established that complies with international humanitarian law and upholds human rights to the extent possible, given the security situation. Future assessments of that process will likely focus upon whether Egyptian negotiations with the Palestinian Authority for a reopening of the Rafah crossing are successful and whether a prisoner exchange agreement can be worked out that includes the release of the Israeli soldier Corporal Gilad Shalit, who has been held captive for more than two years. Encouragement of those negotiations is definitely correlated with the practical prospect of improving the protection of the economic and social rights of the 1.5 million Palestinians living in Gaza, although, from a strictly legal point of view, the obligations of Israel as Occupying Power are unconditional, and not contingent, especially where the fundamental rights of the general Gazan population is concerned.

14. Although the volatile relations of Hamas and Fatah within the Occupied Palestinian Territory are not part of the current mandate, the recent call by President Mahmoud Abbas for talks leading to the establishment of a unity government for all of Palestine moves also in the direction of reducing violence and allowing the civilian population living under Israeli occupation to have somewhat improved prospects that their human rights will be protected. A viable peace process depends, among other

---

5 For an early assessment of the ceasefire, see an article by Joshua Mitnick, "As Gaza ceasefire holds, Israel eases economic blockade," *Christian Science Monitor*, 23 June 2008.

conditions, on achieving unified representation for all Palestinians living under occupation.

15. There have also been some encouraging developments in the region that might indirectly lead to improvements in the occupation regime, although, to date, the developments on the ground have not borne out those hopes. The negotiation of an agreement between Hizbullah and the government of Lebanon offers some basis for greater stability. The ongoing negotiations between Israel and the Syrian Arab Republic, as mediated by Turkey, also suggest a renewed reliance on a diplomatic approach to unresolved conflicts, and some willingness by the State of Israel to explore such a possibility.

16. The end to occupation is the only path to full restoration of the human rights of the Palestinian people. According to doctrine, international law requires an Israeli withdrawal from substantially all Occupied Palestinian Territory, including East Jerusalem, in accordance with the iconic call of Security Council resolution 242 (1967), which was adopted in the aftermath of the 1967 Arab-Israeli war. But withdrawal has been deemed extremely unlikely without bilateral negotiations that address all issues in dispute between Israel and the Palestinian Authority. From that perspective, it had seemed somewhat optimistic to view the Annapolis conference of 27 November 2007 that brought together some 40 concerned governments as a revival of the peace process along the lines set forth by the Quartet in its road map of 2003. At Annapolis, there was a joint understanding of the participating governments that Israel and the Palestinian Authority would seek to resolve all outstanding issues, and there was an apparent shift by the government of the United States towards an encouragement of bilateral negotiations. There have ensued frequent meetings between Israeli Prime Minister, Ehud Olmert, and President of the Palestinian Authority, Mahmoud Abbas, but no sign of notable breakthroughs on final status issues and little prospect that that negotiating track will produce meaningful results. That is a reflection of the weakness of Prime Minister Olmert in view of internal Israeli opposition, his embattled position and his announced plans to resign after the Kadima Party meetings in September 2008.

More fundamentally, Israel has without doubt failed the litmus tests set up at Annapolis for a peace process that involved a complete freeze on Israeli settlement expansion (along with the dismantling of so-called outposts, that is, settler land occupations throughout the West Bank regarded as unlawful under Israeli law) and a reduction of checkpoint constraints on freedom of movement. The pattern since Annapolis is, instead, one of continuous Israeli settlement expansion at an accelerated pace, with no reports of outposts being dismantled, and an increase in the number of cumbersome restraints associated with Israel's network of military checkpoints.

17. The second litmus test set was the reduction of Palestinian violence. Here, the Gaza ceasefire, if it holds, seems extremely relevant, as does the resolve of the Palestinian Authority to implement to the best of its ability a policy of abandoning armed struggle against the Israeli occupation. But without comparable Israeli moves on settlements, the process is likely to be indefinitely stalled or abandoned. At present, there is no basis for optimism that the Annapolis initiative will lead to a timely end to the occupation, to peace or to respect by Israel for the rights of the Palestinian people according to the requirements of international humanitarian law and the legal standards of international human rights.

Right to peaceful assembly: demonstrations against the wall in the West Bank

24. Ni'lin is a village situated in the Ramallah district of the West Bank near the Wall that Israel has been unlawfully constructing on Occupied Palestinian Territory in defiance of the July 2004 Advisory Opinion of the International Court of Justice. It has been the scene of numerous non-violent demonstrations against the construction of the Wall that was built in such a way as to confiscate significant portions of the land belonging to the village. That is part of a longer story of land dispossession that has afflicted the Palestinians.

25. It is estimated that as much as 80 percent of the land belonging to Ni'lin has been incrementally confiscated by Israel,

starting in 1948. After the 1967 war, the location of Ni'lin near the Green Line led to further land confiscations on behalf of West Bank settlements (74 dunams for the settlement of Shalit, then 661 dunams for Mattityahu, 934 dunams for Hashmonaim, 274 dunams for Mod'in Illit, 20 dunams for Menora), which took about 13 percent of the village land. When a further 20 percent of Ni'lin land, belonging to its residents, was officially slated for confiscation by Israel for the construction of the Wall, strong demonstrations took place. Ni'lin became the inspirational center of opposition to the Wall and, during 2003–2004, it was the scene of numerous anti-wall demonstrations. In recent months, there have been protests by people living in the village and supporters from neighboring cities such as Ramallah and Tulkarem, and also by Israeli peace activists who have come to Ni'lin to join in the non-violent demonstrations seeking to prevent the resumption of construction of the wall.

Gaza Occupation Traumas: Operation Cast Lead

Report #2: A/HRC/10/20, 11 Feb. 2009

4. With regard to Gaza, there is a further concern with respect to the nature of the legal obligations of Israel towards the Gazan population. Israel officially contends that, after the implementation of its disengagement plan in 2005, it is no longer an Occupying Power, and is therefore not responsible for observance of the obligations set forth in the Fourth Geneva Convention. That contention has been widely rejected by expert opinion, by the *de facto* realities of effective control and by official pronouncements by, for instance, the United Nations High Commissioner for Human Rights and the Secretary-General (A/HRC/8/17), the General Assembly in its resolutions 63/96 and 63/98, and the Security Council in its resolution 1860 (2009). Since 2005, Israel has completely controlled all entry and exit routes by land and sea and asserted control over Gazan airspace and territorial waters. By

imposing a blockade, in effect since the summer of 2007, it has profoundly affected the life and well-being of every single person living in Gaza. Therefore, regardless of the international status of the Occupied Palestinian Territory with respect to the use of force, the obligations of the Fourth Geneva Convention, as well as those of international human rights law and international criminal law, are fully applicable.

5. The final introductory clarification concerns the relations of international human rights law and international humanitarian law to international criminal law. Not every violation of human rights or infraction of the Geneva Conventions constitutes a war crime or a crime of State. Moreover, criminal intent, by way of mental attitude or through circumstantial evidence, must be established. In essence, "grave breaches" of the Geneva Conventions as defined in article 147 of the Fourth Geneva Convention normally provide a legal foundation for allegations of war crimes. It is to be noted that the role of international criminal law is not only to identify and implement the fundamental obligations of international humanitarian law in wartime, but also to take into account severe violations of human rights arising from oppressive patterns of peacetime governance.

6. The recommended scope of investigation should combine attention to violations of international humanitarian law, the laws of war and general international law (treaty and customary) as it bears on the rights and duties of Israel as the Occupying Power, and Hamas as the party exercising effective political control in Gaza at the present time. It is to be expected that Israel would cooperate with any investigation authorized by the United Nations in accordance with its obligations as a Member State under Article 56 of the Charter of the United Nations calling upon members to cooperate with the Organization, as well as the additional duties contained in the Convention on the Privileges and Immunities of the United Nations. It is disquieting, however, to read that Prime Minister Ehud Olmert and others protect any member of the Israel Defense Forces from being accused, and, if accused, to prevent

indictment and prosecution.[6] Such sentiments seem inconsistent with any expectation of serious official cooperation with a proposed investigation. It may be necessary, given this prospect, to place greater reliance on respected non-governmental organizations compiling evidence and submitting reports and on formal interviews with qualified observers and witnesses.

Inherent illegality: Legally mandatory distinction between civilian and military targets impossible in large-scale sustained attacks on Gaza as commenced by Israel on 27 December 2008

7. It is the view of the Special Rapporteur that the most important legal issue raised by an investigation of the recent military operations concerns the basic Israeli claim to use modern weaponry on a large scale against an occupied population living under the confined conditions that existed in Gaza. This involves trying to establish whether, under the conditions that existed in Gaza, it is possible with sufficient consistency to distinguish between military targets and the surrounding civilian population. If it is not possible to do so, then launching the attacks is inherently unlawful, and would seem to constitute a war crime of the greatest magnitude under international law. On the basis of the preliminary evidence available, there is reason to reach this conclusion.

8. Considering that the attacks were directed at densely populated areas, it was to some extent inevitable and certainly foreseeable that hospitals, religious and educational sites and United Nations facilities would be hit by Israeli military ordnance, and that extensive civilian casualties would result. As all borders were sealed, civilians could not escape from the orbit of harm. For authoritative and more specific conclusions on these points, it will be necessary to mount an investigation based on knowledge of Israeli weaponry, tactics, and doctrine to assess the degree to which, in concrete cases, it would have been possible, given the battlefield conditions, to avoid non-military targets and

---

6 "The soldiers and commanders who were sent on mission in Gaza must know that they are safe from various tribunals and that the State of Israel will assist them on this issue and defend them." *Los Angeles Times*, 26 January 2009.

to spare Palestinian civilians to a greater extent. Even without this investigation, on the basis of available reports and statistics, it is possible to draw the important preliminary conclusion that, given the number of Palestinian civilian casualties and degree of devastation of non-military targets in Gaza, the Israelis either refrained from drawing the distinction required by customary and treaty international law or were unable to do so under the prevailing combat conditions, making the attacks impossible to reconcile with international law. On the basis of existing information, the principal results of the military operation were as follows:

(a) A total of 1,434 Palestinians were killed, of whom 235 were combatants. Some 960 civilians reportedly lost their lives, including 288 children and 121 women; 239 police. Palestinian officers were also killed, 235 in air strikes carried out on the first day. A total of 5,303 Palestinians were injured, including 1,606 children and 828 women (namely, 1 in every 225 Gazans was killed or injured, not counting mental injury, which must be assumed to be extensive).[7]

(b) Homes and public infrastructure throughout Gaza, especially in Gaza City, sustained extensive damage, including several United Nations facilities; an estimated 21,000 homes were either totally destroyed or badly damaged.

(c) A total of 51,000 people were internally displaced in makeshift shelters that provided minimal protection, while others fled to homes of friends and relatives that seemed slightly safer.[8]

---

7 A recent report by Near East Consulting quoted by the Office for the Coordination of Humanitarian Affairs in its Gaza Humanitarian Situation Report of 26 January 2009 concluded that 96 percent of Gaza residents suffer from depression, with intense depression being experienced by 81 percent of the residents of North Gaza and Rafah districts. Such mental deterioration is itself an indication of a failure by the Occupying Power to discharge its basic duty to safeguard the health of civilians living under occupation.

8 Office for the Coordination of Humanitarian Affairs, Field Update from the Humanitarian Coordinator, 9 February 2009, and the Gaza Flash Appeal, 2 February 2009; Palestinian Centre for Human Rights, press release, ref. 36/2009, 12 March 2009.

9. There is no way to reconcile the general purposes and specific prescriptions of international humanitarian law with the scale and nature of the Israeli military attacks commenced on 27 December 2008. The attacks with F-16 fighter bombers, Apache helicopters, long-range artillery from the ground and sea were directed at an essentially defenseless society of 1.5 million persons. As recent reports submitted to the Council by the Special Rapporteur emphasized, the residents of Gaza were particularly vulnerable to physical and mental damage from such attacks as the society as a whole had been brought to the brink of collapse by months of blockade that restricted the flow of food, fuel and medical supplies to sub-subsistence levels, and was responsible, according to health specialists, for a serious overall decline in the health of the population and of the health system. Any assessment under international law of the attacks of 27 December should take into account the weakened condition of the Gazan civilian population resulting from the sustained unlawfulness of the pre-existing Israeli blockade that violated articles 33 (prohibition on collective punishment) and 55 (duty to provide food and health care to the occupied population) of the Fourth Geneva Convention. Considering the obligation of the Occupying Power to care for the well-being of the civilian occupied population, mounting a comprehensive attack on a society already weakened by unlawful occupation practices would appear to aggravate the breach of responsibility described above owing to the difficulties of maintaining the principle of distinction.

10. The deputy head of the embassy of Israel at the European Union, Ambassador Zvi Tal, during discussions with a committee of the European Parliament, sought to defend the attacks on Gaza by describing them as addressing "a very peculiar" situation. In responding to allegations about the bombing of United Nations schools in Gaza, he was quoted as saying: "Sometimes in the heat of fire and the exchange of fire, we do make mistakes. We're not infallible." This is deeply misleading in its characterization of the war zone. It is not a matter of mistakes and fallibility, but rather of a massive assault on a densely populated urbanized setting where the defining reality could not but subject the entire civilian

population to an inhumane form of warfare that kills, maims and inflicts mental harm that is likely to have long-term effects, especially on children, who make up more than 50 percent of the Gazan population.

Non-exhaustion of diplomatic remedies, disproportionality, non-defensive nature of the attacks

11. It is a requirement of international customary law, as well as of the Charter of the United Nations, Article 2, paragraph 4, interpreted in the light of Article 1, paragraph 1, that recourse to force to resolve an international dispute should be a last resort after the exhaustion of diplomatic remedies and peaceful alternatives, even assuming for a moment that an Occupying Power can claim a right to self-defense (see paragraph 28 below). Of course, such an analysis presupposes the rejection of the Israeli contention that Gaza has not been legally "occupied" since the implementation of the disengagement plan in 2005. In the context of protecting Israeli society from rockets fired from Gaza, the evidence overwhelmingly supports the conclusion that the ceasefire in place as of 19 June 2008 had been an effective instrument for achieving this goal, as measured by the incidence of rockets fired and with regard to Israeli casualties sustained.

12. The graph below, based on Israeli sources, shows the number of Palestinian rockets and mortar shells fired each month in 2008, with the period of the ceasefire stretching basically from its initiation on 19 June to its effective termination on 4 November, when Israel struck a lethal blow in Gaza that reportedly killed at least six Hamas operatives. It dramatically demonstrates the extent to which the ceasefire was by far the most secure period with respect to the threats posed by the rockets.

13. The authors of a study based on the data displayed in the graph below[9] concluded that "the ceasefire was remarkably effective; after it began in June 2008, the rate of rocket and mortar fire

9 N. Kanwisher, H. Haushofer and A. Biletzki, "Reigniting violence: how do ceasefires end?," 24 January 2009.

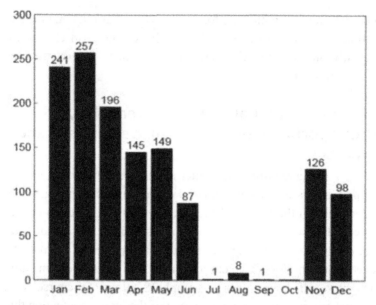

Number of Palestinian rockets and mortar shells fired in 2008

from Gaza dropped to almost zero and stayed there for almost four months." The experience of the temporary ceasefire demonstrates both the willingness and the capacity of those exerting control in Gaza to eliminate rocket and mortar attacks.

14. Beyond this, records show that, during the ceasefire, it was predominantly Israel that resorted to conduct inconsistent with the undertaking, and Hamas that retaliated. According to the above-mentioned study, during a longer period, from 2000 to 2008, it was found that, in 79 percent of the violent interaction incidents, it was Israel that broke the pause in violence. In the course of events preceding the attacks of 27 December, the break-down of the truce followed a series of incidents on 4 November in which Israel killed a Palestinian in Gaza, mortars were fired from Gaza in retaliation, and then an Israeli air strike was launched that killed an additional six Palestinians in Gaza; in other words, the breakdown of the ceasefire seems to have been mainly a result of Israeli violations, although this offers no legal, moral or political excuse for firing of rockets aimed at civilian targets, which itself amounts to a clear violation of international humanitarian law.

15. Furthermore, Hamas leaders have repeatedly and formally proposed extending the ceasefire, including for long periods.[10] It is notable that the president of the United States of America, Barack Obama, has called for this result in a statement accompanying his appointment of a special envoy on the Israel/Palestine conflict: "As part of a lasting ceasefire, Gaza's border crossings should be open to allow the flow of aid and commerce." This assertion is consistent with the call made by the Security Council in its resolution 1860 (2009) for unimpeded provision and distribution throughout Gaza of humanitarian assistance, including food, fuel, and medical treatment, which in effect prescribes the end of the blockade of Gaza that has been maintained by Israel in violation of articles 33 and 55 of the Fourth Geneva Convention.

16. The continuing refusal of Israel to acknowledge Hamas as a political actor, based on the label of "terrorist organization," has obstructed all attempts to implement human rights and address security concerns by way of diplomacy rather than through reliance on force. This refusal is important for reasons already mentioned (see paragraph 3 above), namely, that the population density in Gaza means that reliance on large-scale military operations to ensure Israeli security cannot be reconciled with the legal obligations under the Fourth Geneva Convention to protect to the extent possible the safety and well-being of the occupied Gazan population.

17. There are several relevant conclusions that demonstrate this link between relying on non-violent options and the requirements of international humanitarian law:

(a) The temporary ceasefire was impressively successful in shutting down cross-border violence and casualties on both sides.

---

10 "When this broken truce neared its end, we expressed our readiness for a new comprehensive truce in return for lifting the blockade and opening all Gaza crossings, including Rafah." Khalid Mish'al, "This brutality will never break our will to be free," in *The Guardian*, 6 January 2009. Available at https://www.guardian.co.uk/commentisfree/2009/jan/06/gaza-israel-hamas (accessed 3 March 2009).

(b) The Palestinian side adhered to the ceasefire, with relatively few exceptions, and relied on violence almost exclusively in reactive modes, while Israel failed to implement its undertaking to lift the blockade and seems mainly responsible for breaking lulls in the violence by engaging in targeted assassinations and other violent and unlawful provocations, most significantly by its air strike of 4 November 2008.

(c) The Hamas leadership appears ready at present to restore the ceasefire provided that the blockade is unconditionally lifted, which should in any event happen owing to its unlawful character and should also be accompanied by guarantees against weapons smuggling on the Palestinian side, and a commitment to desist from targeted assassinations on the Israeli side.

(d) If substantiated by further investigation, the overall pattern prevailing at the time the attacks were launched would undermine the claim by Israel that its recourse to force was necessary and defensive, both features of which must be present to support a valid claim under international law of self-defense.

(e) On the above basis, the contention that the use of force by Israel was "disproportionate" should not divert our attention from the prior question of the unlawfulness of recourse to force. If for the sake of argument, however, the claim of self-defense and defensive force is accepted, it would appear that the air, ground and sea attacks by Israel were grossly and intentionally disproportionate when measured against either the threat posed or harm done, as well as with respect to the disconnect between the high level of violence relied upon and the specific security goals being pursued. Israel did little to disguise its policy of disproportionate use of force, thereby acknowledging a refusal to comply with this fundamental requirement of international customary law.[11]

---

11 See, Nidal al-Mughrabi, "Attacks batter Gaza ceasefire," Reuters, last updated 2 Feb. 2009, https://www.reuters.com/article/uk-palestinians-israel/attacks-batter-gaza-ceasefire-idUKTRE5100P520090202

The prime minister of Israel was quoted by the press agency, Reuters, after the ceasefire as saying: "The Government's position was from the outset that if there is shooting at the residents of the south, there will be a harsh Israeli response that will be disproportionate."[12] To the extent that the Prime Minister's comment reflects Israeli policy, it was a novel and blatant repudiation of one of the most fundamental aspects of international law governing the use of force.

21. It needs to be noted once again, and repeated frequently, that the blockade as such is flagrantly and vindictively unlawful given the clear obligation of article 33 of the Fourth Geneva Convention to avoid collective punishment without exception. As such it constitutes a war crime of great magnitude. This denial of access to reconstruction materials appears to be an aggravated violation of article 33, especially severe given the physical and psychological vulnerability of the population in the aftermath of Operation Cast Lead.

22. Once again, the Free Gaza Movement sought to send a ship, *Spirit of Humanity*, containing humanitarian supplies to Gaza as a symbolic expression of the unwillingness on the part of peace activists to respect the unlawful blockade. Six prior ships had succeeded in landing in Gaza, although a prior boat, Dignity, had been rammed by an Israeli naval vessel in December 2008, and prevented from reaching Gaza. The announced purpose of this mission was to deliver needed supplies to Gaza, but also to expose the failures of the United Nations and of the intergovernmental community of States to implement international humanitarian law as obligated by articles 1 and 147 of the Fourth Geneva Convention, as well as article 86(1) of Protocol I.

23. As before, the ship was stopped and boarded in international waters, which constitutes an unlawful operation; the

---

12 This legal sentiment is authoritatively expressed in article 51, subparagraph 5b, of Protocol I to the Geneva Conventions, in which disproportionate attacks are defined as "an attack which may be expected to cause incidental loss of civilian life, injury to civilians, damage to civilian objects, or a combination thereof, which would be excessive in relation to the concrete and direct military advantage anticipated."

passengers were arrested for various periods up to several days, including former American congresswoman and Green Party presidential candidate, Cynthia McKinney. Despite the international site of the incident, 20 passengers were initially charged with "illegally entering Israeli waters" but were eventually released. The Free Gaza Movement vividly reinforces the impression that civil society takes international humanitarian law and international criminal law more seriously in this setting than do governments.

War crimes and accountability

24. There have been several important studies under respected auspices that confirm the earlier suspicions based on journalistic presentations and eyewitness accounts of war crimes associated with Operation Cast Lead. These include:

(a) a comprehensive study prepared by a team of specialists in international humanitarian law led by John Dugard, the former Special Rapporteur on the situation of human rights in the Palestinian Territories Occupied since 1967, as an undertaking of the Arab League, under the title *Report of the Independent Fact-Finding Committee on Gaza: No Safe Place,* presented to the League on 30 April 2009;

(b) the major report on war crimes by Amnesty International, published in July 2009, entitled *Israel/Gaza: Operation "Cast Lead": 22 Days of Death and Destruction,* several reports by Human Rights Watch; and

(c) the ICRC report entitled *Gaza: 1.5 Million People Trapped in Despair,* which is mainly confirmatory of the scale of devastation, and the aggravating impact of the Israeli refusal to lift the blockade.

There is also a major report conducted by the United Nations Board of Inquiry relating to damage done to United Nations facilities and personnel as a result of Operation Cast Lead. A series of conclusions relating to Israeli responsibility and obligations were revealed in the executive summary of the full report; regrettably by order of the Secretary-General the full report has not been released, but its main conclusion is that Israel, without sufficient military justification and with deliberate intention, did serious harm to several United Nations facilities and caused major casualties on the part of those taking shelter in United Nations buildings and schools.

26. As indicated above, despite the overwhelming consensus associated with available materials relating to war crimes allegations directed at Israel and Hamas (as *de facto* governing authority in Gaza), the report of the fact-finding mission led by Judge Goldstone is awaited with great anticipation, and will likely address the same range of issues, and will include the evaluation of testimony received at a series of hearings with victims and other participants; members of this Human Rights Council mandated investigation were also denied entry to Gaza by way of Israel, and were forced to depend on the cooperation of the Egyptian government to obtain access to Gaza; they received no requested cooperation from Israel. Its report is due in September 2009.

27. Whether in response to the incriminating testimony of Israeli soldiers or in anticipation of the report of Judge Goldstone, the Israeli Foreign Ministry announced on 30 July 2009 that it was going to investigate 100 complaints about Operation Cast Lead, including allegations concerning the use of phosphorus artillery shells. This is a welcome recognition by the Israeli government that war crimes allegations are better acknowledged and investigated by Israel than dismissed out of hand. Although one continues to hope for an objective inquiry, Israel's formal announcement of the investigation was coupled with a detailed reassertion and comprehensive explanation of why Operation Cast Lead was a necessary and proportionate response to rocket attacks and suicide bombings over an eight-year period, and that it was carried out with scrupulous regard for international humanitarian law.[13]

28. All of the above developments suggest that once the facts are established and recommendations received, attention will shift to the more difficult question of devising an appropriate

---

13 See Reuters, "Israel says investigating 100 Gaza war complaints," 30 July 2009; for the full text of the report, see "The Operation in Gaza: Factual and Legal Aspects," Israel Ministry of Foreign Affairs, 29 July 2009.

mechanism for assessing accountability for war crimes. For political reasons, it is unlikely that such a mechanism will be established under United Nations auspices although the legal capacity
to do so is definitely present, as illustrated by the establishment
of ad hoc criminal tribunals for former Yugoslavia and Rwanda
in the 1990s. The General Assembly also possesses the constitutional authority under Article 22 of the Charter of the United
Nations to establish subsidiary organs as it deems necessary for
the performance of its functions, and although it has never established a criminal tribunal, there is every reason to suppose that
it possesses the authority to do so. Further, for jurisdictional, as
well as political reasons, it is almost certain that the International
Criminal Court is not available: Israel is not a party and would
undoubtedly refuse all forms of cooperation. Palestine did not attempt to become a party until after Operation Cast Lead and is not
widely thought to have at present the legal credentials to qualify
and be accepted as a "State." It is likely that the only available
form of accountability will result from civil society initiatives
associated with the imposition of sporting and cultural boycotts
and divestment moves involving trade and investment. Once
again it is anticipated that governments and the United Nations
will not follow through at the implementation stage with respect
to international legal obligations.

Breaking the silence

29. *Breaking the Silence: Operation Cast Lead* is a publication containing the responses of combat soldiers who took part in
the military operation.[14] It has received considerable media attention because it confirms from within the Israeli Defense Forces
several disturbing allegations: consistent Forces reliance on
unacceptably loose rules of engagement that meant that international humanitarian law guidelines as to limits on military force in

---

14 Breaking the Silence is an organization of veteran Israeli soldiers that
collects testimonies of soldiers who served in the occupied territories during
the Second Intifadah. *Breaking the Silence: Operation Cast Lead* is available at
https://www.breakingthesilence.org.il/wp-content/uploads/2011/02/Operation_
Cast_Lead_Gaza_2009_Eng.pdf.

relation to civilians and civilian targets became virtually inoperative and were not part of briefings given prior to or during combat; widespread destruction of targets that could not be justified from a military or security perspective; use of phosphorus in densely populated zones; interference with Gazan civilian movement to places of relative safety in Gaza by the fragmentation of the Strip, trapping many within the worst combat sectors; racist pressures brought to bear on soldiers by what was described as the "military rabbinate," dehumanizing Arabs and Palestinians, and treating the conflict as a holy war against a demonic enemy.

30. It should be noted that the testimonies of these Israeli Defense Forces soldiers assumed greater credibility because they were not at all anti-Israeli or anti-Zionist in tone, and many of the soldiers accepted the underlying rationale of Operation Cast Lead as a necessary defensive reaction to Hamas rockets. Also there were some qualifications placed on the condemnation of disregard of the Forces for civilians: there was acknowledgement that Forces warnings were issued, that warning shots were sometimes fired to identify whether individuals were suspicious or to deter Gazans from coming closer to where soldiers were deployed, and that sporadic efforts were made by some Forces commanders to avoid doing as much civilian damage as could have been inflicted. Overall, an impression emerges from the testimonies that many of the tactics relied upon were less designed to kill and injure Palestinian civilians than to protect Israeli soldiers from injury, death, or capture. However, much of this increased the risks of harm inflicted on innocent Palestinians. A typical sentiment in the testimony was the following order given by a field commander to Defense Forces troops: "Not a hair will fall off a soldier of mine, and I am not willing to allow a soldier of mine to risk himself by hesitating. If you are not sure — shoot." Or more generally: "There was a clear feeling, and this was repeated whenever others spoke to us, that no humanitarian consideration played any role in the army at present. The goal was to carry out an operation with the least possible casualties for the army, without its even asking itself what the price would be for the other side."

35. It is the judgment of the Special Rapporteur that Operation Cast Lead discloses that urban warfare, fought on the ground, from air or sea, cannot maintain the legal standards of constraints associated with international humanitarian law, more specifically with the special requirements of the Fourth Geneva Convention and Protocol I associated with the protection of civilians, particularly in circumstances of prolonged occupation. In this respect, the Israeli claim of adherence to the restraints of international law is unconvincing, as demonstrated by the evidence of combat practices and *de facto* rules of engagement; equally unconvincing are contentions that Israeli soldiers in the field should be the main concern of investigation and potential accountability. Instead, the focus should be upon high military commanders and political leaders who devised such an operation, as well as on the limits on military power in the first place.

36. One of the most celebrated legal guidelines on war fighting is contained in article 22 of the annex to the 1899 Hague Convention II on the Laws and Customs of War on Land: "The right of belligerents to adopt means of injuring the enemy is not unlimited." Article 35(1) of Protocol I expresses the same general sentiment: "In any armed conflict, the right of the Parties to the conflict to choose methods or means of warfare is not unlimited."[15] Urban warfare of the sort carried out in Gaza during Operation Cast Lead seems to exceed those limits; however vague they may seem to be as formulated in 1899, the time may have come in 2009 to give them concrete application to the circumstances of modern urban warfare. In other words, it is of great importance to focus on the war itself rather than to limit inquiry to the alleged unlawful practices and tactics.

Settlements in the Palestinian territories and their impact on the enjoyment of human rights

37. The Israeli settlements in occupied Palestine have recently received great attention as a result of President Barack Obama's widely publicized call for a "freeze" on settlement expansion as an

---

15 United Nations, Treaty Series, vol. 1125, No. 17512.

essential step to revive negotiations looking towards a resolution of the underlying conflict. President Obama has also asked Arab governments to reward Israel if it agrees to impose a freeze, implying that Israel would be taking a constructive political step for which it deserves to receive encouragement by way of reciprocity. So far, the Israeli leader, Prime Minister Benjamin Netanyahu, has agreed only to disallow the establishment of new settlements or an expansion of the land area under the control of existing settlements. However, he has insisted that the "natural growth" of West Bank settlements must be allowed, and further, that settlements in East Jerusalem will not be treated as part of any partial freeze. It should be observed that this controversy has been carried on without reference to Palestinian rights under international humanitarian law as if law is irrelevant, and the matter of the settlements is a purely political issue between the parties.

38. For this reason, it is important to recall what has been argued in several previous reports of the Special Rapporteur, that the settlements as such are unlawful under article 49(6) of the Fourth Geneva Convention that clearly states that "The Occupying Power shall not deport or transfer parts of its own civilian population into the territory it occupies."[16] This widely shared legal assessment was authoritatively confirmed by the International Court of Justice in the course of its advisory opinion of 9 July 2004 on the construction of a security wall: "Israeli settlements in Occupied Palestinian Territory, including East Jerusalem, are illegal and an obstacle to peace and to economic and social development...[and] have been established in breach of international law." At present, there are reported to be 121 settlements on the West Bank, 12 situated on land annexed after 1967 by the city of Jerusalem, and about 100 "outposts," which are physical presences established by the settler movement without receiving legal authorization from the Israeli government.

39. From a legal perspective, acknowledging the relevance of Palestinian rights under law, any bilateral understandings between the United States and Israel, such as the Bush/Sharon

---

16 United Nations, Treaty Series, vol. 1125, No. 17512.

exchange of official letters on 14 April 2004, assuring Israel that the large settlement blocs will be incorporated into the future borders of the Israeli State, are completely without legal value. The most important language in the letter of President Bush is the following: "In light of the new realities on the ground, including the existing major Israeli population centres, it is unrealistic to expect that the outcome of final status negotiations will be a full and complete return to the armistice lines of 1949 . . . ." This is even more the case with respect to the effect of supposed informal understandings between the United States and Israel on natural growth of settlements despite the freeze commitments made formally in the Annapolis Declaration of December 2007. According to monitoring groups in actual fact, "tenders for new settlement building increased by 550 percent from 2007. Actual settlement construction has increased by 30 percent since the launching of the new round of peace talks. Settlement building around Jerusalem has increased by a factor of 38."

40. It is an elementary principle of law and equity that any understanding between two parties cannot alter the legal rights of a third party. At most, such an understanding, even in the form of a contract, has only a bearing on the political expectations that exist between the two parties, in this case Israel and the United States. It is also true that within Israel itself the American call for a settlement freeze has aroused passionate forms of opposition, including the renewed efforts by the settler movement to establish in the West Bank settler "outposts" that are illegal even under Israeli law.[17] Rabbi Ovadia Yosef, spiritual leader of the ultra-orthodox Shas Party in Israel, a partner in the ruling coalition, has angrily repudiated the idea of a settlement freeze: "American insidiousness tells us to build here and not to build there as though we were slaves working for them."

41. In point of fact, Israel has, throughout the entire period of the occupation, expanded the population and territorial domain of the settlements: "In the two decades from 1972 to 1993, Israel increased the number of settlers in the West Bank, not including

---

17 See Ethan Bronner, "West Bank Settlers Send Defiant Message to Obama," *The New York Times*, 30 July 2009.

Jerusalem, from 800 to 110,600. In the following ten years—which roughly coincided with the Oslo peace process—the number increased at twice the rate, exceeding 234,000 in 2004. In East Jerusalem, the settler population jumped from 124,400 in 1992 to almost 176,000 in 2002."[18] The most recent estimates of settler population put the number in the West Bank at about 300,000, with an additional 200,000 in East Jerusalem.

42. Further settlement growth, quite apart from the freeze issue as it relates to a resumption of "peace" negotiations, is a continual encroachment on Palestinian right of self-determination, as well as an overall violation of the basic obligations of the occupier under the Fourth Geneva Convention to protect the property and societal prospects of an occupied population. Therefore, during a period when the road map was supposed to curtail settlement growth, actual Israeli behavior went in a quite opposite direction.

43. As summarized in the letter of Palestinian human rights organizations to the Swedish Foreign Minister, Carl Bildt: "The population growth rate of Israeli settlers in the occupied West Bank, including East Jerusalem, is 4.7 percent, compared to an annual growth of the Jewish population in the State of Israel, which is 1.7 percent."

Thus, the smokescreen of "natural growth" is used to mask continuing emigration of Jewish-Israeli settlers to the West Bank, as well as the creation of essentially new settlements appended to existing ones."[8] Some observers argue that these figures exaggerate the threat posed by this settlement growth, insisting that most of the growth is in ultra-orthodox non-Zionist settlements, such as Modi'in Illit and Beitar Illit, currently with 45,000 residents who seem ready to move if given alternative housing within pre-1967 Israel as part of a solution to the underlying conflict.

46. The settlements also pose an additional problem for the maintenance of human rights and compliance with the Fourth Geneva Convention. The location of Israel's unlawful security wall has the effect of placing an estimated 385,000 settlers between the wall and the Green Line, while entrapping approximately 93,000

---

18 See Ali Abunimah, *One Country: A Bold Proposal to End the Israeli-Palestinian Impasse* (Metropolitan Books, November 2006).

Palestinians on the Israeli side of the wall, sometimes cut off from their agricultural lands and parts of their villages, as well as from the West Bank generally.

47. There are several intertwined issues relevant to the mandate:

(a) the settlements, and any further expansion, are a major unlawful impediment to the realization of the Palestinian right of self-determination;

(b) if Israel accepts a freeze on unlawful settlement expansion it seems unreasonable for it to receive some kind of reciprocal gesture from the Arab governments, that is, should Israel be rewarded for doing what it was legally required to do in the first place;

(c) agreements between Israel and the United States are legally irrelevant with respect to the settlements as only the governments of Israel and the Palestinian Authority have the authority to determine their status in the context of peace negotiations;

(d) Israel as Occupying Power has an underlying legal obligation to dismantle existing settlements, including those in East Jerusalem, and not to interfere with Palestinian growth and development. This conclusion has also been reached by B'Tselem, the respected Israeli human rights organization, recommending a "humane" dismantling that respects settlers' human rights, including compensation for any loss.[19]

The Wall and its legal implications

48. The date of 9 July 2009 marked the fifth anniversary of the Advisory Opinion of the International Court of Justice on the security wall, still being constructed mainly on the territory of the occupied West Bank, so designed as to be 86 percent on West Bank territory. The Wall was supposed to extend for 723 kilometers

---

19 See "Land Expropriation and Settlements." Available from The Israeli Information Center for Human Rights in the Occupied Territories, https://www.btselem.org/settlements.

when finished, which is twice the length of building the Wall along the Green Line and which would have saved Israel an estimated $1.7 billion of United States dollars. At present it is reported to be only about 60 percent complete after a construction effort that has gone on for seven years, with latest reports indicating that construction has been suspended for budgetary reasons despite the claimed necessities of security. The Ministry of Defense and public opinion of Israel credit the Wall with improved security within Israel; the significant reduction in terrorist incidents in recent years is invoked to confirm this claim. Critics, including the leadership of the Palestinian Authority, call for the dismantling of the Wall, contending that it is a land grab unrelated to security that has caused great hardship to the Palestinians living near to or on the Western side of the Wall, as well as being unlawful as located.

Israel's unlawful occupation: Crisis of authority in international law

49. Despite the diversity among the 15 judges of the International Court of Justice, they voted 14 against 1 on the main issues of international law concluding: "...the construction of the wall being built by Israel, the Occupying Power, in the Occupied Palestinian Territory... [is] contrary to international law... Israel is under an obligation to cease forthwith the works of construction ...to dismantle forthwith the structure therein situated...to make reparation for all damage caused by the construction of the wall." On 20 July 2004, the General Assembly at its tenth emergency special session voted overwhelmingly to insist that Israel comply with the rulings of the International Court of Justice, and also called upon the General Assembly and the Security Council to consider what further action was required to end the illegal situation resulting from the construction of the wall.[20] The Assembly in its resolution ES-10/15 also called upon all States Member of the United Nations to comply with their obligations as mentioned in the Advisory Opinion of the International Court of Justice, the

---

20 150 Member States voted in favour, and six against (Australia, Micronesia, Israel, Marshall Islands, Palau, United States).

United Nations highest legal body. Attention was particularly called to the obligation of States not to render aid or assistance in maintaining the situation created by such construction. Many subsequent resolutions adopted overwhelmingly by the General Assembly as well as the Human Rights Council have renewed the call on Israel to comply with its legal obligations, as mentioned in the advisory opinion.[21]

50. As is undisputed, Israel has rejected the findings of the International Court of Justice, indicating that it will only adhere to the rulings of its own national judicial system. It has done so, upholding a series of decisions by the Israeli Supreme Court that order the relocation of the Wall so as to lessen the harmful impact on Palestinian communities. It is true that an advisory opinion of the Court is "non-binding" as a direct decision, but it represents an authoritative assessment of the relevant international law. Even though the findings are not directly binding, they present a definitive set of conclusions as to the requirements of international law under the circumstances. When the conclusions reached are so overwhelmingly supported, then there is no basis for "the law" to be inconclusive or contested. Such an assessment is strengthened here because the lone dissenting judge, from the United States, indicated in his Declaration that he accepted most of the legal analysis made by the majority. However, he felt that no firm conclusions could be reached without a better appreciation of the Israeli security arguments for locating the Wall on the occupied territory.

51. As with the confirmed reports of war crimes, the non-implementation of the legal conclusions of the Court is extremely damaging to the authority of international law, of the Court, and of the United Nations generally. An unfortunate message has been delivered: the authority of the international community has been defied by a Member State of the United Nations, harm has been inflicted on a civilian population that is supposed to be under the

---

21 See General Assembly resolution 63/97 (adopted on 5 December 2008 by a vote of 171 to 6, with 2 abstentions), para. 6; see also Human Rights Council resolution 10/18 (adopted on 26 March 2009 by 46 to 1, with no abstentions), para. 8.

protection of international law, and neither States nor the organs of the United Nations do anything about it. As with other aspects of the conflict, the failure to uphold Palestinian legal rights and the treatment of the Court both constitute a crisis of authority and reinforce for the Palestinians the idea that it is no help to have international law on its side.

52. Israel can defy with impunity its international legal obligations. The combination of an insistence that Palestinians renounce all forms of armed resistance and the failure to respect legal rights coupled with United Nations inaction in relation to this failure constitutes the current Palestinian dilemma. What is to be done by the Palestinians under such circumstances? Israeli columnist Gideon Levy explains the currently cynical Israeli approach to peace negotiations as an outgrowth of this situation: "Israelis are not paying any price for the injustice of occupation. Life in Israel is just peachy. Cafes are bustling. Restaurants are packed. People are vacationing. Who wants to think about peace, negotiations, withdrawals—the 'price' that might have to be paid. The summer of 2009 is wonderful. Why change anything?"[22]

53. It should be noted that the issue of unlawfulness arises almost exclusively as a result of building the Wall in the Occupied Palestinian Territory. If the Wall had been built along the Green Line or inside pre-1967 Israel, it might have generated moral and political criticisms associated with such a coercive and hostile form of separation, but not legal objections. The Berlin Wall was not challenged legally, but it was symbolic of what was wrong about East Germany and the Soviet approach to world order. If the Soviet Union had dared to build the wall even a few feet on the West Berlin side of the dividing boundary it could have well provided the trigger of World War III. It is notable that current American fence-building along the Mexican border, while controversial, is scrupulously respectful of Mexican territorial sovereignty. If a State or political community is not as powerless as Palestine, law and respect for territorial rights are generally respected.

---

22 See Jerrold Kessel and Pierre Klochendler, "Mideast: Building Peace on an Incomplete Wall," Inter Press Service, 27 July 2009.

54. Palestinian protests against the Wall continue in several sites in the West Bank, most notably weekly demonstrations near the towns of Bil'in and Nii'iln. Israel has responded with rubber bullets, tear gas, and arrests, with several deaths and many injuries resulting. It would appear that Israeli security forces have been using excessive force in violation of their basic duties the Israeli State, are completely without legal value. The most important language in the letter of President Bush is the following: "In light of the new realities on the ground, including the existing major Israeli population centers, it is unrealistic to expect that the outcome of final status negotiations will be a full and complete return to the armistice lines of 1949 ...." This is even more the case with respect to the effect of supposed informal understandings between the United States and Israel on natural growth of settlements despite the freeze commitments made formally in the Annapolis Declaration of December 2007. According to monitoring groups, in actual fact, "tenders for new settlement building increased by 550 percent from 2007. Actual settlement construction has increased by 30 percent since the launching of the new round of peace talks. Settlement building around Jerusalem has increased by a factor of 38. There is little discussion of the current plight of the refugees living for generations in miserable conditions in Gaza and the West Bank. The Special Rapporteur shares the assessment recently made by Karen Abu Zayd, the Commissioner-General of UNRWA, that for these refugee issues to remain unresolved 60 years after the dispossession and displacement of several hundred thousand Palestinians is unacceptable. In her words the acknowledgement of "the 60-year-old injustice" would be "a first step towards addressing the consequences of that injustice."[23]

Ms. Abu Zayd movingly expresses her concern in the form of an appeal: "As forced displacements continue across the West Bank, as Palestinians are evicted from their homes in East Jerusalem, I ask a simple question. Is it not time for those engaged in the peace process to muster the will and the courage to address the Palestine refugee question."

---

23 See, Karen Abu Zayd, "Creating facts in the mind," *Ammon,* 8 December 2009, https://en.ammonnews.net/article/5179

Boycotts, divestments and sanctions

38. Operation Cast Lead shocked the conscience of humanity, giving rise to feelings of solidarity around the world with the ordeal and struggle of the Palestinian people. These feelings wer-intensified by the awareness that neither the neighboring States nor the United Nations, nor its most powerful Member States, were willing or able to protect the Palestinian people and uphold their rights. The spectacle of a people under siege, as has been the case now for over 30 months in the Gaza Strip, has deepened this sense that there exists some responsibility for people everywhere to take appropriate, non-violent action. Civil society's global Boycott, Divestment and Sanctions (BDS) campaign, aimed at bringing non-violent economic and social pressure to bear to end the Israeli occupation, is the outgrowth of these sentiments, and it has been expanding at a rapid rate during the last few years. This sense of an anti-occupation movement of worldwide scope has come to resemble in many respects the anti-apartheid movement that made important contributions to the transformation of the political climate in South Africa in the late 1980s.

39. The boycott dimension of BDS takes many forms. For example, the boycott in Europe of products produced by Israeli settlements; Britain has now allowed stores to put stickers on food and other products reading "Israeli settlement produce." Soccer games and other athletic events involving Israel have been cancelled or protests mounted. Similar efforts have been made with respect to academic and cultural interaction. Artists and performers have been asked to refuse invitations from Israel, or at least to contribute the proceeds of a performance to Palestinian relief. Stores and companies around the world have been boycotted based on their dealings for profit in the OPT. On the divestment front, contracts have been terminated or bids not made. In addition, a growing number of churches and universities are extending their efforts to invest in a spirit of social responsibility and are excluding companies that are perceived to be profiting from the Israeli occupation. Individuals and NGOs have come out in support of BDS in increasing numbers. It is a central battleground in the

legitimacy war being waged by and on behalf of Palestinians. It is also making use of persuasive and coercive non-violent means to secure the human rights of Palestinians living under oppressive and unlawful conditions of occupation that the actions of diplomacy or the authority of the organized international community seem unable to correct. BDS represents the mobilized efforts of global civil society to replace a regime of force with the rule of law in relation to the OPT.

The De Facto Annexation of East Jerusalem
Report #5: A/HRC/16/72, 10 Jan 2011

15. The Israeli insistence on excluding East Jerusalem from the partial moratorium and its overall attitude toward its status is of further concern to the Rapporteur. Prime Minister Binyamin Netanyahu, along with other Israeli leaders, has repeatedly confirmed continuing rejection by Israel of United Nations resolutions and other relevant aspects of international law recognizing that the Occupied Palestinian Territory includes East Jerusalem. Mr. Netanyahu dramatized this point when he recently stated that "Jerusalem is not a settlement—Jerusalem is the capital of the State of Israel. Israel has never restricted itself regarding any kind of building in the city, which is home to some 800,000 people—including during the 10-month construction moratorium in the West Bank. Israel sees no connection between the peace process and the planning and building policy in Jerusalem, something that hasn't changed for the past 40 years." Although such an assertion amounts to defiance of international law, it is a significant expression of Israeli diplomatic posture, casting further doubt on what could be expected to emerge from a negotiating process that attempts to foreclose a fundamental Palestinian right to have the part of historic Jerusalem occupied by Israeli in 1967 as its national capital. Again, it is disturbing to note the absence of formal objection by the international community and interested governments to such an Israeli posture taken in advance of negotiations.

16. The Rapporteur finds that by December 2010, the pace of settlement expansion in East Jerusalem had in fact escalated. On 4 November 2010, the government of Israel issued tenders for 238 new housing units in the East Jerusalem settlements of Pisgat Zeev and Ramot[24] and the following day announced plans for construction of 1,352 new housing units elsewhere in East Jerusalem. Continued construction in addition to settlers' forcibly taking over Palestinian homes in East Jerusalem has resulted in the expulsion of Palestinian residents from their homes. Palestinian families, some of whom have lived in their homes for generations, have been expelled by Israeli police and settlers. In July 2010, a large Palestinian family that had lived in their home in the Old City for more than 70 years was expelled by police-backed settlers who then took over the house.[25] In November 2010, settler organizations took control of two houses in Palestinian neighborhoods of Jabal al-Mukkaber and al-Tur in East Jerusalem resulting in forcible eviction of several Palestinian families from their homes.[26] The Sheikh Jarrah neighborhood has also been the subject of persistent attempts by Israeli settler groups to take over land and property in order to establish new settlements in the area. As a result, over 60 Palestinians have lost their homes and another 500 remain at risk of forced eviction, dispossession and displacement in the near future.[27] In Silwan neighborhood of East Jerusalem, Israeli families have forcibly taken over Palestinian homes, turning them into guarded settlement compounds flying Israeli flags.[28] Many of the settler organizations are backed by private donors from abroad,[29] raising the issue of international complicity, as well as Israeli State responsibility, with these continuing violations of international law. Moreover, the government of Israel

---

24 Amnesty International UK, "East Jerusalem: Israel's 238 housing units plan threatens Palestinian human rights," 15 October 2010.

25 Ibid.

26 B'Tselem, "New settler enclaves in East Jerusalem," 2 December 2010.

27 Office for the Coordination of Humanitarian Affairs – occupied Palestinian territory (OCHA-OPT), "Fact sheet: The Case of Sheikh Jarrah," October 2010.

28 See, e.g., Wadi Hilweh Information Center Silwan, "Settlers took over a house in Al-Farouq neighborhood in Silwan," 23 November 2010.

29 See "New settler enclaves in East Jerusalem."

and the Jerusalem Municipality support the settlers' actions in Palestinian neighborhoods in East Jerusalem and the Old City by allocating private security guards, paid for by taxes, to protect the compounds; sending security forces to accompany takeover of Palestinian houses; funding and promoting building and development projects in the compounds; and transferring government assets to the control of the organizations.[30] This support further illustrates the institutional and systematic discrimination against the Palestinian residents of Jerusalem by Israel, as well as ongoing Israeli efforts to create what are euphemistically called "facts on the ground" for annexation.

17. The Special Rapporteur believes that the expulsions from East Jerusalem go beyond those linked to house seizures or demolitions—and beyond the immediate dire consequences to individuals and families facing the loss of their homes—and form part of the broader picture of annexation, not as an Israeli legal claim but enacted increasingly as evidence of an Israeli political project. Israel carries out new punishments against Palestinians in Jerusalem, including threats of the revocation of Jerusalem residency rights of Palestinians living legally in Jerusalem.

18. In one of the most egregious examples, in July 2010, four Palestinian citizens of Israel, who were elected members of the Palestinian Legislative Council, including one former Council minister, were given notice that their right to Jerusalem residency was being revoked, after the four politicians refused to renounce their ties to Hamas.[31] Efforts to expel these parliamentarians were resumed in the summer of 2010 and finally, on 8 December 2010, one of these individuals was deported from Jerusalem.[32] The expulsion of the Council's members from Jerusalem is a violation of the article 49(6) of the Fourth Geneva Convention, which explicitly prohibits the forcible transfer of protected persons. It also sets a particularly dangerous precedent for the removal of more

---

30 Ibid.

31 See B'Tselem, "In dangerous precedent, Israel revokes residency of four Palestinians affiliated with Hamas from East Jerusalem and acts to forcibly transfer them," 18 July 2010.

32 Associated Press, "Israel expels Hamas MP jailed over Jerusalem status," 9 December 2010.

than 270,000 Palestinians living in East Jerusalem. As the Special Rapporteur has noted before, it is particularly worrying that Israel appears ready to forcibly transfer these individuals based on their supposed lack of allegiance to the state of Israel. Israel, as an Occupying Power, is prohibited from transferring civilian persons from East Jerusalem and from forcing Palestinians to swear allegiance or otherwise affirm their loyalty to the State of Israel. The revocation of residency permits, home demolitions and evictions, settlement construction, the separation of East Jerusalem from the rest of the West Bank and its annexation to Israel.

Non-implementation of International Law
Report #6: A/HRC/06/358, 13 Sept 2011

4. As usual, there are many more serious human rights concerns associated with the occupation by Israel than can be addressed in this report, which is subject to United Nations guidelines as to a maximum number of words. In order to avoid the impression that earlier concerns no longer persist, the Special Rapporteur stresses that there are continuing violations of international humanitarian law and human rights law arising, inter alia, from the issues discussed below.

5. The recommendations of the report of the United Nations Fact-Finding Mission on the Gaza Conflict[33] (the "Goldstone Report") have not been implemented, despite follow-up reports by the Committee of Independent Experts.[34] The reports of the Committee of Independent Experts took particular note of the failure by Israel to conduct investigations of alleged war crimes in a manner that accords with international standards.

6. The findings and recommendations of the Human Rights Council-mandated fact-finding mission on the incident of the humanitarian flotilla of 31 May 2010,[35] involving naval attacks by

---

33 A/HRC/12/48.

34 A/HRC/15/50 and A/HRC/16/24.

35 See A/HRC/15/21; see also A/HRC/16/73 and A/HRC/17/47.

Israel in international waters, which resulted in the death of nine peace activists on the Turkish vessel Mavi Marmara, have not yet led to appropriate action.[36] It is observed that the failure to follow through on initiatives recommended by competent international experts under the auspices of the United Nations contributes to a lack of accountability for serious allegations of war crimes and human rights violations. The failure is particularly unfortunate given its impact on those living for many years under a regime of belligerent occupation, which has systematically deprived them of the normal rights and remedies associated with a law-abiding society. Without committed and capable international protection, those living under prolonged occupation are exposed to excesses and abuses perpetrated by the occupier, as the realities of the Occupied Palestinian Territories confirm in numerous ways.

7. Concern about non-implementation was underscored by the repudiation by Israel of the near-unanimous advisory opinion of the International Court of Justice in 2004 relating to the construction of the separation Wall in the Occupied Palestinian Territory.[37] This authoritative judicial interpretation of the international obligations of Israel, which was endorsed by the General Assembly in its resolution ES-10/15, has been repudiated by Israel without generating any result-oriented international reaction. Although advisory opinions are non-binding in a formal sense, they have important legal effects because they provide an authoritative interpretation of the issues at stake, which is based on legal reasoning by the world's highest judicial body concerned with international law.[38]

---

36 It is noted that the panel appointed by the Secretary-General to investigate these same events postponed the release of its report until late August 2011.

37 Legal Consequences of the Construction of a Wall in the Occupied Palestinian Territory, Advisory Opinion, I.C.J. Reports 2004 (see also A/ES-10/273 and Corr.1). The International Court of Justice concluded in its advisory opinion that the Fourth Geneva Convention was applicable in the Palestinian territories, which before the 1967 conflict lay to the east of the Green Line and which, during that conflict, were occupied by Israel.

38 See Bekkar, "The United Nations General Assembly Requests a World Court Advisory Opinion on Israel's Separation Barrier," Insights, December 2003.

The advisory opinion is particularly notable in the present instance, since the vote in the Court was 14 to 1—a rare display of consensus among judges drawn from the world's major legal systems and cultural backgrounds. It is worth noting that even the dissenting judge was in substantial agreement with much of the legal reasoning in the advisory opinion, making the conclusions virtually unanimous. While rejecting the authority of international assessments of illegality, the government of Israel has agreed to comply with Israeli law to the extent applicable to the construction of the Wall. Yet in practice Israel has been slow to comply with relevant Israeli judicial decisions ordering the removal and relocation of segments of the Wall. In some instances these judicial directives have been ignored for several years, imposing acute suffering on Palestinian communities that are isolated or cut off from agricultural land.[39] Weekly demonstrations against the Wall have continued, especially in Palestinian villages near Nablus, most prominently in the villages of Ni'lin and Bil'in. As with other issues of violations of international law by Israel, there continues to be a lack of will within the United Nations, and especially among its Member States, to challenge the existence and continuing construction of the Wall, which intrudes so negatively on the lives of many Palestinians living under occupation in the West Bank, especially East Jerusalem.

8. There are two conjoined issues present: the refusal of Israel to adhere to its obligations under international law in administering the Occupied Palestinian Territory, and the failure of the United Nations to take effective steps in response to such persistent, flagrant, and systematic violations of the basic human rights of the Palestinians living under occupation. Yet such steps would seem to be given increased prominence in the light of the adoption of the responsibility to protect doctrine by the Security Council [resolution 1674 ([2006)], and its recent application by

---

39 In June 2011 Israel began dismantling a section of the barrier near the West Bank village of Bil'in, in compliance with a decision of the High Court of Justice of Israel four years earlier. See Office for the Coordination of Humanitarian Affairs, "Protection of Civilians Weekly Report, 8-21 June 2011," 24 June 2011. Available from https://reliefweb.int/report/egypt/protection-civilians-weekly-report-8-21-june-2011.

way of Security Council resolution 1973 (2011) mandating the protection of civilians in Libya.

9. It is worth recalling the language of mutuality and rights emphasized in the Balfour Declaration of 2 November 1917, which underpins the founding of Israel, even now, almost a century after it was issued: " ... it being clearly understood that nothing shall be done which may prejudice the civil and religious rights of existing non-Jewish communities in Palestine." This explicit acknowledgement of support in the contested declaration for the establishment of what was then called "a national home for the Jewish people" is the foundation of the claim of right relied upon in the establishment of the State of Israel, and its recognition and admission to membership by the United Nations in 1948. Although the Balfour Declaration was a colonialist overriding of the right of self-determination that was later recognized in international law, its insistence on showing respect for the reciprocal rights of the non-Jewish communities affected, particularly the Palestinians, should continue to provide political and moral guidance in the search for a peaceful and just solution to the conflict.

Protection of the civilian population living under occupation

12. It is unfortunately necessary to restate the basic obligations of Israel under international humanitarian law as the Occupying Power of the West Bank, including East Jerusalem, and the Gaza Strip. These obligations are mainly set forth in the Geneva Convention relative to the Protection of Civilian Persons in Time of War (Fourth Geneva Convention), to which Israel is party. Most pertinent is section III (arts. 47–78), which addresses issues associated with occupied territories. Of greater detail and more recent origin is the protocol additional to the Geneva Conventions of 12 August 1949 and relating to the protection of victims of international armed conflicts (Protocol I), which entered into force in 1978, particularly part IV, which establishes the legal framework applicable to the civilian population. There are 171 States parties to Protocol I. While Israel is not a party to Protocol

I, it is bound by the provisions of the Protocol because they have become embedded in international customary law, which does not require the explicit consent of a State to be binding. Other highly relevant international legal instruments pertaining to circumstances in the Occupied Palestinian Territory are the Convention on the Rights of the Child, with 197 States parties (including Israel) and the International Convention on the Suppression and Punishment of the Crime of Apartheid, with 107 States parties.

Administrative Detention and Hunger Strikes
Report # 7: A/HRC/20/32, 25 May 2012

7. It was the Special Rapporteur's intention to review the treatment of Palestinians from the Occupied Palestinian Territory being detained in Israeli prisons as a sequel to the analysis of this dimension of occupation contained in a prior report (A/66/358). What was somewhat unanticipated was the urgency emerging in the Occupied Palestinian Territory on this issue, requiring the Special Rapporteur to focus even greater attention on the Israeli practice of holding Palestinians under administrative detention during which evidence, if it exists at all, is held in secret, no charges are filed, and no trials held. The number of detainees in administrative detention rose from 286 in September 2011 to 309 in January 2012.[40] What is now called "administrative detention" was formerly known as "internment." Internment was a colonial procedure used to remove individuals from society even if no criminal charges were made. Administrative detention has been relied upon by a large number of countries, especially in recent years, to detain terrorist suspects who are alleged to pose a threat to domestic security, for whom there is either insufficient evidence or the evidence of supposed criminality cannot be made available without exposing sensitive sources of intelligence or illegal practices (such as torture). The practice is highly controversial, and

40 B'Tselem, *Statistics on Administrative Detention* (updated 24 November 2021), https://www.btselem.org/administrative_detention/statistics.

the Working Group on Arbitrary Detention and respected human rights organizations such as Amnesty International allege that the practice is unacceptable from a human rights viewpoint, as it is so often abused to imprison innocent persons who are prisoners of conscience, opponents of policy or organizers of non-violent protests.[41] On the basis of careful examination of high-profile targets of such detention procedures, it seems to be mainly used by Israel against individuals not engaged in violent activities, and hence they are inappropriately held in administrative detention, even taking into account the highly questionable rationale of a severe and imminent security threat the nature of which is not disclosed.

8. The current Israeli reliance on administrative detention has become particularly controversial for a series of reasons: frequent use and prolonged confinement of people who seemingly do not pose security threats; exceedingly harsh treatment amounting to cruel and unusual punishment accompanying arrest; interrogation and detention in violation of human rights and international humanitarian law obligations; and conflict with fundamental obligations of an Occupying Power to uphold the well-being and normalcy of the civilian population living under occupation, as prescribed by the Geneva Convention relative to the Protection of Civilian Persons in Time of War (Fourth Geneva Convention).[42] There is another issue generally overlooked in the application of administrative detention, given standard Israeli arrest procedures: the terrifying secondary impact of night-time arrests on family members, especially young children. Psychological studies of Palestinian children 12 and under show a disturbingly high correlation between witnessing a parent beaten or humiliated by Israeli soldiers and the loss by the child of a will to live.

9. In opposition to administrative detention, several Palestinians have highlighted their objections to the practice

41 See, for example, reports of the Working Group on Arbitrary Detention A/HRC/4/40 (para. 41) and A/HRC/10/21 (para. 54). See also Amnesty International news and campaigns at https://www.amnesty.org/en/search/Administrative%20Detention/.

42 The basic profile of the use by Israel of administrative detention during the years 2011_2012 has been summarized by B'Tselem and is available from https://www.btselem.org/administrative_detention/statistics.

by engaging in dramatic open-ended hunger strikes that have received widespread international attention from human rights NGOs, public officials, and public opinion, particularly in the region. It should be comprehended that to embark upon a hunger strike of long duration is an extreme form of non-violent protest. It has been used on many past occasions, including famously by Mahatma Gandhi in his struggles against British imperialism and by a group of Irish Republican Army (IRA) political prisoners in the Maze Prison in Northern Ireland, in protest against conditions of their confinement. Ten of these IRA hunger strikers died in prison, with Bobby Sands being the first and most prominent, an event in 1981 that was later credited with leading the British government to change its approach to the IRA, treating it as a political actor rather than as a terrorist organization. This led, a few years later, to the Good Friday Agreement that established an enduring, if fragile, accommodation in Northern Ireland. This background is mentioned to give a political context to the use of hunger strikes as part of the broader Palestinian shift in tactics from armed resistance to an array of non-violent tactics associated with popular resistance.

10. The first of these recent hunger-strike cases involves a Palestinian activist named Khader Adnan, a baker by profession living in a small village near Jenin and spokesperson for the political wing of the Palestinian Islamic Jihad, who had been previously held in administrative detention and was imprisoned by West Bank military authorities on eight separate occasions. Mr. Adnan was arrested at his home at 3 a.m. on 17 December 2011 by a large number of Israeli soldiers, brusquely handled, cuffed and blindfolded in the presence of his pregnant wife and two daughters under the age of 5, and taken off roughly in a military jeep to prison. From the outset of his detention Mr. Adnan commenced a hunger strike, accompanied by a refusal to speak with interrogators until he was released or charged, and similar steps taken to end the practice of administrative detention affecting the hundreds of Palestinians now being held by Israel. Mr. Adnan continued his strike for 66 days, well beyond the time his medical condition was considered to be critical, and despite this, visitors reported

that Mr. Adnan had both legs and one arm shackled to the bed even while under observation in an Israeli prison hospital. After an appeal to a military tribunal was rejected, on the basis of secret evidence, Mr. Adnan's lawyers appealed to the Israeli Supreme Court, but only minutes before court was scheduled to hear arguments, an agreement was reached in which Mr. Adnan ended his strike and Israel agreed to shorten his period of detention by calculating the duration of his term on the basis of the day of arrest rather than the day that his administrative detention was decreed. He was also given reassurance that his detention would not be extended at the date of expiry absent the surfacing of substantial new evidence against him. Since Mr. Adnan resumed eating, he has had various medical difficulties, reported by Physicians for Human Rights-Israel, including surgery to remove an intestinal blockage that was causing great pain. It is not clear whether Mr. Adnan will recover his full health.

11. A second recent case involves a young unmarried Palestinian woman named Hana Shalabi who also lives in a village near Jenin with her family. She had been among those released in the prisoner exchange on 18 October 2011 that traded 1,027 Palestinians for a single Israeli military soldier. In the months subsequent to this release, she had been living quietly with her family, gradually recovering from her prison ordeal that had seemed to render her incapable of normal social interaction, much less militant political activity. Ms. Shalabi was rearrested on 17 February 2012 leading to an administrative detention order of six months, which was subsequently reduced to four months. She was also the victim of an abusive arrest that in some respects resembled the experience of Mr. Adnan, but was even more violent, including to Ms. Shalabi's family members who were present, with as many as 100 soldiers making the arrest at her place of residence, rough physical handling, blindfolding, and humiliating insults, including of a brother who tried to protect his sister. After being taken to the Salem Detention Center, Ms. Shalabi was reportedly subject to further beatings, humiliating treatment, and other clear and severe violations of her rights. She began her hunger strike at the outset of this new period of administrative detention. The parents

of Ms. Shalabi were also on a hunger strike in solidarity with their daughter. After she had gone more than 40 days without food, Ms. Shalabi's physical condition was reported to be life threatening and deteriorating. Respecting her rights to refuse food, medical experts of the Israeli Prison Service formally declined to mandate force-feeding to end the strike. Her appeal was rejected by a military tribunal that refused to shorten her period of administrative detention, citing secret evidence that she constituted a security threat. The Palestinian Authority's Minister of Prisoners' Affairs reported that Israel had offered to release Ms. Shalabi if she could be transferred from her West Bank home to either Gaza or Jordan, in violation of the Fourth Geneva Convention's prohibition against forcible removal of a protected person from the territory under occupation. On 1 April, Ms. Shalabi was indeed transferred to Gaza on this basis, and barred from returning to her home and family in the West Bank for three years. Aspects of Ms. Shalabi's case have the appearance of a being vindictive response by Israel to her strong opposition to the practice of administrative detention.

12. Both of these highly publicized hunger strikes exhibit an extreme dedication to risk life itself to protest against the practice of administrative detention, especially the use of administrative detention absent any proof of a genuine security threat, and the unduly harsh and terrifying Israeli arrest procedures. These developments have called attention to other complaints associated with administrative detention as used against a variety of Palestinians with no known connection to violent activism, as well as to 26 members of the Palestinian Legislative Council who have been detained without charges for several years for no apparent reason other than that they were elected in the 2006 elections. These hunger strikes have not only highlighted the violative use by Israel of administrative detention, but also have mobilized others currently held in detention to engage in open-ended hunger strikes and activated Palestinian solidarity initiatives among Palestinians living under occupation and others elsewhere. For instance, there is a large public mural in a public space in Belfast, Northern Ireland with images of Mr. Adnan and Ms. Shalabi and statistics about overall Palestinian imprisonment. So far, Israel has exhibited no

disposition to abandon, or even review, its reliance on administrative detention as a regular aspect of occupation, or other contentious aspects of its prison policy, including its unlawful transfer of prisoners outside of the territory held under occupation. Israel did relent slightly at the last hour in relation to Mr. Adnan, reaching an agreement with his lawyer, seemingly to avoid having a hunger striker die and become a martyr for his people, which might possibly have sparked Palestinian resistance activity.

13. It is the judgment of the Special Rapporteur that the use of administrative detention, other than in rare circumstances where a demonstration of extraordinary and imminent security justification supported by evidence is made before a judge in conference with the lawyer of the defendant, who is given an opportunity to contest evidence and charges, constitutes a violation of the rights of a protected person under international law. Several provisions of the Fourth Geneva Convention make unlawful the arrest and detention procedures relied upon by Israel in its treatment of Ms. Shalabi. Article 3, paragraph 1, contains the general directive that all persons held by an occupying authority "shall in all circumstances be treated humanely," which is elaborated upon in article 27 in a manner relevant to Ms. Shalabi's treatment: "Protected persons are entitled, in all circumstances, to respect for their persons, their honour, their family rights, their religious convictions and practices, and their manners and customs. They shall at all times be humanely treated and shall be protected especially against all acts of violence or threats thereof and against insults and public curiosity." Further, articles 71 to 73 indicate that any kind of prison sentence must be pronounced by a "competent" court in which the person accused has access to the evidence against them and the opportunity to present evidence with the assistance of legal counsel. Articles 7, 9, and 10 of the International Covenant on Civil and Political Rights are clear in their prohibition of "inhuman and degrading treatment" and of "arbitrary detention" as well of the rights of anyone accused of criminal conduct to have an opportunity to mount a defense in a competent court. For instance, article 9, paragraph 2 declares: "Anyone who is arrested shall be

informed, at the time of arrest, of the reasons for his arrest and shall be promptly informed of the charges against him."

Extrajudicial executions in Gaza by Israel

16. The targeted killing of Palestinian individuals amounts to extrajudicial execution or assassination—a *de facto* form of summary execution of an individual that provides no opportunity for a legal defense or even judicial review, denying the accused any possibility to demonstrate innocence and to receive the comprehensive protection of due process. In the 1990s, Israel strongly rejected accusations that it engaged in targeted killing. The Israel Defense Forces (IDF) issued a statement in response at that time: "There is no policy, and there never will be a policy or a reality, of willful killings of suspects ... the principle of the sanctity of life is a fundamental principle of the IDF."[43] Despite such an affirmation, Israel has subsequently openly and extensively relied on targeted killing, resulting in an estimated 287 Palestinians being killed, mainly in Area A of the West Bank or in Gaza between 2002 and 2008, 234 of whom were targeted, the others being identified as "collateral damage."[44]

17. Clearly demonstrating the falseness of the purported rejection by the IDF of "willful killing of suspects," the Israeli Supreme Court set forth four conditions governing what it deemed to be the lawful recourse to targeted killing.[45] The Supreme Court's finding was based on the idea that the targeted person must be "directly participating in hostilities," and rejected the government's claim that it was permissible to treat suspects as "unlawful combatants" who could be killed regardless of their immediate activity. In subsequent instances of targeted killing, the

---

43 Cited in Lisa Hajjar, "Lawfare and targeted killing: developments in the Israeli and US contexts," *Jadaliyya*, 15 January 2012. Available from https://www.jadaliyya.com/Details/25141.

44 It is noted that these figures do not include killings that occurred during Israel's war on Gaza, Operation Cast Lead.

45 See *The Public Committee against Torture in Israel et al. v. The Government of Israel et al.*, judgement of the Israeli Supreme Court, HCJ 769/02, 13 December 2006. Available from elyon1.court.gov.il/Files_ENG/02/690/007/a34/02007690.a34.htm.

IDF has not conformed to those Supreme Court guidelines, which themselves still stand in violation of the prohibitions of targeted killing under international law.[46] On the contrary, Israel has relied on this tactic, recently using drone attack aircraft, especially in Gaza. Beyond the overarching illegality of targeted assassination, such attacks often kill or wound others than the identified target, and in any event such intrusions of violence spread terror among the general population.

18. The concern of the government of Israel regarding the potential danger facing its citizens who live within the range of rocket and/or mortar fire from Gaza is appropriate but cannot justify provocative actions that are themselves in direct violation of international law in response. It should be noted that one of the most successful examples of the suppression of such rocket fire was enabled by a negotiated ceasefire, namely the one held between Israel and Gaza in 2008, until it was breached by a lethal Israeli bombing attack in Gaza on 5 November 2008. It is also notable and understandable that the world media is attentive to Israeli concerns regarding the reported one million Israelis that live within range of Gaza rocket and mortar fire, a situation which, although rarely resulting in Israeli casualties, definitely spreads acute fear among the general population. What is not reasonable, however, is to ignore the far more insecure, and in fact physically perilous, existence that has been inflicted upon the 1.5 million Gazans who have been living within the confines of a military blockade for more than five years, or to treat as a mere statistic the circumstances of the numerous Palestinians killed or wounded by Israeli military attacks and who die unnecessarily because of restrictions on travel or restrictions on medical services or supplies imposed by Israel. Unlike the Israelis, the Palestinians enduring such vulnerabilities have no "Iron Dome" anti-missile system to offer the population some measure of protection or militarily relevant retaliatory capabilities. The most recent exchange of fire across the Israel/Gaza border shows this vast disparity: 25

---

46 For a detailed and wide-ranging consideration of the status of targeted killing, see the authoritative study by the Special Rapporteur on extrajudicial, summary or arbitrary executions (A/HRC/14/24/Add.6).

Palestinians killed, including several children, with no serious Israeli casualties. What is notably unusual, even gross, is that a sport-like, score-keeping approach has become a popular feature of Israeli media when its military launches attacks against Gaza.[47]

22. There are several conclusions to be drawn in relation to this continued troubled relationship between Israel, the Occupying Power, and the occupied Gaza Strip:

(a) targeted killing is both a violation of international law and understood to be a provocation leading to further lethal violence;

(b) the *de facto* authorities in Gaza do not themselves engage in retaliation and they seek to maintain an effective ceasefire, but seemingly permit or are unable to prevent some militant factions in Gaza from firing rockets in response to a prior Israeli attack;

(c) Israel continues to rely on excessive or disproportionate use of force in Gaza, thereby continuing what was referred to as the Dahiya doctrine in the report of the United Nations Fact-Finding Mission on the Gaza Conflict (A/HRC/12/48), whenever its security interests are engaged—comparative casualty figures bear out this line of reasoning;

(d) there are risks of a second massive Israeli attack on the Gaza Strip, likely to be a larger scale Operation Cast Lead, an attack on Gaza from land, sea and air that continued for three weeks, which inflicted heavy civilian casualties and caused extensive damage to civilian properties, especially homes.[48]

23. The Special Rapporteur believes that there is renewed urgency for the international community to respond to these developments, as well as to the continuing Israeli rejection of negotiated ceasefire in favor of its pattern of reliance on targeted

---

47 For example, on Channel 10 in Israel, a graphic scoreboard was broadcasted depicting the "score" of killings as 25 Palestinians against zero Israelis.

48 For influential public advocacy of such an attack, which is often alluded to by Israeli journalists and officials, see Efraim Inbar and Max Singer, "The Opportunity in Gaza," BESA Center Perspectives Paper No. 167 (Begin-Sadat Center for Strategic Studies), 15 March 2012.

assassination and other extrajudicial killings. The parallel need for "speaking with one voice," so recently heard in the Security Council's statement of 21 March 2012 regarding the Syrian Arab Republic (S/PRST/2012/6), could be applied to the Gaza crisis as well. Relying on the General Assembly-endorsed principle of the responsibility to protect, the Security Council called on the government of the Syrian Arab Republic to "immediately cease troop movements towards, and end the use of heavy weapons in, population centres, and begin pullback of military concentrations in and around population centres ... [and] bring about a sustained cessation of armed violence in all its forms by all parties with an effective United Nations supervision mechanism." The statement continued that "similar commitments would be sought ... from the opposition and all relevant elements to stop the fighting ... and to bring about a sustained cessation of armed violence in all its forms by all parties." If the responsibility to protect is to attain legitimacy as an application of international law, it must be applicable everywhere, in particular the situation of prolonged occupation that prevails in the Occupied Palestinian Territory. Otherwise, the responsibility to protect will be discredited due to selective application.

Human Rights and International Humanitarian Law Obligations and Principles Relevant to Private Corporations in the Occupied Palestinian Territory
Report #8: A/67/379, 19 Sept 2012

Guiding principles on business and human rights

20. On 16 June 2011 the Human Rights Council in its resolution 17/4 unanimously endorsed the Guiding Principles on Business and Human Rights for implementing the United Nations "Protect, Respect and Remedy" Framework, providing—for the first time—a global standard for upholding human rights in relation to business activity. The Guiding Principles were prepared

by the former Special Representative of the Secretary-General on human rights and transnational corporations and other business enterprises, Professor John Ruggie. They provide authoritative normative guidance, clarifying the roles and responsibilities of business enterprises with regard to human rights, and the necessary legal and policy measures to be taken by States arising from their existing human rights obligations to ensure respect for human rights. It is the first normative document on business and human rights to be endorsed by an intergovernmental human rights body.

21. The Guiding Principles highlight the steps States should take to foster respect for human rights by businesses. They provide a framework in which companies should demonstrate that they respect human rights and reduce the risk of abuses. They also constitute a set of benchmarks by which to assess business respect for human rights. The Guiding Principles are organized under the Framework's three pillars:

(a) The State duty to protect against human rights abuses by third parties, including business enterprises, through policies, regulation and adjudication;

(b) The corporate responsibility to respect human rights, which means that business enterprises should act with due diligence to avoid infringing on the rights of others and to address the adverse impacts with which they are involved;

(c) The need for greater access to remedy for victims of business-related abuse, both judicial and non-judicial.

22. The Guiding Principles provide concrete and practical recommendations to implement the Framework. The Guiding Principles do not create new international law obligations but constitute a clarification and elaboration of the implications of existing standards, including under international human rights law, and practices, for both States and business enterprises, integrating them within a coherent framework.[49] In addition to forming part of States' existing international human rights obligations, important elements of the Guiding Principles are also increasingly reflected

---

49 A/HRC/17/31, para. 14.

in national laws, and in global, regional and industry-specific soft law standards and initiatives as well as contractual obligations.

23. Companies can have an impact on all human rights depending on the situation and context of their activities; therefore it is essential that they put in place an effective ongoing human rights due diligence process to assess risks and the potential and actual impact of their activities on human rights, integrate and act on the findings of such assessments, track the effectiveness of their response and communicate on both the assessments and the response. This is in addition to business enterprises expressing a clear public commitment to meeting their responsibility to respect human rights, and to providing for or cooperating with the remediation of any adverse effects that they have caused or contributed to.

24. Human rights may be at heightened risk and should therefore receive greater attention in particular industries and contexts, including humanitarian situations, but businesses should in all cases be encouraged to have a periodic review to assess all human rights affected by their activity. International human rights standards, including the International Bill of Human Rights[50] and the eight core conventions of the International Labour Organization (ILO), as set out in the ILO Declaration on Fundamental Principles and Rights at Work all act as an authoritative list against which to assess the human rights impacts of business enterprises. Impact assessments should also consider, depending on circumstances, additional standards, for instance, relating to the rights of indigenous peoples; women; national or ethnic, religious and linguistic minorities; children; persons with disabilities; and migrant workers and their families, wherever appropriate. Business enterprises should respect the standards of international humanitarian law whenever they operate in a situation of armed conflict. States should exercise even greater oversight with regard to businesses enterprises that they own or control.

25. The Guiding Principles are leading to a convergence of global standards and initiatives on business and human rights, as

---

50 Consisting of The Universal Declaration of Human Rights, the International Covenant on Civil and Political Rights and the International Covenant on Economic, Social and Cultural Rights.

evidenced in reports of the Working Group on the issue of human rights and transnational corporations and other business enterprises and the former Special Representative of the Secretary-General.[51] Examples of regional initiatives include:

(a) The International Organization for Standardization (ISO) has included a chapter on human rights in its guidance on corporate responsibility, which is aligned with the United Nations "Protect, Respect and Remedy" Framework on which the Guiding Principles are based.

(b) The European Commission has issued a communication on corporate social responsibility expressing its expectation that all enterprises should meet human rights responsibility as defined in the Guiding Principles.[52]

(c) It has also stated its intention to publish periodic progress reports on the implementation of the Guiding Principles within the European Union and invited European Union member States to develop national plans for the implementation of the Guiding Principles by the end of 2012.[53]

(d) The Association of Southeast Asian Nations (ASEAN) has announced that the first thematic study by the new Intergovernmental Commission on Human Rights would focus on business and human rights in a manner that is fully compliant with the Guiding Principles.[54]

---

51 Uptake of the United Nations framework and the Guiding Principles has been documented by the Working Group in its first reports to the Human Rights Council (A/HRC/20/29) and the General Assembly (A/67/285), by the Secretary-General in his report to the Human Rights Council (A/HRC/21/21 and Corr.1) and by the former Special Representative of the Secretary- General; see https://www.business-humanrights.org/media/documents/applications-of-framework-jun- 2011.pdf.

52 Available from single-market-economy.ec.europa.eu/industry/sustainability/corporate-social-responsibility-responsible-business-conduct_en.

53 https://eur-lex.europa.eu/LexUriServ/LexUriServ.do?uri=COM:2011:0681:FIN:EN:PDF.

54 Remarks by Rafendi Djamin, rep. of Indonesia to the Intergovernmental Commission on Human Rights of the Association of Southeast Asian Nations, at the Asia Pacific Forum of National Human Rights Institutions Regional Conference on Business and Human Rights, Seoul, 11–13 October 2011.

(e) The Guidelines for Multinational Enterprises of the Organization for Economic Development and Cooperation (OECD), as updated in 2011, are now fully aligned with the corporate responsibility to respect human rights as set out in the Guiding Principles.

Case studies

37. The Special Rapporteur notes that the businesses highlighted in this report constitute a small portion of a wide range of companies that have linked their business operations to Israel's settlements in the Occupied Palestinian Territory. The Special Rapporteur received a large amount of information from stakeholders concerning business practices of companies in relation to Israel's settlements; further investigations will be made to determine whether those allegations are well founded and may lead to additional attention in future reports. The businesses include, inter alia, retailers and supermarket chains, fast food suppliers, wine producers and products that are often labelled "products of Israel" but are in reality produced or extracted from the Occupied Palestinian Territory. They include small, medium and large Israeli-owned companies and multinational corporations. The Special Rapporteur limits coverage to selected illustrative cases; it proved necessary to exclude a significant amount of reliable information at this stage, owing in particular to the word limit imposed by the United Nations on this report.

Conclusion

88. The failure to bring the occupation to an end after 45 years creates an augmented international responsibility to uphold the human rights of the Palestinian people, who in practice live without the protection of the rule of law. In this context, the Special Rapporteur recalls that the General Assembly, as early as 1982,[55] called on Member States to apply economic sanctions against the State of Israel for its unlawful settlement activities.

---

55 Resolution ES-9/1 (5 February 1982); see also resolution 38/180 A (19 December 1983.

89. The Guiding Principles on Business and Human Rights require all business enterprises to respect human rights, which means, in the first instance, avoiding infringing on the human rights of others and addressing adverse impacts on human rights. The Special Rapporteur calls on both States and business enterprises to ensure the full and effective implementation of the Guiding Principles in the context of business operations relating to Israeli settlements in the Occupied Palestinian Territory.

Water and Sanitation in the West Bank and Gaza Strip
Report #9: A/HRC/68/376, 10 Sept 2013

58. During the mission of the Special Rapporteur to the Gaza Strip in December 2012, a number of interlocutors raised serious concerns about the lack of clean water and adequate sanitation facilities in the Gaza Strip. Some of those issues were briefly touched upon in the previous report of the Special Rapporteur to the Human Rights Council.[56] In the context of the near exclusive control by Israel over all underground and surface water resources in Palestine, the Special Rapporteur reiterates his concerns regarding the occupation-induced water and sanitation crisis.

The situation in the Gaza Strip

59. In the Gaza Strip, 90 percent of water in the underlying coastal aquifer beneath the Gaza Strip is unfit for human consumption as a result of pollution caused by raw sewage and rising seawater infiltration. In 2012, the United Nations reported that the coastal aquifer on which the Gaza Strip is almost completely reliant could become unusable as early as 2016, with the deterioration becoming irreversible by 2020. Polluted tap water has forced many families to buy expensive water from external vendors or to rely on desalinated water supplied by the Coastal

---

56 See A/HRC/22/35/Add.1.

Municipalities Water Utility, putting an unreasonable burden on average household incomes, which are already struggling at or below subsistence levels. Under these circumstances, most Gazans consume an average of 70 to 90 litres per person per day, which is well below the global standard set by the World Health Organization.

60. The Israeli blockade of Gaza has exacerbated water scarcity and lack of adequate sanitation facilities. Delays and restrictions on the entry of materials through the Israeli-controlled Kerem Shalom crossing have stalled a number of water and sanitation infrastructure projects. Furthermore, Israel not only extracts a disproportionate share of the water from the coastal aquifer for its own benefit but also blocks the Gazan population from accessing water from the Wadi Gaza, a natural stream that originates in the Hebron Mountains and flows to the Mediterranean Sea.

61. Water scarcity in Gaza has been worsened by the repeated destruction of water and sanitation infrastructure in the course of Israeli military operations. Israel has destroyed at least 306 wells in the Access Restricted Areas of Gaza since 2005.[57]

In this context, the Special Rapporteur strongly condemns the targeting of water and sanitation facilities during Israeli military operations, which cannot be justified as a military necessity, and cannot be explained as a consequence of accidents.

The situation in the West Bank

62. Palestinians in the West Bank are denied their rightful share of water from the underground mountain aquifer and prevented from accessing water from the Jordan River, which are both classified as shared water resources and thus must be shared equitably under customary international law.[58] An estimated

---

57 Emergency Water and Sanitation-Hygiene Group, "Fact sheet 13: Water and sanitation in the Access Restricted Areas of the Gaza Strip" (December 2012). Available from reliefweb.int/report/occupied-palestinian-territory/water-sanitation-access-restricted-areas-gaza-strip-fact-sheet.

58 Palestinian Water Authority, "Palestinian Water Sector: Status Summary Report," prepared for the meeting of the Ad Hoc Liaison Committee (September 2012). Available at reliefweb.int/report/occupied-palestinian-territory/palestinian-water-sector-status-summary-report-september-2012.

500,000 Israeli settlers in the West Bank and East Jerusalem enjoy approximately six times the amount of water used by the Palestinian population of 2.6 million.[59]

Israeli settlers enjoy ample amounts of water channeled directly to the settlements, which allows settlers to irrigate agricultural land and grow water-intensive crops. In contrast, Palestinian farmers depend largely on water supplies transported in tankers or collected by water cisterns, raising agricultural costs and restricting most Palestinian agriculture to unprofitable small-scale operations growing rain-fed crops, which on average is 15 times less profitable than irrigated crops. In this context, only 6.8 percent of land cultivated by Palestinians in the West Bank is irrigated.[60]

63. The unequal distribution of water resources has been sustained by the Joint Water Committee, which was established as part of the Israeli-Palestinian Interim Agreement on the West Bank and the Gaza Strip. Mandated to grant permits for the drilling and rehabilitation of wells and sewage systems, the Committee is also responsible for setting water extraction quotas. The veto power of Israel on decision-making by the Committee has enabled it to constrain the development of water infrastructure for Palestinian communities, particularly in Area C of the West Bank. In addition, all Palestinian water projects located in Area C need to obtain approval from the Israeli Civil Administration. The Special Rapporteur finds it alarming that from 1995 to 2008, the Committee approved Israeli proposals for 3 wells and 108 supply networks and rejected only 1 of 24 proposed wastewater projects, while during the same period it approved only half of all Palestinian proposals for wells.[61]

64. The loss of scarce Palestinian water resources occurs not only through demolitions undertaken by Israeli authorities of "illegal" water collection facilities, including wells and water

59 Elizabeth Koek, *Water for One People Only: Discriminatory Access and "Water-Apartheid" in the OPT* (Ramallah, Al-Haq, 2013). 63.

60 Emergency Water and Sanitation-Hygiene Group, "Fact sheet 14: Water for agriculture in the West Bank" (March 2013). Available from documents.pub/document/water-for-agriculture-in-the-west-bank.html.

61 Elizabeth Koek, *Water for One People Only: Discriminatory Access and "Water-Apartheid" in the OPT* (Ramallah, Al-Haq, 2013).

collection tanks, but also as a result of deep-water drilling activities by Israeli water companies. The Special Rapporteur is also concerned by acts of violence by settlers in the vicinity of Palestinian communities; there are several reports of Palestinian springs being taken over by settlers and fenced off.[62]

65. Israel systematically blocks the development of the Palestinian wastewater and sanitation sector through bureaucratic constraints imposed by the Joint Water Committee and the Israeli Civil Administration. Between 1995 and 2011, only 4 out of 30 Palestinian wastewater treatment plant proposals were approved by the Committee and their construction has been repeatedly delayed. It is of serious concern to the Special Rapporteur that there is only one functioning Palestinian wastewater treatment plant in the West Bank, which has the capacity to treat less than 3 percent of sewage.[63]

66. Meanwhile, Israeli authorities profit from the occupation-induced crisis by treating up to 21 percent of Palestinian sewage in facilities established inside Israel and paid for by Palestinian tax revenues withheld by Israel. The treated wastewater is then reused for the exclusive benefit of the Israeli agricultural sector. The difficulties experienced by Palestinian communities in securing sewage treatment facilities contrasts with the wastewater treatment plants servicing the settlements, which makes a mockery of the relevance of international humanitarian law in the protection of an occupied people.

The Palestinian right to water and development

67. Considering the unlawful policies and practices of Israel that induce a water and sanitation crisis in occupied Palestine, the Special Rapporteur stresses that the Palestinian Authority has neither been able to uphold Palestinian water rights nor to embrace the

---

62 Elizabeth Koek, *Water for One People Only.*

63 Palestinian Water Authority, *Palestinian Water Sector: Status Summary Report,* prepared for the meeting of the Ad Hoc Liaison Committee (September 2012). Available from https://reliefweb.int/report/occupied-palestinian-territory/palestinian-water-sector-status-summary-report-september-2012.

right to development of water and sanitation facilities.[64] Support from the international donor community for ad hoc solutions, such as financing desalination plants and sanitation facilities to meet the immediate needs of the Palestinian population, must go hand in hand with pressure exerted on Israeli authorities to put an end to its discriminatory policies. In sum, the discriminatory pattern disclosed is aggravated by the fact that while the Palestinians are being denied their rights to resources situated within Palestine, settlements have been the beneficiaries of these Israeli policies. In effect, illegality is compounded by illegality, with the result being impending threats of de-development hanging over the Palestinian future in the Gaza Strip, and to a lesser degree in the West Bank.

Gaza Strip
Report #10: A/HRC/23/21, 16 Sept 2013

Operation Pillar of Defense

8. Israel launched Operation Pillar of Defense, the most sustained use of force since Operation Cast Lead, on 14 November 2012, and continued it for eight days. The timeline of the violence leading up to the attack is complex, with no clear relationship of cause and effect.[65] There were incidents of border violence and rocket fire in the days before, yet there is widespread agreement that the definitive moment came when the Hamas military leader, Ahmed Jabari, was assassinated in a targeted killing. It was a safe assumption that the assassination of such a high-value target

---

64 The International Covenant on Economic, Social and Cultural Rights; the Convention on the Elimination of All Forms of Discrimination against Women; the Convention on the Rights of the Child; and the Convention on the Rights of Persons with Disabilities entail obligations for States parties in relation to access to safe drinking water and sanitation. Israel has ratified the aforementioned Conventions except for the Convention on the Rights of Persons with Disabilities, to which Israel is a signatory.

65 "TIMELINE: Israel launches Pillar of Defense amid Gaza Escalation," *Haaretz*, 20 November 2012. Available from https://www.haaretz.com/2012-11-20/ty-article/.premium/timeline-operation-pillar-of-defense/0000017f-e6d9-df5f-a17f-ffdf34140000.

would trigger strong retaliation from Gaza. This was confirmed by widely respected Israeli peace activist Gershon Baskin, who confirmed that Jabari, at the time he was killed, was in the final stages of negotiating a long-term ceasefire with Israel. In an article published during the operation, Baskin pointed out that Israel had tried every military option to crush the capacity and will of Gaza to engage in violent resistance, adding that "the only thing it has not tried and tested is reaching an agreement for a long-term mutual ceasefire."[66] As Baskin pointed out, Jabari had long been in Israeli crosshairs and was known to have masterminded the capture and detention of the Israeli soldier Gilad Shalit. Jabari was the leader who had kept Shalit alive and in good health while in captivity for several years and had prevented rogue militias in Gaza from engaging in violence against Israel. He had also acted to uphold prior ceasefires that had stemmed the level of violence on the Gazan border in recent years, which directly contributed to keeping Israeli casualties at zero since Operation "Cast Lead."

9. Israel justified Operation Pillar of Defense as a defensive response to Gaza rocket fire. The United States of America, along with several European countries, supported this claim. The United States Department of State expressed this sentiment when the attacks started: "We support Israel's right to defend itself, and we encourage Israel to continue to take every effort to avoid civilian casualties."[67] Supporters of Palestine regarded Israel's concerted use of force against urbanized and vulnerable Gaza as "aggression" and "criminal." Israeli military analysts argued that the strategic purpose of Operation Pillar of Defense was to restore deterrence in the light of the recent increase in violence emanating from Gaza and to destroy the capacity of Gazan military forces to launch long-range rockets.[68]

---

66 "Israel's Shortsighted Assassination," *The New York Times*, 16 November 2012. Available from https://www.nytimes.com/2012/11/17/opinion/israels-shortsighted-assassination.html?_r=0.

67 United States. Department of State press statement, 14 November 2012. Available from 2009-2017.state.gov/r/pa/prs/ps/2012/11/200551.htm.

68 Shlomo Brom et al., *In the Aftermath of Operation Pillar of Defense*, Institute for National Security Studies, Tel Aviv, 2012, pp. 7–8.

Both sides claimed victory when the ceasefire agreement brokered by Egypt came into effect on 21 November 2012. The Israeli side avoided a ground attack that had turned the tide of public opinion against its operation in 2009 and took some steps to avoid civilian casualties. On the Gazan side, casualties to police and militants were greatly reduced by avoiding targeted facilities and taking secure shelter, and damage to rocket launchers was reduced by greater mobility and use of underground launching sites. The terms of the ceasefire lend support to the claim of the *de facto* authorities in Gaza that Israel had given ground: agreeing not to engage in future targeted assassinations, and to meet to discuss the opening of crossing points for goods and people. The implementation of the ceasefire agreement is discussed below.

10. The mission of the Special Rapporteur had the objective of gathering information on the situation in the Gaza Strip in the light of a United Nations study that suggested that Gaza's viability would be at serious risk by 2020. The Special Rapporteur did not abandon that goal, and additional concerns arose regarding Operation Pillar of Defense, since the ceasefire went into effect only 10 days before the Special Rapporteur's arrival. Several aspects of the attacks raised serious international humanitarian law issues bearing on the use of excessive force in relation to a population living under conditions of occupation. Although Israel implemented its plan of "disengagement" in 2005, it did not end its legal responsibilities as the Occupying Power. This conclusion reflects Israel's control of entry.[69]

11. The Special Rapporteur conducted three activities during his mission: visits to targeted areas and meetings with families affected adversely by Operation Pillar of Defense; briefings with United Nations officials and with national and international representatives of non-governmental organizations active in Gaza; and meetings with local journalists, doctors and individuals acquainted with the policies and practices of and discussions held at the senior level of the *de facto* authorities. It was an intense yet

---

69 Gershon Baskin, "Israel's Short-sighted Assassination" (op-ed), *The New York Times,* 16 November 2012, https://www.nytimes.com/2012/11/17/opinion/israels-shortsighted-assassination.html.

illuminating means to acquire a direct appreciation of the overall situation of human rights in Gaza.

12. The Special Rapporteur visited Ismail Mohamed Abu Tabiekh Aslan, a neighborhood of Gaza City situated near the border with Israel that had experienced heavy artillery and missile attacks. Some residents reported that drones were used to attack. The Special Rapporteur met with adult residents, mainly men, who spoke of how the attacks had damaged the modest infrastructure (especially electricity and water storage) of this extremely poor neighborhood, and had killed their livestock, which were crucial to their meagre livelihood. They also spoke of their shared sense of vulnerability during the attacks, with no facilities available to offer protection. A deep psychological impact was widely reported, especially affecting young children who were experiencing nightmares, bedwetting, and panic attacks.

13. The Special Rapporteur visited the destroyed residence of the Al Dalou family, which lost 10 family members, including four young children during the attack. Jamel Mahmoud Yassin Al Dalou, the surviving grandfather of the four dead children, described himself as a trader in foodstuffs who lived with his family in the Nasser neighborhood and enjoyed better living conditions than most Gazans. Mr. Al Dalou stated that, during the November attacks:

> Every one of us was a target. The sky was full of Israeli planes and drones, everything that moved could be hit. I left to go to my business by taxi to bring needed food to the family, but while there, people came to me crying and told me my house had been hit, the worst news I've ever received in my life. I rushed home to find many working to remove the rubble of the destroyed house.

On the deaths of his children and grandchildren, Mr. Al Dalou commented:

> If they cannot deal with Islamic militants, should they attack children? We have no problem if Israelis attack

militants, but this was a great injustice. I lost my family.
I sleep on the street. Only my son and I survived. This is
one of the worst crimes. Where is the international court
to prosecute the perpetrators? They destroy our houses,
take our land, and destroy our women and children. To
whom can I complain?

This man's voice represented the pain and grief encountered throughout the visit. Essentially, the other victims and survivors of the attacks with whom the Special Rapporteur spoke told the same story. From the perspective of international humanitarian law, what seems striking is that several of the damaged structures were situated in clearly demarcated residential districts. There is a new yardstick by which to assess responsibility for military strikes on civilian targets. On the one side, missile technology has become more accurate, allowing for less accidental or collateral damage. At the same time, this greater accuracy leads to the presumption that direct hits on civilian residences are deliberate, and thus exhibit criminal intention. In certain instances, there may have been someone acknowledged as a militant living in a residential building, but such a presence does not justify targeting an entire residential complex. In such circumstances, the collateral damage to civilians far outweighs the direct damage inflicted on legally acceptable targets. The Special Rapporteur was informed by several Gazans that rockets were neither stored nor fired from residential districts but were stored underground and launched from open spaces.

The Special Rapporteur was briefed by United Nations officials and civil society representatives who had observed and investigated compliance with human rights law and international humanitarian law during Operation Pillar of Defense. The concerns noted above were affirmed, and the Special Rapporteur's attention was drawn to other important issues. Israel's intentional targeting of journalists covering the military operation was highlighted as a concern that had to be addressed by the international community. The view was repeatedly expressed that Israel's attacks constituted a part of its continuous collective punishment of Palestinians.

In this respect, complaints regarding Israeli impunity for such actions, including the lack of will of the international community to address Israeli impunity firmly, were frequent. One representative insisted that "justice required the accountability of Israelis and upholding the rights of Palestinians." The Special Rapporteur was informed that Israeli attacks had shifted from being restricted to specific targets in the first four days of Operation Pillar of Defense, which appeared to avoid serious civilian casualties and damage, to later attacks on civilian and agricultural targets and a reliance on less accurate forms of weaponry, particularly shelling by naval and land artillery. It was also noted that the attacks had led to the internal displacement of more than 60,000 people, who had no refuge after leaving their place of residence. There was widespread agreement that the possibility of peace depended on an end to the blockade and the shifting of commerce from the tunnels to the crossings. Israel was blamed for its lack of clarity in relation to the definition and breadth of access restricted areas. The Special Rapporteur was left with the strong impression that the ceasefire agreement, even if were to be fully implemented, was merely a stop-gap measure, and that more fundamental changes had to be taken to allow Gaza to focus its energies on long-term viability.

20. Fundamental to the viability of Gaza is the question of food security. The Gaza Strip is 321 square miles, and the latest population estimate is 1.75 million residents, making it one of the most densely populated and impoverished territories in the world. These underlying conditions have been aggravated by Israel's maintenance of a security buffer zone on the Gaza side of the border that deprives Palestinian farmers of 34 percent of available agricultural land. Periodic Israeli incursions have destroyed wells and farm animals and have made it hazardous to work the land. Operation Pillar of Defense inflicted considerable damage on agricultural structures and animal shelters throughout Gaza. The Special Rapporteur was informed that agriculture seemed to have been particularly targeted. To have any hope of achieving long-term viability, the agricultural sector depends on an end to the blockade, improved access to seeds, better irrigation, secure access to the land, a reduced and demarcated buffer zone, and the

renewal of exports of key products in viable quantities. Long-term projections that assume continued population growth and improving living conditions, including less dependence on international donors, are uniformly pessimistic about the future of Gaza, especially if it continues to be cut off from the West Bank and the outside world.

21. The gravity of the situation was dramatized recently by confrontations between Gazans and UNRWA as a result of food shortfalls.[70] The United Nations projection of the collapse of Gaza as a viable entity by 2020 was confirmed by representatives of non-governmental organizations, who even suggested that such a projection was optimistic, especially in relation to water quality and availability, and that 2016 was more realistic. Present conditions are threatening to unleash a health epidemic. There are reports of widespread mental difficulties being experienced by virtually the entire juvenile population. UNRWA felt that it would be only possible to improve the overall situation in Gaza if its annual budget were increased by $200 million to $300 million, which seems unlikely at present. The non-governmental organization Action Against Hunger has noted that any prospect for agricultural sufficiency and livelihood capacity will depend on Gaza reclaiming at least 50 percent of the coastal aquifer.

Health in Gaza

22. The Special Rapporteur met with health experts associated with the World Health Organization, the United Nations Children's Fund (UNICEF) and the Gaza Community Mental Health Programme. They presented a grim picture of the health situation in Gaza. One unexpected finding was their shared assessment that the health effects of Operation Pillar of Defense were more severe than those that followed from Operation Cast Lead, despite fewer casualties. An increased perception of deliberate targeting of neighborhoods and agricultural settings, more fear arising from recollections of past violence, and greater sensitivity

70 Mohammed Omer, "Anger at UNRWA in Gaza grows," *Al Jazeera*, 1 May 2013. Available from https://www.aljazeera.com/humanrights/2013/04/20134294185559594.html.

to extreme vulnerability were cited. Mental health experts referred to the extent to which each major violent incursion in Gaza destroys whatever progress had been achieved in recent years and causes a net depressive mood and reality summarized by the word often encountered in such briefings: "de-development."

23. With regard to medical care, there were reports of an increase in referrals for treatment in Israel and Egypt (for instance, 8,000 in 2007, up from 16,000 in 2011) for persons suffering from cancer and cardiac conditions, as well as other diseases that could not be treated in Gaza. The increase was explained as partly caused by the deterioration of medical equipment in Gaza, the inability to import spare parts and the failure to invest in advanced medical facilities. Despite these shortcomings, health specialists did report some improvement in the overall medical situation following the Mavi Marmara incident in 2010, when it became easier to receive travel permits (95 percent of requests were approved, although often with harmful delays) and to import certain medical equipment. The Special Rapporteur received reports of tragic deaths caused by delays in issuance or denial of travel permits for those needing urgent treatment.

24. During Operation Pillar of Defense, public health facilities were severely strained, and the population came to depend on the assistance of non-governmental organizations, amidst reports of a high incidence of physical and mental injuries. Workers at the Gaza Community Mental Health Programme emphasized the degree to which the impact of the siege and wartime violence on the mental well-being of the civilian population had been both adverse and cumulative. They spoke of the high level of stress observed in most Gazans, with secondary symptoms of despair, hopelessness and powerlessness, and somatic complaints originating with acute stress, such as high blood pressure among children. There were suggestions that the stress and economic challenges of sustaining livelihoods seemed connected with a rise in domestic violence, post-traumatic stress and indications that there occurred refusals by Israeli hospitals to accept patients from Gaza who were unable to pay the exorbitant costs of treatment. One recommendation flowing from the experience was for the creation

of a private patients' fund that could be drawn upon for medical treatment outside of Gaza.

Ceasefire implementation

25. The ceasefire agreement between the *de facto* authorities in Gaza and Israel embodied an understanding that, beyond an immediate cessation of hostilities, Israel would refrain from incursions and targeted assassinations in Gaza and would also allow the movement of people and goods at the crossings. Despite the various interpretations of the ceasefire understanding, with some Israelis contending that it was only an agreement to be discussed, there was a general expectation, at least among Palestinians, that Israel would loosen its stranglehold over the civilian population and make life more tolerable. During the period under review, both sides largely refrained from resuming hostilities, although several developments suggested that Israel had not adhered to the spirit of the ceasefire agreement. There were few signs of a loosening of the blockade and, in latter weeks, targeted assassinations of suspected militants and incursions by the Israel Defense Forces into Gaza resumed. The excessive use of force by the Israeli security forces in the enforcement of access restricted areas continued with disturbing regularity. Several setbacks in recent weeks and months are highlighted below.

26. The Special Rapporteur is disturbed by excessive use of force in the enforcement of access restricted areas on land and at sea, as well as by military incursions with bulldozers into Gaza. He is also concerned at the punitive measures taken by Israel, such as rescinding the fishing zone and closing border crossings, which amount to the collective punishment of the civilian population.

31. While the Occupying Power's continued illegal blockade of Gaza and its failure to uphold its responsibilities to ensure the protection of civilians remain of utmost concern, the Special Rapporteur is alarmed at what appears to be the use of collective punishment on the entire civilian population of Gaza by Israel.

32. The ceasefire agreement will continue to be tested, but the Special Rapporteur is mindful that the continued blockade of

Gaza remains of primary concern to the residents of Gaza. The Israeli stranglehold is such that Gaza's monthly exports consist of a few truckloads of cut flowers, date bars, cherry tomatoes and spices.[71] Israel's blockade is stunting the potential for economic development in the Gaza Strip.

Overview
Report #11: A/HRC/25/67, 13 Jan 2014

1. In his final presentation to the Human Rights Council, the Special Rapporteur on the situation of human rights in the Palestinian Territories Occupied since 1967 would like to under-score the importance of this mandate as providing an independent witness to the evolving effects of the continuing occupation of Palestine by Israel. This exposure is centered upon the presentation of information received on the persistence of severe violations of international humanitarian law and international human rights law. This process of bearing witness provides a record of violations by Israel and its defiant attitude and challenges the United Nations to take steps to ensure compliance. It should be remembered that the suffering of the people of Palestine is inseparably linked to the partition arrangements initially proposed by the United Nations in 1947, and which were never implemented or revised in a manner that takes full account of the rights of the Palestinian people, above all their inalienable right of self-determination.

2. It was unfortunate that Israel refused even minimal co-operation with this mandate to the extent of allowing the Special Rapporteur to have access to occupied Palestine during the past six years or of responding to several urgent appeals addressing specif-ic situations of immediate concern that fell within the purview of the mandate. This Special Rapporteur was expelled in December 2008 when attempting to enter Israel to carry out a mission of the mandate to visit occupied Palestine and detained overnight in

---

71 State of Israel, Ministry of Defense, Gaza Crossing – Weekly Report, 10–16 March 2013.

unpleasant prison conditions. Such humiliating non-cooperation represents a breach of the legal duty of States Members of the United Nations to facilitate all official undertakings of the organization. Although it has been possible to gain information needed to report on the situation confronting Palestinians living under occupation, non-cooperation deprives the mandate of direct interaction, including the receipt of testimony bearing on international law grievances from representatives of the Palestinian people. It is to be hoped that the next Special Rapporteur to be appointed will receive sufficient backing from the Human Rights Council to induce cooperation from Israel and better protection against defamatory attacks by some non-governmental organizations (NGOs) than was the experience of the current mandate holder.

3. *International Law.* An abiding theme of the reports of the Special Rapporteur during the past six years has been the consistent failure of Israel to comply with clear legal standards embodied in the Geneva Convention relative to the Protection of Civilian Persons in Time of War (Fourth Geneva Convention) and elsewhere in international humanitarian law and international human rights law. This pattern, as will be detailed below, is flagrant in relation to the wall, settlements, East Jerusalem, the Gaza Strip, water and land resources, and the human rights of Palestinians living under occupation. Also relevant is the failure of the United Nations to ensure implementation of the recommendations as to international law contained in two high-profile Human Rights Council reports of 2009 and 2013, respectively those of the United Nations Fact-Finding Mission on the Gaza Conflict (A/HRC/12/48) and of the fact-finding mission to investigate the human rights implications of the Israeli settlements (A/HRC/22/63). To the extent such a pattern is tolerated, it undermines respect for international law.

4. *Palestine.* In the light of the General Assembly's recognition of Palestine as a non-member Observer State in Assembly resolution 67/19 of 29 November 2012, it seems appropriate to refer to territory under Israeli occupation as "Palestine" rather than as "Occupied Palestinian Territory." Such a shift in language also emphasizes the inadequacy of the international law framework

available to address a condition of prolonged occupation that has now extended for more than 45 years. Special steps and procedures need to be adopted that will confer rights and establish the rule of law. To sustain indefinitely an oppressive occupation containing many punitive elements also seems designed to encourage residents to leave Palestine, which is consistent with the apparent annexationist, colonialist, and ethnic-cleansing goals of Israel, especially in relation to the West Bank, including East Jerusalem.

5. *Corporate responsibility.* Recent reports have underscored the potential implications for corporations and financial institutions that engage with and profit from Israeli settlements. The establishment and continued development of settlements is in violation of article49(6) of the Fourth Geneva Convention, an assessment reinforced by the International Court of Justice in its advisory opinion of 2004 on the wall. Such an initiative has tried at all times to proceed cooperatively with the economic actors involved and has acknowledged instances of compliance with international law and relevant United Nations guidelines and the encouraging recent indication of governmental and European Union reinforcement of these emergent obligations. This trend also converges with and reinforces the social mobilization of civil society in a variety of initiatives, especially the growing boycott, divestment, and sanctions campaign.

6. *"Legitimacy war."* In the pursuit of Palestinian rights under circumstances of prolonged occupation, there is increasing reason to believe that despite the authority of international law and the expressed will of States Members of the United Nations, the situation is essentially frozen, if not regressing. In addition, Palestinians seem increasingly disillusioned with armed resistance and with traditional intergovernmental diplomacy. Palestinian hopes for the realization of their fundamental rights have now shifted to engagement in a "legitimacy war," which involves a worldwide struggle to gain control over the debate about legal entitlements and moral proprieties in the conflict supported by a global solidarity movement that has begun to sway public opinion. The United Nations has a crucial role to play in this process by lending support to Palestinian claims of rights and providing

assessments of associated grievances resulting from the violation by Israel of international humanitarian law and international human rights principles and standards.

7. *Language.* The Special Rapporteur believes that the language used to consider Palestinian grievances relating to international humanitarian law and international human rights law in Palestine needs to reflect everyday realities, and not remain beholden to technical wording and euphemisms that mask human suffering resulting from violations. It seems therefore appropriate to describe such unlawful impositions on the people resident in the West Bank by reference to "annexation" and "colonial ambitions" rather than "occupation." Whether these impositions constitute "apartheid" is discussed in more detail below. Such clarifications at the level of language reinforce the contention that it is a matter of urgency to pursue more concerted efforts within United Nations venues to implement the rights of the Palestinian people.

8. *Emergency in Gaza.* Developments in the region, combined with an unlawful blockade maintained since mid-2007, has created a serious emergency situation in the Gaza Strip that threatens the entire population. From the perspective of international law, as argued in prior reports (A/HRC/20/32), Gaza remains "occupied," despite the implementation by Israel of its "disengagement" plan in 2005, due to the control of borders, airspace and coastal waters, and periodic military incursions. The present situation is dire, as massive infrastructural failures cause daily hardship for the population, who are also at risk of epidemics. At the time of writing, with insufficient quantities of fuel reaching Gaza, electricity is available only for short periods, making it impossible for hospitals to provide proper treatment for seriously ill patients suffering from cancer and kidney ailments. The situation is aggravated by persisting tensions between the Palestinian Authority and the governing authorities in Gaza, and by the breakdown of cooperation along the border with Egypt. Egyptian security concerns in Sinai have led to greater restrictions at the Rafah crossing, and to the destruction of the tunnel complex in southern Gaza that had eased some of the difficulties caused by the blockade. Some countries, notably Turkey and Qatar, have responded to this situation by

providing emergency relief, but much more assistance is required, including pressure upon Israel to end the unlawful blockade.

9. *Urgency.* The stark reality is that the beleaguered occupied people of Gaza, over half of whom are children, are not receiving the protection to which they are entitled under international humanitarian law, which imposes an overall duty on the Occupying Power to act in such a manner as to protect the civilian population from harm. Given the failure of Israel to live up to these obligations as set forth in the Fourth Geneva Convention, the United Nations and international society generally is challenged to take urgent action. The principles embedded in the concept of the responsibility to protect would seem to have a special applicability to the emergency conditions currently existing in Gaza that are being brought to the attention of the world by graphic pictures of sewage in the streets; widespread flooding; seasonal cold, including snow; and children entrapped by these conditions.

The question of apartheid

51. In 2011, the Special Rapporteur reiterated the call made by his predecessor in 2007 for a referral to the International Court of Justice for an advisory opinion on the question of whether "elements of the [Israeli] occupation constitute forms of colonialism and apartheid."[72] More precisely, he recommended that the Court be asked to assess the allegations that the prolonged occupation of the West Bank and East Jerusalem possess elements of "colonialism," "apartheid" and "ethnic cleansing" inconsistent with international humanitarian law in circumstances of belligerent occupation and unlawful abridgement of the right of self-determination of the Palestinian people.[73]

Since no advisory opinion has been sought following the aforementioned reports of successive Special Rapporteurs, in the present report the Special Rapporteur assumes part of the task of analyzing whether allegations of apartheid in occupied Palestine are well founded. He discusses Israeli policies and practices

---

72 A/HRC/16/72, para. 8, A/HRC/4/17, p. 3.
73 A/HRC/16/72, para. 32(b).

through the lens of the international prohibition of ethnic discrimination, segregation, and apartheid.

Legal framework

52. Apartheid is prohibited under international law, and Israel, as a State and an Occupying Power, is bound by this prohibition. Under Protocol I additional to the Geneva Conventions, which is declaratory of international law and therefore widely regarded as universally binding, "practices of 'apartheid' and other inhuman and degrading practices involving outrages upon personal dignity, based on racial discrimination" are included as grave breaches.[74] Further, the International Law Commission has noted that governments at the United Nations Conference on the Law of Treaties (1968) generally agreed that the prohibitions constituting peremptory norms included apartheid.[75]

53. Apartheid involves the domination of one racial group over another, and some may argue that neither Israeli Jews nor Palestinians constitute racial groups per se. However, article 1 of the International Convention on the Elimination of All Forms of Racial Discrimination, in its definition of racial discrimination, makes it clear that race is in fact not the sole factor, but that racial discrimination may be based on "any distinction, exclusion, restriction or preference based on race, color, descent, or national or ethnic origin." The Committee on the Elimination of Racial Discrimination has stressed that under the definition in article 1 "the Convention relates to all persons who belong to different races, national or ethnic groups or to indigenous peoples."[76]

54. The International Convention on the Suppression and Punishment of the Crime of Apartheid, in article 2, provides a detailed definition of the crime of apartheid, providing that it "shall include similar policies and practices of racial segregation and discrimination as practised in southern Africa," and applies to "inhuman acts committed for the purpose of establishing and maintaining domination by one racial group of persons over

---

74 Art. 85(4)(c), A/HRC/16/72.

75 Art. 85(4)(c), A/HRC/16/72.

76 General recommendation No. 24 (1999), para. 1.

any other racial group of persons and systematically oppressing them." The Rome Statute of the International Criminal Court echoes these core elements (art. 7, para. 2(h)) and further specifies that for such acts to constitute "crimes against humanity" they must be "committed as part of a widespread or systematic attack directed against any civilian population, with knowledge of the attack" (art. 7, para. 1). Without prejudice to any possible differences in the elements of apartheid as an international crime and an internationally wrongful act, apartheid will be treated as a single concept for the purpose of the International Convention on the Suppression and Punishment of the Crime of Apartheid.[77]

Acts potentially amounting to segregation and apartheid

56. In addition, article 3 of the International Convention on the Elimination of All Forms of Racial Discrimination provides that "States Parties particularly condemn racial segregation and *apartheid* and undertake to prevent, prohibit and eradicate all practices of this nature in territories under their jurisdiction."[78]

At the second universal periodic review of Israel in October 2013, South Africa recommended that Israel "prohibit policies and practices of racial segregation that disproportionately affect the Palestinian population in the OPT" (A/HRC/25/15, para. 136.20255. Article 2(a) concerns denial of the right to life and liberty of person, including by (i) murder; (ii) serious bodily and mental harm, infringement of freedom, and torture, and (iii) arbitrary arrest and illegal imprisonment. With respect to article 2(a)(i), continuing excessive use of force by Israeli security forces (ISF) and a lack of accountability for violations of international humanitarian law and international human rights law

---

77 Israel is not a party to the Convention and it is debated whether it was intended to apply exclusively to South Africa. Nonetheless, it continues to inform the prohibition of apartheid in international law.

78 Regardless of the possibility that the Convention's inclusion of apartheid applies exclusively to South Africa, the Convention prohibits all forms of racial segregation. See Committee on the Elimination of Racial Discrimination, general recommendation No. 19 (1995).

is well-documented by successive United Nations resolutions and reports.[79] Palestinians are killed as a result of regular Israeli military incursions into occupied Palestine, lethal use of force against demonstrators, official endorsement of targeted killings, and large-scale military operations.[80]

56. According to B'Tselem, between 1987 and 2000 just under 1,400 Palestinians were killed by ISF.[81] After the year 2000, deaths of Palestinians caused by ISF accelerated, with more than 6,700 deaths, as at October 2013. Of this number, over 3,100 were civilians not involved in hostilities. B'Tselem's statistics show that during Israel's Cast Lead operation in Gaza, of the 344 children reportedly killed, 318 did not take part in hostilities. During the same operation, of the 110 Palestinian women recorded as killed, two were police officers and the remaining 108 did not take part in the hostilities. During Operation Pillar of Defense, approximately 100 Palestinian civilians, a third of whom were children, were reportedly killed as a result of ISF actions (A/HRC/22/35/Add.1, para. 6).

57. Additional deaths were caused by the ISF policy of targeted killing, which resulted in the killing of 369 Palestinians during the period September 2000–December 2013. Moreover, on average, for every person killed as a target of ISF, one or two other persons have been killed in any given operation. Thus, during the same period, 453 Palestinians who were not targets were also killed.[82]

58. Individual accounts by former soldiers of the Israel Defense Forces (IDF), published by the Israeli NGO Breaking the Silence, bear witness to Israeli policy in respect to the occupied people: "'Prevention of terror' is the stamp of approval granted to any offensive IDF action in the territories, obscuring the distinction between the use of force against terrorists and the use of force

---

79 E.g., A/68/502, A/67/372, A/66/356, A/65/366, A/HRC/22/35; General Assembly resolution 67/118; and Human Rights Council resolutions 22/28 and 19/16.

80 Russell Tribunal, *Findings* (2011), para. 5.

81 See https://www.btselem.org/statistics.

82 Ibid.

against civilians. In this way, the IDF is able to justify actions that intimidate and oppress the Palestinian population overall."[83]

59. Under a simple interpretation, the term murder, as referred to in the International Convention on the Suppression and Punishment of the Crime of Apartheid, signifies the unlawful taking of life. Therefore, the taking of lives—outside the limited circumstances in which international humanitarian law and international human rights law do not absolutely prohibit this—potentially constitutes an element of apartheid, in the context of a systematic and institutional regime in which these unlawful killings form part of acts carried out in order to maintain dominance over Palestinians. The relatively high proportion of civilian casualties caused by ISF in occupied Palestine is notable in this respect.

60. In regard to article 2(a)(ii) and (iii), detention by Israel of Palestinians is closely linked to the occurrence of torture and ill-treatment. According to the Prisoner Support and Human Rights Association, Addameer, in September 2013, there were some 5,000 Palestinian political prisoners, including 137 administrative detainees.[84] Many detainees are transferred to prisons in Israel, in violation of the Fourth Geneva Convention (art. 76).[85]

61. In 2012, the Committee on the Elimination of Racial Discrimination urged Israel to end administrative detention, which is discriminatory and constitutes arbitrary detention under international human rights law (CERD/C/ISR/CO/14–16, para. 27). Similar recommendations were made by a number of States during the most recent universal periodic review of Israel (A/HRC/25/15). The Committee further recommended that Israel ensure equal access to justice for all persons living in territories under its effective control, noting that Jewish settlers in occupied

---

83 *Israeli Soldier Testimonies 2000–2010*, p. 26 (https://www.breakingthesilence.org.il/testimonies/publications).

84 See Addameer, Prisoner Support and Human Rights Association, *Administrative Detainees* (December 2018), https://www.addameer.org/the_prisoners/administrative_detainees.

85 See Addameer, "Fact 6: Illegal Transfer of Detainees," *10 Facts about Administrative Detention,* 5 November 2015, https://www.addameer.org/Campaign/sheets-and-reports/10-facts-about-administrative-detention.

Palestine are subject to a civil law regime, while a military regime applies to Palestinians in the West Bank, including East Jerusalem.

62. Despite the absolute prohibition of torture, Palestinians detained by Israel continue to be subjected to torture and ill-treatment (A/68/379). Methods of torture and ill-treatment reportedly include: sleep deprivation, excessive use of handcuffs, beatings, verbal abuse, stress positions, solitary confinement, humiliation, and threats of killing, sexual assault and house demolitions against the detainee or his or her family.[86]

63. In 1999 the Israeli High Court said that using certain methods of physical pressure for the purpose of "breaking" a detainee are unlawful and that interrogation methods must be fair and reasonable, and respectful of human dignity.[87] While representing an important recognition of the illegality of certain methods of torture employed against Palestinian detainees, the decision failed to outlaw torture by allowing the "ticking bomb" or "necessity" defense. According to Addameer, "necessity" is used by interrogators as a blanket defense with little to no accountability.[88] The Public Committee Against Torture in Israel reported that of 701 formal complaints of torture submitted between 2001 and 2010, none resulted in a criminal investigation.[89]

64. Palestinian children are not exempt. In 2013, UNICEF concluded that "Ill-treatment…appears to be widespread, systematic and institutionalized"[90] in the case of Palestinian children held in the Israeli military detention system. Israeli authorities seem to have taken some limited steps towards meeting the UNICEF

---

86 Ibid.

87 See B'Tselem, *Torture and Abuse in Interrogation,* 11 November 2017, https://www.btselem.org/torture/hcj_ruling.

88 See Addameer, "International Torture Day," 26 June 2018, https://www.addameer.org/news/international-torture-day.

89 PCATI, *Accountability Still Denied* (Periodic Update, January 2012), p. 4, available from https://maki.org.il/en/wp-content/uploads/2013/03/www.stoptorture.org.il_files_PCATI_eng_web.pdf. The formal complaints may not be representative of the actual number of victims.

90 UNICEF, *Children in Israeli Military Detention: Observations and Recommendations*, Bulletin No. 1 (October 2013), available from https://kipdf.com/children-in-israeli-military-detention-observations-and-recommendations_5af9a8ca7f8b9a179c8b4588.html.

recommendations,[91] including by piloting test summons in two West Bank areas instead of conducting frightening night arrests of children.[92] While this is clearly a needed development, it also shows just how the regular denial by Israel of the right to life and liberty of significant numbers of Palestinians is reflected in its policies, laws, and practices in occupied Palestine.

66. Article 2(b) refers to the imposition of living conditions calculated to cause a group's physical destruction in whole or in part. It seems unlikely that the policies, laws and practices of Israel can be said to have as their aim the physical destruction of the occupied people.[93]

67. Article 2(c) concerns measures calculated to prevent participation in the political, social, economic and cultural life of the country and the full development of a racial group, including and especially by denying them their rights to work, to education, to leave and to return to their country, to nationality, and to freedoms of movement and residence, opinion and expression, and peaceful assembly and association.

68. Violations of many of these rights have already been touched on in preceding sections. For instance, the violations by Israel of the rights to work, education, freedom of movement and residence, and freedom of expression and assembly have been illustrated in the context of discussing the Wall and its associated regime, and policies and laws related to the development of settlements, including in East Jerusalem. The rights to work, to freedom of movement, and to leave and return to one's country, are particularly relevant to Gaza. In the West Bank, the denial of rights to Palestinians is made possible by the existence of parallel legal systems operating in the same territory: one set of civil and criminal laws for Israeli settlers and another for Palestinian Arabs, subject to Israeli military orders, as well as other laws. While the

---

91 See, UNICEF, *Children in Israeli Military Detention: Observations and Recommendations*, Bulletin No. 1 (October 2013).

92 See also A/68/379 and CRC/C/ISR/CO/2-4.

93 The United Nations has questioned whether Gaza will be a livable place in 2020 ("*Gaza in 2020: A Livable Place?*" 2012). Considering the situation in Gaza, the Russell Tribunal found that Israeli policies aimed at causing displacement of Palestinians, rather than their physical destruction.

Israeli High Court of Justice formally exercises judicial oversight of the Israeli administration in occupied Palestine, according to NGOs, case law illustrates a trend whereby major policy decisions of government, e.g. relating to the Wall and settlements, tend to be immune from judicial intervention, and that human rights and protection under international humanitarian law have not been adequately upheld by the High Court in its rulings.[94] The creation of Israeli legal zones for settlers and the resulting segregation was noted in the 2013 report by the independent fact-finding mission on settlements (A/HRC/22/63). The Committee on the Elimination of Racial Discrimination in 2012 expressed that it was "extremely concerned" at policies and practices amounting to *de facto* segregation and that it was "particularly appalled at the hermetic character of the separation of the two groups" (CERD/C/ISR/CO/14–16, para. 24).

69. It is clear that Israeli measures, in the form of policies, laws and practices, have the effect of preventing Palestinians from full participation in the political, social, economic and cultural life of Palestine and arguably also prevent their full development in both the West Bank and the Gaza Strip.

70. Article 2(d) refers to measures designed to divide the population along racial lines including by the creation of separate reserves and ghettos for the members of a racial group or groups, and the expropriation of landed property. The expropriation of Palestinian land is an obvious part of the expansion of settlements and of the construction of the wall. The fragmentation of Palestinian land and creation of separate reserves and enclaves, including the plans threatening to cut off East Jerusalem from the rest of the West bank, is well documented (A/HRC/22/63). The final conclusions of the Russell Tribunal on Palestine state:

Israel has through its laws and practices divided the Israeli Jewish and Palestinian populations and allocated them different physical spaces, with varying levels and quality of infrastructure, services and access to resources. The end result is wholesale territorial fragmentation and a series of separate reserves and enclaves,

---

94 Information based on Diakonia reporting.

with the two groups largely segregated. The Tribunal heard evidence to the effect that such a policy is formally described in Israel as *hafrada*, Hebrew for "separation."[95] The Special Rapporteur has previously drawn attention to the dual system of roads in the West Bank, as a clear example of segregation, where Palestinians are largely relegated to alternative roads and forced to take long detours (A/HRC/16/72, paras. 20–22).

71. It seems incontestable that Israeli measures do divide the population of the Occupied Palestinian Territory along racial lines, create separate reserves for Palestinians and expropriate their land.

72. Article 2(e) refers to exploitation of labor. There exist historical reports as well as current campaigns and reports[96] which address poor working conditions of Palestinian citizens working in Israel or in settlements. However, it is noted that there has been a sharp drop in Israeli use of Palestinian workers since the 1990s, especially as it is now impossible for Gazans to work in Israel and since in the West Bank the construction of the Wall has further diminished the number of Palestinians working in Israel or for Israeli employers.[97]

73. Article 2(f) concerns persecution of those who oppose apartheid. This provision potentially relates to a wide range of human rights violations against Palestinians in the Occupied Palestinian Territory, who as a people desire self-determination and oppose the segregation, restrictions and discriminatory regime imposed by Israel on them. In this sense, the punitive response often meted out to those who demonstrate against the Wall and its associated regime, or more generally oppose Israeli violations of human rights, arguably fall under this provision.

74. An individual case in point concerns the Palestinian human rights defender Issa Amro, who is a founder of the NGOs Youth Against Settlements and Hebron Defenders. In 2012, Mr.

---

95 Russell Tribunal, *Findings*, para. 5.39.

96 See, "Palestinian children: The invisible workers of Israeli settlements," Defense for Children International–Palestine, 31 August 2013, https://www.dci-palestine.org/documents/palestinian-children-invisible-workers-israeli-settlements.

97 Russell Tribunal, *Findings*, para. 5.40.

Amro was arrested and detained 20 times without charge.[98] At the time of writing, he had been detained multiple times in 2013 and had been hospitalized, allegedly following a beating by ISF while in detention. In August 2013, a number of special rapporteurs, including this Special Rapporteur, expressed deep concern at his alleged ongoing judicial harassment, intimidation and abusive treatment. According to the Special Rapporteur on the situation of human rights defenders: "This is an unacceptable campaign of harassment, intimidation and reprisals against Mr. Amro, and other human rights defenders who peacefully advocate for the rights of Palestinians in the West Bank, including by cooperating with [United Nations] human rights bodies."

75. Omar Saad is an example of an Israeli citizen belonging to the Druze minority, who has reportedly been imprisoned for his conscientious objection to serving in the Israeli army. In an open letter to the Prime Minister and Minister of Defense he explained: "I couldn't imagine myself wearing military uniform and participating in the suppression of my Palestinian people." He asked: "How can I be a soldier standing at Qalandia checkpoint or any other checkpoint, after I experienced the injustices at these checkpoints? How can I prevent someone from Ramallah to visit his city, Jerusalem? How can I guard the apartheid wall? How can I be a jailer to my own people while I know that the majority of prisoners are freedom prisoners and seekers of rights and freedom?[99]

76. It is strongly arguable that those who oppose Israeli measures amounting to apartheid risk persecution because of their opposition.

---

98 See UN press release, "Ninety-third session of the Committee on the Elimination of Racial Discrimination to be held in Geneva from 31 July to 25 August," 27 July 2017, https://www.ohchr.org/en/press-releases/2017/07/ninety-third-session-committee-elimination-racial-discrimination-be-held.

99 See "I'm Omar Saad and I will not be a soldier in your army," *War Resisters International,* https://wri-irg.org/en/programmes/rrtk/co-declaration/2012/im-omar-saad-and-i-will-not-be-soldier-your-army.

Systematic oppression

77. None of the human rights violations discussed in the context of possibly constituting "inhuman acts" for the purpose of the International Convention on the Suppression and Punishment of the Crime of Apartheid or the Rome Statute can be said to be isolated events. Rather, their commission reflects systematic and discriminatory Israeli policies, laws, and practices, which determine where in the occupied land Palestinians may or may not travel, live and work. Laws and policies have also institutionalized just how lightly a civilian Palestinian life may be weighed, when placed on the scales against claims of overarching security concerns, contrasting with the legal protection of the Israeli constitutional system given to unlawful Israeli settlers. The combined effect of the measures designed to ensure security for Israeli citizens, to facilitate and expand settlements, and, it would appear, to annex land, is *hafrada*, discrimination and systematic oppression of, and domination over, the Palestinian people.

CHAPTER SIX

SELECTIONS FROM THE REPORTS OF SPECIAL RAPPORTEUR MICHAEL LYNK

(1 May 2016–30 April 2022)

The Right to Development in the Occupied Palestinian Territory
October 2016 Report (UNGA) – The Right to Development in the Occupied Palestinian Territory (A/71/554)

38. Thirty years ago, the General Assembly adopted the Declaration on the Right to Development.[1] The Declaration, and its subsequent elaborations, state that every human being and all peoples have an inalienable right to economic and social development that is equitable and just, sustainable, participatory and inclusive, non-discriminatory, grounded in the rule of law and fully observant of all human rights and freedoms. The right to development has been recognized as a human right itself, which raises its status to one with universal applicability and inviolability.[2] While the Declaration is not legally binding per se, it encompasses many of the legal rights and obligations—civil, political, economic, social and cultural—that are recognized as binding on all States parties through the various human rights treaties enacted by the international community over the past 70 years.[3] In turn,

1 Resolution 41/128, annex. The right was reaffirmed in subsequent international human rights instruments, including the Vienna Declaration and Programme of Action (1993).

2 Declaration on the Right to Development, article 1, para. 1; Arjun Sengupta, "On the theory and practice of the right to development," *Human Rights Quarterly* 24, no. 4 (2002): 837.

3 The Declaration on the Right to Development is anchored in the International Covenant on Economic, Social and Cultural Rights (United Nations, Treaty

Library).

the Declaration has been expressly incorporated within the 2030 Agenda for Sustainable Development.[4]

39. The Declaration on the Right to Development is particularly relevant to understanding the human rights predicament in the Occupied Palestinian Territory. Among other rights, the Declaration expressly includes the following human rights that are binding in international law:

(a) The self-determination of peoples (art. 1);

(b) The elimination of foreign domination and occupation (art. 5);

(c) The prohibition against discrimination and the flagrant abuse of human rights (art. 6);

(d) The full enjoyment of all human rights and fundamental freedoms, including socioeconomic rights (arts. 6 and 8);

(e) Full sovereignty over one's natural resources (art. 1);

(f) Participatory decision-making in public affairs (arts. 2 and 8).

These rights lie at the core of the binding human rights and humanitarian obligations under international law, which apply in full to the Occupied Palestinian Territory.[5] They establish not only rights for the Palestinian people, but also create obligations for Israel, the Occupying Power, to respect and protect those rights. The Palestinian people's right of self-determination is widely accepted by the international community,[6] and the International

---

Series, vol. 993, no. 14531) and the International Covenant on Civil and Political Rights (United Nations, Treaty Series, vol. 999, no. 4668). For a table linking the rights set out in the declaration to legally binding instruments under international law, see OHCHR, *Frequently Asked Questions on the Right to Development* fact sheet No. 37 (Geneva, 2016).

4 UNGA Resolution 70/1, para. 10.

5 *Legal Consequences of the Construction of a Wall in the Occupied Palestinian Territory*, Advisory Opinion, I.C.J. Reports 2004, paras. 86–114 and para. 149. These rights are also enumerated in binding human rights treaties, including the Universal Declaration of Human Rights, the International Covenant on Civil and Political Rights and the International Covenant on Economic, Social and Cultural Rights

6 See UNGA resolution 70/141.

Court of Justice has stated that "Israel is bound to comply with its obligations to respect the right of the Palestinian people to self-determination and its obligations under international humanitarian law and international human rights law."[7] While the question of development is necessarily complex in the context of occupation, it is essential that human rights and humanitarian law be interpreted in a way that is consistent with the right to development, regardless of the length of occupation.

Economic and social development in the Occupied Palestinian Territory

41. The Palestinian economy is without parallel in the modern world. Its territorial components—the West Bank, including East Jerusalem, and Gaza—are separated physically from one other. Its largest geographic entity, the West Bank, has been divided by Israel into an archipelago of small islands of densely populated areas disconnected from one another by the Wall or by settlements, bypass roads connecting the settlements to each other and to the Israeli transportation system, roadblocks, exclusive zoning laws, restricted areas and military no-go zones. Within these areas occupied by Israel, the local political authority is likewise splintered: the Palestinian Authority has limited rule over a part of the fragmented West Bank, Gaza is governed by a separate political authority not accountable to the Palestinian Authority, and Israel has illegally annexed East Jerusalem.[8] Furthermore, Israel has imposed a comprehensive land, sea, and air blockade on Gaza since 2007. Within the West Bank, Israel exercises full civil and security authority over "Area C," which makes up over 60 percent of this part of the territory and completely surrounds and divides the archipelago of Palestinian cities and towns, a hybrid

---

7 *Legal Consequences of the Construction of a Wall*, Advisory Opinion, para. 149.

8 The Security Council has stated that Israel's annexation of East Jerusalem is contrary to international law, and that East Jerusalem is deemed to be part of the Occupied Palestinian Territory. See Security Council resolution 476 (1980) and resolution 478 (1980).

situation that one human rights group has called "occunexation."[9] The Occupied Palestinian Territory lacks any secure transit access, whether by land, sea, or air, to the outside world. All of its borders, with one exception, are controlled by Israel.[10] No other society in the world faces such an array of cumulative challenges that includes belligerent occupation, territorial discontinuity, political and administrative divergence, geographic confinement and economic disconnectedness.

42. The Oslo Accords of 1993, and the Protocol on Economic Relations between the government of the State of Israel and the Palestine Liberation Organization (the Paris Protocol on Economic Relations, 1994) were meant to be interim arrangements and were considered by Palestine as a diplomatic and economic pathway for Palestinian independence by 1999. During that transitional period, the Oslo Accords left intact the extensive Israeli settlement project and permitted Israel broad authority to act on security concerns throughout the Occupied Palestinian Territory. The Paris Protocol created an economic framework with a significant reliance on Israel for currency, customs-union style trade provisions, foreign exchange arrangements and tax collection capacity that effectively maintained Palestinian dependence on Israel. A final peace settlement between Israel and Palestine has not materialized, and those interim arrangements have now become entrenched. The consequence has been that, while the Palestinian Authority has built much of the administrative and institutional capacity for national governance, it lacks the necessary economic foundation for sovereign development.[11] Since 2000, the Palestinian economy has experienced a volatile economic growth trajectory.

---

9 Association for Civil Rights in Israel, "49 Years of Control without Rights: Human rights of the Palestinians in the West Bank and East Jerusalem – what has changed?," 1 June 2016. Available from https://www.acri.org.il/en/wp-content/uploads/2016/06/49years2016-en.pdf.

10 The only external border point not directly controlled by Israel is the Rafah crossing between Gaza and Egypt. Rafah is used almost exclusively as a civilian crossing, and not as an economic trading junction. Egypt has kept this crossing closed for much of the past three years.

11 World Bank, "West Bank and Gaza: towards economic sustainability of a future Palestinian State—promoting private sector-led growth" (World Bank Group, 2012).

When growth has occurred, it has been judged to be unsustainable because (a) it has been highly dependent upon foreign aid and private consumption of imports,[12] and (b) the Israeli occupation has increasingly separated and shrunk the different regions of the Palestinian territory, creating a dysfunctional economic base deprived of the capacity for autonomous development.[13]

43. The contradictions of attempting to build a sovereign economy under a prolonged occupation, without the realization of genuine self-determination on the foreseeable horizon, have become quite apparent. A stifled and distorted Palestinian economy cannot provide a viable foundation for the sustainable and equitable social development of the Occupied Palestinian Territory. Certainly, Palestine has made steady progress in several important social areas, including maternal mortality, levels of literacy and education, and vaccination rates. Yet, other key indicators point to a serious situation, with social conditions and living standards stagnating or getting worse:

(a) The Palestinian economy has not advanced. In 2014, Palestinian real gross domestic product (GDP) per capita was at virtually the same level as it was in 1999, with Gaza's real GDP per capita standing at only 71 percent of its 1999 level.[14]

(b) Unemployment is growing as a social scourge. In 2016, it stood at 27 percent in the Occupied Palestinian Territory, compared to 12 percent in 1999; in Gaza, the unemployment crisis is particularly acute, where it has reached 42 percent,

---

12 World Bank, "Economic monitoring report to the ad hoc liaison committee" (World Bank Group, April 2016).

13 World Bank, "West Bank and Gaza: towards economic sustainability of a future Palestinian State—promoting private sector-led growth," and UNCTAD/APP/2016/1.

14 In 2014, real GDP per capita income in the Occupied Palestinian Territory (West Bank and Gaza, not including East Jerusalem) stood at $1,737. In 1999, it stood at $1,723. In 2014, Gaza's real GDP per capita income was $971, compared to $1,372 in 1999. All figures are in constant 2004 United States dollars; current (nominal) GDP per capita figures are higher. See data published by the Palestinian Central Bureau of Statistics at https://www.pcbs.gov.ps/default.aspx.

with 58 percent of its youth (aged between 15 and 29) without work, among the highest rates in the world.[15]

(c) Poverty has been increasing among Palestinians since 2012, with 26 percent of the population now deemed to be poor, and 13 percent estimated to suffer from extreme poverty.[16] Food insecurity is endemic: an estimated 2.4 million people in the West Bank and Gaza (57 percent of the population) are projected to require some form of humanitarian assistance in 2016.[17]

(d) The industrial, agricultural and natural resource sectors are steadily shrinking in economic significance and employment size, owing to, inter alia: Israeli restrictions on market access; low confidence among potential investors because of political uncertainty; the significant loss of arable land to the Occupying Power; lack of effective economic planning powers; limited Palestinian control over important natural resources (water, land, stone quarrying, and oil and gas reserves); and the limited access to fishing resources.[18] The economy has become deindustrialized and its ability to export has been undercut by the decline of the agriculture and manufacturing sectors.[19]

---

15 World Bank, "Economic monitoring report to the ad hoc liaison committee" (World Bank Group, September 2016).

16 United Nations Educational, Scientific and Cultural Organization (UNESCO), country programming document for Palestine, 2014–2017.

17 Office for the Coordination of Humanitarian Affairs, "Humanitarian dashboard: 2nd quarter 2016," 18 August 2016. UNRWA reported in March 2016 that 70 percent of the total refugee population in Gaza, over 930,000 people, were dependent on food assistance, dramatically up from 10 per cent in 2000. See Gaza Situation Report 137, 31 March 2016, available at https://www.unrwa.org/newsroom/emergency-reports/gaza-situation-report-137.

18 See UNCTAD/APP/2016/1. The World Bank acknowledged in 2015 that "the competitiveness of the Palestinian economy has been progressively eroding since the signing of the Oslo accords, in particular its industry and agriculture." See World Bank, "Economic monitoring report to the ad hoc liaison committee" (World Bank Group, September 2015).

19 World Bank, "Economic monitoring report to the ad hoc liaison committee" (World Bank Group, September 2016).

(e) The Occupied Palestinian Territory continues to be a captive trading market for Israel, as it has been throughout the occupation: in recent years, about 85 percent of Palestinian exports have gone to Israel, and it received 70 percent of its imports from Israel. The restrictions and imbalance in the trading relationship contributed to maintaining a chronic trade deficit in the Palestinian economy of $5.2 billion in 2015, some 41 percent of GDP.[20]

(f) Symptomatic of the Palestinian government's precarious economic management powers are the substantial fiscal leakages that the Palestinian government and the Palestinian economy suffer under the current revenue-sharing and collection agreements with Israel. These arrangements are estimated by the World Bank and the United Nations Conference on Trade and Development (UNCTAD) to cost the Palestinian economy at least $640 million annually (amounting to 5 percent of GDP).[21]

(g) UNCTAD has estimated that, without the occupation, the economy of the Occupied Palestinian Territory could double its GDP, with significant reductions not only in the unemployment and poverty levels, but also in the chronic trade and budget deficits.[22]

Shrinking Space for Human Rights Defenders
March 2017 Report (UNHRC) – Human Rights Defenders (A/ HRC/34/70)

38. In compiling the evidence for the present report, the Special Rapporteur has been in direct communication with human rights organizations in Palestine and Israel. Their common observation was that the protections and respect accorded to them,

---

20 UNCTAD/APP/2016/1. All amounts are in United States dollars.

21 See World Bank, "Economic monitoring report to the ad hoc liaison committee" (World Bank Group, April 2016) and UNCTAD/APP/2016/1.

22 UNCTAD/APP/2016/1.

which were already precarious by the end of 2008, had declined precipitously after Operation Cast Lead in Gaza in December 2008 and January 2009. This hostile atmosphere for human rights defenders has since become even more overtly toxic and harsh since 2015, in the aftermath of Operation Protective Edge in Gaza in 2014 and the subsequent initiation by the International Criminal Court of a preliminary investigation, with the cooperation of a number of Palestinian human rights defenders, into possible war crimes and crimes against humanity committed during the most recent Gaza conflict and by the Israeli settlement project. In the words of one leading human rights group: "We are seeing a general assault by the government and right-wing groups on those parts of Israeli society that are still standing up for democratic values. The aim is to silence us."[23]

39. Palestinian human rights organizations report that they have endured a repressive working environment in recent years, with their day-to-day operations stymied by concerted efforts from the government of Israel, the Israeli military, private Israeli organizations and unknown individuals or groups to discredit and sabotage their work.[24] The escalation in threats and physical assaults, cyberattacks, arrests and incarceration under military and administrative orders and bans and restrictions on movement is exacerbated by the absence of any effective means for remedies or protection. A report by the Human Rights Defenders Fund in 2015 found that the Israeli military and the occupation authorities had employed a promiscuous range of criminal, security, and legal tools to harass and constrain the entirely legitimate and peaceful activities of human rights defenders in the Occupied Palestinian Territory. As the author observed:

---

23 Sarit Michaeli, spokeswoman for B'Tselem, quoted in David Shulman, "Israel: the broken silence," *The New York Review of Books*, 7 April 2016.

24 The Special Rapporteur's mandate, as defined in resolution 1993/2, is focused on violations of the law committed by Israel as the Occupying Power and thus the present analysis is limited to that discussion. There are undoubtedly other groups, such as the Government of the State of Palestine, who similarly have an obligation to respect and protect human rights, including those of human rights defenders.

In addition to draconian legislative attempts and ongoing efforts to depict them as public enemies, many human rights defenders, particularly activists, are the target of systematic criminalization efforts. Protesters are arrested and detained even when they do not break the law, they are subjected to strict conditions of release and are often indicted simply for their efforts to promote human rights.[25]

40. Al-Haq, a leading Palestinian non-governmental human rights organization, has endured a grievous pattern of threats and cyberattacks and a campaign of attempted interference with its work by persons unknown. Beginning in the autumn of 2015 and continuing into 2016, a series of detailed letters from either anonymous individuals or individuals impersonating someone else were sent to donors and partners of Al-Haq, purporting to raise serious concerns about fraud, corruption, financial disarray, lack of transparency and organizational disunity at the organization. Al-Haq was obliged to expend considerable resources refuting the unfounded allegations, including having its auditors, Ernst and Young, assure the partners and donors that there had been no financial or institutional malfeasance. Other messages contained explicit threats to the lives or well-being of various Al-Haq employees, including its General Director, Shawan Jabarin.

41 The Al-Mezan Center for Human Rights, based in Gaza, received a series of anonymous e-mail messages, Facebook posts and calls in 2015 and 2016, sent to staff, donors and partners in which institutional corruption and mismanagement were alleged and explicit threats to the lives and safety of its employees were made. Like Al-Haq, Al-Mezan has been active since 2015 in advocating accountability before the International Criminal Court for possible war crimes.

---

25 See Palestinian Human Rights Organizations Council, "PHROC Presents Oral Statement of Culture of Impunity in Israel," *Al-Haq,* 24 September 2012, https://www.alhaq.org/palestinian-human-rights-organizations-council/6832. html. (Submission to UN SR on the OPT Re HRDs November 2016); Human Rights Defenders Fund, "Disturbing the peace: the use of criminal law to limit the actions of human rights defenders in Israel and the Occupied Palestinian Territories" (2015), p. 63.

42. Youth against Settlements, a Hebron-based human rights organization, has had its center raided several times by Israeli soldiers and it has been effectively closed on occasions after the Israeli military declared the neighborhood surrounding it to be a closed military zone.[26] In November 2016, the Israeli military conducted a night raid on the Health Development Information and Policy Institute, a Palestinian health advocacy organization based in Ramallah. They seized computers, servers, and security camera footage, and left the offices in a shambles. In accordance with the Oslo Accords, the Palestinian Authority is supposed to have complete political and security control in Ramallah and other parts of Area A of the West Bank, but the Israeli military routinely tramples over this nominal Palestinian sovereignty.[27]

46. Human rights organizations working in Gaza face a unique array of obstacles to the conduct of their work. Among the biggest is their non-existent freedom of movement, as described in detail above. For human rights defenders in Gaza this means that they are rarely allowed to journey to Israel, the West Bank or abroad. They cannot travel to regional or international human rights meetings and forums; they cannot attend external training programs; their ability to participate by videoconferencing is restricted by the sporadic electricity supply in Gaza and the limitations of the medium; and their ability to interact, inform and work with the rest of the world is likewise diminished. This enforced isolation substantially impairs the protection and advancement of human rights in Gaza.[28]

47. Israeli human rights defenders who work on the many issues related to the Occupied Palestinian Territory are also experiencing an increasingly virulent environment. A moment that exemplifies this turning of the screw was in October 2016,

---

26 Submissions from human rights organizations to the Special Rapporteur.

27 Marsad, "Israeli forces invade Ramallah offices of health work NGO," 16 November 2016, available from https://www.marsad.ps/en/2016/11/16/israeli-forces-invade-ramallah-offices-healthwork-ngo/

28 Communications with leaders of the Palestine Center for Human Rights and the Al-Mezan Center for Human Rights; and Gisha, "Split apart. Palestinian civil society in its own words on the impact of the separation policy and the potential should the policy be reversed," March 2016.

when Hagai El-Ad, the Director-General of B'Tselem, delivered a presentation to the Security Council in New York. He warned of the expanding settlement enterprise and the deteriorating human rights situation for the Palestinians in the Occupied Palestinian Territory, and cited the need for effective international intervention to bring the Israeli occupation to an end.[29] In response, many in the Israeli political leadership stridently denounced B'Tselem, casting it as unpatriotic, traitorous and a political outcast. Prime Minister Benjamin Netanyahu condemned Mr. El-Ad for joining the "chorus of slander" against Israel, stating: "What these organizations cannot achieve through democratic elections in Israel, they try to achieve by international coercion."[30] The Likud Member of the Knesset and whip for the governing coalition, David Bitan, demanded that Mr. El-Ad be stripped of his Israeli citizenship.[31] Danny Danon, Permanent Representative of Israel to the United Nations, said: "It is a shame that Israeli groups have been drafted into the diplomatic terror war that the Palestinians are waging against us."[32]

48. Notwithstanding these toxic attacks and the failure of the government to provide the protections and space for civil society to operate, several prominent Israeli intellectuals and advocates publicly defended B'Tselem and American Friends of Peace Now for their presentations at the Security Council. Professor Ze'ev Sternhell stated that: "The one who forced the civil society groups to turn to international public opinion and international institutions is the government of Israel itself," while Michael Sfard, a human rights lawyer, wrote that "the occupation is not an internal Israeli

---

29 See "Hagai El-Ad's address in a special discussion about settlements at the United Nations Security Council," 2016 October 14, https://www.btselem.org/settlements/20161014_security_council_address; and "APN's Lara Friedman Addresses the United Nations Security Council on Settlements," 2016 October 14, *APN*, peacenow.org/page.php?name=lara-addresses-the-unsc#.WNJ9UG_ytpg.

30 See Jonathan Lis, "Netanyahu's Coalition Whip to Push Bill Barring Calls for Sanctions Against Israel in Int'l Forum," Haaretz, 22 October 2016, https://www.haaretz.com/israel-news/1.748737.

31 See https://www.haaretz.com/israel-news/1.748609.

32 Dov Benovadia, "Netanyahu: Leftist Groups That Testified at U.N. Security Council 'Beyond the Pale,'" *Hamodia,* 16 Oct 2016, hamodia.com/2016/10/16/netanyahu-leftist-groups-that-testified-at-u-n-security-council-beyond-the-pale/.

matter. And even if it were, human rights are always a matter for the entire international community."[33]

62. The 50-year occupation of the Palestinian territories, which becomes more pervasive by the day with no end even remotely in sight, has been profoundly corrosive of human rights and democratic values. How could it be otherwise? To perpetuate an alien rule over almost 5 million people, against their fervent wishes, inevitably requires the repression of rights, erosion of the rule of law, the abrogation of international commitments, the imposition of deeply discriminatory practices, the hollowing-out of well-accepted standards of military behavior, subjugation of the humanity of the "other," denial of trends that are plainly evident, the embrace of illiberal politics and—the focus of the present report—the scorning of those civil society organizations that raise uncomfortable truths about the disfigured state of human rights under occupation.

63. A government that honors human rights and democratic values and takes seriously its obligations under the Declaration on Human Rights Defenders would protect and encourage the work of human rights defenders, not ostracize and isolate them. It would publicly denounce any incitement against human rights defenders and would certainly not engage in inflaming the public against them. It would recognize the fundamental status in law of the freedoms of association, assembly, expression, and opinion, and of movement, and would do all that it could to enable human rights defenders to enjoy them. Such a government would respect the critical scrutiny of their work, even if their reports and allegations excoriated the conduct of that government. It would treat all NGOs equitably. It would enact legislation to enlarge the freedoms of human rights defenders and it would never impose discriminatory statutes or programs that impaired their work. If it was to criticize human rights defenders, its comments would be measured and constructive. If and when threats or acts of violence were directed towards human rights defenders, its military and

---

33 Zeev Sternhell, "Yes, Israelis, we must air our dirty laundry in public," *Haaretz*, 21 October 2016; Michael Sfard, "It's every Israeli's right, and duty, to speak up – including at the UN," *Haaretz*, 24 October 2016.

police services would act promptly to impartially investigate and prosecute. It would strive to build collaborative relationships with human rights defenders and take advantage of their experience and expertise to deepen the respect of the public for human rights and their defenders. And such a government—even one conducting a long-term occupation—would accept that human rights can be infringed only as a last measure and then only in a minimally impairing manner that is subject to meaningful judicial review.

64. In all these respects, the government of Israel has been significantly deficient in honoring its obligations under the Declaration on Human Rights Defenders. On the evidence gathered for the present report, its treatment of human rights defenders, be they Palestinian, Israeli, or international, who work on the vital issues arising from the occupation, has been contrary to the basic guarantees of international human rights law. Nor is the situation improving. As the occupation becomes further entrenched,[34] and as human rights defenders persist with their intrepid activism to investigate and oppose the regime of human rights violations that is integral to the occupation, all indications are that they will continue to be among the prime targets of those who are intolerant of their criticisms and alarmed by their effectiveness.

Legal Framework of Occupation: Is the Israeli Occupation Illegal?

October 2017 Report (UNGA) – The Legality of the Israeli Occupation (A/72/556)

General principles of international law and occupation

20. Two decades into the twenty-first century, the norm that guides our global community is that people are citizens,

---

34 See Ian Fisher, "Israel passes provocative law to retroactively legalize settlements," *New York Times*, 6 February 2017; and Isabel Kershner, "Emboldened by Trump, Israel approves a wave of West Bank settlement expansion," *New York Times*, 24 January 2017.

not subjects, of the State that rules them. Accordingly, they are entitled to express their legal identity and their inalienable rights through their sovereign State. Colonialism, occupation and other forms of alien rule are very much the exception to this norm, and they can only be justified in law and international practice as a short-term and abnormal condition that is leading unhesitatingly towards self-determination and/or sovereignty. Most other forms of alien rule would be, *ipso facto*, unlawful.

21. In our modern world, fundamental rights and protections (including protections under international humanitarian law, civil and political rights such as the right of self-determination, and economic, social and cultural rights) are to be given a purposive and broad interpretation and a liberal application. This is because they embody the rights and freedoms that go to the core of our humanity and are meant to be universally available to, and actionable by, all of us.[35] Conversely, exceptions to these fundamental rights (such as military necessity, significant threats to national security or public emergencies) are to be interpreted and applied in a measured and narrow fashion, so as not to unduly impair the breadth, accessibility and enjoyment of these fundamental rights by all peoples.[36]

22. Created in the aftermath of the bitter experiences of total war and extreme civilian suffering in the nineteenth and twentieth centuries, international humanitarian law is embodied in the Regulations annexed to the Convention respecting the Laws and Customs of War on Land of 1907 (the Hague Regulations), the Geneva Convention relative to the Protection of Civilians in Time of War of 12 August 1949 (the Fourth Geneva Convention) and the Protocol Additional to the Geneva Conventions of 12 August 1949 and relating to the protection of victims of international armed conflicts of 1977 (Protocol I), among other instruments, as well as in the practices of the modern world. Three of the core purposes of

---

35 International Covenant on Civil and Political Rights and International Covenant on Economic, Social and Cultural Rights

36 International Covenant on Civil and Political Rights, art. 4 ("...may take measures derogating from their obligations under the present Covenant to the extent strictly required by the exigencies of the situation ..."); and International Covenant on Economic, Social and Cultural Rights, art. 4.

modern international humanitarian law as related to foreign military occupation are: (a) to closely regulate an occupation to ensure that the territory achieves, or is restored to, a state of sovereignty; (b) to prevent the territory from becoming a fruit of conquest; and (c) to safeguard the protected people under occupation. As with other areas of international law, international humanitarian law is constantly evolving—within the natural scope of its foundational instruments, principles and purposes—to address new challenges in humanitarian protection in situations where the answers are not always expressly laid out in these primary documents.[37]

25. Israel has occupied the Palestinian territory (the West Bank, including East Jerusalem, and Gaza) since June 1967. As such, the Fourth Geneva Convention applies in full. This legal determination has been affirmed by the Security Council on a consistent and regular basis, starting at the very beginning of the occupation in June 1967 and restated most recently in December 2016. This is also the position stated at a 2014 Conference of High Contracting Parties to the Fourth Geneva Convention.[38] As such, the Palestinians in the occupied territory are "protected persons" under international humanitarian law, and are entitled to all of the protections of the Fourth Geneva Convention.[39] Israel has denied the application of the Fourth Geneva Convention and does not recognize the Palestinian territory as being occupied,[40] a position that the international community has widely rejected.[41]

---

37 Eyal Benvenisti, *The International Law of Occupation* (Princeton, New Jersey: Princeton University Press, 2004) (". . . it [is] not simply a task of looking up the relevant articles in The Hague Regulations or the Fourth Geneva Convention. International law has evolved significantly since the time these two instruments were drafted.").

38 A/69/711-S/2015/1, annex, para. 4.

39 Article 4.

40 Israel, Ministry of Foreign Affairs, "Israel settlements and international law," 30 November 2015 ("In legal terms, the West Bank is best regarded as territory over which there are competing claims which should be resolved in peace process negotiations"). Available from https://www.mfa.gov.il/mfa/foreignpolicy/peace/guide/pages/israeli%20settlements%20and%20international%20law.aspx.

41 See UNGA resolution 71/96, affirming the applicability of the Fourth Geneva Convention to the Occupied Palestinian Territory, adopted by a vote of

26. With these principles and observations in mind, a four-part test is proposed to determine whether an occupier is administering the occupation in a manner consistent with international law and the laws of occupation, or whether it has exceeded its legal capacity and its rule is illegal.

Test as to whether a belligerent occupier remains a lawful occupant

27. As the Israeli occupation of the Palestinian territory has lengthened in time, and with many of its features found to be in flagrant violation of international law, some international legal scholars have raised the issue of whether an occupation that was once regarded as lawful can cross a tipping point and become illegal. Professor Eyal Benvenisti has written that: ". . . it would seem that an occupant that in bad faith stalls efforts for a peaceful ending to its rule would be considered an aggressor and its rule would be tainted with illegality."[42] Professors Ben-Naftali, Gross and Michaeli take a broader view, arguing that violation of any of the fundamental legal principles of occupation (listed below) "renders an occupation illegal per se."[43] Professor Gross has extended this argument more recently to emphasize the importance of analyzing whether an indefinite or permanent occupation has become illegal, so as to counter "... the risk of occupation becoming conquest or a new form of colonialism while hiding behind an imagined temporality."[44] They have provided the intellectual foundation for the following test.

28. The four elements of the lawful occupant test are:

(a) The belligerent occupier cannot annex any of the occupied territory

---

168 to 6 with 6 abstentions. See also Aeyal Gross, *The Writing on the Wall: Rethinking the International Law of Occupation* (Cambridge University Press, 2017)

42 Benvenisti.

43 Orna Ben-Naftali, Aeyal M. Gross and Keren Michaeli, "Illegal Occupation: Framing the Occupied Palestinian Territory," *Berkeley Journal of International Law* 23, no. 3 (2005): 55.

44 Gross, *The Writing on the Wall.*

(b) The belligerent occupation must be temporary and cannot be either permanent or indefinite; and the occupant must seek to end the occupation and return the territory to the sovereign as soon as reasonably possible

(c) During the occupation, the belligerent occupier is to act in the best interests of the people under occupation; and

(d) The belligerent occupier must administer the occupied territory in good faith, including acting in full compliance with its duties and obligations under international law and as a member of the United Nations.

Application of the legality test to Israel's occupation

Prohibition against annexation

45. Israel's formal annexation of East Jerusalem in 1967 and 1980, and its *de facto* annexation of significant parts of the West Bank, are intended to solidify its claim for sovereignty. This constitutes a flagrant breach of the absolute prohibition against annexation and violates Israel's obligations under international law.

46. After capturing the Palestinian territory (the West Bank, including East Jerusalem, and Gaza) in the June 1967 war, Israel annexed East Jerusalem and parts of the West Bank in late June 1967 by a Cabinet decision. In July 1967, the General Assembly unanimously denounced the annexation and called upon Israel to rescind the measures that would alter the status of Jerusalem.[45] Subsequently, in July 1980, the Israeli Knesset adopted the Basic Law on Jerusalem, declaring Jerusalem to be the "complete and united" capital of Israel. The Security Council in August 1980 censured Israel "in the strongest terms" for its enactment of the Basic Law, affirmed that the Law was in breach of international law, and determined that Israel's annexation was "null and void" and "must be rescinded forthwith."[46] Israel remains non-compliant with all United Nations resolutions on Jerusalem; there are presently

---

45 UNGA Resolutions 2253 (ES-V) and 2254 (ES-V).
46 UNSC Resolutions 476 (1980) and 478 (1980).

about 210,000 Israeli settlers living in Occupied East Jerusalem, and Israel has stated that it will not leave East Jerusalem.[47]

47. Beyond Jerusalem, Israel is actively establishing the *de facto* annexation of parts of the occupied West Bank. The International Court of Justice, in the Advisory Opinion on the Construction of a Wall, warned that the reality of the Wall and the settlements regime was constituting a fait accompli and *de facto* annexation.[48] The Association for Civil Rights in Israel has characterized Israel's regime in the West Bank as an "occunexation."[49] Professor Omar Dajani has observed that, given the absolute prohibition today in international law against conquest, acquisitive States have an incentive to obfuscate the reality of annexation.[50] In the West Bank, Israel exercises complete control over Area C (making up 60 percent of the West Bank), where its 400,000 settlers live in approximately 225 settlements. The settlers live under Israeli law in Israeli-only settlements, drive on an Israeli-only road system, and benefit greatly from the enormous sums of public money spent by Israel on entrenching, defending and expanding the settlements. Few of these benefits, except incidentally, flow to the Palestinians in Area C. Only 1 percent of Area C is designated for Palestinian use, notwithstanding the approximately 300,000 Palestinians who live there.[51] What country would invest so heav-

---

47 Prime Minister of Israel, Benjamin Netanyahu, in 2015: "Forty-eight years ago, the division of Jerusalem was ended and we returned to be united...We will keep Jerusalem united under Israeli authority." See Oren Liebermann, "Benjamin Netanyahu: Jerusalem will remain united city," *CNN*, 2015 May 17, https://www.cnn.com/2015/05/17/middleeast/israel-netanyahu-united-jerusalem/.

48 *Legal Consequences of the Construction of a Wall*, Advisory Opinion, para. 121.

49 The Association for Civil Rights in Israel, "49 Years of Control without Rights: Human rights of the Palestinians in the West Bank and East Jerusalem—What has changed?" (2016), https://www.acri.org.il/en/wp-content/uploads/2016/ 06/49years2016-en.pdf.

50 Omar Dajani, "Israel's creeping annexation," *American Journal of International Law Unbound* 111 (January 2017): 51–56.

51 Orhan Niksic, Nur Nasser Eddin and Massimiliano Cali, *Area C and the Future of the Palestinian Economy* (Washington, D.C.:World Bank, 2014); and Diakonia International Humanitarian Law Resource Centre, "Planning to fail: The planning regime in Area C of the West Bank—an international law perspective" (2013).

ily over so many years to establish so many immutable facts on the ground in an occupied territory if it did not intend to remain permanently?[52]

Occupations must be temporary, and not indefinite or permanent

48. Israel's occupation is 50 years old and counting. The duration of this occupation is without precedent or parallel in today's world.[53] Professor Adam Roberts has stated that an occupation becomes prolonged if it lasts longer than five years into a period, closely resembling peacetime, when hostility is reduced.[54] Modern occupations that have broadly adhered to the strict principles concerning temporariness, non-annexation, trusteeship and good faith have not exceeded 10 years, including the American occupation of Japan, the Allied occupation of western Germany and the American-led coalition's occupation of Iraq.[55]

49. Employing the precept that the longer the occupation, the greater the onus on the Occupying Power to justify its continuation, Israel lacks any persuasive reason to remain as the occupant after 50 years. Israel has signed peace treaties with Egypt (1981) and Jordan (1994) that have stood the test of time, and the absence of peace agreements with its other two neighbors (the Syrian Arab Republic and Lebanon) cannot be invoked to justify its continuing

---

52 Prime Minister of Israel, Benjamin Netanyahu, in 2017: "We are here to stay forever. There will be no further uprooting of settlements in the Land of Israel . . . This is our land." See Noga Tarnopolsky, "Netanyahu says Israel won't retreat on Jewish settlements: 'We are here to stay forever,'" *Los Angeles Times,* 2017 August 28, https://www.latimes.com/world/middleeast/la-fg-israel-netanyahu-settlements-20170828-story.html.

53 Yoram Dinstein, *The International Law of Belligerent Occupation* (Cambridge University Press, 2009).

54 Adam Roberts, "Prolonged military occupation: the Israeli Occupied Territories since 1967," *American Journal of International Law* 84, no. 1 (January 1990): 44–103.

55 These three occupations are sometimes cited as examples of "transformative" occupations, which raise separate legal questions that are not addressed in the present report. See generally, Gregory Fox, "Transformative occupation and the unilateralist impulse," *International Review of the Red Cross* 94, no. 885 (March 2012): 237–266.

occupation of the Palestinian territory. Contrary to the repeated declarations by many Israeli leaders, the Palestinian Authority is accepted by the international community as a legitimate negotiating partner for peace. The primary engine of Israel's ongoing occupation—the settlement enterprise—detracts from, rather than enhances, Israel's security.[56] Professor Gershon Shafir has written that: "A circular logic is in play here: Israel is able to use the stipulation of the temporary character of occupation to make long term changes in the name of extended security risks, many of which are the result of the violations of the law of occupation."[57]

50. The only credible explanation for Israel's continuation of the occupation and its thickening of the settlement regime is to enshrine its sovereign claim over part or all of the Palestinian territory, a colonial ambition par excellence. Every Israeli government since 1967 has pursued the continuous growth of the settlements, and the significant financial, military and political resources committed to the enterprise belies any intention on its part to make the occupation temporary.[58] Every Israeli government since 1967 has left office with more settlers living in the occupied territory than when it assumed office. (Certainly, in various peace negotiation rounds in the 1990s and the 2000s, Israeli leaders had proposed to withdraw from some of the West Bank, but even in the most advanced of these negotiations—under Prime Minister Ehud Olmert between 2006 and 2008—Israel insisted on keeping many of its settlements in East Jerusalem and the West Bank in any final agreement.)[59] The current Israeli government is strongly committed to deepening the settlement enterprise.[60] Professor

56 Israeli Council for Peace and Security (June 2012), quoted in Gershon Shafir, *A Half Century of Occupation: Israel, Palestine, and the World's Most Intractable Conflict* (University of California Press, 2017), 98.

57 Shafir, *A Half Century of Occupation*. 155.

58 Idith Zertal and Akiva Eldar, *Lords of the Land: The War Over Israel's Settlements in the Occupied Territories, 1967–2007* (Nation Books, 2007).

59 Dajani, "Israel's creeping annexation."

60 Samantha Power, "Permanent Representative of the United States of America to the United Nations," speech after abstention on anti-settlement vote, New York, 23 December 2016. ("The Israeli Prime Minister recently described his government as 'more committed to settlements than any in Israel's history.'") Available at https://www.timesofisrael.com/full-text-of-us-envoysamantha-powers-speech-after-abstention-on-anti-settlement-vote/.

Shafir observes that "temporariness remains an Israeli subterfuge for creating permanent facts on the ground," with Israel able to employ the seemingly indeterminate nature of the occupation's end-point to create a "permanent temporariness" that intentionally forestalls any meaningful exercise of self-determination and independence by the Palestinians.[61]

51. The Israeli occupation has long exceeded the temporariness principle under international law. It has not acted in a manner consistent with the requirement that it take all necessary steps to bring the occupation to a successful close in as reasonable and expeditious a time period as possible. Indeed, far from it. Whether the occupation is said to be indefinite or permanent, the lack of a persuasive justification for its extraordinary duration places Israel, as the Occupying Power, in violation of international law.

Best interests/trust principle

52. Under international law, Israel is required to administer the Occupied Palestinian Territory in the best interests of the Palestinian people, the protected people under occupation, subject only to justified security concerns. It is prohibited from governing the occupied territory in an acquisitive or self-interested manner. Contrary to these requirements, Israel has acted in its own expansionary interests unaccompanied by most of the responsibilities attached to a belligerent occupier.

53. The social and economic impact of the occupation on the Palestinians in the occupied territory, which had always been disadvantageous, has become increasingly dire in recent years. According to recent reports by the World Bank[62] and the United Nations,[63] the expanding Israeli settlement enterprise and the supporting apparatus of occupation has deepened the already separate and distinctly inferior civil and economic conditions imposed upon Palestinians in the West Bank. There, the Palestinians are subject to a harsh and arbitrary legal system quite unequal to that enjoyed

---

61 Shafir, *A Half Century of Occupation*.

62 World Bank, *Area C and the Future of the Palestinian Economy* (2013).

63 Office for the Coordination of Humanitarian Affairs, Occupied Palestinian Territory, "Fragmented lives: humanitarian overview 2016" (2017).

by the Israeli settlers.[64] Much of the West Bank is off-limits to Palestinians, and they regularly endure significant restrictions on their freedom of movement through closures, roadblocks, and the need for hard-to-obtain travel permits.[65]

54. Access to the natural resources of the occupied territory, especially to water, is disproportionately allocated to Israel and the settlers.[66] Similarly, the planning system administered by the Occupying Power for housing and commercial development throughout the West Bank, including East Jerusalem, is deeply discriminatory in favor of settlement construction, while imposing significant barriers on Palestinians,[67] including ongoing land confiscation,[68] home demolitions and the denial of building permits.[69] Israel employs practices that in some cases may amount to the forcible transfer of Palestinians, primarily those living in rural areas, as a means of confiscating land for settlements, military weapons training areas and other uses exclusive to the Occupying Power that have little or nothing to do with its legitimate security requirements.[70]

55. As for East Jerusalem, the occupation has increasingly detached it from its traditional national, economic, cultural and family connections with the West Bank because of the Wall, the growing ring of settlements and related checkpoints, and the discriminatory permit regime. It is neglected by the municipality in

---

64 L. Yehuda et al, "One rule, two legal systems: Israel's regime of laws in the West Bank" (Association for Civil Rights in Israel, 2014).

65 See Human Rights Watch, *World Report 2017: Events of 2016*. Available from https://www.hrw.org/world-report/2017/country-chapters/israel/palestine.

66 Amnesty International, "Troubled waters: Palestinians denied fair access to water" (London, 2009).

67 Human Rights Watch, "Separate and unequal: Israel's discriminatory treatment of Palestinians in the Occupied Palestinian Territories," 19 December 2010. Available from https://www.hrw.org/report/ 2010/12/19/ separate-and-unequal/israels-discriminatory-treatment-palestinians-occupied.

68 A. Aloni, *Expel and Exploit: The Israeli Practice of Taking Over Rural Palestinian Land* (B'Tselem, 2016)

69 Office for the Coordination of Humanitarian Affairs, "Fragmented lives."

70 Simon Reynolds, *Coercive Environments: Israel's Forcible Transfer of Palestinians in the Occupied Territory* (Badil Resource Centre for Palestinian Residency and Refugee Rights, 2017).

terms of services and infrastructure,[71] the occupation has depleted its economy and the Palestinians have only a small land area on which to build housing.[72]

56. In Gaza, Israel vacated its formal presence in 2005, but its effective control over the Strip—through its dominance over Gaza's land and sea frontiers and its air space—means that it retains its responsibilities as an occupier. As Tamir Pardo, former head of Israel's Mossad, stated recently: "Israel is responsible for the humanitarian situation [in Gaza], and this is the place with the biggest problem in the world today."[73] Since 2007, Israel has maintained a suffocating economic and travel blockade that has driven Gaza back to the Dark Ages. More than 60 percent of the population of Gaza is reliant upon humanitarian aid, it is unable to secure more than one third of the electrical power that it requires, it will soon exhaust its sources of safe drinking water and, virtually unique in the world, its gross domestic product is actually lower than it was in 2006.[74]

57. All these restrictions in the civil and commercial life of the Palestinians have created a shattered economic space which has resulted in a highly dependent and strangled economy, mounting impoverishment, daily impositions and indignities, and receding hope for a reversal of fortune in the foreseeable future.[75]

58. On the probative evidence, Israel, the Occupying Power, has ruled the Occupied Palestinian Territory as an internal colony,

---

71 Association for Civil Rights in Israel, "East Jerusalem: facts and figures 2017," 21 May 2017.

72 United Nations Conference on Trade and Development (UNCTAD), "The Palestinian economy in East Jerusalem: enduring annexation, isolation and disintegration," 9 May 2013.

73 Gili Cohen, "Ex-Mossad chief says occupation is Israel's only existential threat," *Haaretz*, 22 March 2017. Available from https://www.haaretz.com/israel-news/1.778650.

74 United Nations Country Team in the Occupied Palestinian Territory, *Gaza Ten Years Later,* July 2017. Available from https://unsco.unmissions.org/sites/default/files/gaza_10_years_later_-_11_july_2017.pdf.

75 UNCTAD, "Report on UNCTAD assistance to the Palestinian people: developments in the economy of the Occupied Palestinian Territory," document UNCTAD/APP/2016/1. In this report, UNCTAD estimated that the Palestinian economy would be twice its present size in the absence of the Israeli occupation.

deeply committed to exploiting its land and resources for Israel's own benefit, and profoundly indifferent, at very best, to the rights and best interests of the protected people.[76] As such, Israel is in breach of its obligations to administer the occupation as a trustee for the well-being of the protected people under occupation.

Good faith

59. For an Occupying Power to govern an occupied territory in good faith, it must not only comply with the three principles stated above, but it must also be fully compliant with any specific directions issued by the United Nations or other authoritative bodies pertaining to the occupation. Further, it must comply with the specific precepts of international law, including humanitarian law and human rights law, applicable to an occupation.

60. Since 1967, the Security Council has adopted, in clear and direct language, more than 30 resolutions pertaining to Israel's occupation of the Palestinian territory. On the settlements, the Council has variously stated that they "have no legal validity," they must be "dismantled" and they constitute a "flagrant viola-tion under international law," and that settlement activities must "immediately and completely cease" and they "are dangerously imperilling the viability of a two-state solution."[77] Similarly, the Council has affirmed, with specific reference to the Israeli oc-cupation, that the acquisition of territory by war or by force is inadmissible.[78] The Council has censured "in the strongest terms" Israel's annexation of East Jerusalem; it has "deplored" Israel's "persistence in changing the physical character, demographic composition . . . and status of the Holy City of Jerusalem"; it has

---

76 D. Kretzmer, *The Occupation of Justice: The Supreme Court of Israel and the Occupied Palestinian Territories* (State University of New York Press, 2002). ("On the political level, the government relates to the Occupied Territories as colonies, with all that this entails: exploitation of their resources and markets for the benefit of the home country and its citizens and a clear distinction between the status of the 'natives' and those of the settlers.")

77 See UNSC resolutions 2334 (2016), 465 (1980), 452 (1979) and 446 (1979)

78 See UNSC resolutions 2334 (2016), 497 (1981), 478 (1980), 476 (1980), 298 (1971), 267 (1969), 252 (1968) and 242 (1967).

called these changes a "flagrant violation" of the Fourth Geneva Convention; and it has stated that these changes "must be rescinded."[79] Repeatedly, the Security Council has affirmed that the Fourth Geneva Convention applies to the Occupied Palestinian Territory and has called upon Israel to "scrupulously" abide by it.[80]

61. In the face of the persistent Israeli refusal to accept and apply any of these resolutions, the Security Council has "strongly deplored the continued refusal of Israel, the Occupying Power, to comply with the relevant resolutions of the Council and the General Assembly."[81] Immediately following the adoption of resolution 2334 (2016) by the Council in December 2016 condemning the settlement enterprise and Israel's failure to apply the Fourth Geneva Convention, Mr. Netanyahu sharply criticized the resolution and announced that Israel would not submit to it.[82] In October 2017, the United Nations Special Coordinator for the Middle East Peace Process reported to the Council that Israel was not complying with the resolution and that indeed its settlement activity was continuing at a high rate.[83]

62. Israel has been deemed to be in breach of many of the leading precepts of international humanitarian and human rights law. Its settlement enterprise has been characterized as illegal by the Security Council.[84] The prohibited use of collective punishment has been regularly employed by Israel through the demolition of Palestinian homes of families that are related to those suspected of terrorism or security breaches and by extended closures of Palestinian communities (which resumed in 2014, after a

---

79 See UNSC resolutions 2334 (2016), 478 (1980) and 476 (1980).

80 See UNSC resolutions 2334 (2016), 478 (1980), 476 (1980), 471 (1980), 465 (1980), 452 (1979) and 446 (1979).

81 See UNSC resolutions 478 (1980), 476 (1980) and 446 (1979).

82 I. Kershner, "Netanyahu promises retribution for 'biased' U.N. resolution," *New York Times*, 24 December 2016.

83 N. Mladenov, Special Coordinator for the Middle East Peace Process, "Briefing to the Security Council on the situation in the Middle East: Report on Council resolution 2334 (2016)," 25 September 2017.

84 See UNSC resolutions 2334 (2016), 478 (1980), 476 (1980), 471 (1980), 465 (1980), 452 (1979) and 446 (1979).

moratorium lasting since 2006).[85] Bedouin communities in the West Bank and East Jerusalem are the latest Palestinian communities to be at risk of forcible transfer instigated by the Occupying Power.[86] The right to liberty, with its accompanying right not to be subjected to arbitrary arrest, are violated by the high rates of arbitrary detention, including administrative detention, and the revocation of the residency rights of many thousands of Palestinians.[87] Freedom of movement is impaired through a complex system of administrative, bureaucratic and physical constraints that affects virtually every aspect of daily life for the Palestinians.[88] And above all, the entrenched and unaccountable occupation—through its denial of territorial integrity, genuine self-governance, a sustainable economy and a viable path to independence—substantively violates, and undermines, the right of the Palestinians of self-determination, the platform right that enables the realization of many other rights.

63. Whether measured by the criteria of substantive compliance with United Nations resolutions or by the satisfaction of its obligations as occupier under the framework of international law, Israel has not governed the Occupied Palestinian Territory in good faith. As a United Nations Member State with obligations, it has repeatedly defied the international community's supervisory authority over the occupation. As the occupant, it has consciously breached many of the leading precepts of international humanitarian law and international human rights law that govern an occupation.

---

85 See https://www.btselem.org/topic/punitive_demolitions.

86 Office for the Coordination of Humanitarian Affairs, "Demolition and seizure of service infrastructure in Palestinian communities in Area C exacerbates risk of forcible transfer," 11 October 2017.

87 Human Rights Watch, "Israel: 50 years of occupation abuses," 4 June 2017.

88 Office of the United Nations High Commissioner for Human Rights, "Freedom of movement: human rights situation in the Occupied Palestinian Territory, including East Jerusalem" (February 2016).

Conclusion

64. International law is the promise that States make to one another, and to their people, that rights will be respected, protections will be honored, agreements and obligations will be satisfied, and peace with justice will be pursued. It is a tribute to the international community that it has sustained this vision of international law throughout its supervision of Israel's occupation of the Palestinian territory. But it is no tribute that—as the occupation deepened, as the occupier's intentions became crystal clear, and as its defiance grew—the international community recoiled from answering Israel's splintering of the Palestinian territory and disfiguring of the laws of occupation with the robust tools that international law and diplomacy provide. International law, along with the peoples of Palestine and Israel, have all suffered in the process.

65. States who administer another territory under international supervision—whether as an occupier or a mandatory power—will cross the red line into illegality if they breach their fundamental obligations as alien rulers. The International Court of Justice in its advisory opinion on Namibia supports this conclusion. The Special Rapporteur submits that Israel's role as occupant has crossed this red line. The challenge now facing the international community is to assess this analysis and, if accepted, to devise and employ the appropriate diplomatic and legal steps that, measure by measure, would completely and finally end the occupation. As Amos Schocken, the publisher of *Haaretz*, has written about his own country's leadership: ". . .international pressure is precisely the force that will drive them to do the right thing."[89]

66. A determination that Israel's role as occupant is now illegal would serve several significant purposes. First, it would encourage Member States to take all reasonable steps to prevent or discourage national institutions, organizations, and corporations within their jurisdiction from engaging in activities that would invest in, or sustain, the occupation. Second, it would encourage

---

89 Amos Schocken, "Only international pressure will end Israeli apartheid," *Haaretz*, 22 January 2016.

national and international courts to apply the appropriate laws within their jurisdiction that would prevent or discourage cooperation with entities that invest in, or sustain, the occupation. Third, it would invite the international community to review its various forms of cooperation with the Occupying Power as long as it continues to administer the occupation unlawfully. Fourth, it would provide a solid precedent for the international community when judging other occupations of long duration. Most of all, such a determination would confirm the moral importance of upholding the international rule of law when aiding the besieged and the vulnerable.

The Right to Health in the Occupied Palestinian Territory

March 2018 Report (UNHRC) – The Right to Health in the OPT (A/HRC/37/75)

27. A 4-year-old girl in Gaza suffering from heart failure dies after Israeli authorities deny her permission to return to East Jerusalem for pediatric cardiology treatment that is unavailable in Gaza. Access to safe and sufficient drinking water in the Occupied Palestinian Territory is severely compromised by the discriminatory access to sources of water in the West Bank, and by the depleted and contaminated water aquifers in Gaza. The principal Palestinian hospital in East Jerusalem is raided repeatedly by heavily armed Israeli soldiers and police who fire stun and sponge grenades, resulting in mayhem and fear among patients and staff. Significant stocks of essential drugs are exhausted in Gaza hospitals and are unable to be replaced, even as emergency services in local hospitals are reduced because of political decisions to cut electricity supplies to the territory. Health workers in the West Bank are frequently impeded in their ability to reach patients and hospitals because of interference by Israeli security forces, including delays at checkpoints and the requirement to transfer patients

from Palestinian ambulances to Israeli-registered ambulances before entering East Jerusalem.

28. Those recent examples, among many others, raise serious concerns about the fulfilment of the right to health in the Occupied Palestinian Territory. In recent years, civil society organizations and international agencies have extensively documented the significant and chronic challenges to health care and well-being related to the occupation of the Palestinian territory. Relying upon the World Health Organization's (WHO) definition of health as "a state of complete physical, mental and social well-being and not merely the absence of disease or infirmity"[90] and understanding health within the context of human security and the enlargement of dignity and human choices,[91] this portion of the Special Rapporteur's report examines the impediments to the realization of the right to health in the Occupied Palestinian Territory.

Right to health under international law

29. The right to health is one of the most fundamental and widely recognized human rights. The right touches on everything that we do as humans, and its robust promotion is one of the most effective tools available to reduce the scourges of social and economic inequalities, gender disparities, discrimination, and poverty. Reflecting the indivisibility and interdependence of all human rights, the right to health is inextricably linked to the realization of other recognized rights, including the rights to water, housing, food, work, education, life and human dignity. As WHO has stated: "Without health, other rights have little meaning."[92]

30. The right to health is well anchored within international law.[93] Article 25 of the Universal Declaration of Human Rights states that: "Everyone has the right to a standard of living adequate for the health and well-being of himself and his family." Article

---

90 Constitution of the World Health Organization.

91 Rajaie Batniji and others, "Health as human security in the Occupied Palestinian Territory," *The Lancet* 373, no. 9669 (28 March 2009): 1133–43.

92 Quoted in Steven D. Jamar, "The international human right to health," *Southern University Law Review* 22, no. 1 (1994): 1–68.

93 John Tobin, *The Right to Health in International Law* (Oxford University Press, 2012).

12 (1) of the International Covenant on Economic, Social and Cultural Rights establishes the broad nature of States' obligations to ensure the availability of, access to, and acceptability and quality of health services in its proclamation of "the right of everyone to the enjoyment of the highest attainable standard of physical and mental health." In its General Comment No. 14, the Committee on Economic, Social and Cultural Rights linked the right to health not only to the availability of quality health-care services but to a wide range of socioeconomic determinants that together promote the conditions by which people can lead a healthy life.

32. For protected peoples living under occupation, their right to health is also guaranteed by international humanitarian law and the laws of occupation. In particular, the Geneva Convention relative to the Protection of Civilian Persons in Time of War of 12 August 1949 (the Fourth Geneva Convention), together with the Additional Protocols and customary international law, places the overall responsibility for civilian access to health care in an occupied territory upon the Occupying Power.[94] Among the extensive responsibilities assumed by the Occupying Power for the civilian population are: the protection and respect for the wounded, sick and infirm;[95] the protection of civilian hospitals and their personnel;[96] the assurance that the medical supplies for the population are adequate;[97] the maintenance of the medical and hospital establishment and services, public health and hygiene of the territory;[98] and the facilitation of medical personnel of all categories to fulfil their duties.[99] In addition, the Security Council has stated that all parties to a conflict must ensure that medical and humanitarian staff and health facilities are not attacked.[100]

---

94 See generally, Andrew Clapham et al. (eds.), *The 1949 Geneva Conventions: A Commentary* (Oxford University Press, 2015), especially chaps. 37, 39 and 40.

95 Fourth Geneva Convention, arts. 15 and 16.

96 Ibid., arts. 18 and 20.

97 Ibid., art. 55.

98 Ibid., art. 56.

99 Ibid., arts. 23 and 56

100 UNSC Resolution 2286 (2016).

33. Israel, as the Occupying Power, has specific and significant obligations under international law to ensure the health and welfare of the Palestinian population under its control. As a State party to the International Covenant on Economic, Social and Cultural Rights and as an Occupying Power, Israel is required to observe international human rights law throughout the Occupied Palestinian Territory.[101] And as a State party to the Geneva Conventions of 1949 and as the Occupying Power, Israel is bound under international treaty and customary law to scrupulously apply the Fourth Geneva Convention and the other obligations of international humanitarian law.[102]

Situation of health in the Occupied Palestinian Territory

34. The unprecedented length and character of Israel's 50-year acquisitive occupation, driven by the logic of demographic engineering and territorial annexation, both *de jure* and *de facto*, has badly fragmented the Palestinian territory. The consequence has been the political separation and geographic isolation of the West Bank, East Jerusalem and Gaza from one another, significantly impinging upon the Palestinians' internal freedom of movement. That fragmentation likewise splinters the delivery of Palestinian health services and deforms the social determinants of health throughout the Occupied Palestinian Territory.[103] Because the Occupied Palestinian Territory lacks any reliable frontier with a neighboring country, Israel completely controls the Palestinians' external freedom of movement as well.[104]

---

101 International human rights law applies to a territory under occupation: see *Legal Consequences of the Construction of a Wall,* Advisory Opinion, paras. 111–113.

102 UNSC Resolution 2334 (2016). See also Aeyal Gross, "Litigating the Right to Health under Occupation: Between Bureaucracy and Humanitarianism," *Minnesota Journal of International Law* 27, no. 2 (2018): 421–491.

103 Physicians for Human Rights–Israel, "Divide and conquer: inequality in health," January 2015.

104 The only direct frontier between the Occupied Palestinian Territory and a State other than Israel is the Rafah crossing between Gaza and Egypt. The exit crossing is only open intermittently: in 2015, it was open for 24 days; in 2016, for

35. In the West Bank, health care is primarily delivered by the Palestinian Authority and UNRWA, while in Gaza, the governing authority and UNRWA are the principal providers of health services. Palestinian private health providers and Palestinian and international non-governmental organizations also play an important role in health delivery. Nonetheless, the extensive control exercised by the Israeli occupation over the daily lives and movements of the Palestinian population decisively and adversely affects the health services and health outcomes in those areas. In East Jerusalem, where the Israeli health-care system is available to the resident Palestinians, their standard of living and their access to health services is considerably inferior to that enjoyed by Jewish Israeli residents.[105]

Conclusions

63. An Occupying Power has the duty, under international law, to ensure that the right to health—the enjoyment by the protected population of the highest attainable standard of physical and mental health—is fulfilled during the temporary period of occupation, consistent with its reasonable security needs. While fully respecting its legal obligation not to act covetously towards the territory and resources of the Occupied Palestinian Territory, it would actively work to restore and enhance the health-care system for the people under its effective control. It would not obstruct access by patients and medical staff to hospitals and health clinics, either physically or bureaucratically. It would strive to create conditions of stability and security, so that the social determinants of health can advance, rather than retard, the flourishing of physical and mental well-being. It would promote equality of access to health care for all, with particular attention paid to the vulnerable and marginalized. The Occupying Power would actively work with the health institutions of the protected population to chart a

---

38 days; and in 2017, for only 21 days, see WHO, "Health Access for Referral Patients from the Gaza Strip," monthly report, December 2017.

105 United Nations Conference on Trade and Development, "The Palestinian Economy in East Jerusalem: Enduring annexation, isolation and disintegration," document UNCTAD/GDS/APP/2012/1.

progressive health-care strategy for the future that also respected the coming restoration of full sovereignty. It would not discriminate. It would not torture or mistreat prisoners and detainees. It would not impose collective punishments of any sort. As a priority, it would provide all the necessary health services and supplies that the medical institutions of the protected population were unable to deliver themselves. Ultimately, the Occupying Power would understand that leaving behind a thriving health-care system, aligned with robust social determinants, at the end of the occupation provides the best opportunity for peace and prosperity to endure.

64. Measured against those obligations, Israel has been in profound breach of the right to health with respect to the Occupied Palestinian Territory. Its avaricious occupation—measured by the expanding settlement enterprise, the annexation of territory, the confiscation of private and public lands, the pillaging of resources, the publicly stated ambitions for permanent control over all or part of the Territory and the fragmentation of the lands left for the Palestinians—has had a highly disruptive impact upon health care and the broader social determinants for health for the Palestinians. While the Palestinian Authority (which governs in parts of the West Bank) and the authority in Gaza have some agency over the state of health care in the Occupied Palestinian Territory, Israel's conduct of the occupation bears the ultimate responsibility. At the heart of this chasm between the right to health and the harrowing conditions on the ground is what Dr. Paul Farmer has called the "pathologies of power": the enormous gap in situations of structured inequality between those who control the power to decide and those without power who must bear the consequences of these rapacious decisions, until some combination of a vision for justice, an organized opposition and the display of an international conscience can bring these disparate relationships to an end.[106] Palestinian, Israeli and international human rights organizations have persuasively demonstrated both the inequities in the health and social conditions in the Occupied Palestinian Territory and

---

106 Paul Farmer, *Pathologies of Power: Health, Human Rights, and the New War on the Poor* (University of California Press, 2004).

their substantive relationship to Israel's occupation. That leaves to the rest of us the obligation to act decisively and effectively.

The Prohibition Against Annexation in International Law and the Israeli Occupation of Palestine

October 2018 Report (UNGA) – The Prohibition against Annexation and the OPT (A/73/447)

Annexation

24. The annexation of territory is strictly prohibited in modern international law. Indeed, that prohibition has acquired the status of a *jus cogens* norm in international law, meaning that it is accepted as a fundamental principle of law by the international community, for which no exception or derogation is permitted.[107] Territorial conquest and annexation are now regarded as intolerable scourges from darker times, because they invariably incite devastating wars, political instability, economic ruin, systematic discrimination and widespread human suffering.[108] Although annexation has yet to be completely eradicated in the modern world, its occurrence has become much more infrequent since the creation of the United Nations, with the international community refusing to recognize annexation claims in many cases.

25. Nevertheless, annexation remains a burning issue in the Israeli-Palestinian conflict. Israel, the Occupying Power, has twice formally annexed occupied territory under its control: East Jerusalem (in 1967 and 1980) and the Syrian Golan Heights (in 1981).[109] Its refusal to relinquish the two territories in the face of widespread condemnation by the international community

---

107 R. Hofmann, "Annexation," in *Max Planck Encyclopedia of Public International Law* (Oxford University Press, 2013), paras. 21 and 38.

108 R. Jennings, *The Acquisition of Territory in International Law* (Manchester University Press, 1963, 2017).

109 These de jure annexations have been condemned by the UN Security Council in its resolutions 478 (1980) and 497 (1981).

has contributed to regional instability and severely limited the efficacy of international law. Furthermore, throughout the years of occupation since the June 1967 war, Israel has continuously entrenched its *de facto* annexation of the West Bank by imposing intentionally irreversible changes to occupied territory that are proscribed by international humanitarian law: the establishment of 230 settlements, populated by more than 400,000 Israeli settlers; the physical and political enclosure of the 2.6 million West Bank Palestinians; the extension of Israeli laws to the West Bank and the creation of a discriminatory legal regime; the unequal access to natural resources, social services, property and land for Palestinians in the occupied West Bank; and the explicit statements by a wide circle of senior Israeli political leaders calling for the formal annexation of parts or all of the West Bank. Those annexation trends have only intensified over the past two years. As one Israeli human rights lawyer recently stated, "[the Government of Israel] is peeling away the last remnants of loyalty to the notion of the occupation as temporary and to any obligation to negotiate with the Palestinians. The goal is clear: a single State containing two people, only one of which has citizenship and civil rights."[110]

Annexation in modern international law

27. After 1945 and the bitter experience of decades of global wars fuelled by ambitions of territorial expansionism, the international community resolved to forbid war, conquest and annexation as instruments of national policy. The Charter of the United Nations, in its Article 2 (3) and (4), requires States Members of the United Nations to settle their differences by peaceful means, with the corollary that annexation had now become illegal.[111] The Declaration on Principles of International Law concerning Friendly Relations and Cooperation among States in accordance with the Charter of the United Nations (the Declaration on Friendly Relations), adopted unanimously in 1970 by the General Assembly, declares that no territorial acquisition or special advantage resulting from the

---

110 Michael Sfard, "Israel and annexation by lawfare," *The New York Review of Books*, 10 April 2018.

111 Hofmann, "Annexation," para. 14.

threat or use of force shall be recognized as legal. From 1967, the Security Council has expressly affirmed the inadmissibility of the acquisition of territory by war or force on at least eight occasions.[112] The inadmissibility principle has also been endorsed repeatedly by the General Assembly and the Human Rights Council.[113] The International Court of Justice stated in 2004 that this principle has achieved the status of customary international law.[114] Leading international legal scholars are widely in agreement that the prohibitions against conquest and annexation are cornerstones of modern international law.[115] Annexation is incompatible with the foundational principles of the laws of occupation, which stipulate that the Occupying Power's tenure is inherently temporary, not permanent or even indefinite, and that it must rule the territory as a trustee for the benefit of the protected population under occupation and not for its own aggrandizement.[116] Annexation is also profoundly in breach of the fundamental right to self-determination, an *erga omnes* obligation under international law.[117]

Effectiveness of the prohibition

28. Recently, scholars have affirmed that the legal and diplomatic prohibition of conquest and annexation has had a significant dampening effect on its occurrence in the post-1945 period. In

---

112 The latest is Security Council Resolution 2334 (2016).

113 Most recently in UNGA Resolution 72/14 and UN HRC Resolution 37/36.

114 *Legal Consequences of the Construction of a Wall in the Occupied Palestinian Territory*, Advisory Opinion, I.C.J. Reports 2004, para. 87.

115 For example: M. Shaw, *International Law*, 8th ed. (Cambridge University Press, 2017), p. 372. "No territorial acquisition resulting from the threat or use of force shall be recognized as legal"; R. Jennings, *The Acquisition of Territory in International Law*, p. 56: "Conquest as a title to territorial sovereignty has ceased to be a part of the law."

116 O. Ben-Naftali, M. Sfard and H. Viterbo, *The ABC of the OPT: A Legal Lexicon of the Israeli Control over the Occupied Palestinian Territory* (Cambridge University Press, 2018), p. 399: "The normative framework limits the occupant's powers in terms of both material scope and time, forbidding it to act in a manner intended to generate permanent results . . . the occupation does not confer title to the territory; . . . it is to be managed as a trust; and . . . it is temporary."

117 *Legal Consequences of the Construction of a Wall*, paras. 88 and 155.

the period 1816–1928, until the signing of the General Treaty for Renunciation of War as an Instrument of National Policy (the Briand-Kellogg Pact), there had been an average of 1.21 conquests per year, with the acquisition of an average of 295,486 square kilometers annually. Between 1928 and 1948, during the initial period following the Pact, only a slight decline in the patterns of conquest and annexation were evident: there was an average of 1.15 conquests per year, involving an average of 240,739 square kilometers. However, since 1948, with the emergence of the United Nations and the consolidation of the prohibitions within international law, there has been a dramatic decline: only 0.26 conquests per year, amounting to an annual average of 14,950 square kilometers. Most importantly, many of the modern conquests and annexations have not been recognized by states. Thus, while war may still sometimes produce a military victory, it does not often yield lasting legal victories.[118]

Annexation and East Jerusalem

34. Several weeks after the military occupation of East Jerusalem and the West Bank — among other territories—by Israel in the June 1967 war, Israel formally extended its law and administration to East Jerusalem and 28 surrounding Palestinian villages in the West Bank, creating a much-enlarged Jerusalem municipality. The 1967 annexation absorbed not only the 6,400 dunams of East Jerusalem — previously ruled by Jordan — but also 65,000 dunams in the West Bank, attaching them to the 38,000 dunams belonging to West Jerusalem. In General Assembly Resolutions 2253 (ES-V) and 2254 (ES-V), the international community immediately and overwhelmingly rejected that de jure annexation. Israel refused to comply with those resolutions and began to establish permanent demographic, structural and institutional facts on the ground to consolidate its sovereignty claim.

35. Subsequently, in July 1980, the Israeli Knesset enacted the quasi-constitutional Basic Law: Jerusalem, Capital of Israel,

---

118 O. Hathaway and S. Shapiro, *The Internationalists: How a Radical Plan to Outlaw War Remade the World* (Simon and Schuster, 2017), chap. 13

which proclaimed that Jerusalem, "complete and unified," was the capital of Israel. Again, the international community, this time through the Security Council, condemned the annexation in the strongest terms and declared that the Basic Law was a violation of international law and a threat to peace and security. Furthermore, in its Resolution 478 (1980), the Council determined that all legislative and administrative measures and actions taken by Israel, the Occupying Power, that had altered or purported to alter the character and status of Jerusalem were null and void and must be rescinded.

36. The United Nations, by Council Resolution 2334 (2016) and Assembly Resolution ES-10/19, has recently reaffirmed those declarations, establishing the illegality of the formal Israeli annexation of East Jerusalem.

37. As part of its continuing efforts to ensure that its *de jure* annexation of East Jerusalem is irreversible, Israel has over the past five decades extended its national laws and civil authority to the occupied section of the city; issued numerous declarations of permanent sovereignty; transformed the physical features and historic character of East Jerusalem; moved some of its national institutions, including the Ministry of Justice; and embarked upon an intensive programme of creating and expanding Israeli settlements.[119]

Annexation and the West Bank

48. Israel has yet to declare its formal annexation of any part of the Occupied West Bank, as it presently lacks international political support from any quarter for such a move.[120] Its official

---

119 Prime Minister Ehud Barak stated in November 2000, "maintaining our sovereignty over Jerusalem and boosting its Jewish majority have been our chief aims, and toward this end Israel constructed large Jewish neighbourhoods in the eastern part of the city, which house 180,000 residents, and large settlements on the periphery of Jerusalem, like the city of Ma'aleh Adumim and Givat Ze'ev." See http://mfa.gov.il/MFA/PressRoom/2000/Pages/Address%20by%20PM%20Barak%20on%20the%20Fifth%20Anniversary%20of%20th.aspx.

120 N. Landau and others, "White House strongly denies as 'false' Netanyahu's claims of talks with U.S. on annexing West Bank settlements," *Haaretz*, 12 February 2018.

position to the rest of the world is that, while it denies that the West Bank (which it refers to as "Judea and Samaria") is occupied and it has rejected the applicability of the Fourth Geneva Convention, it remains willing to negotiate its future status with the Palestinians.[121] However, in practice, Israel has taken multiple steps consistent with establishing a sovereign claim over the West Bank since shortly after the occupation began in June 1967, and those steps have escalated significantly in recent years.

52. What civil society organizations once called the "creeping Israeli annexation" of the West Bank has now been relabelled "leaping annexation"[122] and "occup'annexation."[123] The Israeli political leadership has perceived that the current international environment—particularly its relationship with the present United States administration—is conducive to its aspirations to solidify its permanent domination over the West Bank, notwithstanding the lack of support for formal annexation. As a result, there has been a flurry of soft-annexation legislation since early 2017, which appears to be laying the foundation for hard-annexation legislation in the future. In a recent editorial, *Haaretz*, the leading liberal daily in Israel, stated that the Government has been practising legal annexation through its recent application of "more and more Knesset laws to the West Bank while erasing the Green Line," resulting in two different and unequal legal systems for the two peoples residing in the territory. "This phenomenon has a name," it stated, "and Israel will no longer be able to renounce reality and deny to the international community that it is an apartheid State, with all that this implies."[124]

---

121 Ministry of Foreign Affairs: https://www.mfa.gov.il/mfa/foreignpolicy/peace/guide/pages/israeli%20settlements%20and%20 international%20law.aspx.

122 Americans for Peace Now, "From creeping to leaping: Annexation in the Trump-Netanyahu era," April 2018.

123 11.11.11, "Occup'annexation: The shift from occupation to annexation in Palestine," Brussels, 2017.

124 "The Knesset wants apartheid," *Haaretz*, 1 June 2018.

Conclusion

60. A fundamental tenet of modern international law is the legal maxim *ex turpi causa non oritur actio*: a lawbreaker cannot benefit from his or her illegal act.[125] In 1967 and again in 1980, the international community clearly stated that the annexation by Israel of East Jerusalem breached international law and was null and void.[126] It has also spoken decisively about the illegality of the Israeli settlement enterprise,[127] which is the political and de-mographic engine that has transformed the Israeli occupation into an annexation. However, those repeated condemnations of Israeli annexationist actions have lacked any meaningful steps by the international community to insist upon accountability. Despite the ongoing record of Israel of non-compliance with the directions of the international community, it has rarely paid a meaningful price for its defiance, and its appetite for entrenching its annexationist ambitions in East Jerusalem and the West Bank has gone largely unchecked. A deep-rooted problem at the heart of the conflict has not been the clarity of international law, but the unwillingness of the international community to enforce what it has proclaimed. As one academic stated succinctly: "The problem is not international law per se, but its lack of enforcement; that in the Middle East, international law is closer to power than to justice."[128] Nothing could more effectively refute that judgment than for the interna-tional community to act on the overwhelming evidence before it and insist that Israel either fully annul its annexations and relin-quish its occupation, or be prepared to bear the full consequences of accountability for its mocking of international law.

---

125 L. Oppenheim, *International Law: A Treatise*, 8th ed., vol. 1, Peace (Longmans, Green and Company, 1955), p. 574.

126 UNSC Resolution 2334 (2016), UNGA Resolution 72/14 and UNHRC Resolution 37/36.

127 UNSC Resolution 2334 (2016).

128 Victor Kattan, *From Coexistence to Conquest: International Law and the Origins of the Arab-Israeli Conflict*, 1891–1949 (London: Pluto Press, 2009), p. 4.

Accountability, Impunity and the Responsibility of the International Community

October 2019 Report (UNGA) – Accountability and the Israeli Occupation (A/74/507)

28. Accountability—the duty to account for the exercise of power—is an indispensable cornerstone of the rule of law and a rules-based international order. No legal system, domestic or international, can acquire and sustain popular legitimacy if it cannot impose effective sanctions and provide restorative remedies when its laws are breached. Without accountability, power trumps law, justice becomes a hollow promise and those without power are left either to suffer or to pursue irregular and even violent means outside the legal order to achieve their own rough measure of justice. A right without a remedy is ultimately no right at all.

29. The enemies of accountability are impunity and exceptionalism. As was stated recently in the Security Council: "International law is not an à la carte menu."[129] Those who maintain that they are exempt from the directions of the international legal and diplomatic order not only defy the rule of law, but also fail the test of political realism—for no country can sustain for long its standing and influence among the community of nations if it asserts special arguments forbidden to others,[130] and no international rules-based order can command the requisite compliance with its laws and directions if it allows defiance and exceptionalism to thrive unchallenged. Impunity anywhere is a danger to justice everywhere.

30. An acute problem in the modern world is not the absence of laws, but the absence of international political will. As the Deputy Permanent Representative of the United Kingdom of Great Britain and Northern Ireland, Jonathan Allen, pointed out during a Security Council briefing on international humanitarian

---

129 Christoph Heusgen, Permanent Representative of Germany to the United Nations, statement at the Security Council open debate on the Middle East, 23 July 2019.

130 Benjamin R. Barber, *Fear's Empire: War, Terrorism and Democracy* (W.W. Norton and Company, 2003).

law in April 2019: "We do not lack law, we lack enforcement and accountability."[131] Far too often, accountability has been applied by the international community in a selective and partisan fashion to many serious issues, reflecting a dispiriting mixture of design and indifference, collusion and apathy. On too many occasions, defiance has been ignored and outliers have been excused or appeased. This deficit of accountability erodes popular trust in the efficacy of international law, thereby jeopardizing a precious common good.

31. The 52-year Israeli occupation of the Palestinian territory—Gaza and the West Bank, including East Jerusalem—is a bitter illustration of the absence of international accountability in the face of the systemic violations of Palestinian rights under human rights and humanitarian law. Accountability is the key to opening the titanium cage that is the permanent occupation, and its principled application is the best path to a just and durable settlement. Israel, a relatively small country in terms of geography and population and with a particular dependence on the international community for both trade and investment and diplomatic cooperation, could not have sustained such a prolonged and repressive occupation in clear violation of international law without the active support and malign neglect of many in the industrialized world. While the international community has issued numerous resolutions and declarations critical of the unending occupation by Israel and its steady designs for annexation, such criticisms have rarely been matched by any meaningful consequences. In a comment that aptly applies to the wider world, the former European Union Special Representative for the Middle East, Miguel Moratinos, stated with regard to the Israeli occupation: "We Europeans excel at declarations. It is compensation for our scarcity of action."[132]

---

131 Jonathan Allen, Deputy Permanent Representative of the United Kingdom of Great Britain and Northern Ireland to the United Nations, "International humanitarian law: we lack enforcement and accountability," statement at the Security Council briefing on international humanitarian law, 1 April 2019.

132 Akiva Eldar, "Israel can't afford to postpone Mideast peace much longer," *Haaretz*, 12 November 2010.

Lack of accountability in the conduct of the Israeli occupation

United Nations calls for accountability

65. In a variety of forums, the United Nations has frequently called upon the international community to ensure accountability and to end impunity with respect to the Israeli occupation.

66. In four major independent reports commissioned by the Human Rights Council since 2009, the constant theme has been the serious violations of human rights and humanitarian laws by Israel, the necessity to ensure Israeli accountability and the prevailing culture of exceptionalism.[133] It was stated in the report on the conflict in Gaza in 2008 and 2009 that: "Justice and respect for the rule of law are the indispensable basis for peace. The prolonged situation of impunity has created a justice crisis in the Occupied Palestinian Territory that warrants action" (A/HRC/12/48, para. 1958). In its report of 2013 on the implications of the Israeli settlements, the independent international fact-finding mission called upon Israel "to ensure full accountability for all violations ... and to put an end to the policy of impunity" (A/HRC/22/63, para. 114). In the report on the conflict in Gaza in 2014, concern was expressed that "impunity prevails across the board for violations of international humanitarian and human rights law allegedly committed by Israeli forces. ... Israel must break with its recent lamentable track record in holding wrongdoers accountable" (A/HRC/29/CRP.4, para. 664). Furthermore, in the report of 2019 on the protests in Gaza in 2018, it was found that "to date, the Government of Israel has consistently failed to meaningfully investigate and prosecute commanders and soldiers for crimes and violations" and that "scarce accountability measures arising out of Operations Cast Lead and Protective Edge ... cast doubt over the State's willingness to scrutinize the actions of military and civilian leadership."[134]

---

133 Alessandro Tonutti, *International Commissions of Inquiry and Palestine: Overview and Impact—Study Analysis* (Ramallah, Al-Haq Centre for Applied International Law, 2016).

134 A/HRC/40/74, para. 111.

67. The General Assembly and the Human Rights Council have both accentuated the necessity for accountability by Israel, the Occupying Power, in recent years. In a resolution on the Israeli settlements, the Assembly called for the consideration of measures of accountability, in accordance with international law, in the light of continued non-compliance [by Israel] with the demands for a complete and immediate cessation of all settlement activities.[135] Similarly, the Human Rights Council, in March 2019, expressed its alarm and emphasized "the need for States to investigate and prosecute grave breaches of the Geneva Conventions of 1949 and other serious violations of international humanitarian law, to end impunity, to uphold their obligations to ensure respect and to promote international accountability."[136]

68. Impunity and the lack of accountability by Israel in its conduct of the occupation have also been addressed by the Secretary-General. In 2016, the former Secretary-General, Ban Ki-Moon, stated that:

> the lack of any significant movement towards a political resolution and ongoing violations of international human rights and humanitarian law were exacerbated by the lack of accountability for previous violations. and that tackling impunity must be the highest priority.[137]

69. The lack of accountability has also been a central concern of the United Nations High Commissioner for Human Rights. In a comprehensive report on accountability issued in June 2017,[138] the former High Commissioner, Zeid Ra'ad Al Hussein, reviewed 551 recommendations issued since 2009 by relevant Human Rights Council mechanisms to determine the degree of compliance and cooperation by Israel with respect to the human rights situation in the Occupied Palestinian Territory. Of the 178 recommendations issued regarding accountability and access to

135 General Assembly Resolution 73/98, para. 6.
136 See Human Rights Council Resolution 40/13.
137 A/71/364, para. 6.
138 A/HRC/35/19.

justice, Israel had implemented 2, had partially implemented 8 and had not implemented 168 (90 percent). A similarly sparse record of compliance by Israel regarding the implementation of recommendations on the arrest and detention of Palestinians (91 percent not implemented and 8 per cent partially implemented), on settlements (100 per cent not implemented) and on freedom of movement (97 percent not implemented) was also reported. In total, Israel had fully implemented less than 0.5 per cent of the human rights recommendations presented to it. In his conclusions, the High Commissioner reminded the international community that "all stakeholders must recognize that compliance with international law is a sine qua non condition for peace."[139]

70. In a report published in March 2019 on accountability,[140] the current High Commissioner, Michelle Bachelet, gave details of the long pattern of impunity throughout the Israeli occupation, including:

- In Gaza in 2014, where she noted that the Israeli Military Advocate General had closed a number of cases without any criminal investigation, despite serious allegations and prima facie evidence of international law violations

- In Gaza in 2018 and 2019, where she noted the excessive use of force by Israeli security forces that had killed and wounded a large number of Palestinian demonstrators outside the context of hostilities

- In the case of human rights defenders, in which she pointed to a prevailing atmosphere of intimidation, threats and arrests of human rights defenders and civil society actors by Israel

- In the report, the High Commissioner addressed the international community's responsibility to take measures to prompt States to act in compliance with international humanitarian law. She concluded by

---

139 (A/HRC/35/19, para. 81.
140 A/HRC/40/43.

observing that the "lack of accountability compromises chances for sustainable peace and security" and urged that addressing impunity should be the "highest priority."[141]

71. The paradox of accountability is as striking as it is tragic. The international community has knowingly, on countless occasions, either voted for resolutions in United Nations forums or accepted public reports from independent commissions of inquiry and from senior United Nations officials in which the acute lack of accountability, coupled with the abundant impunity that has characterized Israeli conduct of the five-decade-long occupation, have been recognized. It has also displayed extraordinary lethargy in enforcing what its own laws and decisions, its binding humanitarian obligations and its political precedents would compel it to do. It is therefore necessary to ask whether it is simply to be accepted that, with this occupation, international law is closer to power than it is to justice.

Conclusion

77. No occupation in the modern world has been conducted with the international community so alert to its many grave breaches of international law, so knowledgeable about the occupier's obvious and well-signalled intent to annex and establish permanent sovereignty, so well informed about the scale of suffering and dispossession endured by the protected population under occupation, and yet so unwilling to act upon the overwhelming evidence before it to use the tangible and plentiful legal and political tools at its disposal to end the injustice.

78. An international community that took seriously its legal responsibilities to challenge and end internationally wrongful acts would have concluded long ago that Israel, the Occupying Power, was not sincere about seeking to end the occupation. It would have drawn the necessary lessons from the many unfulfilled Security Council and General Assembly resolutions, the inordinate duration of the occupation, the innumerable facts on the ground and

141   A/HRC/40/43, para. 54.

the aimless rounds of negotiations. It would have determined that the status quo of this occupation and annexation was endlessly sustainable without decisive international intervention because of the grossly asymmetrical balance of power on the ground. It would accept that its duty was not to oversee the management of the occupation, but to end it. Such an international community would take the prudent and necessary steps to collectively construct a list of effective countermeasures that would be appropriate and proportional to the circumstances. Should the Occupying Power remain unmoved, the international community would apply and escalate the range of its targeted countermeasures until compliance had been achieved. It would realize that bold measures and the determination to enforce accountability in these circumstances would greatly improve the chances that the next obstinate occupier would not likely want to test its resolve.

Collective Punishment and the Israeli Occupation

March 2020 Report (UNHRC) – The Prohibition against Collective Punishment and the OPT (A/HRC/44/60)

24. Collective punishment is an inflamed scar that runs across the entire 53-year-old Israeli occupation of the Palestinian territory. In this time, two million Palestinians in Gaza have endured a comprehensive air, sea and land blockade since 2007, several thousand Palestinian homes have been punitively demolished, extended curfews have paralysed entire towns and regions, the bodies of dead Palestinians have been withheld from their families, and critical civilian supplies—including food, water and utilities—have been denied at various times. Notwithstanding numerous resolutions, reports and reminders critical of its use, Israel continues to rely upon collective punishment as a prominent instrument in its coercive toolbox of population control.

25. A fundamental tenet of any legal system—domestic and international—that respects the rule of law is the principle that the

innocent cannot be punished for the crimes of others. Punishment without crime is abhorrent. A corollary of this tenet is that collective punishment of communities or groups of people for offences committed by individuals is absolutely prohibited under modern law. Individual responsibility is the cornerstone of any rights-based legal order, as explained by Hugo Grotius, the seventeenth century Dutch legal philosopher: "No one who is innocent of wrong may be punished for the wrong done by another."[142]

26. Throughout history and in contemporary times, belligerent armies, colonial authorities and Occupying Powers have commonly employed a spectrum of collective punishment methods against civilian populations hostile to their alien rule.[143] The methods used have included executions of civilians, sustained curfews and closures of towns, food confiscation and starvation, punitive property destruction, the capture of hostages, economic closures on civilian populations, the cutting off of power and water supplies, the withholding of medical supplies, collective fines and mass detentions.[144] These punishments are, in the words of the International Committee of the Red Cross (ICRC), "in defiance of the most elementary principles of humanity."[145]

International law

28. To protect these principles of humanity and justice, international humanitarian law has expressly forbidden the use of collective punishment against civilian populations under occupation.

---

142 Stephen C. Neff (ed.), *Hugo Grotius on the Law of War and Peace: Student Edition* (Cambridge University Press, 2012), p. 298.

143 In response, art. 1, para. 4, of *Protocol I Additional to the Geneva Conventions of 1949* has expressly extended the protection of international humanitarian law to armed conflicts involving colonial domination, alien occupation and racist regimes, in relation to people's exercise of their right of selfdetermination.

144 See, generally, C. Klocker, *Collective Punishment and Human Rights Law: Addressing Gaps in International Law* (Routledge, 2020); and S. Darcy, *Collective Responsibility and Accountability Under International Law* (Martinus Nijhoff, 2007).

145 See International Committee of the Red Cross, *Treaties, States Parties and Commentaries,* https://ihl-databases.icrc.org/applic/ihl/ihl.nsf/ 1a13044f3bbb5b8ec12563fb0066f226/ 36bd41f14e2b3809c12563cd0042bca9..

The Regulations respecting the Laws and Customs of War on Land (the Hague Regulations), of 1907, prohibited the imposition of general penalties on the occupied population. Expanding on this protection, article 33 of the Fourth Geneva Convention provides that:

> No protected person may be punished for an offence he or she has not personally committed. Collective penalties and likewise all measures of intimidation or of terrorism are prohibited. Pillage is prohibited. Reprisals against protected persons and their property are prohibited.[146]

29. This prohibition has been further entrenched by Protocol I Additional to the Geneva Conventions of 1949. Article 75 thereof establishes "fundamental guarantees" in respect of the treatment of protected people under occupation. Among these fundamental guarantees is prohibition of collective punishment, which is "prohibited at any time and in any place whatsoever, whether committed by civilian or by military agents."[147]

31. The ICRC commentary on the prohibition on collective punishment found in Protocol I Additional to the Geneva Conventions of 1949 establishes that its protection is to be given a large and liberal application. This is consistent with the purpose of international humanitarian law to provide wide protection to civilian populations in a range of vulnerable circumstances occasioned by conflict and alien rule:

> The concept of collective punishment must be understood in the broadest sense: it covers not only legal sanctions but sanctions and harassment of any sort, administrative, by police action or otherwise.[148]

---

146 See www.refworld.org/docid/3ae6b36d2.html.

147 See www.refworld.org/docid/3ae6b36b4.html.

148 Y. Sandoz, C. Swinarski, and B. Zimmermann (eds.), *Commentary on the Additional Protocols of 8 June 1977 to the Geneva Conventions of 12 August 1949* (International Committee of the Red Cross, 1987), para. 3055.

35. International human rights law does not expressly prohibit collective punishment in any of its treaties or conventions. However, collective punishment likely breaches universally accepted human rights such as equality before and under the law, and the rights to life, dignity, a fair trial, freedom of movement, health, property, liberty and security of person, adequate shelter, and an adequate standard of living.

Collective punishment in the Occupied Palestinian Territory

36. Over the past 25 years, the Security Council,[149] the General Assembly,[150] ICRC[151] and Palestinian,[152] Israeli[153] and international human rights organizations[154] have criticized Israel, the Occupying Power, for its recurrent use of collective punishment against the protected Palestinian people. Former Secretaries-General of the United Nations Kofi Annan[155] and Ban Ki-moon[156] both deplored the practice by Israel of collective punishment, while in office.

37. Subsequently, important United Nations reports on the human rights situation in the Occupied Palestinian Territory have

---

149 UNSC Resolution 1544 (2004).

150 UNGA Resolution 58/99.

151 See International Committee of the Red Cross, "Gaza closure: Not another year!" ICRC News Release 10/103, 14 June 2010, https://www.icrc.org/en/doc/resources/documents/update/palestine-update-140610.htm.

152 See Al-Haq, *Collective Punishment in Awarta,* 20 July 2011, https://www.alhaq.org/publications/8083.html.

153 See B'Tselem, "Demolition for Alleged Military Purposes - Collective Punishment," 1 January 2011, https://www.btselem.org/razing/collective_punishment.

154 See Human Rights Watch, "Israel's Closure of the West Bank and Gaza Strip," HRW report, 1 July 1996, https://www.hrw.org/report/1996/07/01/israels-closure-west-bank-and-gaza-strip.

155 See OCHA, "Israeli destruction of buildings in Gaza is illegal, Annan and UN envoy say," 27 October 2003, *reliefweb,* https://reliefweb.int/report/israel/israeli-destruction-buildings-gaza-illegal-annan-and-un-envoy-say.

156 See National Human Rights Committee, State of Qatar, "UN Says Israel Collective Punishment Against Palestinians in Gaza Unacceptable," June 2016, https://nhrc-qa.org/en/un-says-israel-collective-punishment-against-palestinians-in-gaza-unacceptable/.

drawn attention to the ongoing use by Israel of collective punishment. In 2009, the United Nations Fact-Finding Mission on the Gaza Conflict held that the conditions of life in Gaza, resulting from the "deliberate actions" of the Israeli armed forces during the 2008–2009 conflict and the "declared policies" of the Government of Israel towards Gaza "cumulatively indicate the intention to inflict collective punishment on the people of the Gaza Strip."[157] In 2016, the Committee against Torture stated that punitive home demolitions constituted a breach of article 16 of the Convention against Torture and Other Cruel, Inhuman or Degrading Treatment or Punishment, and requested Israel to cease the practice.[158]

Punitive home demolitions

38. Since the occupation began in 1967, Israel has punitively demolished or sealed approximately 2,000 Palestinian homes in the occupied territories.[159] These targeted homes have included not only dwellings owned by a purported perpetrator of a crime, but also homes where he or she lived with his or her immediate family or other relatives and/or where the family home concerned was rented from a landlord. These demolitions proceeded even though the families or owners were not proved to have played a role in the alleged offence, having never been charged, let alone convicted. In the vast majority of cases, the home was not involved in the commission of the purported act.

Closure of Gaza

53. In June 2007, Israel initiated a comprehensive air, sea and land closure of Gaza, which it maintains to this day. This followed victory by Hamas in the 2006 Palestinian elections, the imposition of international sanctions against the Hamas-led Palestinian Authority and the subsequent political split between Fatah and Hamas, each with nominal control over a fragmented

---

157 A/64/490, para. 1331.

158 CAT/C/ISR/CO/5, para. 41.

159 B'Tselem, *Home Demolition as Collective Punishment,* 11 November 2017, https://www.btselem.org/punitive_demolitions.

segment of the Palestinian territory.[160] Subsequently, Gaza has suffered through three devastating rounds of conflict—in 2008–2009, 2012 and 2014, as well as sustained protests at the Gaza frontier in 2018–2019, all of which resulted in significant numbers of civilian deaths and injuries and in widespread property destruction.

54. The impact of the 13-year closure by Israel has been to turn Gaza from a low-income society with modest but growing export ties to the regional and international economy to an impoverished ghetto with a decimated economy and a collapsing social service system. In 2012, the United Nations wondered whether Gaza, given its trajectory, would still be liveable by 2020.[161] In a follow-up report in 2017, the United Nations found that life in Gaza was deteriorating even faster than anticipated.[162] In 2020, the United Nations Special Coordinator for the Middle East Peace Process and Personal Representative of the Secretary-General to the Palestine Liberation Organization and the Palestinian Authority observed that "the immense suffering of the population" in Gaza had continued.[163]

Conclusions

80. Collective punishment is a tool of control and domination that is antithetical to the modern rule of law. It defies the foundational legal principle that only the guilty should incur penalties for their actions, after having been found responsible through a fair process. Prohibitions of collective punishment are found in virtually all legal systems across the globe. The deeds of a few

---

160 Tareq Baconi, *Hamas Contained: The Rise and Pacification of Palestinian Resistance* (Stanford University Press, 2018); and Sara Roy, *The Gaza Strip*, 3rd ed. (Institute for Palestine Studies, 2016).

161 See "Gaza in 2020: A Liveable Place?", a report by the United Nations Country Team in the Occupied Palestinian Territory (August 2012), *The Question of Palestine,* https://www.un.org/unispal/document/auto-insert-195081/.

162 *Gaza Ten Years Later – UN Country Team in the Occupied Palestinian Territory Repor,* available from https://www.un.org/unispal/document/gaza-ten-years-later-un-country-team-in-the-occupied-palestinian-territory-report/.

163 See "Paper to the Ad-Hoc Liaison Committee 2 June 2020 - Office of the United Nations Special Coordinator for the Middle East Peace Process," available from: https://reliefweb.int/report/occupied-palestinian-territory/paper-ad-hoc-liaison-committee-2-june-2020-office-united.

cannot, under any circumstances, justify the punishment of the innocent, even in a conflict zone, even under occupation, even during times of popular discontent and security challenges. As is the case with torture, there are no permissible exceptions in law to the use of collective punishment. And, as is the case with torture, the use of collective punishment flouts law and morality, dignity and justice, and stains all those who practise it.

81. An Occupying Power has a duty to maintain order and public safety, and is entitled to punish individuals who breach enforceable laws. But these practices, these laws and these procedures must be consistent with the elevated standards of international human rights law and international humanitarian law. Accordingly, an occupation must be administered through a rights-based approach, subject only to actual and genuine security requirements. And behind these rights-centred responsibilities is an indelible lesson from history: an Occupying Power that ignores its solemn obligations towards the protected population or disregards its binding duty to end the occupation as soon as reasonably possible only fertilizes popular resistance and rebellion. And the more that it employs unjust and illegal measures—such as collective punishment—to sustain its alien rule, the greater the defiance that it sows.

Accountability, Impunity and the Responsibility of the International Community (II)

October 2020 Report (UNGA)—Accountability and the Israeli Occupation (A/75/532)

31. The international supervision of the 53-year-old Israeli occupation of Palestine illustrates that, between international law and accountability, there is an enormous gap between promise and performance. The tragic paradox is that there has been no other conflict in the modern world to which the United Nations has contributed so decisively to the development of international law in such a large number of significant areas—providing depth

and breadth to the rights of refugees, the application and meaning of belligerent occupation, the strict prohibition against the annexation of occupied territory, the legal status of civilian settlements in occupied lands and the centrality of the right of self-determination, among other areas—while delivering such a paucity of actual protections to the occupation's many victims.[164]

32. The United Nations and other authoritative international institutions have spoken, often with lucidity and incisiveness, about the incompatibility of the Israeli occupation with international law and basic rights-based principles. On a number of occasions, they have warned Israel about its defiance of, and non-compliance with, Security Council, General Assembly and Human Rights Council resolutions. Rarely, however, have they actually taken steps to hold Israel accountable—through effective countermeasures and sanctions—for its obstructive policies and practices concerning the occupation.

33. The purpose of this call for consequential accountability is plainly obvious: Israel has been operating a largely cost-free occupation for decades, with every available indicator—whether it is the unrelenting growth in the settlement population, the confiscation of more and more Palestinian public and private lands for settlements and the Israeli military, the repeated proclamations by Israeli political leaders that the occupied lands are Israeli by right, or the refusal by Israel to acknowledge that its rule over the Palestinian territory is governed by the laws of occupation—pointing to an unremitting occupation. The former head of the Israeli Shin Bet (the country's internal security unit), Carmi Gillon, recently observed, with regret, that "the *status quo* is good for Israel, because Israel gets all it wants without paying a price."[165]

34. Israel is a rational actor, and it understands that, if the incentives to thicken its occupation are high and the deterrents

---

164 Susan M. Akram, Michael Dumper, Michael Lynk, and Iain Scobbie (eds.), *International Law and the Israeli-Palestinian Conflict: A Rights-Based Approach to Middle East Peace* (Routledge, 2011).

165 Natash a Mozgovaya, "No Chance for Peace With Netanyahu, Ashrawi Says," *Haaretz*, 2010 April 7, https://www.haaretz.com/middle-east-news/palestinians/.premium-the-palestinians-got-screwedthey-are-now-a-non-issue-1.896

from the international community are virtually non-existent, it can continue to devour the territory meant for a Palestinian State unimpeded. If impunity continues to be indulged and even rewarded by the international community, then it is magical thinking to expect an acquisitive Occupying Power would do anything else but further expand its settlement enterprise, prepare even more assiduously for a future de jure annexation claim, doom the Palestinians to a future without hope and write the obituary for the two-state solution.

Security Council and the Israeli occupation

Introduction

36. Over the past five decades, the Security Council has repeatedly and unambiguously endorsed three fundamental principles with respect to the Israeli occupation of the Palestinian territory (the West Bank, including East Jerusalem, and Gaza). First, Israel is the Occupying Power, the Fourth Geneva Convention of 1949 applies in full, and Israel is required to fulfil all of its obligations under the Convention.[166] Second, the acquisition of territory by force or war is inadmissible.[167] Third, the creation and expansion of the Israeli settlements is a serious violation of the absolute prohibition under international law of the Occupying Power transferring parts of its civilian population into the occupied territory.[168] All three of these principles were expressly reaffirmed by the Council in its resolution 2334 (2016). These three principles are among the most settled and widely-accepted tenets of modern international law.

37. At no time have any of these three principles been accepted or applied by Israel. The Security Council has spoken, at times sharply, about the defiance of Israel, but it has not imposed any consequences in the face of the ongoing obstructiveness of Israel. There is no other grave international human rights situation, and

166 The Security Council first referred to the applicability of the *Fourth Geneva Convention* to the Israeli occupation in its Resolution 237 (1967), adopted within a week of the end of the war of June 1967.

167 See UNSC Resolution 242 (1967).

168 UNSC Resolution 446 (1979).

no other insubordinate State actor in the world today, about which the Security Council has spoken in such quantity and with such critical clarity, but acted with such passivity.[169] And yet, even as Israel has deepened its obstinacy in recent years, the Security Council has not only failed to act, it no longer even speaks on the issue with the regularity it had before: since January 2009, the Council has adopted only two resolutions critical of the Israeli occupation,[170] even as human rights conditions on the ground have progressively worsened.

Security Council and accountability

45. Under Article 24 (1) of the Charter of the United Nations, the Security Council has the responsibility of maintaining international peace and security. With that responsibility comes the authority, under Article 41 of the Charter, to apply a broad range of enforcement mechanisms, short of military action, in order to compel errant States and actors to cooperate with international law (such as the 1991 Iraqi invasion of Kuwait), to contain a perceived threat to international peace and security (such as regional nuclear proliferation) or to address the malign actions of specific international, national or subnational actors (such as Islamic State in Iraq and the Levant, Al-Qaida and the Taliban).[171] Since 1966, the Security Council has established 30 sanctions regimes, and currently maintains 14 ongoing regimes. While Security Council sanctions have had a varied record in effectiveness and have been criticized on occasion for their adverse humanitarian impact,[172] more recent history has demonstrated that—when applied with precision, purpose, unity, and the flexibility to vary and escalate

---

169 Kofi Annan, in his memoirs, observed that "the Council's aggressive stance against the Syrian presence in Lebanon stood in stark contrast to its passivity regarding Israel's occupation of Arab lands...the perception of double standards in the Middle East undermined the United Nations." See Kofi Annan, *Interventions* (Penguin Books, 2012), p. 298.

170 UNSC Resolutions 1860 (2009) and 2334 (2016).

171 Larissa van den Herik, *Research Handbook on UN Sanctions and International Law* (Edward Elgar Publishing, 2017).

172 Jeremy Matam Farrall, *United Nations Sanctions and the Rule of Law* (Cambridge University Press, 2007).

accountability measures—United Nations–led sanctions can produce meaningful changes in behaviour by states and other actors.[173]

46. The defiance of Israel—as termed by the Security Council[174]—of the direction of the international community is a serious challenge to the rules-based international order. The resolutions and decisions of the Security Council, along with those of the General Assembly, are the bedrock of the international legal consensus on the Israeli occupation of Palestine. As a solemn condition of joining the United Nations, Member States commit themselves to accepting and carrying out the decisions and directions of the Security Council.[175] If the rule of law matters, then so does accountability. If the Security Council is to speak with authority, then the disobedience of Council directions must have consequences.

47. Similarly, the inertia of the Security Council in meaningfully responding to the non-compliance of Israel with its resolutions and directions—particularly on the three fundamental principles it has so frequently endorsed—is also a body blow to the efficacy of international law.[176] In his memoirs, Kofi Annan was disturbed by the "prolonged and sometimes brutal occupation" by Israel, and lamented the timidity of the Security Council's response: "Even when the Council took positions, it did not establish mechanisms to enforce its will."[177] He also identified a leading source for the

---

173 Enrico Carisch, Loraine Rickard-Martin, and Shawna R. Meister, *The Evolution of UN Sanctions: from a Tool of Warfare to a Tool of Peace, Security and Human Rights* (Springer, 2017)

174 UNSC Resolutions 608 (1988), 636 (1989) and 641 (1989).

175 *Charter of the United Nations*, Article 25.

176 In 2020, Peter Mulrean, retired Ambassador of the United States of America, observed that the international community's "words were never matched by action, however, especially because the United States ensured through pressure on other countries and through the United Nations Security Council veto that Israel was never meaningfully punished by or even harshly criticized in that potentially influential forum." (See, Ambassador Peter Mulrean (ret.), "Trump's '"Deal of the Century' is Bibi's Dream Come True," 2020 April 30, *Just Security,* https://www.justsecurity.org/69925/trumps-deal-of-the-century-is-bibis-dream-come-true/.)

177 Annan, *Interventions*, p. 256.

Council's paralysis: the "unhealthy possessiveness of the Middle East peace process" by the United States of America.[178] Since 1973, the United States has cast 31 vetoes at the Security Council against draft resolutions critical of the Israeli occupation; in each case, it has been the only Council member casting a negative vote. No other permanent member of the Security Council has vetoed a Council resolution critical of the Israeli Occupation.[179]

Private corporations and the Israeli settlements

Introduction

48. In 2011, the Human Rights Council unanimously adopted the Guiding Principles on Business and Human Rights (A/HRC/17/31, annex). The Guiding Principles are a set of non-binding norms to influence corporate decision-making in integrating human rights principles into daily business operations. The Principles are intended to apply to all commercial and corporate sectors and to all geographic regions. They are part of a larger global initiative—including major statements by the International Committee of the Red Cross[180] and the Organization for Economic Cooperation and Development[181]—to mainstream a responsive and vibrant human rights culture within the corporate world. The Guiding Principles set out three pillars as part of the United Nations "Protect, Respect and Remedy" Framework to advance human rights practices and compliance:

(a) The duty of States to protect human rights, including against abuses by corporations;

---

178 Ibid, p. 290.

179 See https://research.un.org/en/docs/sc/quick.

180 See International Committee of the Red Cross, *Business and international humanitarian law,* 30 November 2006, https://www.icrc.org/en/doc/resources/documents/misc/business-ihl-150806.htm.

181 See *OECD Guidelines for Multinational Enterprises - Responsible Business Conduct Matters,* https://www.oecd.org/corporate/mne/responsible-business-conduct-matters.htm.

(b) The corporate responsibility to respect human rights, including by acting with due diligence to avoid violating the rights of others;

(c) The need for greater access to effective remedies for victims of business-related abuses.

49. The Guiding Principles are not law, and most international human rights treaties do not contain specific obligations with respect to corporations. Nonetheless, a number of states have extended criminal and/or civil liability to corporations domiciled within their jurisdictions through their domestic laws, many of which reflect international human rights standards (see A/HRC/17/31, annex, commentary on Principle 12). Some states have also issued national guidance policies and advisories to corporations regarding their compliance with human rights standards internationally. The rich body of modern international human rights legal instruments—regarding labor rights, environmental rights and the rights of vulnerable groups, such as minorities, women, children and persons with disabilities, among other guarantees—is the North Star for directing corporations on how to satisfy their human rights responsibilities.

Corporations and the Israeli settlements

53. The Israeli settlements are a profound breach of international law, as determined by the leading deliberative and judicial organs of the United Nations, including the Security Council,[182] the General Assembly,[183] the Human Rights Council[184] and the International Court of Justice.[185] Other influential international bodies—including the European Union,[186] the International

---

182 UNSC Resolution 2334 (2016).

183 UNGA Resolution 71/97.

184 UNHRC Resolution 43/31.

185 *Legal Consequences of the Construction of a Wall in the Occupied Palestinian Territory*, Advisory Opinion, I.C.J. Reports 2004, at para. 120.

186 Council of the European Union, "Council conclusions on the Middle East peace process" (18 January 2016).

Committee of the Red Cross[187] and the High Contracting Parties to the Fourth Geneva Convention[188]—concur. More seriously, the settlements are a presumptive war crime under the Rome Statute.[189]

54. The disfiguring human rights consequences of the settlements upon the Palestinians in East Jerusalem and the West Bank are pervasive. The United Nations High Commissioner for Human Rights has determined that the human rights violations emanating from the settlements include: land confiscation and alienation, settler violence, discriminatory planning laws, the appropriation of natural resources, home demolitions, forcible population transfer, labour exploitation, forced evictions and displacement, physical confinement, discriminatory law enforcement, and the imposition of a two-tiered system of unequal political, social and economic rights based on ethnicity. Above all, the settlements serve the broader goal of the government of Israel of staking an impermissible sovereignty claim over parts of the Occupied Territory while simultaneously denying Palestinian self-determination (see A/HRC/43/67; see also A/HRC/22/63). The Israeli settlements and the corresponding shrinking space for Palestinians have created a "coercive environment" in the Occupied Palestinian Territory, according to the United Nations.[190]

55. The United Nations Conference on Trade and Development has found that the territorial restrictions imposed by the settlements—the separate road systems for settlers and Palestinians; the hundreds of roadblocks, checkpoints and obstructions throughout the West Bank; settler violence; and regular area closures and curfews—have created a shattered economic space in the Occupied Palestinian Territory. This has resulted in

187 Peter Maurer, "Challenges to international humanitarian law: Israel's occupation policy" *International Review of the Red Cross* 94, no. 888 (2012): 1503.

188 Declaration of the Conference of High Contracting Parties to the Fourth Geneva Convention, 17 December 2014, available from https://www.un.org/unispal/document/auto-insert-187192/.

189 Ghislain Poissonier and Eric David, "Israeli settlements in the West Bank: a war crime?"*La Revue des droits de l'homme.* 17 (2020).

190 See, "Palestinians trapped in 'coercive environment', says UN rights official," *UN News,* 11 December 2018, https://news.un.org/en/audio/2018/12/1028241.

a highly dependent and captive Palestinian economy, mounting impoverishment, daily impositions and indignities, and an accelerating trend towards economic de-development.[191] In 2018, a leaked memorandum by European Union diplomats in Jerusalem highlighted the "systematic legal discrimination" imposed by the Israeli Occupation and its settlement enterprise against the Palestinian people.[192]

56. Corporate and business activities contribute significantly to the economic viability of the Israel settlement enterprise.[193] It is private corporations that, through tenders issued by the Israeli government agencies that administer the settlement enterprise, construct the settlements and build and maintain the roads and utility infrastructure that service them. Businesses operating in the settlements and the industrial parks—in particular, manufacturing and service industries, and wineries—provide jobs and commercial activity that economically sustain the settlements, while paying taxes to settlement municipalities. Private security companies guard many of the settlements, and those companies and high-tech businesses supply surveillance and identification equipment. Banks and financial institutions facilitate the fiscal infrastructure to arrange residential mortgages and to lend capital to businesses operating in the settlements. Law firms offer legal services to the settlements, settlers and settlement businesses. Real estate firms coordinate the sale and purchase of residential and commercial properties in the settlements. Agricultural corporations grow a range of foodstuffs for domestic and export markets, utilizing large-scale farming and modern technology.

191 *The Economic Costs of the Israeli Occupation for the Palestinian People: Cumulative Fiscal Costs* (United Nations publication, Sales No. E.20.II.D.6)

192 Andrew Rettman, "No EU cost for Israeli 'apartheid' in West Bank," EUobserver, 1 February 2019.

193 Paras. 56–58 are informed by the comprehensive overviews of the corporate dimensions of the Israeli settlement economy provided in Amnesty International, *Think Twice* (2019); Amnesty International, *Destination: Occupation* (2019); Farah, *Business and Human Rights in Occupied Territory*; Profundo and 11.11.11, *Doing Business with the Occupation* (2018); Human Rights Watch, *Bankrolling Abuse* (2018); Human Rights Watch, *Occupation, Inc.* (2016); and Diakonia, *The Unsettling Business of Settlement Business* (2015). See also the work of Who Profits, at https://www.whoprofits.org/.

Domestic and international tourism is an emerging sector for the settlements, along with hotels and accommodation rentals. Retail store chains operate in the settlements. Transportation companies link the settlements to each other and to communities within Israel. Extraction companies exploit the Occupied Palestinian Territory's natural resources, including minerals and water. Equipment companies supply the heavy machinery needed to construct residential and commercial building structures. Waste management companies service both municipalities and industrial enterprises in the settlements. The construction and maintenance of the separation Wall through occupied territory solidifies an illegal situation.

57. Many of the corporations and businesses supplying commercial services in or to the settlement economy are Israeli companies. However, a number of international corporations also contribute to and profit from the settlement economy. International banks and financial institutions underwrite loans to or invest in businesses with operations in the settlements. Other companies sell goods and services to the settlements, such as construction materials, heavy machinery and solar power technology, or they excavate non-renewable natural resources. Major international transportation companies have participated in the building of the Jerusalem light rail system (which connects a number of the illegal East Jerusalem settlements to West Jerusalem) and the high-speed rail connection between Tel Aviv and Jerusalem (which passes through parts of the Occupied Territory). Major international accommodation booking companies advertise housing rentals in the Israeli settlements. Goods and services from the Israeli settlements, including manufactured goods, wines and foodstuffs, are exported in quantity to the international market.

58. Without this extensive corporate involvement, the settlements—the engine of the Occupation—would be an unsustainable economic burden for the government of Israel. These businesses—domestic and international—benefit greatly from the illegal confiscation by Israel of Palestinian land and natural resources, from the discriminatory Israeli two-tier system of rights, benefits and opportunities between the settlements and Palestinian people, and from Palestinian impoverishment (and the resulting

employment of low-cost Palestinian labor in the settlements) that is the inevitable consequence of a settlement implantation enterprise.[194] The question becomes whether companies can become or remain involved with the Israeli settlements and still honor their human rights commitments.

62. The Special Rapporteur takes the view that any form of corporate involvement—whether Israeli or international, whether direct or indirect, whether intentional or incidental—with the Israeli settlements is wholly incompatible with human rights obligations, with the Guiding Principles and with any purposive definition of enhanced due diligence. Three reasons inform this view. First, the Israeli settlements are a flagrant violation and a grave breach of the Fourth Geneva Convention and a presumptive war crime under the Rome Statute. These are among the most serious of contraventions under international human rights, humanitarian and criminal law. Second, corporations and businesses operating in, or benefiting from, the settlements provide the indispensable economic oxygen for their growth. Whatever positive benefits are cited by companies in defending their engagement with the settlements—often, the employment of Palestinian labor, or the payment of local taxes[195]—are far outweighed on the human rights ledger by the scale of gross violations inherent in the settlement enterprise. Third, the settlements are the primary political instrument—the pervasive "facts on the ground"—employed by the Government of Israel to advance its *de facto* and *de jure* annexation claims and to deny Palestinian self-determination. Annexation is a crime of aggression,[196] and self-determination is the *primus inter pares* of human rights.[197]

---

194 Yael Ronen, "Responsibility of businesses involved in the Israeli settlements in the West Bank," January 2015.

195 Maha Abdullah and Lydia de Leeuw, *Violations Set in Stone* (Al-Haq, 2020).

196 *Rome Statute of the International Criminal Court* (last amended 2010), 17 July 1998, article 8 bis, para. 2 (a).

197 Self-determination is the very first human right cited in both the *International Covenant on Economic, Social and Cultural Rights* and the *International Covenant on Civil and Political Rights.*

The Legal Status of the Israeli Settlements Under the Rome Statute

July 2021 Report (UNHRC) – The Israeli Settlements and the Rome Statue (A/HRC/47/57)

26. In July 1998, delegates from 120 states voted in favour of the negotiated text of the Rome Statute of the International Criminal Court. The Rome Statute created, for the first time, a permanent international court to try alleged perpetrators of war crimes, crimes against humanity and other serious international crimes. It built upon the legacy of the Nuremberg and Tokyo military tribunals established after the Second World War, as well as the war crimes tribunals for Rwanda, the former Yugoslavia, Cambodia, and Sierra Leone set up in the 1990s and 2000s. The International Criminal Court came into being in July 2002.

28. Among the war crimes expressly listed in the Rome Statute is the transfer, directly or indirectly, by an Occupying Power of parts of its own population into the territory it occupies.[35] Its inclusion was deliberate, appropriate, and linear. The prohibition against settler implantation by an occupying power was first entrenched in international law through the Fourth Geneva Convention of 1949. It was subsequently characterized as a "grave breach" and a "war crime" in the 1977 Protocol Additional to the Geneva Conventions of 12 August 1949 and relating to the Protection of Victims of International Armed Conflicts.

29. The phenomenon of settler implantation has historically involved the transfer by an empire or expansionary state of some of its own citizens or subjects into lands that it has acquired through conquest or occupation. These lands may have been already swept clean of their inhabitants, but more commonly they are still populated by some or all of the indigenous peoples. The objectives of the conquering power in implanting settlers have been to solidify its political and military control, augment its economic penetration, and ultimately bolster its legal claim to permanent sovereignty over the subjugated lands. The transferred settlers are almost always willing citizens or subjects of the dominant power, motivated by government inducements, enhanced

economic prospects, special legal and political privileges in the subjugated lands and, on occasion, by nationalist, religious or civilizing missions.[198]

30. The flip side of the coin of settler implantation is the rupture of the established relationship between the indigenous population and its traditional territory and lands through demographic engineering. The common bond of any original society is the link between community and territory. Accordingly, the exercise of the right of self-determination is substantially abrogated if that link is disrupted through territorial alienation, the deliberate loss of majority status or the inability of an occupied or subjugated people to control its political destiny. Indeed, the rupture of this link is not only the frequent consequence of settler implantation, but invariably its very purpose. Needless to say, settler implantation projects throughout history have invariably occurred regardless of, and almost always against, the wishes of the indigenous population.[199]

Fourth Geneva Convention of 1949

35. The purpose of the Fourth Geneva Convention is to protect civilians during situations of armed conflict. Among its many protections, the Convention expressly prohibits an Occupying Power from implanting civilian settlers of its own population into the occupied territory in article 49 (6): "The Occupying Power shall not deport or transfer parts of its own civilian population into the territory it occupies."

36. The objective of article 49 is to preserve the demographic and social structure of the occupied territory and to forbid attempts by an Occupying Power to treat the territory as a fruit of conquest.[200] Article 147 of the Convention establishes the gravity of the prohibition.

198 Claire Palley, "Population transfers," in Donna Gomien (ed.), *Broadening the Frontiers of Human Rights: Essays in Honour of Asbjorn Eide* (Scandinavian University Press, 1993).

199 E/CN.4/Sub.2/1994/18, para. 131.

200 At a conference of the High Contracting Parties to the Fourth Geneva Convention in December 2001, the Intl. Committee of the Red Cross issued a statement, in which it stated (para. 3): "Being only a temporary administrator of occupied territory, the Occupying Power must not interfere with its original economic and social structures, organization, legal system or demography."

38. The temporary nature of an occupation and the full preservation of national rights and the territorial integrity of the ousted sovereign—the protected population—lie at the very core of international humanitarian law. In his 1958 commentary on the Fourth Geneva Convention, Jean Pictet stated that "the occupation of territory in wartime is essentially a temporary *de facto* situation, which deprives the occupied power of neither its statehood nor its sovereignty."[201] As for annexation, the Security Council has affirmed on at least 11 occasions since 1967, consistent with Article 2 (4) of the Charter of the United Nations, that the acquisition of territory by war or force is inadmissible.[202] Neither conquest nor occupation confer title.[203] The occupying power must administer the occupation in good faith, consistent with international law, and it must seek to fully terminate the occupation as soon as reasonably possible.[204] The very raison d'être of settler implantation—the creation of demographic facts on the ground to solidify a permanent presence, a consolidation of alien political control and a claim of sovereignty—tramples upon the fundamental precepts of humanitarian law.

International human rights law

39. The logic and the dynamic of settler implantation—rupturing the relationship between an indigenous people and its territory—is the denial of the right of self-determination. Self-determination is both a *jus cogens* right (a fundamental principle of international law), and a right *erga omnes* (a right owed to all).[205] This right has been placed in the opening articles of the Charter of the United Nations, the International Covenant on Civil and Political Rights and the International Covenant on Economic, Social and Cultural Rights precisely to underscore the fact that

201 See https://docplayer.net/213339157-Advance-unedited-version.html.

202 Most recently in UNSC Resolution 2334 (2016).

203 Christian Tomuschat, "Prohibition of settlements," in A. Clapham et al. (eds.), *The 1949 Geneva Conventions: a Commentary* (Oxford University Press, 2015).

204 A/72/556, paras. 32–38

205 *Legal Consequences of the Construction of a Wall in the Occupied Palestinian Territory*, Advisory Opinion, para.155.

the realization of all other individual and collective human rights depends upon the ability to exercise this cornerstone right.[206] Flowing from this cardinal principle, the international community has prohibited the demographic manipulation of a territory through settler implantation because it is incompatible with the fundamental rights of a people to retain its distinct identity and to freely determine its destiny on its own territory.[207]

40. In addition to self-determination, settler implantation projects frequently violate a range of protected individual and collective rights in international human rights law to which the indigenous population is entitled. As the Special Rapporteur on the human rights dimensions of population transfer, including the implantation of settlers and settlements, for the Commission on Human Rights (and later a judge on the International Court of Justice), Awn Al-Khasawneh, concluded in a 1997 report: "The range of rights violated by population transfer and the implantation of settlers places this phenomenon in the category of mass violations of human rights."[208]

Israel, the occupation and the settlements

52. The creation and expansion of Israeli settlements in the Occupied Palestinian Territory is the state's largest and most ambitious national project since its founding in 1948.[209] Starting with the very first Israeli settlements that were erected in the months

---

206 Both Covenants state in article 1 (1) that: "All peoples have the right of self-determination."

207 Eric Kolodner, "Population transfer: the effects of settler infusion policies on a host population's right to self-determination," *New York University Journal of International Law and Politics* 27, no. 1 (1994).

208 E/CN.4/Sub.2/1997/23, para. 16.

209 Menachem Klein, Opinion: "Any Solution to the Israeli-Palestinian Conflict Will Lead to Civil War," *Haaretz*, 15 June 2019: "Israel's territorial expansion project and control over the Palestinian population is the largest state/national project the country has ever carried out ... Almost the entire state is invested in this project. This does not refer only to the ideological investment and the transfer of settlers into the Palestinian territories. It's also about jobs for hundreds of thousands or millions of Israelis, as well as profits from exporting technological know-how and security products that maintain Israel's control over the Palestinian population and territory."

following the war of June 1967, the full apparatus of the state—political, military, judicial and administrative—has provided the leadership, financing, planning, diplomatic cover, legal rationale, security protection and infrastructure that has been indispensable to the incessant growth of the enterprise.[210]

54. To incentivize Israeli and diaspora Jews to live in its settlements in the Occupied Territory, the government of Israel actively offers a range of financial benefits, including advantageous grants and subsidies for individuals and favorable fiscal arrangements for settlements. These include subsidized housing benefits and premium mortgage rates, venture benefits for agricultural development, education and welfare benefits, and the designation as a national priority area. It also makes available attractive business incentives for industrial zones in the settlements, such as discounted land fees, employment subsidies, and reduced corporate taxes.[211] Beyond this, the settlements are treated as an integral part of the municipal and regional governance system of Israel, with budgetary funding for education, utilities, infrastructure, housing, water, transportation, and other services.

55. The spatial placement of the Israeli settlements badly fragments Palestinian contiguity in East Jerusalem and the West Bank. In East Jerusalem, the 12 Jewish settlements are located primarily around the northern, eastern and southern perimeters of the city, blocking any Palestinian territorial continuity with the West Bank. In the West Bank, the settlements are organized into two main settlement blocs. South of Jerusalem is the Gush Etzoin bloc, stretching from Bethlehem to Hebron. The northern bloc is spread out from the Ramallah area to Nablus. There are also smaller settlement blocs just east of Jerusalem and in the Jordan Valley. In order to provide efficient transportation between the settlements and to Israeli urban areas, and to encourage new settlers and settlement expansion, the government of Israel has invested heavily in building a dense network of highways through the West

---

210 Zertal and Eldar, *Lords of the Land.*

211 B'tselem, "This is ours – and this, too: Israel's settlement policy in the West Bank" (March 2021).

Bank and East Jerusalem, which is built on confiscated Palestinian lands and services only the settler population.[212]

56. Aside from 150 officially recognized settlements in East Jerusalem and the West Bank, there are another 150 so-called settlement outposts built without formal State authorization and which Israel does not officially recognize.[213] However, it has granted retroactive authorization to dozens of these outposts, and it actively supports virtually all of the other remaining outposts. The 2005 Sasson report, commissioned by the Government, determined that Israeli state bodies had been discreetly funnelling significant public funds for decades to these outposts for housing, roads, education, utilities and security. Although the author of the report observed that this amounted to a "bold violation of laws" and recommended that criminal charges be brought against state officials, no charges were ever initiated and virtually all of the outposts remain thriving settlements today.[214]

57. Beyond the expansive support for the settlements provided by the Government of Israel, several significant international private organizations play a seminal role in supporting settler implantation. The Settlement Division of the World Zionist Organization, which is substantially funded by the Government, acts as a government agent in assigning land to Jewish settlers in the West Bank, including settlement outposts.[215] The Jewish National Fund has actively sought to purchase Palestinian lands in the West Bank and support infrastructure development, tourism, and roads in the Israeli settlements.[216]

58. While the Israeli settlements have flourished and provide an attractive standard of living for the settlers, they have created

---

212 Israeli Centre for Public Affairs and Breaking the Silence, "Highway to annexation. Israeli road and transportation infrastructure development in the West Bank" (December 2020).

213 B'Tselem, "This is ours – and this, too: Israel's settlement policy in the West Bank" (March 2021).

214 Daniel Kurtzer, "Sleight of hand: Israel, settlements and unauthorized outposts" Middle East Institute, October 2016.

215 Yotam Berger, "World Zionist Organization Settlement Division finances illegal West Bank outposts," *Haaretz*, 7 December 2018.

216 Peace Now, "KKL-JNF and its role in settlement expansion," April 2020.

a humanitarian desert for the Palestinians, reaching every facet of their lives under occupation.[217] Human rights violations against Palestinians arising from the Israeli settlements are widespread and acute,[218] and settler violence has created a coercive environment.[219] There is an apartheid-like two-tier legal system granting full citizenship rights for the Israeli settlers while subjecting the Palestinians to military rule.[220] Access to the natural resources of the Occupied Territory, especially to water, is disproportionately allocated to the settlements[221] and the fragmented territory left to the Palestinians has resulted in a highly dependent and strangled economy, mounting impoverishment, daily impositions and indignities, and receding hope for a reversal of fortune in the foreseeable future.[222]

Do the Israeli settlements violate the Rome Statute?

68. The Rome Statute requires three elements of the war crime of transfer of a civilian population in an occupied territory to be satisfied. The first two elements constitute the material element of the crime:

(a) The transfer by the perpetrator of parts of its own population into the Occupied Territory;

(b) The conduct took place arising from an international armed conflict.

69. In the case of the Israeli settlements, both the material elements are met. Israel captured the West Bank, including East Jerusalem, and Gaza in June 1967 as part of an international armed conflict. Virtually the entire international community accepts the designation of the Israeli control of the Palestinian territory as an

---

217 A/HRC/22/63.

218 A/HRC/40/42.

219 Yesh Din, "Settler crime and violence inside Palestinian communities, 2017–2020" (May 2021)

220 Association for Civil Rights in Israel, *One Rule, Two Legal Systems: Israel's Regime of Laws in the West Bank* (October 2014).

221 A/HRC/40/73

222 See TD/B/67/5.

occupation, to which the full scope of international humanitarian law and international human rights law continues to apply.[223]

70. In addition, the historical and contemporary evidence is abundantly clear that the senior political, military and administrative officials of the government of Israel, as well as important international private organizations, have actively developed and implemented a practice of transferring hundreds of thousands of Israeli citizens into the Occupied Palestinian Territory through enabling large-scale housing, commercial and infrastructure construction, providing advantageous State funding and ensuring military security, in order to establish an immovable demographic presence.[224]

71. The third element of the crime is the mental element that the perpetrator was aware of the factual circumstances of the crime of transfer that established the existence of an armed conflict. In other words, the perpetrator has both the intent and the knowledge of the crime.[225]

72. In this case, the mental element is satisfied. The political, military and administrative leadership of Israel has directly and knowingly supported the decades-long state policy of encouraging and sustaining the growth of the settlements. Throughout those decades, the leadership has been fully aware of the clear direction from the international community that such activities violate fundamental prohibitions in international law.

73. It is the finding of the Special Rapporteur that the policy of settler implantation meets the definition of "war crime" under international humanitarian law and the Rome Statute. The Special Rapporteur also endorses the view that the Israeli settlements

223 UNSC Resolution 2334 (2016) *and Legal Consequences of the Construction of a Wall in the Occupied Palestinian Territory*, Advisory Opinion, paras. 101 and 111–114.

224 Ghislain Poissonnier and Eric David, "Israeli settlements in the West Bank, a war crime?" *Revue des droits de l'homme* 17 (2020): paras. 72–102.

225 Diakonia International Humanitarian Law Resource Centre, "Litigating settlements: The impact of Palestine's accession to the Rome Statute on the settlement enterprise" (December 2015).

constitute a continuing crime and therefore fall within the temporal jurisdiction of the International Criminal Court.[226]

The Responsibility of International Actors
October 2021 Report (UNGA) – The Responsibility of International Actors (A/76/3187)

Introduction

23. The international community—and particularly, but not only, the United Nations—has long accepted that it bears a special responsibility for supervising the question of Palestine, fully ending the Israeli occupation, realizing Palestinian self-determination and ensuring that all of the issues related to the conflict are brought to a just and durable resolution.[227] These issues have understandably taken on an immense political, legal and popular resonance which ripples well beyond the Levant. Kofi Annan, the former Secretary General of the United Nations, recalled in his memoirs that: "...the Israeli-Palestinian conflict is not simply one unresolved problem among many. No other issue carries such a powerful symbolic and emotional charge affecting people far from the zone of conflict."[228]

International responsibility for the deepening occupation

27. In recent years, the now 54-year-old Israeli occupation of Palestine—always repressive, always acquisitive—has been metastasizing into something much harsher and more entrenched: the permanent alien rule of one people over another, encased in a two-tiered system of unequal laws and political rights. More than

---

226 Uzay Yasar Aysev, "Continuing or settled? Prosecution of Israeli settlements under article 8 (2) (b) (viii) of the Rome Statute," *Palestine Yearbook of International Law* 20, no. 1 (2019).

227 UNGA Res. 75/23 (2 December 2020): "Reaffirming that the United Nations has a permanent responsibility towards the question of Palestine..."

228 Kofi Annan, *Interventions: A Life in War and Peace* (Penguin Books, 2012), 254.

680,000 Israeli settlers living in segregated and privileged settlements amidst five million stateless Palestinians. Asymmetrical wars. Geographic fragmentation. A smothered and heavily aid-dependant economy. Separate networks of roads and utilities. Impoverished and fenced-in ghettos unique in the modern world. A coercive environment. The growing amount of violence required to maintain the occupation. The denial of self-determination. The deeply lopsided access to property, social, health and employment rights. All of this based entirely on nationality and ethnicity.[229] All of this should be unthinkable in the 21st century.

29. Yet, the international community has been perplexingly unwilling to meaningfully challenge, let alone act decisively to reverse, the momentous changes that Israel has been generating on the ground. This is a political failure of the first order. Let us recall that this very same international community—speaking through the principal political and legal organs of the United Nations—has established the widely accepted and detailed rights-based framework for the supervision and resolution of the Israeli occupation of Palestine.[230] Accordingly, the protracted Israeli occupation must fully end.[231] Both the Palestinians and Israelis are entitled to live in peace and security and enjoy the right to self-determination, including sovereign, secure and viable states, within the boundaries of mandate Palestine, based on the 1967 border.[232] Annexation of occupied territory is illegal.[233] All of the more than 280 Israeli settlements in East Jerusalem and the West Bank are a flagrant violation under international law.[234] East Jerusalem has

---

229 See the recent reports of Al-Haq, B'Tselem, Human Rights Watch, Amnesty International, and the West Bank Protection Consortium.

230 Kofi Annan stated in 2002: "There is no conflict in the world today whose solution is so clear, so widely agreed upon, and so necessary to world peace as the Israeli-Palestinian conflict." https://news.un.org/en/story/2002/03/30872-arab-summit-annan-urges-sharon-arafat-lead-their-peoples-back-brink

231 UNSC Res. 476 (30 June 1980) ("*Reaffirms* the overriding necessity to end the prolonged occupation of Arab territories occupied by Israel since 1967, including Jerusalem").

232 UNSC Res. 1850 (16 December 2008); UNGA Res. A/73/159 (December 17, 2018).

233 UNSC Res. 2334 (23 December 2016).

234 UNSC Res. 2334 (23 December 2016).

been illegally annexed by Israel and remains occupied territory.[235] The Palestinian refugees from the 1948 and 1967 wars have the right to choose to return to their homeland.[236] Gaza is an integral part of Palestine, it remains occupied, and the Israeli blockade is a prohibited form of collective punishment.[237] Let us also recall the political and legal duty of accountability: the international community bears the responsibility to challenge and vanquish erious violations of international law and human rights,[238] for which it possesses abundant political and legal powers to sanction violators until they have complied with their obligations.[239]

30. Alas, the international community's remarkable tolerance for Israeli exceptionalism in its conduct of the occupation has allowed *realpolitik* to trump rights, power to supplant justice, and impunity to undercut accountability. This has been the conspicuous thread throughout the Madrid-Oslo peace process which began in 1991. Israel, with little resistance from major international actors, has been able to successfully insist that negotiations with the Palestinians are to be conducted outside of the framework of applicable international law and the prevailing international consensus,[240] notwithstanding the imperatives of the rules-based international order. This has enabled Israel to maintain an obdurate bargaining stance, with the endgame of formalizing its claims to East Jerusalem and to most, if not all, of its West Bank settlements, while acquiescing to a Potemkin statelet for the Palestinians that would enjoy neither meaningful territory nor

---

235 UNSC Res. 2334 (23 December 2016).

236 UNGA Res. A/73/92 (7 December 2018); UNGA Res. A/73/93 (December 7, 2018).

237 UNSC Res. 1860 (January 8, 2009). And see the remarks by UN Secretary-General Ban Ki-Moon, June 28, 2016: https://www.un.org/sg/en/content/sg/press-encounter/2016-06-28/secretary-generals-remarks-press-encounter.

238 *Articles on Responsibility of States for Internationally Wrongful Acts* (2001), Articles 40 & 41 https://www.refworld.org/pdfid/3ddb8f804.pdf. Also see J Crawford, *State Responsibility* (Cambridge University Press, 2013)

239 Jeremy Farrall, *United Nations Sanctions and the Rule of Law* (Cambridge University Press, 2009); International Committee of the Red Cross: https://ihl-databases.icrc.org/applic/ihl/ihl.nsf/Comment.xsp?action=open Document&documentId=72239588 AFA66200C1257F7D00367DBD.

240 Khaled Elgindy, *Blind Spot* (Brookings Institution, 2019).

sovereignty.[241] For the international community, this has created a troubling paradox: while there is no conflict zone in the world where the United Nations has pronounced with as much frequency and detail on the framework for conflict resolution, this framework has rarely informed the various Oslo-related peace process initiatives—including the 1993 Declaration of Principles, the 1995 Oslo II agreement, the 2000 Camp David negotiations, the 2001 Clinton parameters, the 2003 Quartet principles, the 2007 Annapolis formula, the 2013–14 Kerry initiative and the 2020 Trump Peace for Prosperity plan—that have successively collapsed in the absence of any sturdy legal scaffolding and political will to sustain a rights-based resolution.

31. The cost of the international community's failure to insist upon its own rights-based framework and to enforce its many resolutions has been the evaporation of what lingering possibilities remain for a genuine two-state solution. In its place has emerged what the European Union has acknowledged to be a one state reality of unequal rights,[242] and what regional and international human rights groups have declared to be apartheid.[243] The United Nations Security Council warned in 2016 that Israel's settlement activities were ". . .dangerously imperilling the viability of the two-state solution based on the 1967 lines."[244] Former United Nations Secretary-General Ban Ki-Moon stated in June 2021 that: "Israel has pursued a policy of incremental *de facto* annexation in the territories it has occupied since 1967, to the point where the prospect of a two-state solution has all but vanished."[245] The minimalist pink lines that the international community has drawn for Israel—no further *de jure* annexations, no new settlements,

---

241 Seth. Anziska, *Preventing Palestine* (Princeton University Press, 2018); Jeremy Sharon, "Netanyahu calls for Palestinian 'state-minus,'" *The Jerusalem Post*, 24 October 2018.

242 "Israel's land-grab law entrenches One state Reality of Unequal Rights," *Haaretz*, 7 February 2017.

243 Human Rights Watch, *A Threshold Crossed* (April 2021); Al Haq, *The Legal Architecture of Apartheid* (April 2021); B'Tselem, *This is Apartheid* (January 2021).

244 UNSC Resolution 2334 (23 December 2016).

245 *Financial Times* (29 June 2021).

no destruction of Palestinian communities—have hardly slowed down the growth of Israel's settler population, the expansion of its transportation and utility infrastructure linking the settlements, its hermetic sealing of Gaza, or the regularity of declarations by many in its political leadership that East Jerusalem and the West Bank belong to Israel by right and will never be yielded. The ritual avowals by major international actors that they remain committed to a two-state solution have become a diplomatic pantomime, a cover for paralysis rather than a declaration of resolve which is occurring with everyone's eyes wide open about the dynamic reality on the ground.

36. To assess the effectiveness of the international community's supervision of the occupation, the Special Rapporteur is proposing five foundational criteria to measure the role of these leading actors. These criteria are important to accentuate, because they go to the heart of the disparate relationship between Israel and Palestine. Any efforts by the international community, collectively or individually, to create a framework for supervising and ending the occupation that does not place these criteria at or near the core of its endeavours will almost certainly crash upon the shoals of Middle East realism:

i. **Because of the vast asymmetry in power between Israel and the Palestinians, active international intervention is indispensable.** *Militarily*, Israel has the strongest armed forces in the region. *Economically*, Israel enjoys a European-level GDP per capita that is 12 times higher than that of the Palestinians. *Diplomatically*, Israel relies upon the enduring support of major international actors. *Territorially*, Israel enjoys complete military freedom of action between the Mediterranean and the Jordan. Only on *demography* do the Palestinians have the edge: they now constitute a slight majority of the population between the Sea and the River. Without active and decisive international accountability measures to counter the abuse of this overwhelming power, Israel's vast advantages will continue to dictate what happens on the ground and at any negotiating table.

ii. **The framework for fully ending the Occupation must employ a rights-based approach, anchored in international law and human rights.** Yesterday's diplomatic playbook—relying on the *realpolitik* of Israel's "facts on the ground," Palestinian weakness and the absence of law—has only led to repeated diplomatic *cul-de-sacs*, while enabling the patterns of human rights abuses and an endless occupation to continue largely unimpeded.[246] Ignoring the established international framework on occupation and rights only accelerates this downward trajectory.[247] Only a rights-based approach can engage the considerable tools of accountability and the already widely-endorsed body of international law, including human rights and humanitarian law, to end impunity and advance the interests of both Palestinians and Israelis.

iii. **The end goal must be the realization of Palestinian self-determination.** Israel already exists, and has since 1948. The missing key to enduring peace has always been the denial of Palestinian self-determination.[248] But the *de facto* and *de jure* annexation of occupied territory by Israel, primarily led by the relentless expansion of its settlements, has undercut any meaningful exercise of self-determination on what remains of Palestinian land. Self-determination is at the heart of modern human rights, and it is the *sine qua non* for a just and final peace. Palestinian self-determination must be based on the 1967 borders and the realization of authentic sovereignty, if a genuine two-state solution remains a possibility. If not, then self-determination must be centred on individual and collective equality rights for all those living between the Mediterranean and the Jordan.

---

246 *Ha'aretz* editorial (22 December 2019): "Even harder to understand is the claim that the issue of the Israeli-Palestinian conflict must be left for dialogue and negotiations and the legal process will only harm it, while it is clear to all that there is no such process on the table because the Israeli government is not interested in it."

247 Dimitris Bouris & Nathan J. Brown, "The Middle East Quartet's Quest for Relevance," *Carnegie Europe,* 20 July 2016.

248 UNGA Res. 75/172 (16 December 2020).

iv. **Israel is a bad-faith occupier.** This is the inescapable conclusion from Israel's conduct of its 54-year-old occupation of the Palestinian territory. Its non-compliance with hundreds of United Nations resolutions from the Security Council, the General Assembly and the Human Rights Council regarding the occupation, and its refusal to apply the Fourth Geneva Convention, is not an honest policy difference with the world, but a sustained show of defiance meant to preserve the fruits of its conquest. To assume that Israel is a responsible occupier, marred only by an errant and unfortunate policy towards the Palestinians, is to indulge in the magical thinking that has led to the past diplomatic failures.

v. **The occupation must end with all deliberate speed.** Occupations are designed in international law to be temporary, and to last only for the period of time necessary for the Occupying Power to re-establish state and social institutions and civic life in the occupied territory, and for the territory to be then returned to the displaced sovereign (the people under occupation).[249] Alien rule in the 21st century can only be justified in exceptional and highly conditioned circumstances. Modern international law and effective international statecraft do not tolerate an indeterminate clock for injustice to end, particularly for an avaricious occupation that has long ago slipped the restraining bonds of legitimacy.

---

249 UNSC Res. 1483 (22 May 2003), which welcomed the commitment of the powers occupying Iraq to restore sovereignty to the people of Iraq "as soon as possible," and which "must come quickly." Also see UNGA Res. 75/172 (16 December 2020): "Stressing the urgency of achieving without delay an end to the Israeli occupation. . . ."

From Occupation to Apartheid
March 2022 Report (UNHRC) – Apartheid in the Occupied Palestinian Territory (A/HRC/49/87)

A Legal Definition of Apartheid

22. Only the 1973 International Convention on the Suppression and Punishment of the Crime of Apartheid[250] and the 1998 Rome Statute of the International Criminal Court[251] provide legal definitions of apartheid. The two instruments were drafted and adopted in distinct eras, which likely explains the differences in their respective terminology. The Convention Against Apartheid's drafting in the early 1970s reflected the international community's focus on the specific practices of racial supremacy in southern Africa. When the Rome Statute was drafted and adopted 25 years later, the apartheid era in southern Africa had already ended, and the statute's purpose was to provide a forward-looking definition with a universal application. In particular, it made no reference to South Africa or southern Africa. Given this approach, there is no reasonable basis to think that the existence of apartheid is limited either in time or in geography. Furthermore, while the historical practice of apartheid in southern Africa provides useful reference points for assessing the possible existence of apartheid elsewhere, such historical and political comparisons are never exact, and cannot be expected to be.[252] Rather, the legal and political starting point to determine the presence of apartheid in another time and place is the application of a commonly-accepted definition, drawn from the Convention and the Statute.

23. Amnesty International's report correctly notes that there are two secondary differences between the definitions of apartheid

---

250 (1973), 1015 UNTS 243, entered into force 18 July 1976. As of 1 February 2022, 110 states had ratified the Convention. The State of Palestine ratified the Convention in 2014. Israel has not ratified it.

251 (1998), 2187 UNTS 3, entered into force 1 July 2002. As of 1 February 2022, 123 states had ratified the State. The Statute was ratified by the State of Palestine in 2015. Israel has not ratified it.

252 John Dugard and John Reynolds, "Apartheid, International Law and the Occupied Palestinian Territory," *European Journal of International Law* 24, no. 3 (August 2013):883–84.

in the Convention Against Apartheid and the Rome Statute.[253] First, the Statute requires the existence of "an institutionalized regime of systematic oppression and domination by one racial group over any other racial group," with the intent of maintaining that regime. In contrast, the Convention takes a less-specific approach in that it does not refer to an "institutionalized regime." Nonetheless, since the Convention specifically mentions the "similar policies and practices" that were applied in southern Africa during the apartheid era, it stands to reason that these practices amounted to the sort of 'institutionalized regime' that the Statute has in mind. The second difference goes to the broader list of "inhuman acts" proscribed in the Convention. However, a purposive reading of the respective lists indicates that there is considerable overlap, and the broad language used in the Statute—i.e, "other inhumane acts"—can reasonably be said to include the same prohibited provisions that are found on the Convention's list.

24. These differences between the Convention and the Statute are secondary and reconcilable. Accordingly, the construction of a definition of the "crime against humanity of apartheid" that draws from, and is consistent with, both instruments would be made up of the following three features: (i) There exists an institutionalized regime of systematic racial oppression and discrimination; (ii) established with the intent to maintain the domination of one racial group over another; and (iii)which features inhuman(e) acts committed as an integral part of the regime.

This definition has been accepted by scholars and human rights organizations who have assessed the contemporary meaning of apartheid in international law.[254] It must be noted that all three features are required: examples or patterns of racial discrimination by themselves are insufficient.

---

253 Amnesty International, *Israel's Apartheid against Palestinians* (February 2022).

254 Dugard and Reynolds, note 24; Human Rights Watch, *A Threshold Crossed* (April 2021); Amnesty International, note 25; Harvard Law School, International Human Rights Clinic and Addameer, *Apartheid in the Occupied West Bank* (February 2022).

An institutionalized regime of systematic racial oppression and discrimination

42. At the heart of Israel's settler-colonial project is a comprehensive dual legal and political system which provides comprehensive rights and living conditions for the Jewish Israeli settlers in the West Bank, including East Jerusalem, while imposing upon the Palestinians military rule and control without any of the basic protections of international humanitarian and human rights law.[255] Against the grain of the 21st century, Israel assigns, or withholds, these rights and conditions on the basis of ethnic and national identity.

43. Politically and legally, Jewish Israeli settlers enjoy the same fulsome citizenship rights and protections as Israeli Jews living inside the country's 1949 borders. The 475,000 Israeli settlers in the West Bank, all of whom live in Jewish-only settlements, have the full panoply of laws and benefits of Israeli citizenship extended to them personally and extra-territorially. Like Israelis in Tel Aviv or Eilat, the West Bank settlers have the same access to health insurance, national insurance, social services, education, regular municipal services and the right of entry into and out of Israel and around much of the West Bank. They also received targeted benefits and incentives from the Israeli government to live and work in the settlements.[256] The settlers are an integrated part of a wealthy society with a European standard of living.[257] The utilities and services which the settlements enjoy—water, power, housing, access to well-paid jobs, roads and industrial investment—are far superior to those available to the Palestinians. If settlers are charged with a crime, they are tried in an Israeli court with the full protection of Israeli criminal law. These settlers have the right to vote in Israeli elections, even though Israeli laws formally

---

255 The Association for Civil Rights in Israel, *One Rule, Two Legal Systems* (October 2014); D. Kretzmer and Y. Ronen, *The Occupation of Justice* (2nd ed.) (Oxford, 2021).

256 B'Tselem, *This Is Ours - And This, Too: Israel's Settlement Policy in the West Bank*, joint report with Kerem Navot (March 2021), https://www.btselem.org/publications/202103_this_is_ours_and_this_too

257 World Bank: Israeli GDP per capita in 2020 was $44,168 (USD).

restrict the ability of Israeli citizens who live outside the country's territory to vote. To be sure, there are some citizenship rights possessed by an Israel citizen that are not automatically extended territorially to the West Bank settlers, particularly regarding property, planning and building laws. However, Israeli military orders have been created to assign these rights to the local and regional settler councils in the West Bank, which effectively bridges the gap. These settler councils are regarded by Israel as equivalent to municipal councils inside Israel, and they are allocated substantial benefits and budgets by the Israeli government accordingly. The major para-statal institutions that have been given the authority to operate in the Occupied Territory—the Jewish National Fund, the Jewish Agency, the World Zionist Organization and a multitude of foreign charities—work solely for the benefit of consolidating the presence of Israeli Jews in the settlements.

44. In sharp contrast, the 2.7 million Palestinians living in the West Bank enjoy none of the rights, protections and privileges possessed by the Israeli Jewish settlers living among them. They can vote in elections (when they are held) for the Palestinian Authority, but it has exceptionally limited powers. They have no democratic or political rights to hold accountable the Occupying Power which exercises the overwhelming control over their lives. The ubiquitous barriers to freedom of personal and commercial movement throughout the occupied territory has resulted in a structurally de-developed economy. The United Nations Conference on Trade and Development has estimated that Israeli closures, the confiscation of land and resources, rapacious settlement growth and military operations have cost the Palestinian economy $57.7 billion (USD) in arrested development since 2000.[258] Yet, notwithstanding the travails of the occupation, Palestinian society has become highly literate and quite well-educated.[259] The result is a dynamic and talented population whose economy has become depleted and impoverished by a protracted military occupation,

---

258 "Economic costs of the Israeli occupation for the Palestinian people: Poverty in the West Bank between 2000 and 2019," https://unctad.org/system/files/official-document/a76d309_en_0.pdf.

259 Palestine Central Bureau of Statistics, *Palestine in Figures 2020* (2021).

which is heavily dependent on international aid and which has only 1/13th the GDP per capita of Israel.[260]

45. The lives of the Palestinians in the West Bank are governed by more than 1800 military orders issued since 1967 by the Commander of the Israeli Defence Forces, covering such issues as security, taxation, transportation, land planning and zoning, natural resources, travel, and the administration of justice. In particular, Israel has imposed a military legal system in the West Bank which applies to Palestinians, but not the Jewish settlers. The focus of the military legal system is the regulation of security, which covers such offenses as participating in protests and non-violent civil disobedience, standard criminal acts, traffic violations, terrorism, membership in over 400 banned organizations, taking part in political meetings and engaging in civil society activities. Palestinians arrested for security offences can be detained without charge for a much longer time period than Israeli settlers. The military legal system is presided over by Israeli military judges, trials are conducted in Hebrew (which many Palestinians detainees do not speak), it offers very few of the procedural and substantive protections of a purposive criminal legal system, the prisoners' lawyers are significantly restricted in their access to evidence, and the conviction rate is over 99 percent.[261] Even more draconian, there are, at any one time, hundreds of Palestinians imprisoned indefinitely through administrative detention, where they are incarcerated without the façade of a formal proceeding, that is: without charges, evidence, a trial or a conviction, and whose detention can be extended indefinitely. Investigations by Israel's military into deaths and serious injuries rarely result in any accountability.

46. A central strategy of Israeli rule has been the strategic fragmentation of the Palestinian territory into separate areas of population control, with Gaza, the West Bank and East Jerusalem physically divided from one another. The West Bank itself is further splintered into 165 disconnected enclaves. This strategic

---

260 According to the World Bank, Palestinian GDP per capita in 2020 was $3,239 (USD). (The World Bank only measures the West Bank and Gaza, and excludes East Jerusalem.)

261 Judge_Jury_Occupier_report_War_on_Want.pdf (waronwant.org)

fragmentation—*divide et impera*—is geographically enforced by Israel through an elaborate series of walls, checkpoints, barricades, military closure zones, Palestinian-only roads and Israeli-only roads.[262] Israel closely monitors Palestinian society through advanced cyber-surveillance and its full control over the Palestinian population registry. The Occupied Palestinian Territory lacks any secure land, sea or air access to the outside world, with Israel controlling all of its borders (with the exception of the Rafah crossing between Gaza and Egypt). Palestinians require difficult-to-obtain special permits from the Israeli military to travel between the West Bank, East Jerusalem and Gaza.[263] This geographic division not only severs the Palestinians under occupation from each other socially, economically and politically, but also from Palestinians living in Israel and in the wider world.[264] As the Special Rapporteur has previously observed: "No other society in the world faces such an array of cumulative challenges that includes belligerent occupation, territorial discontinuity, political and administrative divergence, geographic confinement and economic disconnectedness."[265]

47. In the West Bank and East Jerusalem, Palestinian lands—the single most important natural resource in the territory—are being steadily expropriated by Israel for Jewish-only use and settlement, buttressed by discriminatory planning laws and military orders. Since 1967, Israel has confiscated more than two million dunams of Palestinian land in the West Bank,[266] which have been used to build settlements, Israeli-only highways and roads, recreational parks, industrial centers, and military bases

262 Regarding the separate highway system, see Highway-to-Annexation-Final.pdf (breakingthesilence.org.il)

263 Gisha, *Separating Land, Separating People* (June 2015).

264 Former prime minister Benjamin Netanyahu explained in 2019 that: ". . . maintaining a separation policy between the Palestinian Authority in the West Bank and Hamas in Gaza helps prevent the establishment of a Palestinian state." Lahav Harkov, "Netanyahu: Money to Hamas part of strategy to keep Palestinians divided," *The Jerusalem Post,* 12 March 2019, https://www.jpost.com/arab-israeli-conflict/netanyahu-money-to-hamas-part-of-strategy-to-keep-palestinians-divided-583082.

265 A/71/554, para. 41.

266 Metric dunam is 1,000 square metres.

and firing zones, all for the purpose of cementing a permanent and immovable demographic presence. Israel has employed three primary methods for land confiscation: (i) the appropriation of land for "military needs," some of which have later been converted for civilian Jewish settlements; (ii) the designation of land for "public needs," with the purpose of primary or exclusive Jewish Israeli use; and (iii) the declaration of "state land," with the ultimate aim of using these lands primarily for Jewish Israeli purposes. According to Peace Now in 2018, the allocation of 99.76 percent of state land has been for the exclusive use of Israeli settlements.[267] Unlike Jewish settlers, Palestinians have no representation or voice on decision-making over zoning and property use throughout most of the West Bank. The United Nations has observed that, because permits for construction for Palestinian homes and property in East Jerusalem and Area C of the West Bank "are nearly impossible to obtain," Palestinians often build without one. In turn, the Israeli military frequently orders the demolition of Palestinian homes and property built without a permit: the number of structures demolished in 2020 and 2021 are the second and third highest annual rates since these figures were first recorded in 2009.[268] And outside of official expropriation policies are the tolerated actions of Israeli settlers, who violence has been regularly employed to seize Palestinian land or make its use untenable.[269]

48. In East Jerusalem, the 360,000 Palestinians have a more enhanced social and legal status than Palestinians on the West Bank, but their position is still greatly inferior to the 230,000 Jewish settlers, who live among them in Jewish-only settlements. The Jewish settlers are regarded by Israel as residing in sovereign Israeli territory (arising from its two-stage illegal annexation of East Jerusalem in 1967 and 1980)[270] and, as such, they enjoy

---

267 *State Land Allocation in the West Bank – For Israelis Only,* Peace Now, 17 July 2018.

268 *Data on demolition and displacement in the West Bank*, United Nations Office for the Coordination of Humanitarian Affairs, https://www.ochaopt.org/data/demolition.

269 B'Tselem, *State Business: Israel's misappropriation of land in the West Bank through settler violence* (November 2021).

270 UNSC Resolutions.476, 478 and 2334.

full citizenship rights, benefits, and privileges. Almost all East Jerusalemite Palestinians possess residency status as opposed to Israeli citizenship; while this entitles them to some Israeli social rights (including health insurance), this residency status could be cancelled if they leave Jerusalem for a period of time, a threat which Jewish Israelis do not face. Approximately 75 percent of Palestinian families in East Jerusalem live below the poverty line, compared to 22 percent of Jewish families. Around 38 percent of land in East Jerusalem—mostly private Palestinian land, but some of it public land—had been expropriated by 2017 by the Israeli government for Jewish-only use, leaving Palestinian Jerusalemites with a diminished land base to accommodate tis growing population.[271] The Palestinian neighborhoods in East Jerusalem live with significant shortages in schools, much higher housing congestion, the discriminatory application of zoning and housing permits and much poorer access to municipal services (including sewage and water) than the Jewish settlers in their midst. Around 120,000–140,000 Palestinian Jerusalemites have been forced to live on the West Bank side of the separation Wall, physically separated from access to the city and its services.[272] The intentionally discriminatory neglect of Palestinians in East Jerusalem is best illustrated by the Jerusalem Master Plan, which has created a target of maintaining a Jewish demographic majority of a 60:40 ratio, after having failed to maintain an earlier target of 70:30.[273]

49. In Gaza, Israel's apparent strategy is the indefinite ware-housing of an unwanted population of two million Palestinians, whom it has confined to a narrow strip of land through its

---

271 UN Habitat, *Right to Develop: Planning Palestinian Communities in East Jerusalem* (2015).

272 The Association for Civil Rights in Israel, *East Jerusalem: Facts and Figures 2021*, https://www.english.acri.org.il/post/__283.

273 International Crisis Group, "Reversing Israel's Deepening Annexation of Occupied East Jerusalem," Report No. 202, *Middle East & North Africa*, 12 June 2019, https://www.crisisgroup.org/middle-east-north-africa/eastern-mediterranean/israelpalestine/202-reversing-israels-deepening-annexation-occupied-east-jerusalem.

comprehensive 15-year-old air, land, and sea blockade[274] (with further restrictions by Egypt on Gaza's southern border). Ban Ki-Moon has called this political quarantining of the population a "collective punishment,"[275] a serious breach of international law.[276] The World Bank reported in 2021 that Gaza has undergone a multi-decade process of de-development and deindustrialization, resulting in a 45-percent unemployment rate, a 60-percent poverty rate and with 80-percent of the population dependent on some form of international assistance, in significant part because of the hermetic sealing of Gaza's access to the outside world.[277] Gaza's coastal aquifer, its sole source of natural drinking water, has become polluted and unfit for human consumption because of contamination by seawater and sewage, substantially driving up water costs for an already destitute population. The Strip is heavily dependent on external sources—Israel and Egypt—for power, and Palestinians live with rolling power blackouts of between 12–20 hours daily, severely impairing daily living and the economy. The entry and export of goods is strictly controlled by Israel, which has throttled the local economy. Gaza's health care system is flat on its back, with serious shortages of health care professionals, inadequate treatment equipment and low supplies of drugs and medicines. Palestinians in Gaza can rarely travel outside of the Strip, a denial of their fundamental right to freedom of movement. More acutely, they have endured four highly asymmetrical wars with Israel over the past thirteen years, with enormous loss of civilian life and immense property destruction. Gaza's suffering was

---

274 Al-Mezan, note 26; Gisha report: *Area G: From Separation to Annexation,* 29 June 2020; Donald MacIntyre, *Gaza: Preparing for Dawn* (Oneworld Pubs., 2017).

275 Reuters, "UN chief Ban Ki-Moon calls for Israel to end 'collective punishment' blockade of Gaza," Middle East News, *Haaretz.com,* 29 June 2016, https://www.haaretz.com/middle-east-news/2016-06-29/ty-article/ban-ki-moon-calls-for-israel-to-end-blockade-of-gaza/0000017f-e36f-d9aa-afff-fb7fd58f0000.

276 Fourth Geneva Convention, Article 33.

277 World Bank, *Economic Monitoring Report,* 17 November 2021. These are among the highest rates of any economic unit in the world monitored by the Bank.

acknowledged by Antonio Guterres in May 2021 when he said: "If there is a hell on earth, it is the lives of children in Gaza."[278]

The intent to maintain the domination of one racial group over another

50. Across most of Israel's political spectrum is a widely-held consensus: Israel will keep East Jerusalem and either most or all of the West Bank, whether or not there is a peace agreement, and the Palestinians will remain under its permanent security control. Former prime minister Benjamin Netanyahu said in 2019: "A Palestinian state will endanger our existence. . . . I will not divide Jerusalem, I will not evacuate any community [settlement] and I will make sure we control the territory west of Jordan."[279] Before he became prime minister, Naftali Bennett stated that: "The world does not respect a nation that is willing to give up its homeland. We need to apply Israeli law in Judea and Samaria."[280] Defence Minister Benny Gantz declared in 2019 that: "We will strengthen the settlement blocs and the Golan Heights, from which we will never retreat. The Jordan Valley will remain our eastern security border."[281] Minister of Transportation Merav Michaeli, when campaigning in 2019, stated: "No one thinks that half-a-million settlers will be evacuated from Judea and Samaria."[282] And before he became foreign minister, Yair Lapid explained in 2016 that:

278 "Gaza children living in 'hell on earth' UN chief says, urging immediate end to fighting," UN News Release, 20 May 2021, https://news.un.org/en/story/2021/05/1092332.

279 "Netanyahu Says Will Begin Annexing West Bank if He Wins Israel Election," *Haaretz,* 7 April 2019, http://www.haaretz.com/misc/article-print-page/netanyahu-says-will-annex-west-bank-in-next-term-1.7089387

280 Alex Traiman, "On AIPAC sidelines, Israeli ministers express support for settlements," Jewish News Syndicate, 6 March 2018, https://www.jns.org/on-aipac-sidelines-israeli-ministers-express-support-for-settlement.

281 "Benny Gantz, Netanyahu Rival, Gives Campaign Launch Speech - Full English Transcript," *Haaretz,* 30 January 2019, https://www.haaretz.com/israel-news/elections/benny-gantz-netanyahu-rival-campaign-launch-speech-full-english-transcript-1.6892617.

282 Tovah Lazaroff, Michaeli: No one thinks half a million settlers will be evacuated," *Jerusalem Post,* 9 March 2021, https://www.jpost.com/israel-news/labor-party-head-no-one-thinks-half-a-million-settlers-will-be-removed-661353.

"My principle says maximum Jews on maximum land with maximum security and with minimum Palestinians."[283] Among recent and current Israeli political leaders, the only debate regarding the Palestinians has come down to tertiary issues: whether the Palestinians will be granted a shrunken statelet with its own postage stamps and a seat at the United Nations, or alternatively be kept in their present state of statelessness. Either way, the intent is for the Palestinians to be encased in a political ossuary, a museum relic of 21st century colonialism.

51. Except for a few weeks immediately following its 1967 occupation of the West Bank, East Jerusalem and Gaza, Israel has never accepted the international community's wall-to-wall consensus that the Palestinian territory is occupied, the Geneva Conventions apply, and therefore the strict rules of international humanitarian law apply.[284] Israel's refusal to accept the international community's direction is not a honest difference over the interpretation of international law, but the obfuscation of an acquisitive occupier determined to maintain permanent control over the land and its indigenous population.. Within a few months of the June 1967 war, the Israeli cabinet was debating not whether to return the territory, but whether to either keep all of it or return only the major Palestinian cities to Jordan in a condominium arrangement.[285] In the summer of 1967, Israel initiated the construction of its first civilian Jewish settlements, covertly at first, and then openly. The most reliable route for an alien power that covets the territory it occupies is to establish irreversible facts on the ground through the creation of civilian settlements. This not only establishes a thickening demographic footprint that consolidates the planting of the national flag, but it also generates a growing domestic political constituency which will support the embryonic claim for territorial annexation. Israel's intention in building the

283 Gil Stern Stern Hoffman, "Yair Lapid: US helped Iran fund its next war against Israel," *Jerusalem Post,* 26 January 2016, https://www.jpost.com/israel-news/politics-and-diplomacy/lapid-us-helped-iran-fund-its-next-war-against-israel-442791.

284 Theodor Meron, "The West Bank and International Humanitarian Law" *American Journal of International Law* 111, no. 2 (May 2017): 357.

285 Zertal & Eldar, *Lords of the Land.*

settlements was never primarily about security or increasing the incentive of neighboring Arab states to negotiate a final peace agreement, but rather to ensure that it retained as much of the land as possible. As Yigal Allon, the Israeli Minister of Labour and a leading proponent of the settlements explained in 1969: "Here, we create a Greater Eretz Israel from a strategic point of view and establish a Jewish state from a demographic point of view."[286] Today, 10 percent of Israel's Jewish citizens live in settlements in the Occupied Palestinian Territory, and the political constituency among Israeli Jews in support of settlement expansion continues to grow ever larger.

Inhuman(e) acts committed as an integral part of the regime

53. Israel's administration of its occupation has been replete with a range of inhuman(e) acts prohibited by the Convention Against Apartheid and the Rome Statute. In summary form, these acts would include:

i.   **Denial of the right to life and liberty**: Israel's rule is requiring increasingly more violence and confinement to be maintained: between January 2008 and February 2022, 5,988 Palestinians have been killed in the context of the occupation and conflict. (262 Israelis have died during the same time period). 2021 has been the deadliest year for Palestinians since 2014.[287] State-sanctioned extra-judicial killings by Israel continues to be part of its toolbox, including the killings of civilians posing no immediate threat to Israeli troops, and with little or no internal accountability.[288] In addition, Israel's military courts incarcerate thousands of Palestinians on security charges through a judicial system that offers few of the international protections regarding due process, and the

---

286 Robert I. Friedman, *Zealots for Zion* (Random House, 1992).

287 Data on casualties | United Nations Office for the Coordination of Humanitarian Affairs – Occupied Palestinian Rerritory (ochaopt.org)

288 A/HRC/40/74; Al-Haq Sends Urgent Appeal to UN Special Procedures on Israel's Extrajudicial Killing of Three Palestinian Men in Nablus (alhaq.org)

prevention of arbitrary arrest and detention.[289] Additionally, hundreds of Palestinians languish in administrative detention under open-ended confinement.[290] Collective punishment is frequently employed, whether it is the blockade of Gaza, the demolition of family homes of terror suspects, or the withholding of bodies.[291]

ii. **Denial of Full Participation in All Features of a Society**: Palestinians not only have no voice or vote to hold accountable the military regime which governs much of their lives, they are also severely restricted through Israeli military orders in the exercise of their inherent rights to freedom of expression, assembly, association, and movement within their own society. They are confined in travel by hundreds of checkpoints and separate roads and by the permit and ID system. They are restricted in their ability to leave and return to Palestine. Their right to work is impeded by a smothered economy, travel restrictions and the fragmentation of their territory. Hundreds of political and civil organizations are banned, and leading human rights organizations have been designated as 'terrorist' groups. Israel has imprisoned members of the (dormant) Palestinian Legislative Council. Fragmentation divides Palestinians and ensures more comprehensive control by Israel.

iii. **Measures which Divide the Population along Racial Lines**: Israel has created hundreds of Jewish-only settlements in East Jerusalem and the West Bank, living separate and apart from Palestinian Arabs. The Israeli settlers enjoy substantially superior rights, benefits, privileges and standards of living. In 2022, the Israeli Knesset adopted The Citizenship Law, which restricts the ability of Palestinians from Israel to marry

---

289 Luigi Daniele, "Illegality: Israel's Military Justice in the West Bank," *The Israeli Military Justice System and International Law, Questions of International Law,* 30 Novemer 2017, http://www.qil-qdi.org/enforcing-illegality-israels-military-justice-in-the-west-bank/.

290 Addameer, *On Administrative Detention* (July 2017), https://www.addameer.org/israeli_military_judicial_system/administrative_detention.

291 A/HRC/44/60.

spouses from the West Bank or Gaza; this does not apply to Israel Jews.[292] The Israeli military application of land, zoning and property rules in East Jerusalem and the West Bank discriminatorily benefits Israeli Jewish settlers and significantly disadvantages Palestinians. Separate settler and Palestinian highways run throughout the West Bank, and Jewish settlers do not encounter the myriad checkpoints and travel obstructions throughout the West Bank. Separate legal systems govern Israeli Jews and Palestinians.

iv. **Exploitation of Labor of a Racial Group**: Palestinians have become a reserve labor force for Israel and for its settlements. Israel recently announced that it is planning to issue up to 10,000 permits for Palestinians in Gaza to work in Israel.[293] Similarly, around 90,000 Palestinians in the West Bank have permits to work in Israel.[294] Another 35,000 Palestinians work in the Israeli settlements.[295] Many more work without permits. These jobs are almost all menial unskilled and semi-skilled positions in construction, agriculture, and manufacturing, at the low end of Israel's labor market, highly precarious, with no union protection and involving long journeys each day. Palestinians working in

---

292 Noa Shpigel, "Israel just re-banned Palestinian family unification. What does this law do, and how can it be fought?" Israel News, Haaretz.com, 12 March 2022, https://www.haaretz.com/israel-news/2022-03-12/ty-article/.premium/whats-new-in-the-citizenship-law-whats-the-next-step-in-fighting-it/0000017f-e938-d62c-a1ff-fd7b25010000. In supporting the *Law*, the Israeli Interior Minister said: "There's no need to mince words. The bill also has demographic reasons."

293 Emanuel Fabian, "Israel to boost number of Palestinian workers from Gaza, Gantz says" *The Times of Israel,* 1 March 2022, https://www.timesofisrael.com/israel-to-boost-number-of-palestinian-workers-from-gaza-gantz-says/.

294 Daniel Avis, "Israel to Offer More Work Permits for Palestinians, Bennett Says," *Bloomberg,* 18 January 2022, https://www.bloomberg.com/news/articles/2022-01-18/israel-considering-expanding-number-of-work-permits-for-gazans.

295 Mark Samander, *Captive Markets, Captive Lives: Palestinian Workers in Israeli Settlements* (Al-Haq, 2021), https://www.alhaq.org/cached_uploads/download/2021/05/01/palestinian-workers-in-israeli-settlements-webversion-1-page-view-1619871735.pdf.

Israel are paid more than their counterparts in the occupied territory, but their working conditions and wages are considerably inferior to Israelis in the Israeli labor market, and they are subject to an abusive permit brokerage system. A 2021 report by the International Labour Organization noted the exceptionally harsh impact that the Covid-19 pandemic had on Palestinian employment and working conditions, given that Palestinian society lacks the social shock absorbers possessed by Israel to manage the abrupt labor crisis.[296]

v. **Other Inhuman(e) Acts Causing Great Suffering**: Although strictly prohibited under international law, torture continues to be used in practice by Israel against Palestinians in detention. Methods of torture include sleep deprivation, beating and slapping, humiliation, unhygienic conditions and extended shackling in contorted position.[297] Challenges to the Israeli Supreme Court against its use have been unsuccessful.[298] Beatings by Israeli soldiers of Palestinians during an arrest are regularly reported, with little accountability.[299]

59. This is apartheid. It does not have some of the same features as practiced in southern Africa; in particular, much of what has been called "petit apartheid" is not present. On the other hand, there are pitiless features of Israel's "apartness" rule in the occupied Palestinian territory that were not practiced in southern Africa, such as segregated highways, high walls and extensive checkpoints, a barricaded population, missile strikes and tank

---

296 International Labour Organization, *The situation of workers of the Occupied Palestinian Territories,* Report of the Director-General at the International Labour Conference 109th Session, 2021, https://www.ilo.org/wcmsp5/groups/public/---ed_norm/---relconf/documents/meetingdocument/wcms_793285.pdf.

297 PCATI, "Torture in Israel 2021: Situation Report" (information sheet), available at דף-מידע--2021הוועד-נגד-עינויים-אנגלית-סופי.pdf (stoptorture.org.il).

298 "It's now (even more) official: torture is legal in Israel," OMCT Blog, 21 March 2019, https://www.omct.org/en/resources/blog/its-now-even-more-official-torture-is-legal-in-israel.

299 B'Tselem, *Torture and Abuse in Interrogation,* 11 November 2017, https://www.btselem.org/torture.

shelling of a civilian population, and the abandonment of the Palestinians' social welfare to the international community.[300] With the eyes of the international community wide open, Israel has imposed upon Palestine an apartheid reality in a post-apartheid world.

---

300   John Dugard, *Confronting Apartheid* (Jacana, 2018).

PART III

Accomplishments and Frustrations

CHAPTER SEVEN

ACCOMPLISHMENTS, FRUSTRATIONS, AND THE FUTURE

John Dugard

I like to think that I made a difference to the human rights mandate on Palestine in three respects during my term of office. First, I transformed the mandate from a diplomatic exercise to a robust exercise in critical monitoring and reporting. Second, I took the mandate to the people of Palestine. Third, my reports on the Wall Israel is (still) building in Palestinian territory helped to discredit this venture.

From diplomatic report to robust criticism

Three men had held the post of special rapporteur on the human rights situation in the Occupied Palestinian Territory between the establishment of the Mandate in 1993 and my election: Rene Felber (1993–1995), a Swiss politician who had served as President of the Swiss Confederation in 1992, Hannu Halinen (1996–1998), a Finnish diplomat and ambassador, and Georgio Giacomelli, an Italian diplomat and ambassador who had been Commissioner-General of UNRWA from 1985 to 1991. In common they were highly respected figures well versed in diplomacy. Each one of them resigned after a mere two years in office, citing dissatisfaction with the one-sidedness and political nature of the mandate. Their reports were characterized by discretion and careful assessment of the situation.

I lacked the diplomatic skills or experience of my predecessors. My time in apartheid South Africa had taught me that if criticism was to be effective it should be bold and robust, inevitably indiscreet, and undiplomatic. Diplomats and UN officials in New York did not like my forthright criticism of Israel, which accused Israel of violating international law, practicing apartheid and committing international crimes. They had no hesitation in telling me that I was part of the problem and not the solution, and that I should desist from criticism of this kind.

I have little doubt that my approach was more effective. On the negative side it gave rise to a stream of hate mail and strong rebuke, particularly from Israel and European and American diplomatic officials. On the positive side, it undoubtedly succeeded in highlighting Israel's violation of human rights and promoting a public awareness of its wrongdoing. Palestinians applauded this new approach as did UN officials in occupied Palestine, who resented the way in which their own frank criticisms of Israel were translated into gentle admonitions by officials in New York and Geneva. My annual report to the Third Committee of the General Assembly in New York assumed the character of gladiatorial combat with the delegates in the crowded hall delighted to hear the United States and Israel openly confronted.

My successors have followed my approach and the Human Rights Council appears to agree that diplomats are not suited for this mandate. Consequently, it is today accepted that the human rights mandate for Palestine requires a special rapporteur who will not mince his or her words.

Presenting the United Nations to the people of Palestine

It is interesting to compare the attitudes towards the United Nations of black Namibians and South Africans under apartheid to those of Palestinians under occupation. The apartheid regime of Southern Africa refused to allow UN agencies to operate in either Namibia or South Africa. Attitudes and expectations were shaped by an awareness, on the basis of news reports, of a growing determination of the United Nations to bring an end to apartheid, and of the actions it had taken to achieve this, in particular the isolation and sanctioning of the apartheid state. Consequently, they believed, with good reason, that salvation lay with the United

Nations and the international community. Palestinians, on the other hand, are regularly exposed to the benevolence of the United Nations through its agencies such as UNRWA, OCHR, WHO, UNICEF, WFP etc. From this they know that the United Nations is concerned about their well-being. But then, they also realize that the United Nations is not willing to confront Israel on the big issues of the occupation, the Wall, settlements, seizure of land, assaults on Gaza, the blockade of Gaza, and so on. Inevitably this has bred a cynicism about the United Nations. In short, while black Namibians and South Africans had high expectations of the United Nations, which were subsequently realized, Palestinians, sadly, have low expectations as a result of disappointment over many years.

Where did I fit into this picture? I was not part of a UN welfare scheme able to dispense material assistance. Instead, I was in some ways a representative of the political arm of the United Nations that was strong on language but weak on action, a political placebo.

Despite this, I think, perhaps naively, that my presence achieved something.

When I visited farmers in homes overlooking fields captured by the Wall, Bedouins whose structures had been destroyed by the IDF, refugees whose houses had been bulldozed by the IDF, cave-dwellers in the South Hebron Hills under constant threat of eviction, school teachers whose class rooms had been damaged by the IDF, farmers whose olive trees had been uprooted by settlers, health workers struggling to cope with the wounded and owners whose homes had been demolished, I really believe that they received some comfort from the knowledge that someone who held a position of some importance in the United Nations was concerned about their plight and prepared to listen to their grievances. Although I might not herald action on the part of the UN, they hoped that I would inform decision-makers in the assembly halls of the United Nations of their frustrations and disappointments. They placed their confidence in me to tell it how it is. It was my duty to not to disappoint them.

The Wall

Undoubtedly my greatest achievement as special rapporteur was my role in opposition to the Wall Israel began to construct in Palestinian territory in 2002 and in the 2004 Advisory Opinion of the International Court of Justice, which declared that the Wall was illegal and should be dismantled. The failure of the United Nations and states to comply with this Opinion was undoubtedly my greatest disappointment.

In Part One I have described the way in which the Wall dominated my reports from 2002 to 2007. Early reports focused on the illegality of the Wall as an act of annexation and the harmful effects it had on Palestinians in the shadow of the Wall. Reports after the International Court had rendered its Advisory Opinion welcomed the Opinion and stressed that although it was advisory only, it nevertheless bound the United Nations, which had endorsed it. I repeatedly called upon Israel, the Quartet and the Security Council to comply with the Opinion. I later stressed that statements from the Israeli government confirmed that the Wall had replaced the Green Line as the boundary between Israel and Palestine, which meant that the annexation of Palestinian land was abundantly clear. At the same time, I continued to monitor the growth of the Wall, its ongoing harmful consequences, and the impact it had had on Jerusalem and Bethlehem.

The response of the United Nations to this Opinion was initially encouraging when the General Assembly, including the Russian Federation and European Union member states, approved the Court's Opinion.[1] But this euphoria was short lived when the Security Council, Quartet and Secretariat combined to ensure that it would not even guide the UN in its approach to the Palestine issue, let alone bind it to take action.

The approach of the Security Council and the Quartet, at the instigation of the United States, was simply to ignore the Opinion as if it had never happened. The Secretary-General also had an important role to play, both as representative of the United Nations in the Quartet and as executive officer of the United Nations.

---

1 Resolution ES-10/15, adopted by 150 votes to 6, with 10 abstentions.

Undoubtedly, he could have made a difference by endorsing the Opinion and urging the Quartet and the political bodies of the UN to give their support to the Opinion.

I found the silence of the Secretary-General, Kofi Annan, difficult to understand, not only because it seemed to run counter to his vision of the world order, but also because when I met him whenever I was at UN headquarters in New York, he expressed support for my work and by necessary implication, for my campaigning for compliance with the Opinion. The most likely explanation for this was the extent of pressure on him exerted by the United States, the United Kingdom and the Israeli lobby. That the Israeli lobby, supported by the United States, was a powerful influence in the UN Secretariat was confirmed when I approached Lakhdar Brahimi, a seasoned UN insider, then special adviser to the Secretary-General, to find out whether my suspicions that members of the Secretariat were particularly well disposed towards Israel were well-founded. He told me that the United States controlled the United Nations and determined how Israel was be treated. This, he said, was "a given" of the United Nations with which one had to live.

Kiernan Prendergast, the British Under Secretary-General for Political Affairs, appeared to play a major role in the decision-making of the Secretary-General on Israel/Palestine in general and on the approach to adopt towards the advisory opinion in particular. I was surprised when he told me without hesitation when we met that "we do not think the ICJ Opinion was a good idea."[2] This provided me with an explanation for why the UN Legal Counsel had not participated in the advisory proceedings, as had been done in other important cases of this kind. Later I learned that Prendergast had asked the UN Office of Legal Affairs for a legal opinion on "actions and positions which the Secretariat...could take pursuant to the Court's Opinion" and that this had resulted in an opinion not from the Legal Counsel himself but his deputy, Ralph Zacklin. This brief and superficial opinion, which paid little attention to legal principle or UN precedent, advised that the

---

2 Meeting of 29 October 2004.

Secretary-General was under no legal obligation to pronounce on the merits of the Opinion, to reiterate the Court's finding on the illegality of the Wall or to call upon Israel to dismantle the Wall. In effect this meant that the Secretary-General was in law obliged to do nothing. Strangely this important opinion which provided a legal basis for the silence of the Secretary-General on the Court's Opinion has received virtually no attention. Searches for this opinion on the internet are of no avail.[3]

My disillusionment with officers of the law was now complete. In 1966 I had been shaken by the failure of the judges of the International Court of Justice to find South Africa accountable for its administration of Namibia on the basis of a specious technicality.[4] Now the Office of Legal Affairs had undermined my faith in the United Nations with a thoroughly bad opinion that has resulted in successive Secretary-Generals doing nothing to promote compliance with the ICJ Opinion.

The future of the mandate

Accountability

A question which troubled me throughout my mandate was that of accountability. To whom was I accountable? The United Nations? Or the wider international community?

Clearly a view prevailed in the UN Secretariat in New York that a special rapporteur is accountable to the United Nations with the consequence that he or she, like an employee or paid consultant, is obliged to follow UN directives and to refrain from criticism of the UN. This approach saw the UN as a club, of which special rapporteurs—although unpaid and purportedly independent—are members and expected to place the reputation

---

3 The only references I have found to this opinion are references to my criticisms of the opinion in Marcelo Kohen and Laurence Boisson de Chazournes (eds.), *International Law and the Quest for its Implementation:* Liber Amicorum *Vera Gowlland-Debbas* (Brill, 2010), 403.

4 *South West Africa Cases, Second Phase,* 1966 ICJ Reports 6. See my criticisms of this decision in John Dugard, *The South West Africa/Namibia Dispute, Documents and Scholarly Writings on the Controversy between South Africa and the United Nations* (University of California Press, 1973), 332–374.

of the United Nations as an institution above considerations of justice and community interest. This was brought home to me on a number of occasions.

I found it strange that UN officials were not allowed to meet with Hamas officials. After all, in similar conflict situations, such as South Africa, the UN had treated parties with different ideologies equally, even if a party espoused violence. Obviously, this was yet another policy dictated by the United States. I took the position that as an independent expert I was not bound by this policy and proceeded to arrange to meet with Ismail Haniyeh, the leader of Hamas in Gaza. I was then warned by a bureaucrat in the Office of the High Commissioner for Human Rights that I was not permitted to do this. I simply went ahead and met Haniyeh, with whom I had a very insightful discussion. I complained to the UN Special Envoy, Alvaro de Soto, about the UN policy towards Hamas. He failed to respond. Later he was to denounce this policy in his End of Mission statement In May 2007.

My criticisms of the failure of the UN to take a more proactive position on Palestine grew louder as my term neared an end. In October 2007 I was scolded for my criticisms of the UN by the Under Secretary-General for Political Affairs, Lynn Pascoe, who told me that as special rapporteur I was a UN insider and should keep my criticisms within the organization.[5] He seemed surprised when I told him that I believed that had a wider responsibility.

Kofi Annan accepted that I was required to account to a wider constituency than the UN. I met with him regularly in my visits to New York and he listened attentively to my concerns about the UN without any suggestion that I had exceeded my mandate in my criticisms of the UN. In 2006 I wrote to him expressing my concerns about the decision of the UN to impose sanctions on Palestine after the 2006 elections in which Hamas had triumphed. I warned him that this decision and the participation of the UN in the Quartet had undermined the credibility of the UN as an independent arbiter in occupied Palestine. He wrote a warm letter in which he expressed an appreciation for my "frank assessment

---

5 Meeting of 29 October 2007.

of the situation" and stated that "in your role as special rapporteur, you are acting as an independent expert, with a mandate to speak out on human rights issues. I fully respect your mandate."[6]

My experience with Secretary-General Ban Ki-Moon was very different. In September 2007 as my mandate was coming to an end, I gave an interview to *Al Jazeera* (Arabic) which was conducted in English but translated into Arabic. I spoke about the pro-Israel bias of the Quartet, that it was a tool of the United States and suggested that the UN should withdraw from the Quartet. I also said that the Secretary-General should distance himself from the United States. I chose my words carefully as I knew that I was treading on dangerous ground. The translator was, however, less concerned about the nuances of my language and simply translated me as having said that the Secretary-General was biased and took instructions from Washington. The Secretary-General was furious and called on Louise Arbour, the High Commissioner for Human Rights, to dismiss me immediately. Louise replied, quite correctly, that I was an unpaid expert, not employed by the UN, who had been appointed by the Human Rights Council. This was followed by an investigation of the translation which showed that the translator had indeed given a loose translation to my words. I could not, however, seriously fault him as he had captured the essence of what I wished to convey, albeit in more careful language. Thereafter I tried to schedule a meeting with Ban Ki-Moon to discuss the issue, but he refused to see me.

These incidents raised the question of the limits of a special rapporteur's independence. Does a special rapporteur, an expert not on the pay roll of the UN, have an obligation to refrain from criticism of the institution or does he or she have a wider constituency to which he or she is accountable? Clearly Kofi Annan believed that a special rapporteur served a wider interest, namely the promotion and protection of human rights. Unfortunately, this view was not shared by all. This is a matter that deserves attention. It should be made clear that a special rapporteur is not only free

---

6 Letter of 13 July 2006.

but obliged to criticize the UN if it undermines international law and fails to protect human rights.

The status of the special rapporteur

I occupied an unusual position in the UN system. On the one hand, I was a member of the International Law Commission, a 34-member body of independent and unpaid experts, elected by a vote in the General Assembly, charged with task of codifying international law. On the other hand, I was a special rapporteur of the Human Rights Council, also an independent and unpaid expert. In the former capacity I enjoyed the same status as heads of mission accredited to international organizations in Geneva. More importantly, I was treated with respect and helpfulness by the staff of the UN Codification Division which administered sessions of the International Law Commission in Geneva. As special rapporteur I was extremely well received by the heads and staff of UN agencies in Palestine. Successive UNRWA commissioners-general were particularly hospitable and helpful. I had no complaints about the way in which I was received and treated in Palestine by UN staff. Nor did I have complaints about the treatment I received from Israeli officials.[7] It was a different story in Geneva. I had excellent relations with the High Commissioners for Human Rights—Mary Robinson, Sergio Vieira de Mello, Bertrand Ramcharan (Acting High Commissioner after Sergio's death in Iraq, 2003) and Louise Arbour, and I was fortunate to have wonderful special assistants and security advisers. On the other hand, staff members of the Office of the High Commissioner for Human Rights with whom I was required to deal in Geneva often seemed determined to obstruct my mission by telling me who I might meet in Palestine, trying to prevent me from presenting my report on the Wall, removing Darka Topali as my assistant in the last year of my mandate and generally being unhelpful. There appeared to be a culture of unhelpfulness verging on obstruction

---

7 Israeli soldiers, as opposed to Israeli officials, at checkpoints were routinely rude and wished to inspect the contents of our vehicle until they were reminded that the Convention on the Privileges and Immunities of the United Nations prohibits such searches.

towards special rapporteurs on the part of many bureaucrats in Geneva.

The need for a statute on the office and function of special rapporteurs

The election, role and functions of the International Law Commission are spelled out in a Statute adopted by the General Assembly. A Statute of this kind adopted by the Human Rights Council on the election, independence, travel expenses and subsistence allowances, privileges and immunities,[8] staff assistance and functions is something worth considering. Such a Statute would place the role, rights, responsibilities, and status of special rapporteurs on a firmer basis. It would make it clear that special rapporteurs are accountable to the international community as a whole, rather than to the United Nations or Human Rights Council. It might also ensure that staff of the Office of the High Commissioner for Human Rights were more respectful and helpful to special rapporteurs.

Dissemination of reports

The purpose of the reports of special rapporteurs is to influence governments, civil society and public opinion. The effective dissemination of reports is therefore of paramount importance. All special rapporteurs, whether their focus is on a special human rights subject or specific country, have an interest in a wider dissemination of their reports. All face obstacles specific to their particular mandate. The Palestine mandate is, however, confronted by greater problems in this respect on account of the international conspiracy to portray criticism of Israel as anti-Semitism.

The UN's chief method of dissemination of reports is publication on the UN website. That this is not an ineffective means of dissemination was brought home to me every time a report was

---

8 Special rapporteurs are entitled to certain immunities in terms of Article VI, section 22, of the Convention on the Privileges and Immunities of the United Nations. This has been confirmed by the International Court of Justice in the cases of *Mazilu*, 1989 ICJ Reports 177 and *Cumaraswamy*, 1999 ICJ Reports 62.

published in this way. Suddenly I was inundated with hate-mail. There is no doubt, however, that more could be done to disseminate reports. At present the UN does not see it as its task to publish shortened versions of a report which highlight the main findings and issues of concern to the international community. Every effort should, however, be made to persuade the UN to publish such a press release. The press release published by the International Court of Justice of its decisions provides a useful precedent.

A special rapporteur should be given an opportunity to engage with civil society. Side events at Geneva sometime provide special rapporteurs with such an opportunity but what is needed is a more structured and substantial meeting that enables special rapporteurs to explain reports and answer questions.

When I was in Palestine, I regularly addressed a meeting of representatives of UN agencies. This allowed me to obtain the views and suggestions of agencies working in Palestine, many of which were later included in my report. Although such a meeting in Geneva would lack information from those working in the field, it would allow special rapporteurs to engage with a wider section of the UN family than is represented in the Human Rights Council.

The Special Rapporteur on the situation of human rights in the Palestinian territory occupied since 1967 faces a unique problem relating to dissemination of reports. It is common knowledge that many newspaper editors and media outlets deliberately suppress criticism of Israel for fear of being labeled as anti-Semitic. Even the most carefully researched and cautiously expressed criticisms are often suppressed. It thus becomes a challenge to the special rapporteur to reach his or her audience by other means, such as the avenues of social media. The United Nations itself might do more to disseminate the reports of the Special Rapporteur on Palestine in the light of this obstacle. One fears, however, that the United States and Israel lobby will ensure that such a dissemination does not occur.

Visits to occupied Palestine

I had the good fortune to be able to visit occupied Palestine. Despite its strong criticisms of my reports, and its refusal to meet with me, the Israeli government at no time suggested that I would be prohibited from carrying out my mandate in occupied Palestine. On the contrary, it took care to ensure that I was never obstructed or even seriously inconvenienced in pursuing my mandate. Although it refused to engage with me it did on occasion arrange for me to meet persons outside government who presented the government's position to me. This surprised me as I recalled that the South African apartheid regime consistently refused to allow UN officials to visit South Africa at all.

I have no knowledge as to why Israel reversed its policy in this respect when Richard Falk was appointed to succeed me. I suspect that Israel was testing the waters to see how the UN would react to such a decision. Had the UN Secretary-General complained to Israel about this decision I believe that there is good reason to believe that the decision would have been reversed. It is not too late for such action. It seems, however, that the present Secretary-General, like his predecessor, lacks the courage to publicly confront Israel (and the United States) in this regard. This is unfortunate. To fulfill her task properly the present Special Rapporteur, Francesca Albanese, should not be denied access to the people and territory who her mandate seeks to protect.

CHAPTER EIGHT

CHALLENGES AND RESPONSES

Richard Falk

In retrospect my six years as special rapporteur was the most challenging professional experience of my life, not only because Israel impeded my factfinding missions, but due to the informal politics that swirled about the homeland struggles of two peoples for land, basic rights, and international legitimacy. It was also personally challenging as I was defamed by pro-Israeli militants from the time my UN appointment until my term expired in 2014. At the same time, it was deeply rewarding to be given such an opportunity to serve the UN in this manner as an unpaid official engaged in a meaningful effort to document Israeli violations of the human rights of Palestinians living under harsh conditions of prolonged occupation. Additionally, in the course of the six years, I was brought into contact with many congenial and courageous persons within the UN and in the countries neighboring Israel and Palestine who lent various kinds of support for this work. These collaborative features of the work more than offset the personal attacks by NGOs at the UN, and by diplomats from a few countries most closely allied with Israel, including my own, and by the malicious Zionist civic activism that was directed toward me.

On a practical level, my role as SR was much more affected by Israel's hostility to the mandate than was experienced by John Dugard, my predecessor. John had the benefit of Israel's tacit and sullen acceptance of his role, allowing him entry to the Occupied Palestinian Territory (OPT) by way of Ben Gurion Airport, which ensured access to the West Bank and East Jerusalem, as well as to the Gaza Strip. I was not only denied entry in December 2008 but expelled after some hours of detention in a prison cell, with the clear implication that I would not be allowed entry for as long as I held the position.

This exclusion from the OPT meant that I was deprived of the benefit of periodic factfinding visits that included opportunities for direct observation of the operational features of the occupation with respect to such sensitive issues as the checkpoints, settlements, house demolitions, exclusionary roads, separation Wall, and security regime, as well as interaction with Palestinians, Israelis, and others, including diplomats who had useful firsthand knowledge about human rights issues. Carrying out the mandate without being able to visit the OPT periodically influenced the tone and approach taken in my annual reports to the HRC and the Third Committee of the General Assembly but had little impact on my legal analysis assessing the legality of Israeli practices in the OPT, and the resulting policy recommendations.

My experience in Gaza was different than that in either the West Bank or Gaza. This was because I could enter Gaza from Egypt without passing by Israeli checkpoints that not only blocked access by way of Israel but also via Jordan. After my experience at Ben Gurion, I would undoubtedly have been denied entry if proceeding by way of Jordan. Even before the Arab Spring the Egyptian government was cooperative in a low-profile manner with the HRC mandate with respect to Gaza. It facilitated my access to Gaza, as well as lent some diplomatic support in Geneva, but my first two attempts to visit Gaza were blocked, nonetheless, by logistical reasons unrelated to Israel. First, there were security concerns about the drive from Cairo to the Rafah crossing in southern Gaza that went through a part of Egypt where criminal gangs kidnapped foreigners for ransom. Then, there was a temporary UN prohibition on travel to Gaza that was put in place after the assassination of a UN civil servant in Cairo. Finally, on my third visit to Egypt, I managed to carry out a mission in Gaza, shortly after an eight-day major Israeli military operation that began on November 14, 2012 (Operation Pillar of Defense), making it an opportune time to grasp what the "occupation" actually meant for the civilian population of Gaza, and more pointedly, whether and to what extent the tactics and weaponry used by Israel violated international humanitarian law and the Fourth Geneva Convention governing belligerent occupation.

As with the personal attacks, there were compensations arising from the denials of entry to the OPT. This enabled me to visit Egypt, Jordan, and Lebanon under generally favorable factfinding conditions, witnessing the effects of long-term dispossession of Palestinians from their homeland. I also had the opportunity to meet with Hamas leaders living in exile in Doha and Cairo, and with several refugee communities in Jordan and Lebanon, as well as in Gaza. Furthermore, some indirect factfinding took place especially in Amman as a result of Palestinian human rights NGOs agreeing to meet with me and feeling freer to cooperate with my mandate than if the meetings had taken place within the OPT under watchful Israeli eyes. The NGO delegations were often accompanied by Palestinians who had endured abuses associated with the occupation, especially in the West Bank. Many of the more serious abuses of international human rights were either a matter of well-documented public record or already addressed in Israel's own official reports on its administration of the West Bank and Jerusalem, the establishment and expansion of settlements, or the compilation of reports on Palestinian prisoners and prison conditions. The careful and comprehensive reports prepared by Palestinian and Israeli NGOs were also of great help, reflecting the participation of international law and human rights experts, reinforced by systematic gathering of evidence bearing on allegations of Israeli violations of international humanitarian law.

Despite my ability to adapt to Israel's refusal to permit entry, the lack of direct access had negative effects on the quality of the reports during my time as SR. The prevention of existential contact with the occupation represents a serious barrier to the ability of an SR to fulfill the overall purposes of the UN mandate. Israeli non-cooperation in relation to official UN activities was a violation of its obligations as a member of the UN, and expressive of its wider pattern of defiance of international law—rendered more serious because of an absence of adverse consequences. Israel's pattern of achieving impunity had an overall effect of weakening respect for international law and the authority of the UN. Such negative fallout was accentuated in my case by the unwillingness of the UN to do more to insist on my access to the OPT, which confirmed for me the extent of UN weakness when, as here, faced with strong geopolitical pressures.

I came to understand that even at the Human Rights Council, where Israel was not a member and a pro-Palestine consensus dominated the agenda, Israel with U.S. backing, and sometimes EU backing, exerted formidable soft power influence behind the scenes that discouraged any strenuous effort to implement international law obligations involving Israel that extended *beyond* the factfinding stage. That is, opposition to UN factfinding involving Israel could be overcome, as was the case with the establishment of the OPT Mandate, and the dozen special commissions of inquiry devoted to Israel's administration of occupied Palestine, but when it came to enforcement of any kind Israel, with the help of its friends, could block UN efforts even if the calls for implementation were grounded on exceedingly well-evidenced findings by highly credible level commissions of inquiry. I believe this distinction between factfinding capabilities and implementation failures is key to an accurate appreciation of the UN, illustrating both its value and its limitations. Such a distinction makes it irresponsibly wrong to conclude that the UN is worthless because of its lack of enforcement capabilities vis-à-vis Israel. And at the same time, it is hopelessly naïve to expect the UN to be able to overcome determined geopolitical resistance to its assessments, and hence alter the abusive conditions facing the civilian population of Gaza on a daily basis.

A further dimension of this hotly contested interface between factfinding and enforcement helps account for the attention given to the Israel/Palestine agenda item and the UN-bashing that pushes back against such persistence. The lack of enforcement and continuing non-compliance generates more effort to exert whatever pressures can be mounted, and this means that Israel feels more criticized and investigated than other countries which also perpetrate supposedly acute abuses of human rights. The attention given to Israeli violations of human rights is deflected by a broad campaign to label critics, including institutional venues, as "anti-Semitic," and indeed this has produced support for the International Holocaust Remembrance Alliance (IHRA) re-definition of anti-Semitism to include what is deemed excessive criticism of the state of Israel.

In the background, partly explaining the UN preoccupation, is the fact that unlike other unresolved conflicts in the world, except maybe that in Western Sahara, the UN accepted from the United Kingdom in 1948 responsibility for a just solution to the competing claims of Jews and Arabs over the territory of Palestine, and failed miserably to complete the mission in ways that safeguarded basic Palestinian rights. The UN record over the years is far from blameless. The UN neither insisted on maintaining the unity of Palestine nor managed to achieve its own preferred "two-state solution," presupposing Palestinian statehood existing in sovereign equality with the state of Israel. Little was done by to implement the partition solution proposed by the UN and formally accepted by Israel. Even partition interfered with the Palestinian basic right of self-determination, having never been endorsed by the majority resident Palestinian population and opposed by the Arab countries in the Middle East.

Marginalizing the Goldstone report

This failure of the political will to implement international law against Israel was probably most prominently exhibited by the events that surround the so-called Goldstone Commission. The commission was established by the HRC after Operation Cast Lead in early 2009 when there was widespread criticism of Israel's use of advanced military weaponry against a defenseless and thoroughly vulnerable and entrapped civilian population supposedly under the protective control of Israel as the Occupying Power. The distinguished South African jurist, Richard Goldstone, was named chair of the commission that included three other highly qualified members. A detailed and impressive report was produced and received praise from impartial sources. The report was balanced even to the extent of declaring Hamas' retaliatory rockets as violations of the laws of war, although they caused minimal damage because of their indiscriminate trajectories. The findings of the Goldstone Commission were unanimous, yet the reaction of Israel, supported by the U.S., was one of outrage. It was accompanied by a vicious character attack on Goldstone by the highest government officials in Israel, and a major pushback by the U.S. government, leading even the Palestinian Authority to shrink from exerting pressure for implementation of its recommendations and findings. In this atmosphere, Goldstone took the extraordinary step of publishing a journalistic retraction of the most damaging finding against Israel in the *Washington Post*. Goldstone declared that if he had known, when preparing the report, what he later learned, he would never have found Israel in deliberate violation of international law. None of the three other internationally known members of the commission joined Goldstone or were consulted in advance of his notorious retraction. On the contrary, they issued a statement reaffirming the findings and recommendations of the detailed report as presented to the HRC.

This Goldstone retraction highlighted UN problems of implementation and also the vulnerabilities facing SRs addressing situations in which human rights norms are systematically violated. The salience of this pattern in the aftermath of Cast Lead made obstacles to the implementation of international law more transparent but had a disillusioning effect on the international efforts to uphold legal obligations. This pattern was often misinterpreted, including by Palestinians, as evidence that international law had not proved helpful in their liberation struggle. Palestinians and their supporters argued that having international law on their side for all major issues resulted in no mitigation of the prolonged suffering and subjugation that the Palestinians experienced over the course of decades.

For myself, in contrast, it made clear that violations of international law could nonetheless be articulated within the confines of the UN despite interference from governments enjoying a right of veto and possessing geopolitical clout, albeit when it came to enforcement, the primacy of geopolitics could nullify the behavioral impact of even the most authoritative finding of unlawfulness.

I interpreted this dichotomy as creating a distinction between the symbolic domain of lawfulness and unlawfulness, and the substantive impact of power politics upon behavioral compliance with legal norms. In inter-governmental circles this distinction was often ignored. In civil society, however, respected findings of unlawfulness or criminality rendered behavior "illegitimate," thereby justifying activism and opposition, and indirectly exerting influence on governments, including on their foreign policy and on public opinion. The symbolic domain is not sufficiently appreciated as having significant indirect effects on unresolved conflicts, including those of the Israeli/Palestine variety. Israel and its supporters have shown an increasing appreciation of incurring setbacks with respect to Israeli policies and practices relied upon in the OPT. In particular, Israel is acutely aware that the apartheid regime in South Africa collapsed not because of a lack of sufficient police and military capability but because it lost the "legitimacy war" within the symbolic domain. I came to appreciate that the contributions of my work as SR were confined to the symbolic domain, but that this aspect of UN activity was generally underestimated as of value to the eventual implementation of international law standards. The anti-colonial wars of liberation show that, over and over again, the side with the weaker military and police capabilities, but victorious in the struggle for legitimacy controlled the political outcome of such struggles. Gandhi's understanding of how important making time for international journalists and winning over international public opinion was to his nonviolent movement, has provided an iconic model for activists, attesting to the utility of pursuit of victory in the symbolic domain functioning as a prelude to a substantive victory on the ground.

General observations

The politics of the Palestinian Authority

I was aware that support by the Palestinian Authority (PA) although not a member of the HRC, was crucial to my selection as SR in 2008. What I found unacceptable was the PA's initial sense of entitlement with respect to the manner in which I discharged the role. Perhaps I invited some of this PA pushback by suggesting in my first report to the HRC that the mandate be expanded to include Palestinian violations of human rights and international humanitarian law, a generally unwelcome suggestion on my part that was rejected by all governments in Geneva that were sympathetic with Palestinian grievances. I learned my lesson, and although unconvinced on the merits, dropped the suggestion altogether.

However, my more serious troubles with the PA lay ahead during my first year as SR. The PA made no secret of their deep objections to any mention of Hamas and its governance role in Gaza as a result of its electoral victories in 2006 and subsequent displacement of Fatah. The PA sought to block the release of my report, and later urged me to resign as SR, which is something not even UN Watch (UNW), with its campaign to portray me as an anti-Semite, had proposed. I resisted both sets of pressures, and the PA then, for whatever reasons, decided to cooperate with me. For the next five years the PA respected my independence, during which time I maintained a cordial supportive relationship with the highly capable PA diplomatic representatives in Geneva and New York. However, in retrospect, it was the PA more than Israel that directly objected to my way of fulfilling the duties of SR, while Israel and UN Watch were intent on publicly discrediting me personally, wounding the messenger to divert attention from the message, which was part of a broader Israeli tactic that I described as "the politics of deflection." In essence, this meant shifting the political conversation from the substantive issues raised by Israel's occupation policies and practices to the alleged bias of individual and institutional critics.

What I learned was that political independence was vital for a responsible performance in the role of SR for a hotly contested mandate such as mine, and that such independence could not be taken for granted just because the UN didn't regard the position as subject to the discipline imposed on salaried international civil servants. The SR must be willing to resist pressures from interested governments and civil society organizations and adhere to professional standards of performance and the guidance provided by conscience.

Policy recommendations

It has been customary to add recommendations for action by the HRC or the UN generally at the end of SR periodic reports. These were to be made in light of the analysis of patterns of behavior that violated international human rights standards and the norms of international humanitarian law within the scope of the mandate.

In preparing reports, I accorded considerable effort to framing policy recommendations at the end each report, proposing ways to exert more pressure on Israel to comply with human rights in the OPT. For example, I proposed recourse to the International Court of Justice on matters pertaining to the unlawful establishment and expansion of Israeli settlements on the West Bank and East Jerusalem. I was often told by diplomats stationed in Israel, always on a not-for-attribution basis, that the settlements were the most important obstacle to achieving success within the Oslo diplomatic framework, and I tried to highlight such issues in the framing of recommendations, including suggestions of advocating recourse to the ICJ for an Advisory Opinion on the lawfulness of Israeli settlements, and their security and logistical infrastructure.

What at first disappointed and even surprised me was that although my reports were generally well received, the recommendations were uniformly ignored. Only in retrospect do I link this observation to my earlier commentary on what the UN can and cannot do. The issue here relates to a presumed division of labor between relying on experts for the *facts,* and on governments for *policy.* This parallels the assertion that the UN plays an integral role in symbolic politics but cannot follow through substantively if geopolitical forces resist. In contrast, when geopolitical consensus exists as in the First Gulf War (1991) or the Libyan Intervention (2011), the UN is quite capable of acting beyond the constraints of its own Charter and of international law, if necessary to fulfill the mission characteristically being implemented by a coalition of the willing. This happened in the Libyan instance when a limited mission to protect the city of Benghazi by establishing a No Fly Zone was delineated on the authority of the Right to Protect (R2P) norm in the Security Council. The implementation of the mission was entrusted to NATO, which then ignored the limits and proceeded to engage in a regime-changing intervention.

The fate of the Goldstone Report is symptomatic of this broader issue. Even the critics of its findings spent little energy disputing the exhaustively documented findings, concentrating instead on nullifying the recommendations. Israel itself undertook a major effort to discredit the process, perhaps its excessive fury reflecting anger that such a previously respected international figure as Richard Goldstone, who also happened to be a lifelong Zionist, should be associated with such a UN undertaking that was damaging to Israel's top PR goal of presenting the IDF as "the most moral armed forces in the world."

Overall assessment

After a lapse of seven years since my second term as SR ended, the situation in the OPT more than ever warrants the attention of a SR mandate from the UN HRC. The situation on the ground, besides being prolonged, seems to have no end in sight. As at this writing, armed struggle has not featured prominently in the conflict in recent years, although the May 2021 major Israeli military attack on Gaza, the tepid international response, and the resultant civilian casualties suggests that an objective accounting of the events from the perspective of international law is more needed and useful than ever. And it is impossible to rule out the possibility that a subsequent Palestinian leadership will rely on its right of resistance to justify recourse to an armed liberation movement, having been so long frustrated in its attempt to find a solution that is based on compromise and basic rights.

Both the Palestinians and Israelis have become alive to the centrality of the lawfare dimensions of Israeli occupation and Palestinian resistance. Israel has exhibited sensitivity to setbacks in the legitimacy war being waged by Palestine and its supporters in the symbolic domain, responding less via lawfare of its own devising than by continuing attacks on its critics. Perhaps, the most flagrant expression of this way of proceeding was the 2021 classifications of six leading Palestinian NGOs operating in the OPT as terrorist organizations, a move apparently designed to inhibit funding and other forms of support from foreign sources as well as the capabilities of these voluntary organizations to carry on their work effectively. Such action taken against NGOs with such strong international reputations of professionalism is a new Israeli tactic supplementing its reliance on defamatory tactics of UN-bashing and treating criticisms of Israeli state practices as expressions of anti-Semitism.

On the Palestinian side there has been more stress on lawfare, that is, expressing grievances by appeals to legal assessments of rights and international institutional procedures, especially within the broader reach of the UN system. Most notably, there has been an increasing consensus in international circles of opinion that Israel is an apartheid state of settler colonial origins, established and maintained in violation of international criminal law. The related acceptance in 2021 by the International Criminal Court of a PA request that specific Israeli violations of international criminal law in the OPT since 2014 be investigated by the ICC Prosecutor for possible further action is another significant factor. These are major Palestinian victories in the ongoing legitimacy war, adding credibility and support to global solidarity initiatives, most notably the BDS Campaign.

It has become evident that the role of SR is an integral part of this ongoing struggle. By giving reliable and comprehensive confirmation of Palestinian grievances, SRs provide a professional underpinning to the basic contention that Israel is depriving the Palestinian people of their basic rights. They contribute a vital influential basis for keeping Palestinian grievances on the UN and civil society agenda, and challenge purported democracies to reconcile their foreign policy stance with their abstract championship of human rights. It is relevant to take note of the fact that South Africa has shaped its foreign policy more than any other country to align toward Israel/Palestine in the spirit of continuing the anti-racist struggle that unexpectedly led to the collapse from within of the apartheid regime in South Africa.

338 | PROTECTING HUMAN RIGHTS IN OCCUPIED PALESTINE

In the near future, Palestinian victories in the legitimacy war are not likely to become decisive in ending Israeli apartheid or achieving a sustainable peace based on finally recovering the inalienable right of self-determination enjoyed by the Palestinian people. The geopolitical alignment supportive of Israel is presently too strong and inflexible and is held in place by domestic U.S. pro-Israel lobbying groups and the media influence Israel continues to enjoy in leading Western countries. Beyond this Israel is a wily opponent and has learned from the collapse of the South African state resulting from largely nonviolent global pressures. Israel continues to benefit diplomatically from the lingering sense of guilt in the liberal democracies about their inadequate response to Nazi genocide, and fascist anti-Semitism in Europe more generally. For these reasons the struggle ahead may be long with many bends in the road, but throughout the UN role will remain a test of whether in the end international justice or the politics of domination prevails.

CHAPTER NINE

LOOKING BACKWARD, LOOKING FORWARD

Michael Lynk

Introduction

When I was selected as special rapporteur by the Human Rights Council in March 2016, a great advantage in my favor was the solid foundation established by two of my recent predecessors, John Dugard and Richard Falk. Their reporting had consistently combined judicious human rights commentary with rigorous legal analysis regarding Israel's increasingly entrenched occupation of Palestine. In the initial weeks following my selection, amidst the noisy backlash generated by private organizations in North America and Europe that vigorously supported Israel's occupation, I spoke on a number of occasions with both of them. Although I had not previously met either John or Richard, they extended a tremendous generosity of spirit in helping me adjust to the sudden spotlight. As special rapporteurs, they both had been subjected to the same bitter criticisms that I was now facing for the principled positions similar to those they had advanced in their UN reports and their public commentary.

Distilled into a pithy piece of advice, John and Richard told me in those early days that, to be an effective human rights expert for the OPT mandate within the UN system, I had to keep two indispensable duties always in mind. First, I would have to be *fearless* in my reporting and commentary. The special rapporteur mandate on Palestine is one of the most difficult and challenging positions within UN Special Procedures. In part, this is because the Israeli occupation is an integral part of the longest-lasting and most visible conflict zone in the modern world.[1] Any human rights reporting on Israel and Palestine invariably attracts heightened public and political attention. And, in part, this is because the mandate draws the close scrutiny of a well-funded lobby that is deeply allergic to any criticism of Israel's occupation. No small amount of nerve is required to face down this relentless vilification. Accordingly, a capable rapporteur in this position has to be prepared to employ language that is sharp, analysis that is boundary-pushing and perspectives that are incisive and stirring. Because political leaders and opinion-makers in the West have grown entirely comfortable with the relegation of Israel's subjugation of Palestine to the diplomatic backburner, the special rapporteur for the OPT has an outsized duty to constantly push against this antipathy with boldness and mettle, stamina and strategic patience.

The second essential working duty stressed by Richard and John was that I would have to be *responsible* in my work as special rapporteur. Accuracy in facts and evidence. Finding the right tone in my reporting. Anchoring my analysis in a solid yet accessible reading of international law. Working well with other special rapporteur mandates. Writing reports that challenge *shibboleths* and tired thinking. Using vivid expressions and lucid analogies, while running away from the dreary and stifling language endemic in UN documents. Always thinking positively, because human rights cannot be realized without optimism. And understanding that the special rapporteur for the OPT has multiple audiences to engage with. These included political decision-makers. Senior diplomats. Both mainstream and progressive media. Civil society organizations globally and in the region. UN officials at various ranks. And, most important, the vulnerable and the forsaken in Palestine. Trying to master this duty would become a never-ending work-in-progress during my six years in the mandate.

1 At the United Nations General Assembly, the consequences from the 1947–49 and 1967 Arab-Israeli wars and the Israeli occupation of Palestine are arguably the single most debated issue, according to this interactive table on UNGA resolutions created by Al-Jazeera: How has my country voted at the UN? | Al Jazeera English. interactive.aljazeera.com/aje/2019/how-has-my-country-voted-at-unga/index.html

David Remnick, the long-time editor of *The New Yorker*, once described the job of his staff artists was to go "too-far enough" in creating relevant and provocative covers for the magazine.[2] I first read that phrase shortly after my UN appointment, and I thought it elegantly summed up these duties of fearlessness and responsibility. Special rapporteurs, in their reports and advocacy, have to explore the very edge of the possible, while knitting together the practical with the visionary. They must lead the critical thinking within the UN system to place human rights at the center of the search for solutions to the world's many social and political problems. Equally important, they have to develop creative and impactful paths forward on how this can be achieved. Not for nothing did Kofi Annan once call the UN Special Procedures the "crown jewel" of the UN human rights system.[3] If the ingrained habit of any foreign ministry is to see the world only as it is, then special rapporteurs and human rights experts always have to be walking far enough ahead to visualize the world as it should be.

The significance of informed impartiality

Impartiality is one of the most important qualities required by the United Nations of a special rapporteur.[4] That said, in the world of international human rights, this term requires some unpacking. Special rapporteurs are deeply knowledgeable human rights experts, who bring experience, judgment, independence and understanding to their particular mandate. In this milieu, impartiality means a dispassionate and rigorous adherence to international law and UN resolutions. This means understanding the broader context of the issues at the heart of their human rights mandate. This means going as far as what the reliable evidence allows. And this

---

2 "New Yorker's Magazine Covers Shift From Polite to Provocative," *The New York Times*, 28 September 2014.

3 "Annan calls on Human Rights Council to strive for unity, avoid familiar fault lines," *UN News*, 29 November 2006.

4 OHCHR | Special Procedures of the Human Rights Council. https://www.ohchr.org/en/special-procedures-human-rights-council/special-procedures-human-rights-council#:~:text=Special%20Procedures%20are%20individual%20experts&text=They%20undertake%20to%20uphold%20independence,do%20not%20receive%20financial%20remuneration.

means advocating fresh thinking and new conclusions whenever the changing realities on the ground require this.

But impartiality in the human rights context is not a symmetrically balanced scale. This does not mean "both-sidesism" or a sterile neutrality that treats a human rights crisis like a football game, with evenly matched teams on a level playing field. Nor does this mean seeking a false balance between two opposing viewpoints, when the evidence clearly points to an identifiable source generating the gross harm. Such an illusionary equilibrium only exacerbates a human rights predicament by misinforming us about both why the suffering exists, and what has to be done to cut off the oxygen fueling the injustice.

The former Chief Justice of Canada, Beverley McLachlin, has written that the traditional image of the blindfolded judge searching for an abstract truth must be supplemented by the concept of "informed impartiality" in the contemporary courtroom.[5] The modern judge has to understand the different lived experiences in the diverse and evolving society where her or his decision-making takes place. This means that judges in our era must be alive to the historical and present-day inequalities and social fissures that shape the litigation which comes before them. Consciously appreciating these systemic disadvantages and injustices within one's society makes for better judging and a more responsive and equitable legal system.

Mutatis mutandis, special rapporteurs in the international human rights system also work within this realm of informed impartiality. Modern liberal thinking no longer accepts a *faux* equivalence when reporting climate change, medical efficacy in a global pandemic, the health effects of tobacco or the relationship between gun laws and violence in any society. We do not accept a human rights equivalence in the Rohingya crisis in Myanmar, the Russian invasion of Ukraine or the slaughter of civilians in Syria

---

5 Judging: the Challenges of Diversity. Remarks of the Right Honourable Beverley McLachlin, P.C. Chief Justice of Canada. docplayer.net/62981676-Judging-the-challenges-of-diversity-remarks-of-the-right-honourable-beverley-mclachlin-p-c-chief-justice-of-canada.html

and Yemen. And we should not accept it with respect to Israel's subjugation of the Palestinians.

When I became special rapporteur for the OPT, there already existed a virtual wall-to-wall consensus by the international community, speaking through the United Nations, regarding Israel's many violations of international human rights and humanitarian law. Israel's annexation of East Jerusalem is illegal.[6] Its settlements are a profound breach of the Fourth Geneva Convention.[7] The location of its 700-kilometer separation wall is unlawful.[8] Its presence in Palestine is as a belligerent Occupying Power, and the Fourth Geneva Convention applies in full,[9] something Israel thoroughly rejects. Its administration of the occupation is teeming with human rights and humanitarian violations.[10] Its persistent defiance of Security Council and General Assembly resolutions and requests for cooperation is deplorable.[11] Its blockade of Gaza must be lifted.[12] The Palestinian refugees have a right to return to their homeland.[13] Numerous commissions of inquiry created by the Human Rights Council since 2009 have concluded that Israel has likely committed war crimes during its various assaults on Gaza, and its refusal to hold its commanders and soldiers accountable for these crimes and violations is unacceptable.[14] And its denial of Palestinian self-determination is a breach of its obligations

---

6 UN Security Council Resolutions 476 (30 June 1980) and 478 (20 August 1980).

7 UN Security Council Resolutions 465 (1 March 1980) and 2334 (23 December 2016); UN General Assembly Resolution 71/97 (6 December 2016).

8 *Advisory Opinion Concerning Legal Consequences of the Construction of a Wall in the Occupied Palestinian Territory*, International Court of Justice (9 July 2004).

9 UN Security Council Resolutions 242 (22 November 1967) and 672 (12 October 1990); UN General Assembly Resolution 71/96 (6 December 2016).

10 UN General Assembly Resolution 71/98 (6 December 2016).

11 UN Security Council Resolutions 478 (20 August 1980) and 673 (24 October 1990).

12 UN Security Council Resolution 1860 (8 January 2009); UN General Assembly Resolution 71/98 (6 December 2016).

13 UN General Assembly Resolution 194 (11 December 1948), reaffirmed annually. It is the most re-affirmed resolution in the history of the General Assembly.

14 A/HRC/12/48 (2009); A/HRC/29/52 (2015); A/HRC/40/74 (2019).

as an Occupying Power.[15] These are among the most settled legal-political issues in the modern world, and these violations only intensified during my mandate as special rapporteur.

Insisting upon international law and a rights-based framework as the basis for supervising and ending the Israeli occupation is neither a flight from reality nor an inflexible impediment to engaged diplomacy. Rather, given my mandate as special rapporteur for the OPT, this insistence was both my duty and the very essence of informed impartiality. Such a framework establishes the clear legal and political boundaries for permissible and impermissible behavior that all states and international actors—large and small, strong and weak, democratic and authoritarian—have committed themselves to follow through their signatures on modern treaties and conventions and their membership in the United Nations. All of this applies to Israel.

Add to this the numerous and comprehensive reports on the Israeli occupation of Palestine issued by the United Nations and by well-respected organizations such as Human Rights Watch, Amnesty International, Al-Haq, Addameer, Al-Mezan, B'Tselem, Gisha and Yesh Din, and a deeply troubling *exposé* of Israel's systemic human rights abuses emerges. To be sure, human rights violations have been also committed by the Palestinian Authority and Hamas (more on this later), but impartiality that is informed by the dynamic tools of probative evidence and the framework of international law requires the identification of the primary source of this human rights crisis. Undeniably, that is Israel and its settler-colonial enterprise.

Lessons looking forward

In my work as special rapporteur for the OPT, I regularly encountered a wide spectrum of issues, organizations and challenges while trying to advance the purposes of my mandate. Three matters in particular merit specific comment, all of which offer germane human rights lessons going forward.

---

15 UN General Assembly Resolution 71/98 (6 December 2016), para. 5.

The Trump Plan

In January 2020, the Trump Administration released its Peace to Prosperity Plan,[16] which purported to provide a two-state solution for Israelis and Palestinians that would successfully end the conflict. In the maps which accompanied the Plan, it was clear what a rotten deal was being offered to the Palestinians. No capital in Jerusalem. A moth-eaten statelet in parts of the West Bank with no territorial contiguity, divided and enclosed by Israeli walls, Israeli-only highways and Israeli checkpoints. The continued Israeli blockade of Gaza, only modestly alleviated by an underground tunnel to the West Bank. Tracts of empty sand dunes near the border with Egypt as land compensation to the Palestinians for Israel's annexation of all of its 300 settlements in East Jerusalem and the West Bank. No external border with the world, except for the existing (and often-closed) Rafah crossing with Egypt. And no rights-based solution for the millions of Palestinian refugees.

Several days after its release, I issued a public statement through the United Nations rebuking the Plan. I wrote:

> What the Trump Plan offers is a one and a half state solution. This Potemkin state—lacking most of the commonly understood attributes of sovereignty beyond the right to fly its flag and issue stamps—would become an entirely new entity in the annuls of modern political science.

Among my greatest concerns about the Trump Plan was its trampling upon the cornerstone foundations of international law that had been articulated by the United Nations for decades. The Plan endorsed both the Israeli annexation of Palestinian territory and the legalization of the settlements, making a travesty of the law. I noted this in my statement:

> This Plan would turn the rules-based international order on its head and would permanently entrench the tragic

---

16 Peace to Prosperity, trumpwhitehouse.archives.gov/peacetoprosperity/

subjugation of the Palestinians that is already existing on the ground. The abandonment of these legal principles threatens to unravel the long-standing international consensus on the conflict, favoring *realpolitik* over rights, power over justice and conflict management over conflict resolution.

The Trump Plan was heavily criticized by many international figures. The European Union said that the Trump Plan broke with "internationally agreed parameters,"[17] while Pope Francis warned about the "danger of inequitable solutions."[18] Nonetheless, Israeli Prime Minister Benjamin Netanyahu declared that his government would proceed to unilaterally annex those parts of the Occupied Territory granted to it by the Plan in the summer of 2020.

In June 2020, in one of my proudest moments as special rapporteur for the OPT, 66 other UN special rapporteurs and human rights experts joined me in a public statement condemning the looming annexation plan. The statement was widely cited in the international media and by civil society organizations for months afterwards. It warned that, given that Israel was claiming permanent security control between the Mediterranean Sea and the Jordan River under the Trump Plan: "...the morning after annexation would be the crystallization of an already unjust reality: two peoples living in the same space, ruled by the same state, but with profoundly unequal rights. This is a vision of a 21st century apartheid."

Israel's *de jure* annexation of parts of the West Bank was subsequently forestalled by American pressure, with even the Trump Administration recognizing that the Plan had gone too far. The substitute was the proclamation of the Abraham Accords in August 2020, with Bahrain, the United Arab Emirates, Morocco, and Sudan agreeing to establish diplomatic and trade relations with Israel in exchange for the withdrawal of the Trump Plan.

---

17 Reuters, "EU rejects Trump Middle East peace plan, annexation," 4 February 2020.

18 Justine Coleman, "Pope Warns of 'Inequitable Solutions' after release of Trump Mideast peace plan," *The Hill*, 23 January 2020.

But the Accords, which the Biden Administration subsequently endorsed, did nothing to bring Palestinian self-determination even a millimeter closer. Unsurprisingly, in the two years following the Accord, Israel continued to expand its settlements and deepen its *de facto* annexation of the West Bank, encouraged the efforts of Israeli settlers to remove scores of Palestinian families from their homes in East Jerusalem and maintained its comprehensive blockade of Gaza. Indeed, part of the Abraham Accord's *quid pro quo* for the recognition of Israel was the Trump Administration's acceptance of Morocco's illegal annexation of most of Western Sahara, a sordid scratch-my-back which united two disreputable belligerent occupiers and their diplomatic patron together.[19]

Even though the Trump Plan was withdrawn, its dead hand lives on. After assuming office in January 2021, President Joe Biden undid very little of the Trump legacy respecting Israel/Palestine. The relocation of the American embassy to Jerusalem has been left undisturbed, even though it defied the direction of the UN Security Council.[20] Likewise, the American recognition of Israel's illegal annexation of the Syrian Golan Heights has not been reversed.[21] The American consulate in East Jerusalem remains shuttered. The building of more settlements is largely un-challenged. The intense American hostility towards the investiga-tions against Israel at the International Court of Justice continues. And the Biden Administration has effectively given the two-state solution its kiss of death, even if it has declined to issue its offi-cial obituary. During his speech to the UN General Assembly in September 2021, President Biden said that: "I continue to believe that a two-state solution is the best way…[but] we're a long way from that goal at this moment…"[22]

---

19 Rina Bassist, "Israeli minister backs Moroccan claims to Western Sahara sovereignty," *Al-Monitor,* June 22, 2022, https://www.al-monitor.com/originals/2022/06/israeli-minister-backs-moroccan-claims-western-sahara-sovereignty.

20 UN Security Council Resolution 478 (20 August 1980).

21 UN Security Council Resolution 497 (17 December 1981).

22 Remarks by President Biden Before the 76th Session of the United Nations General Assembly | The White House (21 September 2021) https://www.whitehouse.gov/briefing-room/speeches-remarks/2021/09/21/

Indeed, having Europe and the United States continuing to speak about the importance of an imaginary two-state solution is Israel's sweet spot. Even as its intensive settlement enterprise and its barricading of the Palestinians has reduced the possibility of a genuine Palestinian state to a mirage, the Israeli political leadership is entirely comfortable with the international community's ongoing mantra of two states, notwithstanding its own public opposition to a Palestinian state. For Israel, this mantra perpetuates the illusion that such a solution is still within reach, and all that is needed is the right diplomatic magic sauce to make it happen, thus reducing any effective international diplomatic pressure on Israel. And, in the increasingly unlikely scenario that the United States would push Israel into a new round of peace negotiations in the future, Israel would be assured that it would be playing chess with a full board of pieces while the Palestinians would have only a handful of pawns.

Canada, Ireland and Norway: Three middle powers and their contrasting positions on Palestine

In June 2020, the UN General Assembly was set to vote for five new non-permanent members of the Security Council for a two-year term beginning in January 2021. Two of the seats were designated for the Western Europe and Other States grouping. Three countries—Norway, Ireland and Canada—had been campaigning for a number of years to secure these two seats. Norway and Ireland are small European countries in terms of population (around 5 million each), but both punch above their weight in terms of an impactful international presence. Norway has used some of its oil wealth to become a substantial contributor to the UN as well as to fund creative international assistance projects, while Ireland has been a regular provider to UN peace-keeping missions. As well, Ireland is a member of the European Union, while Norway has an associate status with the EU.

remarks-by-president-biden-before-the-76th-session-of-the-united-nations-general-assembly/

Canada, in contrast, has devoted a very low percentage of its national wealth to international assistance, and has completely withdrawn in recent decades from what was once a very active role in UN peace-keeping assignments in conflict zones. Yet, Canada also had some significant advantages over Norway and Ireland in its campaign for the Council seat: it is a much bigger country (38 million), it is home to large immigrant diasporas from many countries, and it enjoys a wide international network through its memberships in the G7, the G20, the Commonwealth, the Organization of American States, the Francophonie, and the Comprehensive and Progressive Agreement for Trans-Pacific Partnership (CPTPP).

One visible advantage had emerged by the spring of 2020 which blew wind into the sails of the Norwegian and Irish campaigns: their more principled and critical stances towards the Israeli occupation of Palestine. Over the previous decade, both Norway and Ireland had voted consistently in favor of most of the annual resolutions respecting Palestinian rights debated at the General Assembly every December. In contrast, between 2011 and 2019, Canada voted against the series of UNGA resolutions on Palestine 123 times, abstained nine times, and cast only one affirmative vote.[23] When the Canadian foreign minister visited Israel in November 2018, she publicly stated to an influential foreign policy audience that, if Canada won a seat on the Security Council, it could be "an asset for Israel and can strength our collaboration."[24] And in the months leading up to the election at the General Assembly, both Norway[25] and Ireland[26] spoke up strongly against Israel's plans to annex parts of the West Bank, as endorsed

---

23 UN Dashboard – CJPME – English. https://www.cjpme.org/un_dashboard?utm_campaign=em_2020_11_11_un_dashboard&utm_medium=email&utm_source=cjpme

24 Chrystia Freeland, "Perspectives on Canada–Israel Relations," *Israel Journal of Foreign Affairs* 12, no. 3 (2018): 367.

25 "SC: The situation in the Middle East, including the Palestinian question," *Norway in the UN*, 22 April 2020, https://www.norway.no/en/missions/UN/statements/security-council/2020/unsc-the-situation-in-the-middle-east-including-the-palestinian-question/

26 Statement on Behalf of Ireland, *UN Security Council Debate on the Middle East*, Department of Foreign Affairs and Trade, 23 April 2020, https://www.

by the Trump Peace Plan. Canada, in contrast, issued a vanilla statement declaring that it would "carefully examine the details of the U.S. initiative for the Middle East peace process."[27]

As the General Assembly vote was nearing, the Canadian foreign ministry recognized that its regressive position towards Palestinian self-determination at the United Nations had become a sizable albatross. Canadian civil society organizations critical of Canada's position on Israel and Palestine had initiated a substantial letter-writing campaign to UN member states, arguing that it did not deserve a seat on the Security Council. In direct response, the Canadian ambassador to the UN, Marc-André Blanchard, wrote a letter to every UN member state in early June 2020, seeking to justify its tepid stance on Palestine.[28] The letter stated that Canada believed "there are too many General Assembly resolutions on the Israeli-Palestinian conflict," and many of them were "too one-sided." It ignored the fact that the prevailing problem is not that there are too many resolutions on the Israeli occupation, but that far too little has been done to implement any of these resolutions. It said nothing about the human rights abuses central to Israel's rule over Palestine, and it did not even use the word "occupation." Nor did it make any commitment to re-align or re-think its position regarding Israel's suppression of Palestinian rights. Too late, and much too little.

On 17 June 2020, the UN General Assembly voted for Norway and Ireland on the first ballot. Canada lost its bid for a Security Council seat for the second time in a decade, with its outlier position on the plight of the Palestinians as a contributing factor in both cases. As special rapporteur for the OPT working frequently with diplomats at the UN, I was gratified to see that

dfa.ie/pmun/newyork/news-and-speeches/speeches/2019/un-security-council-debate-on-the-middle-east.html.

27 Statement by Foreign Minister on the release of U.S. Middle East Peace Plan, Global Affairs Canada, 2020 January 28, https://www.canada.ca/en/global-affairs/news/2020/01/statement-by-foreign-minister-on-the-release-of-us-middle-east-peace-plan.html.

28 Marc-André Blanchard, Letter to UN Missions, New York, 10 June 2020, https://www.ceasefire.ca/wp-content/uploads/2020/06/blanchard-to-ambassadors-on-annexation-letter.pdf.

this positive position of UN member states towards Palestinian self-determination could assist with their bids for leadership roles on the international stage.

During their subsequent tenure on the Security Council, Norway and especially Ireland have been reliable voices providing critical perspectives from within Europe regarding the importance of an ongoing international spotlight on Palestine. At the Council, Ireland has proclaimed that Israel's occupation of Palestine is illegal, a first for a European country.[29] While Norway has been less demonstrative and bold, it has regularly stated at the Council that Israel's continuing settlement activities are illegal, and its ongoing evictions of Palestinians from their homes and communities must be reversed.[30] The ability of Ireland and Norway as non-permanent members to shape the Security Council's accountability measures towards Israel is very limited, but their willingness to ground their analysis in international law and regularly bring attention on such an influential world forum to the inexorable harshness of the occupation through a European lens is a step forward.

During my years as special rapporteur, I enjoyed very good relationships with civil society organizations in both Ireland and Norway that oppose the occupation. Ireland has a political culture that is quite unique in Europe, given its long and deeply remembered history as a repressed and rebellious colony of England. Six of the seven political parties elected to the Irish Dáil Éireann (lower house) in 2020 ran on election platform statements that strongly supported Palestinian rights. Irish civil society—which includes solidarity campaigners, international aid organizations and trade unions—spearheaded support in the Oireachtas (Irish legislature) for the Occupied Territories Bill, which would ban goods and

29 Statement by Amb. Byrne Nason – UNSC Briefing on the Middle East, Including the Palestine Question, Department of Foreign Affairs, 30 November 2021: "Illegal settlement activity further entrenches the illegal Israeli occupation, undermining the right of the Palestinian people to self-determination…" https://www.dfa.ie/pmun/newyork/news-and-speeches/securitycouncilstatements/statementsarchive/statement-by-amb-byrne-nason---unsc-briefing-on-the-middle-east-including-the-palestinian-question-2.html

30 Statement by Norway on behalf of the five Nordic countries in the Sixth Committee meeting on Cluster I of the Report of the International Law Commission, 25 October 2022, *Norway in the UN*, https://www.norway.no/en/missions/UN/statements/general-assembly-committees/2022/6c-joint-statement/.

services produced by colonial settlements in occupied territories, a first in Europe.[31] Although a clear majority of members in both the Dáil and the Seanad (Irish upper house) endorsed the Bill, its passage into law has since been stalled by the leadership of Fine Gael, one of Ireland's traditional and largest political parties. In another success for Irish civil society, the Dáil unanimously adopted a motion in May 2021 stating that "Israel's actions amount to unlawful *de facto* annexation of [the Palestinian] territory." When the motion passed, the Irish Minister of Foreign Affairs stated that this was "a clear signal of the depth of feeling across Ireland."[32] This sentiment was obvious during my mission as special rapporteur to Ireland in March 2022, where I met with the Irish President, the foreign affairs minister, and a large number of members from many parties and from both houses of the legislature. I also held meetings with a wide cross-section of civil society organizations, whose advocacy for Palestine has become a model for human rights activism in the West.

Norway also has a vibrant civil society movement for Palestinian rights. Its successes are not as numerous as those in Ireland, but campaigners for Palestine have developed deep ties with the Norwegian trade union movement, faith-based organizations, and international development organizations. These continually press the Norwegian government to take stronger stands internationally and domestically to oppose the Israeli occupation. One of its most significant achievements to date has been to successfully campaign for heightened due diligence by Norwegian investors, as evidenced by divestments of holdings from companies linked to Israeli settlements by the Norwegian sovereign wealth fund and asset managers, such as Storebrand and KLP.[33]

31 Control of Economic Activity (Occupied Territories) Bill 2018 (No. 6 of 2018), Houses of the Oireachtas, https://www.oireachtas.ie/en/bills/bill/2018/6/.

32 "Dáil passes motion condemning Israel's *de facto* annexation of Palestinian land," *thejournal.ie*, 2021 May 26, https://www.thejournal.ie/dail-vote-expulsion-of-israeli-ambassador-defeated-5449176-May2021/.

33 "Norwegian pension fund sells off groups linked to Israeli settlements," *France 24*, 2021 July 5, https://www.france24.com/en/live-news/20210705-norwegian-pension-fund-sells-off-groups-linked-to-israeli-settlements.

In April 2022, I visited Norway as special rapporteur, and found a growing tension between the lingering glow of the intrepid diplomacy celebrated by Norwegian political leaders and diplomats respecting the country's role in initiating the Oslo peace process between Israel and the Palestinians in the early 1990s, and Norwegian civil society's demand for more concrete steps to be taken to oppose Israel's permanent occupation, such as a ban of settlement goods and products and recognition of Palestine as a state. Norway is the long-standing chair of the Ad Hoc Liaison Committee (AHLC), a relic of the Oslo process which promotes international financial support for Palestinian institutions and its economy as the pathway to statehood. During my meeting with a senior diplomat in Oslo in April 2022, I pointed out that, in 2012, Jonas Gahr Stoere, then the Norwegian foreign minister (and by 2022 Norway's prime minister), had said in an interview with *Haaretz* that "once it will be clear to everyone that the donors' mechanism is perpetuating the *status quo* rather than contributing to peace, we will have to reconsider [this form of support]. We are not quite there yet."[34] I noted to the Norwegian diplomat that, given the consolidation of the Israeli *de facto* annexation of, and permanent rule over, the OPT in the intervening decade, and the enormous growth in the settlement population, the *status quo* was more deeply entrenched than ever. Was it not finally time to re-consider? The diplomat replied, with a trace of cynicism, that: "Well, we are still not quite there yet." Alas, even for some of the more liberal countries in the West, the Israeli occupation has become a clock with no alarm.

Canada, my home country, also has a small but energetic civil society movement supporting Palestinian rights, but without the weight to move the political needle nearly as far as have their counterparts in Ireland and Norway. Although recent public opinion polls indicate that Canadians favor a more critical position against the Israeli occupation,[35] this has not yet filtered upwards

34 Akiva Eldar, "We don't want peace, but we want the world to keep funding the occupation," *Haaretz*, 23 November 2021.

35 *A Survey on Canadians' Views Toward Israel/Palestine,* EKOS Research Associates, 2 March 2017, https://d3n8a8pro7vhmx.cloudfront.net/cjpme/

into meaningful changes within political debates on Canadian foreign policy or within mainstream media coverage. In recent years, both the Liberal and Conservative parties—which have been the only two parties ever to hold federal power in Canada—have maintained strong relationships both with the Israeli political leadership and with a well-organized domestic pro-Israel lobby.[36] As special rapporteur for the OPT, the ease with which doors opened for me to speak with senior diplomats and political decision-makers from Europe or the developing world was never the case in Ottawa. The lessons from Canada's past two unsuccessful campaigns for a Security Council seat have neither been accepted nor absorbed into conventional Canadian politics, leaving a gap bordering on willful blindness between the country's proclaimed adherence to human rights everywhere and its refusal to apply those very principles to Israel's conduct of its occupation.

The Palestinian Authority and Hamas

An important, if secondary, issue that faces every special rapporteur for the OPT is the nature of the relationship that he or she builds with the Palestinian Authority. The PA is the internationally recognized political representative of the Palestinian people. It delivers the basic public services—including education, health, welfare, the judicial system, infrastructure, policing, and security—to the Palestinians in the slivers of the West Bank where the Palestinian Authority has nominal jurisdiction. It is the diplomatic representative for the Palestinians internationally, and many countries have established embassies, consulates or representatives' offices in Ramallah or East Jerusalem. Insofar as it is the Palestinians' subjugation that is at the core of this human rights crisis, developing an effective rapport with the official representatives of the Palestinians is key to the success of the

---

pages/2537/attachments/original/1488423127/EKOS_Poll_Results_Report_R2_-_2017-03-02-Final-v1.pdf?1488423127.

36 Steven Seligman, "Canada's Israel Policy under Justin Trudeau: Rejecting or Reinforcing the Legacy of Stephen Harper?" *American Review of Canadian Studies* 48, no. 1 (2018): 80.

special rapporteur's mandate, guided as it must be by impartiality, professionalism and an arm's length relationship.

The Palestinian Authority operates under extraordinarily challenging circumstances that are unique in the modern world. Its governmental writ extends on paper only to the 40 percent of the West Bank that it was granted under the "temporary" Oslo agreements in the early 1990s. It has no authority in East Jerusalem (where Israel exercises sovereign rule flowing from an illegal annexation), nor in Gaza (where Hamas rules, although the PA channels funding for some public services). In the West Bank, the area governed by the PA is cut up into 165 separated islands of land, divided by Israeli checkpoints, settlements, high walls, Israeli-only highways, roadblocks and forbidden military zones. This means that its rule is contingent on the overriding military control exercised by Israel over the entire area from the Mediterranean Sea to the Jordan River. This allows the Israeli military to enter the areas governed by the Palestinian Authority at will.

The Palestinian Authority last held national elections in 2005, and legislative elections in 2006. Hamas won the 2006 legislative elections but was ousted from power following a brief but violent clash with the PA in 2007. Hamas is the *de facto* governing authority in Gaza. The Palestinian Legislature Council was suspended in 2007, with President Mahmoud Abbas ruling by executive fiat ever since. Legislative elections were scheduled for May 2021, but President Abbas postponed them in late April, citing the refusal by Israel to commit to allowing campaigning and voting to take place in East Jerusalem. In response, I joined two other special rapporteurs in issuing a UN statement, saying that:

> The Palestinian elections present a monumental opportunity to renew the democratic process, to address the long-standing internal political divisions, to build up accountable institutions and to take an important step towards achieving the fundamental national and individual rights of the Palestinian people.

We call upon Israel to clearly state that it will allow the full democratic participation of Palestinians in East Jerusalem in the planned elections. As the Occupying Power in East Jerusalem, it must interfere as little as possible with the rights and daily lives of the Palestinians.

We also stated that we did not underestimate the challenges facing the Palestinian leadership in holding free and fair democratic elections while under an entrenched occupation. Notwithstanding, we called upon the Palestinian authorities, the PA and Hamas, to remove any unnecessary barriers inhibiting the full and free participation of Palestinians in the democratic process, such as unnecessary restrictions on candidates and political parties registering to contest the elections.

The deep split between Fatah and Hamas acts as a significant impediment to augmenting the very weak bargaining position of the Palestinians vis-à-vis Israel and the international community. That said, I never thought that this split should be treated by the international community as a free pass for Israel to engage in conflict-management, rather than conflict-resolution. In 1990, when Nelson Mandela was released from prison and negotiations began to replace the apartheid regime with a new democratic South Africa, the anti-apartheid movement—which included the African National Congress, the Inkatha Freedom party and the Pan-Africanist Congress, among many others—was badly divided. Yet, political creativity enabled the participation, not without bumps, of all of these parties in the negotiations leading to the end of apartheid in 1994.[37] Ending apartheid did not depend upon the absolute unity of the political opposition. Likewise, political divisions among the Palestinians should not be used as a diplomatic pretext for initiating a genuine peace process and not imposing meaningful accountability to Israel to bring the occupation to a just end. And as ghastly as some of Hamas' actions have been, refusing to incorporate it within a meaningful conflict-resolution

---

37 Patti Waldmeir, *Anatomy of a Miracle: The End of Apartheid and the Birth of the New South Africa* (Rutgers University Press, 1998).

strategy—as was done in Columbia and Northern Ireland—has become a self-defeating approach.[38]

This political division and the dire need for elections were not the only issues that I had addressed as special rapporteur regarding the Palestinian leaderships. Violations of human rights by both the Palestinian Authority and Hamas were an ongoing concern. In several of my semi-annual reports, I pointed out the arrests of political activists and journalists in Gaza by Hamas and by the PA in the West Bank.[39] With the ubiquity of social media in recent years, criticism of the Palestinian authorities by human rights activists has grown exponentially, which was too often followed by security crackdowns on free expression. Respected Palestinian and international human rights organizations have issued disturbing reports on violations by Hamas and the PA against their critics and opponents.[40]

Perhaps the most visible recent incident of this type of serious human rights violation was the murder in June 2021 of Nizar Banat by Palestinian security forces near Hebron. Banat, a trained lawyer, was a vocal critic of the Palestinian Authority and had previously been arrested and threatened several times for his scathing on-line commentary regarding purported corruption and abusive conduct by the Palestinian leadership in the West Bank as well as its close security relationship with Israel in the OPT. In June 2021, he was arrested by the PA's security forces during a raid on his residence and badly beaten with steel batons. He died several hours later in their custody. In a joint UN statement released by several special rapporteurs, we condemned Banat's murder and said that:

---

38 Hugh Lovatt, "Why the UK's blacklisting of Hamas hurts its own peace policy." +972 Magazine, 2021 November 25, https://www.972mag.com/hamas-uk-terrorism-peace/.

39 A/75/532, at paras. 25-26; A/HRC/44/60, at paras. 21-22; A/74/507, at para. 18.

40 "Palestinian Authorities in the West Bank and Gaza Strip Must Uphold the Right to Freedom of Opinion and Expression," Al-Haq, 26 October 2020, https://www.alhaq.org/advocacy/17477.html; Independent Commission for Human Rights (Palestine), The Status of Human Rights in Palestine, Executive Summary 2020 (Ramallah, 2021); Human Rights Watch & Lawyers for Justice, Joint Submission to the UN Committee against Torture (30 June 2022).

The obligation to respect, protect and fulfill human rights rest with the competent authority exercising power. Notwithstanding a harsh occupation by Israel, Palestinian civil society has every right to demand that its own political and security leaders live up to their solemn promises to abide by international human rights commitments.

Hamas also has a troublesome human rights record. It retains the death penalty in Gaza, with 176 persons sentenced to death between 2007 and June 2022, although many of these sentences had yet to be carried out.[41] Human Rights Watch and Amnesty International have both cited Hamas for torture, arbitrary detention and violations of freedom of assembly and expression.[42] It has perpetuated or condoned acts of terrorism against Israeli civilians and, in times of intense combat in Gaza, it has fired explosive rockets, recklessly or intentionally, into Israeli civilian population areas, a probable war crime.[43]

As I ended my UN mandate in April 2022, the Palestinian Authority was sitting on a precarious precipice. Three primary issues defined this predicament. First, there is no political horizon for Palestinian freedom, which contradicts the *raison d'être* of the Palestinian Authority as the state-in-waiting. The international community has ensured that the PA's head remains (barely) above water, but it has never provided it with a boat to reach dry land. Back in 2011, the United Nations, the World Bank and

---

41 "Two Death Sentences in One Week: PCHR Demands Respect for Palestine's International Obligations to Abolish Death Penalty," Palestinian Centre for Human Rights, 23 June 2022, https://pchrgaza.org/en/two-death-sentences-in-one-week-pchr-demands-respect-for-palestines-international-obligations-to-abolish-death-penalty/.

42 Human Rights Watch, note 40; Amnesty International, "Everything you need to know about human rights in Palestine (State of)" Amnesty International, https://www.amnesty.org/en/location/middle-east-and-north-africa/palestine-state-of/report-palestine-state-of/.

43 "Human Rights Watch, Palestinian Rockets in May Killed Civilians in Israel, Gaza," Human Rights Watch, https://www.hrw.org/news/2021/08/12/palestinian-rockets-may-killed-civilians-israel-gaza.

the International Monetary Fund had concluded that, given the quality of its political institutions, Palestine was ready to assume statehood.[44] No serious steps were ever taken to build upon this, thanks not only to the vehement obstruction of the Israeli political leadership, but also because of American obeisance and the international community's self-inflicted feebleness. By 2022, a genuine Palestinian state was further away than at any time during the 55-year-old occupation. If there is no pathway to self-determination, no one should be surprised if repeated patterns of both low and high intensity violence—borne of despair and the shackles of colonialism—fill this swelling political vacuum in Palestine.[45]

Second, the ability of the PA to generate any economic prosperity is illusionary in the face of the shattered geographic space that it governs and its imposed dependency on the Israeli economy.[46] In 1993, on the eve of the Oslo peace process, the World Bank released a prominent six volume study—*Developing the Occupied Territories: An Investment in Peace*—which was intended to advance the economic and social capabilities of the Palestinian territory.[47] The most disquieting feature of this report is that its description of the dilapidated Palestinian economy in 1993—its high unemployment, stagnant incomes, deep poverty, overstretched public institutions and meager public services, subordinate integration into the Israeli economy, vulnerability to Israeli political retaliation and the enormous disparities in wealth and income between Israelis and Palestinians—remains equally true in 2022, even after 29 years of substantive institution building and billions of dollars in aid. The United Nations Conference on

---

44 Joel Greenberg, "U.N. Report: Palestinian Authority ready for statehood," *The Washington Post*, 12 April 2011.

45 *Universal Declaration of Human Rights* (1948), Preamble: "Whereas it is essential, if man is not to be compelled to have recourse, as a last resort, to rebellion against tyranny and oppression, that human rights should be protected by the rule of law…"

46 United Nations Conference on Trace and Development, *Report of UNCTAD assistance to the Palestinian people* TD/B/EX(71)/2 (20 September 2021).

47 *Developing the Occupied Territories: An Investment in Peace – Volume I: Overview* – World Bank report (September 1993), https://www.un.org/unispal/document/auto-insert-196019/.

Trade and Development (UNCTAD) estimated in 2019 that Israel's occupation had cumulatively cost the Palestinian economy $57.7 billion (U.S.) since 2001.[48] The pervasiveness and destructiveness of the Israeli occupation far outpaces the ability of international funding to build a sovereign Palestinian economy, which explains why we are witnessing not a state-in-the-making, but a broken territory encased in formaldehyde.

And third, the Palestinian political leadership has become increasingly sclerotic and unable to mount effective strategies to counter the occupation's tightening vise. The popular legitimacy of the PA wanes with every year that its indefinite rule continues without free and fair elections.[49] It also loses popular trust through its deeply integrated security relationship in the West Bank with the Israeli military, which provides safety for both Israeli settlers and troops, while damping any genuine popular mobilization against the occupation.[50] Perhaps the most important strategic issue for the Palestinian leadership to address, which it has avoided to date, is whether it remains worthwhile to continue to advocate for a two-state solution, when the reality on the ground tells us that a one-state apartheid reality has been created. Civil society in Palestine and elsewhere has long ago moved beyond any serious support for a two-state solution, given its impracticability, but their ability to move international political and diplomatic opinion towards the vision of a different future for Israelis and Palestinians will be stymied as long as the Palestinian leadership itself does

---

48 UNCTAD, *The Economic Costs of the Israeli Occupation for the Palestinian People* (Geneva, 2019).

49 Opinion polling in March 2022 by Dr. Khalil Shikaki found that a strong majority of Palestinians (72%) supported the holding of presidential and legislative elections in the near future, but only a bare majority (51%) would vote in a presidential election if the choice was between the current leaders of Fatah (Abbas) and Hamas (Ismail Haniyeh). Issues of corruption and the improved delivery of public services ranked among the highest issues of popular concern. As well, a growing majority of Palestinians (60%) believed that a two-state solution was no longer practical. Press Release: Public Opinion Poll No (83), Palestinian Center for Policy and Survey Research (22 March 2022), https://www.pcpsr.org/en/node/902.

50 Hugh Lovatt, "The end of Oslo: A New European Strategy on Israel-Palestine," European Council of Foreign Relations, 9 December 2020.

not promote such a vision. If Israel disregards the boundaries of 1967, why should the Palestinians not be able to address the 1948 division of Palestine as the root cause? The world is waiting for the Palestinian leadership to arrive at its South African moment: to move beyond political nationalism and the demand to end the occupation, and instead seek to provide for all those who live between the Mediterranean Sea and the Jordan River an alternative future, one based on equality, democracy and shared prosperity that can inspire people to recognize their common humanity.[51]

Conclusion

In the third decade of the 21st century, 75 years after the European empires began to crumble amid the rise of anti-colonial movements for self-determination and the universality of human rights, Palestine has become an anachronistic exception, a settler-colonial reality in a world that has moved largely beyond alien domination and non-consensual foreign rule. In every meaningful sense that counts—economically, diplomatically, politically, and especially militarily—Israel exercises overwhelming and abusive control over the Palestinians. Throughout my mandate, Israel's appetite for more land grew, its strategic objective to deepen the fragmentation of the Palestinians intensified, its need and ability to inflict ever greater levels of violence in order to maintain its occupation deepened, and its erasure of any lingering political horizon for a genuine two-state solution was achieved. Listen carefully to any argument that seeks to justify or excuse this state of affairs, and you will hear a claim with no moral core and no legal anchor.

My overwhelmingly sense, after six years in the UN human rights system, is that what the West wants—and here I include Europe, the United States, Canada, Japan, and Australia—is for the Palestinians to resolve the predicament of confronting Israeli exceptionalism and impunity entirely by themselves, without any international cavalry coming to their rescue. With no political will among the leadership in these countries to meaningfully

---

51 Mahmood Mamdani, "The South African Moment," *Journal of Palestine Studies* 45, no. 1 (2015): 63.

demand that Israel reverse and end its manifestly illegal activities in the OPT beyond issuing some reproaches *sotto voce,* the West is wordlessly wishing for the Palestinians to finally yield to the overwhelming power it is up against, agree to the Bantustan that is on offer, admit that the conflict is completely over, and thereby extricate the West from the embarrassment it finds itself in regarding its paralysis towards Israel's calcifying occupation.

I wrote earlier that optimism is an essential pre-requisite for a human rights movement. At the beginning or the middle of a prolonged struggle, it can be exceedingly difficult to imagine how ending an embedded reign of injustice can be accomplished and how realizing the triumph of rights and freedom can come about. And when thinking about Israel's punitive, lengthy and, to date, seemingly successful subjugation of the Palestinians, there are so many reasons for dejection. But during my time as special rapporteur, I saw many reasons to be buoyant. The Palestinians have never accepted their fate, and they continue to demand, through many forums, a complete end to their bondage. The international human rights movement has adopted the position of Palestinian civil society that the current Israeli systemic reality is apartheid, which introduces a new, clarifying, and invigorating framework into the global debate on Israel and Palestine. There is a growing bridge between human rights organizations in Palestine and Israel: they speak the same rights-based language, they have come to the same conclusions respecting the nature of Israeli rule, and they insist upon a common future based on the principles of freedom and equality. And international law is firmly on the side of those who are seeking justice in Israel and Palestine. In any hand of cards, these are winning suits.

PART IV

Joint Concluding Statement

CHAPTER TEN

FUTURE PROSPECTS

Richard Falk, John Dugard,
Michael Lynk

There has been little progress over the course of our three experiences as Special Rapporteurs on the situation of human rights in the Palestinian territory occupied since 1967 in reaching an effective peace process or in securing Israeli compliance with Palestinian basic rights as proclaimed in international humanitarian law, international human rights law, and international criminal law.[1] Efforts to curtail war crimes, to dismantle apartheid, to end the blockade of Gaza, to freeze settlement expansion, to stop collective punishment, and to bring a halt to prolonged belligerent occupation have met with little success. We jointly agree that Israel's failure as the Occupying Power to comply with applicable international law with regard to its underlying obligation to protect the civilian population of an occupied society and the fact that this occupation has now lasted over 55 years with no end in sight has created an emergency situation deserving of urgent attention by the United Nations.

A dynamic international context

There have been major contextual changes in recent years brought about by regional and international developments. Notably, in 2021 a pre-trial chamber of the International Criminal Court (ICC) concluded that the tribunal possesses the legal authority and jurisdiction to proceed with an investigation of criminal charges of alleged Israeli offenses after 2014 made by the State of

---

1 The Indonesian diplomat, Makarim Wibisono, served briefly as special rapporteur during 2014–15. Wibisono resigned citing Israel's failure to fulfill its promise to him that it would cooperate with him if selected by the HRC as SR by at least approving visits to the OPT.

Palestine. Abundant evidence had been submitted by the State of Palestine and NGOs to the ICC on crimes relating to excessive use of force in Gaza, settlement expansion and apartheid in the West Bank and East Jerusalem and other violations of human rights law and international humanitarian law in Gaza, the West Bank and East Jerusalem.

Since the ICC decision there has been considerable direct and indirect pushback by the United States, Israel, a number of European States, Canada, and Australia which questions the jurisdictional authority of the ICC with respect to states that are not party to the Rome Statute and the validity of an initiation of a criminal investigation into Israel's conduct in occupied Palestine. However, the future of this proceeding has arisen due to the election of a new prosecutor at the ICC, Karim Khan of the United Kingdom, who took over in June 2021, and has yet to disclose whether he will vigorously pursue the investigation and institute a prosecution within a reasonable time or will find some specious legal rationale for discontinuing or delaying the investigation.

While not altering the fundamental substantive or diplomatic realities mentioned above, changes in the leadership of both Israel and the United States are also worth further comment. The new Biden leadership in Washington has displayed renewed rhetorical support for the international consensus on a two-state solution, which had been effectively abandoned in the Trump "deal of the century" proposals, which did not produce serious negotiations when put forward, and has voiced mild opposition to Israel's annexation of Occupied Palestinian Territory, expansion of settlements, and the excessive use of force. On the other hand, it has demonstrated a strong bias in favor of Israel by refusing to return the U.S. Embassy from Jerusalem to Tel Aviv, failing to challenge Israel's annexation of the Golan Heights, continuing to fund Israel militarily, failing to make a serious effort to halt Israel's May 2021 unprovoked assault on Gaza, accepting Israel's refusal to negotiate a peace settlement with the State of Palestine, being unwilling to demand full accountability from Israel for the killing of the Palestinian-American journalist Shireen Abu Akleh in May 2022, and generally failing to express its opposition to Israel's denial of human rights and violations of international humanitarian law.

Washington's determination to respect Israel's demands is well illustrated by its handling of relations with Iran. Although it has attempted, over Israel's objections, to negotiate a renewal of U.S. participation in the 2015 Iran Nuclear Agreement (also known as the Joint Comprehensive Plan of Action or JCPOA), which would entail a return by Iran to compliance with its obligations to restrict its nuclear program to the development of peaceful uses of nuclear energy (which Iran ultimately suspended after the Trump administration's withdrawal from the JCPOA), the U.S. Government is intent on not overly distressing Israel and pro-Israel domestic public opinion. Consequently, the U.S. has sought a number of new restrictions on Iran's behavior with respect to levels of enrichment and number of centrifuges, and at this point negotiations drag on with as yet no clear outcome.

In Israel, Naftali Bennett has been more forthright than Netanyahu about his opposition to any form of Palestinian statehood. He has continued to expand settlements, to dispossess Palestinians of their homes, and to exercise the brutal occupation policies of his predecessor. He has publicly indicated his opposition to the JCPOA, despite Washington's elaborate attempts to reassure Israeli officials that its security interests will be protected. Bennett provocatively contended that the Middle East will become more burdened by violent conflict if sanctions on Iran are lifted in the aftermath of an agreement on the terms of renewed participation by the U.S. in the JCPOA.

Disappointments at the UN

There were two categories of disappointment arising from the interaction between ourselves and the UN, especially on the occasions when our annual reports were presented to the Human Rights Council (HRC) in Geneva and the Third Committee of the General Assembly in New York. The first and more trivial disappointment involved the failure of successive presidents of the HRC to ensure that SRs were spared the defamatory remarks by spokespersons for pro-Israel NGOs during the "interactive dialogues" between SRs, country delegations, and NGOs, with the latter having submitted formal requests to participate. This was particularly troublesome in Geneva. UN Watch invariably (mis)used its allotted time in the interactive dialogue following upon the oral presentation of periodic reports of the SR, to launch attacks on the personal credibility of the SR. Such remarks should have been ruled out of order so that the interactive dialogues might serve their purpose of allowing debate on the report itself, and raising questions relating to substance, keeping the focus on the message, and not allowing diversions as to the credibility of the messenger. We believe it is feasible to avoid future misuses of the interactive dialogue segment of the reporting procedure by conveying "rules of order" guidelines to the presiding official.

The second matter is more substantive, and hence more difficult to correct: the failure of the UN to show greater respect for the recommendations of its appointees, in this instance special rapporteurs, particularly those charged with investigating human rights violations that collide with the policy priorities of geopolitical actors. Our recommendations were seldom acted upon, or even discussed, in the political organs of the UN. Such a fate seems systemic within the UN system, and has diminished the credibility of the HRC, confirming cynical impressions that it can talk but not act.

More publicly visible similar instances of this pattern routinely occurred in response to far reaching findings of HRC factfinding inquiry commissions headed by internationally respected public figures. A flagrant instance was the disregard of the recommendations of the Goldstone Report in 2009 in an inquiry set up by the HRC to investigate the massive IDF military attack by Israel on Gaza in 2008–2009. The issuance of the report unleashed a storm of personal abuse against Richard Goldstone, the chair of the process. Goldstone's subsequent unilateral public repudiation of sections of the report[2] reinforced our experience that, when it comes to behavioral implementation of international

2 "Reconsidering the Goldstone Report on Israel and War Crimes," *Washington Post*, 1 April 2011. The three other commissioners, Christine Chinkin, Hina

humanitarian law or international human rights standards, the primacy of geopolitics controls behavior at the expense of implementing applicable law. Undoubtedly the failure of the UN to act on the recommendations of the Goldstone Report did lasting damage to the reputation of the UN as an effective guardian of human rights.

Symbolic successes

The shortcoming of the UN when it comes to implementation of recommendations of special rapporteurs and commissions of inquiry has often led to a deeper, unwarranted dismissal of the UN as "worthless" when it comes to addressing internationally controversial questions. On the other hand, the HRC generally, and to a certain extent the whole UN system, possesses a special kind of influence on behavior because of its contributions to the *symbolic* domains of politics, which have proved to be crucial determinants of political outcomes in conflict situations since World War II. This source of influence tends to be overlooked because it falls outside the boundaries of conventional and prevailing ideas about the nature of power, authority, and political realism. It is notable that the symbolic aspect of the anti-colonial wars and the dismantling of South African apartheid undoubtedly contributed to the victory to the weaker side in terms of military capabilities and geopolitical leverage, although regrettably often at great cost to the people struggling for their basic rights.

In the context of the struggle for Palestinian basic rights, above all, the right of self-determination, the symbolic domain is crucial for both sides.

Israel has itself gained a major symbolic victory, with some substantive underpinnings, through the "Abraham Accords," normalizing diplomatic relations with several previously hostile Arab states. Israel's feverish, and sometimes successful, efforts of recent years to criminalize and discredit the BDS campaign and other global peaceful solidarity initiatives in the United States and

Jilani and Desmond Travers publicly expressed their full endorsement of the Report and rejected Goldstone's repudiation of sections of the Report.

some European countries by labelling them as anti-Semitic is a further example of this type of symbolic victory.

The Palestinian people have also gained important symbolic victories, including access to the ICC to address criminal grievances. The greatest symbolic gain for Palestine in recent years has been the publication of a series of reports endorsing allegations that Israel practices apartheid in violation of the 1973 International Convention on the Suppression and Punishment of the Crime of Apartheid and the Rome Statute of the International Criminal Court. As early as 2007 John Dugard's report to the HRC alleged that Israel had indeed relied on an apartheid regime of control to maintain Israel's occupation of the Palestinian territories. The reports of the UN Economic and Social Commission for West Asia (ESCWA) (2017), the widely respected Israeli human rights defenders, Yesh Din (2020) and B'Tselem (2021), the Palestinian NGO, Al Mezan (2021), the two most influential international human rights organizations, Human Rights Watch (2021), and Amnesty International (2022), and the final report of Special Rapporteur Michael Lynk to the Human Rights Council (2022) provide evidence which convincingly establishes that Israel applies apartheid in both Palestine and Israel itself.

Giving such credibility to the apartheid allegations has put Israel on the defensive with regard to its status as a legitimate state, and as a democracy. The fact that South Africa supports these allegations against Israel provides another dimension of credibility. According to international criminal law and the 1973 Apartheid Convention, legal responsibilities arise for the UN and its membership, as well as civil society, and from such flow legal obligations. So far, the principal Members of the UN have not confronted the challenge posed to its fair dealing and its legitimacy by failing to address Israeli apartheid in a manner similar to its earlier very robust anti-apartheid campaign directed at the South African government. In the period ahead the SRs will have further opportunities to exert pressure by dwelling on developments pertaining to the apartheid aspects of Israeli governance of the Palestinian people. Although international public opinion and civil society increasingly recognize that Israel practices apartheid the majority of states seem determined to resist this obvious truth. Politicians are unduly sensitive to false accusations of anti-Semitism, which may compel them to resist acknowledging that Israel is a state that practices apartheid. The South African experience shows, however, that ultimately international opinion will prevail, and states will have no alternative but to conclude that Israel, like South Africa, is guilty of instituting an apartheid system.

Contributions of the SR reports

There are currently 58 special rapporteurs and independent experts covering a variety of themes and in a few cases specific countries, such as Palestine. In our instance, the mandate for Palestine is formally titled The Situation of Human Rights in the Palestinian Territory Occupied since 1967. It is a distinctive mandate in several respects.

First of all, it was established in 1993 over the vehement and continuing objections of Israel and the United States, as well as several UN members from Western Europe. Such geopolitical pressures test the political independence of the UN System as a whole. In line with our prior commentaries, these pressures have blocked the *substantive* protection and realization of human rights but have not been able to blunt the impact of the work of the SR for the OPT in relation to the *symbolic* domain, which has grown considerably over time.

Second, due to the polarization of public opinion with respect to the Israel/Palestine conflict, the SR biannual reports to the HRC and the Third Committee of the General Assembly, based on expert knowledge, regular missions and factfinding, have gained respect as objective summaries of Israel's failure to comply with international law in the OPT as well as the presentation of informed commentary and analysis. This has been confirmed for us by positive feedback from government foreign offices, mainstream NGOs and other civil society entities such as churches, universities, and labor unions. For analogous reasons, the otherwise routinely pro-Israel mainstream media platforms became increasingly receptive to our press releases and sought interviews.

Third, the impacts of our reports and activities were felt in relation to specifying and extending the contours of responsible political discourse within the UN system and in civil society. More concretely, the language employed by the SRs in their reports and public activities exerted a discernable influence, including some success in normalizing previously taboo formulations. Among the most notable of these were addressing the establishment of Israel as shadowed by "colonial" legal entitlements (e.g., the Balfour Declaration); "settler colonialism" as descriptive of subsidized and induced immigration of Jews with the primary of intention of establishing a Jewish state in a non-Jewish society; and "apartheid" as increasingly accepted by credible civil society actors. Reports changed the narrative of the conflict by calling into question the illegal occupation by Israel's administration of the OPT in view of its prolonged character and by repeatedly stressing Israel's record of flagrant violations of international law and its defiant attitude towards pronouncements on international law by the UN, ICJ, and ICC.

Fourth, SR interactions by way of side events at UN Headquarters with such actors as the ICRC, World Council of Churches, HRW, and Amnesty International were mutually beneficial. There has long been lamentation about insufficient connection between the UN and peoples of the world, as especially represented by an assortment of civil society actors. We think it is reasonable to claim that the SRs contributed to a fruitful interaction between the UN and civil society of increasing relevance. Civil society actors were provided with valuable inputs on the Israel/Palestine conflict through reports and exchanges. The influence of SRs on international opinion was apparent in publications, conferences, webinars and interviews.

Fifth, the UN accepted without protest Israel's refusal to allow SRs access to the OPT after 2008. While John Dugard was permitted to visit the OPT freely throughout his mandate, both Richard Falk and Michael Lynk were denied access to the OPT. This meant that Falk and Lynk were obliged to collect evidence from other sources. In order to do this, the UN allowed SRs to conduct missions to neighboring states where they were able to meet Palestinian NGOs and interlocutors, visit Palestinian refugee camps, exchange views with resistance leaders in exile and to hold discussions with leaders of neighboring states. This broadening of the territorial scope of the mandate undoubtedly added to the value of the work done by the SRs, although in no sense did it adequately substitute for direct observation by visits to the three territories comprising the OPT, which would have provided opportunities for direct contact with Palestinian inhabitants and the receipt of testimony as to their human rights grievances. John Dugard, in his concluding essay in this volume, observes that he found these mission visits indispensable to his understanding of Israel's failure to uphold human rights in the OPT. It was the misfortune of Richard Falk and Michael Lynk to be denied such direct contact with the OPT and its inhabitants during their tenure as SR.

Sixth, it follows from what has been enumerated above, that this mandate dedicated to monitoring compliance with human rights obligations in the OPT was shaped by the need to surmount the obstructive tactics of Israel, including harassment of SRs by pro-Israeli NGOs and media outlets. Notably, many delegates at the HRC and GA, as well as many UN civil servants, went out of their way to facilitate the work of SRs precisely because they were being obstructed. This facilitation was often carried on below the radar of public awareness because of an institutional reluctance to antagonize the U.S. and Israel by openly opposing their objections to the mandate. In our judgment SRs, independent experts who serve the UN on a voluntary basis without salary, deserve protection in the performance of their tasks by the UN and Member states, and obstructive behavior by pro-Israel NGOs should not be tolerated.

The likelihood of a continued need for the mandate

It seems certain that there will be no fundamental changes of circumstances in the near future that might allow the termination of this OPT mandate. Only Israel's withdrawal from Palestinian Territories Occupied since 1967 or the achievement of viable

Palestinian statehood formally accepted by Israel would justify terminating the mandate. A converse possible fundamental change might be the Israeli annexation of most of the OPT, excluding Gaza; the grant of limited autonomy to the major Palestinian cities in the West Bank; and the conferral of limited citizenship rights on the Palestinians who find themselves living in an expanded Israel. Such a political dispensation, however, would obviously not justify termination of the mandate.

Our assumption is that the status quo will persist in the form of occupation, apartheid, collective punishment, the brutal suppression of human rights and the denial of social and economic development. As long as such conditions exist, there will be a need for the continuation of the mandate to ensure that the human rights situation in the Palestinian Territories Occupied since 1967 is properly monitored.

Future special rapporteurs on the human rights situation in the OPT will continue the task of collecting, analyzing and reporting on the evidence of human rights violations in the OPT. In addition, they will have to devise new strategies to fulfil their mandate. These might include initiating a request for an advisory opinion from the International Court of Justice on an issue such as the legality of the occupation; concerted pressure on the Prosecutor of the International Criminal Court to prosecute Israeli political and military leaders for war crimes and crimes against humanity; and active support for economic sanctions against Israel, including an end to more arms sales.

The characterization of Israel as an apartheid State has been given new impetus by recent reports and may well constitute the Achilles heel of Israel's occupation and annexation ambitions. Continued emphasis on this subject will resonate with civil society activism and embolden and legitimize Palestinian resistance. This in turn might encourage the UN to blur the lines between symbolic and substantive action, and act to reduce the discrepancies between its response to South African apartheid and Israeli apartheid.

INDEX

About the Authors

 RICHARD FALK is a leading international law professor, prominent activist, prolific author, and a pioneer thinker dedicated to peace and justice. During forty years at Princeton University Falk was active in seeking an end to the Vietnam War, a better understanding of Iran, a just solution for Israel/Palestine, and improved democracy elsewhere. He also served as UN Special Rapporteur for Occupied Palestine.

 JOHN DUGARD is a South African who lives in The Hague, Netherlands. He holds law degrees from the Universities of Stellenbosch and Cambridge. In South Africa he directed the Centre for Applied Legal Studies, attached to the University of the Witwatersrand, which engaged in human rights advocacy, research and litigation during the apartheid years. More recently he has taught at the Universities of Cambridge and Leiden. He served as a member of the UN International Law Commission from 1997 to 2011, and as a judge ad hoc of the International Court of Justice from 2000 to 2018.

 MICHAEL LYNK is a law professor at Western University in London, Ontario, where he teaches labour law, domestic and international human rights law and constitutional law. He has law degrees from Dalhousie University and Queen's University in Canada. He started his legal career as a labour lawyer, acting primarily for trade unions. Later, he became a labour arbitrator and mediator, and presently serves as an arbitrator for the Ontario Grievance Settlement Board. He has published extensively on Canadian labour law and human rights law.